THE
LEGACY OF INDIA

A SHIP

From the Buddhist sculptures on the *stūpa* of Borobodur, Java.   8th century A.D.

THE
LEGACY OF INDIA

Edited by

G. T. GARRATT

With an Introduction by

THE MARQUESS OF ZETLAND

OXFORD
AT THE CLARENDON PRESS

Oxford University Press, Amen House, London E.C. 4

GLASGOW NEW YORK TORONTO MELBOURNE WELLINGTON
BOMBAY CALCUTTA MADRAS CAPE TOWN

Geoffrey Cumberlege, Publisher to the University

FIRST PUBLISHED 1937
REPRINTED 1938

Reproduced lithographically in Great Britain
at the University Press, Oxford, 1945, 1948, 1951

CONTENTS

LIST OF ILLUSTRATIONS

4085

INTRODUCTION

THE legacy of India; how rich a heritage, drawing contributions, as it does, from diverse races and from many epochs both preceding and following the great Aryan incursion from the lands lying beyond the snow-capped ranges of the Hindu Kush. From the prehistoric civilization of the Indus valley, brought to light by excavations at Harappa and Mohenjodāro, to British India in the twentieth century is a span in all probability of from five to six thousand years. During all these centuries the peoples of India have lived their lives and evolved their civilization in comparative isolation; for if we except the invasion of Alexander of Macedon and of the Bactrian Greeks who followed him during the second century B.C. it is only during a comparatively brief period, and that the most recent of this immense arc of time, that European influences have made themselves seriously felt in the sub-continent. Yet so momentous are the consequences of the impact of Great Britain upon India during the past one hundred and fifty years that it comes as something of a shock to discover from the concluding chapter of this volume how little has been added during that time to the legacy of India in the sense in which that word is here employed. In the sphere of administration, of jurisprudence, of engineering achievement, and of political science it would be difficult to exaggerate the consequences of the contact of the two peoples, yet throughout the pages which he devotes to Indo-British civilization Mr. Garratt is chiefly at pains to show that no such thing exists, in the shape, that is to say, of what he refers to as 'some new form of civilization' derived from 'the close contact between India and England'.

Nevertheless it would be a mistake to dismiss as wholly irrelevant to the subject-matter of this volume the influence exerted upon the culture of India by the advent of the British.

The legacy of India is not static, it is an organism growing in richness and content, and for generations yet unborn it may well be that the contribution made to it by the British people may prove to have been an incalculable one. Even to-day the influence of the English language upon the development of the vernaculars is plainly apparent, while the effect of English political tradition as a force moulding the mind of modern India has been profound. Purity and efficiency of administration; the equality of all men in the eyes of the law; these together with ideals of liberty and of the sovereignty of the people expressing itself through representative institutions have been sown by Englishmen upon Indian soil. What will come of them? Will they prove to be purely exotic plants which when no longer tended by those who sowed the seed will wither and die? Or has the genius of the Indo-Aryan race that in it which will enable them to draw new life from the soil in which they have been planted? Some indications of the probable answers to these questions are provided by the legacy of India as we see it to-day.

We know, indeed, that political science—*arthashastra* in San-skrit—was a favourite subject with Indian scholars some centu-ries before the Christian era. The social contract as an origin of kingship is discussed in the now famous work attributed to Kautilya, the chief Minister of the Emperor Chandragupta, about the year 300 B.C. And it would seem that the people who contracted for a king in these early days did so in order that there should be some external authority capable of insuring that the laws and regulations of the various corporate bodies which had come into existence were respected. 'The King', wrote Yajnavalkya, 'must discipline and establish again on the path of duty all such as have erred from their own laws, whether families, castes, guilds, associations. . . .' It is probable that the tendency towards self-government evidenced by these various forms of corporate activity received fresh impetus from the Buddhist rejection of the authority of the priesthood and further by its doctrine of equality as exemplified by its repudiation of caste. It is, indeed, to the Buddhist books that we have to turn for an account of the manner in which the affairs of these early examples of representative self-governing institutions were conducted. And it may come as a surprise to many to learn that in the Assemblies of the Buddhists in India two thousand years and more ago are to be found the rudiments of our own parliamentary practice of the present day. The dignity of the Assembly was preserved by the appointment of a special officer —the embryo of 'Mr. Speaker' in our House of Commons. A second officer was appointed whose duty it was to see that when necessary a quorum was secured—the prototype of the Parliamentary Chief Whip in our own system. A member initiating business did so in the form of a motion which was then open to discussion. In some cases this was done once only, in others three times, thus anticipating the practice of Parliament in requiring that a Bill be read a third time before it becomes law. If discussion disclosed a difference of opinion the matter was decided by the vote of the majority, the voting being by ballot.

Many centuries later inscriptions, probably of the tenth century A.D., in the Vaikuntha Perumal temple at Uttaramallur in southern India, provide us with a picture in great detail of the system of village self-government, including the principle of election, then in force, and it seems probable that, though submerged by the flood of disorders which accompanied the break-up of the Mughal Empire, the principle of representative self-government, whether expressed in the form of village *panchayats* or of other small units such as those to which reference has been made, has persisted through the vast vicissitudes of at least two and a half millennia of Indian history. If this be so, the inference to be drawn, however tentatively, would seem to be that the seed now sown will prove capable of drawing nourishment from the soil—an inference supported by the success of numerous Indian public men in those branches of parliamentary art which the constitutional system in force during the past thirty years has necessarily tended to encourage, such as rhetoric, dialectical ability, obstruction—all those weapons in short which may be said to be the especial prerogative of the politician doomed to function in perpetual opposition.

Let me now return to those aspects of the contact between Great Britain and India with which in the concluding chapter Mr. Garratt is more particularly concerned. He dismisses quite rightly the charge too often brought that the British deliberately destroyed a flourishing Indian civilization; but he does lay at the door of British rule in India failure, where success ought presumably to have been achieved, to effect a union of Hindu and European learning. This failure, he argues, has been due in the main to the fact that England has never seriously considered India as a *colonie de peuplement* but only as a *colonie d'exploitation*. This is doubtless true, yet there are many Indians who have drunk deep at the wells of Western civilization, and some Englishmen at least who have acquired a deep insight into the Indian mind, and there must be, one would suppose, some more fundamental explanation of the almost complete absence of the kind of cultural synthesis that might be expected from the close contact over a considerable period of time of two civilizations such as those of the British and of the Hindus. Can it be said, in fact, that it is in the case of the British only that such a fusion has not taken place? Is there, for example, a distinctive Hindu-Muslim civilization? The contact of the Muslims with the Hindus has been of far greater duration and from the point of view of numbers on a far greater scale. Moreover, they have treated India as a *colonie de peuplement* and not as a *colonie d'exploitation*. Of course the two civilizations have reacted the one upon the other. Muslim architecture owes something to earlier Hindu design and much to earlier Hindu craftsmen, as Mr. Briggs tells us in his chapter on the subject, and it was no doubt the impact of the monotheism of Islam upon the pan-

theism of the Hindus that gave rise in due course to the cult of
the Sikhs. Urdū with its distinctive literature was, as Sir Abdul
Qadir reminds us, a direct and striking product of the inter-
mingling of the two peoples. But, broadly speaking, Muslims and
Hindus remain to this day peoples apart with their own distinctive religions, languages, literature, and social systems; and
it is, surely, a remarkable thing that though the first serious incursion of the Muslims into India took place about the time of the
Norman Conquest of England there never has been any such
fusion of races in the case of the Muslims and the Hindus as has
gone to the making of the English people. What, then, is the
explanation of so surprising a state of affairs? A main cause,
surely, is the caste system of the Hindus which—particularly in
the case of the higher and more cultured classes of the people—
not only stands in the way of any admixture of blood with that
of other peoples but renders intimate social intercourse impossible. In such circumstances the existence side by side of two
distinct civilizations, even at the end of a thousand years of close
juxtaposition, becomes intelligible. And if it be objected that
iconography as an Indian art is a product of the fusion of
European and Indian influences of the kind which beyond India's
western boundaries gave birth to Sassanian art and within them
to Gandharan sculpture, it has to be observed that the Buddhists
who supplied the Indian influence rejected caste, and that in
the case of the Hindus themselves caste had not in those early
days acquired the complexity, the rigidity, or the exclusiveness of later times. Perusal of Mr. Masani's chapter on caste
and the structure of society will serve to show how formidable
are the barriers in the way of that intimate intercourse between
the Hindu and other peoples out of which alone some new form
of civilization could be expected to emerge.

But this is not to say, of course, that those races which, though
living in India, have not amalgamated with the Hindu people
have not contributed to the legacy which India has bequeathed

to mankind. Nor, indeed, would Mr. Garratt suggest any such thing. On the contrary it is probable that the legacy of India would have been the poorer for any such fusion of races as has occurred in our own country. Had the Muslims, for example, adopted the Hindu practice in the matter of the disposal of their dead, the peerless mausoleum at Agra, admittedly one of the outstanding buildings of all time, might never have seen the light of day.

Here, then, is one cause of what the reader of this book, when the last page has been turned and the volume itself laid down, will undoubtedly conclude is a striking characteristic of the legacy of India, namely, its infinite variety. But this is not the only cause. There are, each contributing to it, the three Indias of which Mr. Codrington writes, the India of the great cities standing out in contrast with the India of the hill and forest peoples, and between these two the India of the villages serving as a link between life in its complex and life in its primitive forms. The thought characteristic of these three Indias, ranging from simple aboriginal superstitions through the variegated beliefs of an agricultural and pastoral people to the subtle metaphysics and philosophies of the intellectuals, has found expression both in literature and in art. How great has been the influence of agricultural India on the evolution of her culture is evidenced by the widespread worship of the *lingam* and the *yoni* and by such religious celebrations of the present day as that of the *Holi*, the great festival of spring; or again by the place which the *Jātaka* tales occupy in Buddhist literature and by much of the subject-matter of the great epics, the *Rāmāyana* and the *Mahābhārata*. Neither is this all, for the thought springing from these three fountains poured in very early days, long before Islam came to add still further to the diversity of Indian civilization, through different filters, Brahmanical, Buddhist, and Jain, acquiring in the process, despite the fact that it maintained one basic belief unaltered—that of *karma* and transmigration—new and widely differing characteristics. A typical illustration of this diversity is to be found in the religious architecture of Brahmanical Hinduism and of Buddhism. In the case of the former outstanding features are the shrines to the infinitely diverse deities of the Hindu pantheon; in the case of the latter the chapter-hall derived from the Buddhist practice of assembly and the *stūpa* representing the cenotaph of the founder of the Order. One thing the Hindu, Buddhist, and Jain builders had in common, whether hewing their temples out of the great rock escarpments at such places as Ajanta and Ellora, or building them of wood or stone; they were sculptors as well as architects. And during a period extending over many centuries they covered the land with buildings whose very structure they often hid under an amazing exuberance of ornamentation, just as the Indian musician is apt to hide the tune by the plethora of grace notes with which he delights to embellish it. Hence the contrast with the architecture of the Muslims, whose religious practice forbade the sculpture of images and whose architects and craftsmen relied for effect upon the symmetry and proportion of their buildings and upon mural design in letters such as the beautiful kufic script for their ornamentation. But the buildings of the Muslims, as has already been indicated, differed from those of the Hindus not only in style but to a considerable extent in purpose also. While the Hindu burns his dead and scatters the ashes upon the waters of his sacred rivers, the Muslim follows the practice of burial, with the result that tombs are to be found amongst his most famous buildings. And in this connexion it may be noted in passing that the method of disposing of the dead in the case of yet another fragment of the Indian people, the Parsees, has provided India, in the Towers of Silence, with yet one more distinctive type of building. Then again, Muslim worship is congregational, hence the spacious courts of his mosques and the pulpits of his imams; Hindu temple worship on the other hand is individual, hence the multiplicity of shrines housing the images before which the worshipper performs his genuflexions and on whose altars he lays his offerings.

For the visitor to India it is these many and various buildings—Dravidian, Brahmanical, Buddhist, Jain, and Muslim—deriving from different sources, racial, religious, and social, their varying characteristics, that constitute the outward and visible part of the legacy of India. For descriptions of its many other facets the reader must turn to the chapters devoted to particular subjects, wherein he will find accounts of the contributions made by India both to science and to the arts. But it may not be thought to be inappropriate to an introductory chapter of a general character that something should be said in conclusion of the less tangible and more elusive aspect of India's legacy. For the legacy which she bequeathes is not exhausted with its material assets. It is characterized by a particular attitude towards life on the part of her people which can best be described as other-worldliness. It is true that the inflow of the virile though to a large extent materialistic civilization of Europe in the nineteenth century was accompanied by a great churning of the ocean of thought in India; yet below a surface of froth thrown up in the process still lie the deep waters of the spiritual life of her peoples. Throughout the centuries peasant and philosopher, Hindu, Buddhist, and Jain, has set before himself one immediate goal—that of bringing to an end the relentlessly revolving cycle of birth, old age, death, and rebirth. What lay beyond the cycle itself was a matter for impotent speculation, since not even those who had burst their bonds asunder and had thereby acquired complete enlightenment could render the beyond and the hereafter intelligible to those who remained within the automatically revolving cage of sentient existence—and necessarily so, for were the infinite to be comprehended by the finite it could only mean that the infinite had ceased to be the infinite. The striving of man was concentrated, therefore, upon release from an existence governed inexorably by the iron law of cause

INDIA IN EUROPEAN LITERATURE AND THOUGHT

NOTHING is more misleading than a half-truth, and it would be hard to find a more apposite illustration of this than the old adage about East and West never meeting. No statement could be more inaccurate. In spite of geographical, linguistic, and racial obstacles, the intercourse between India and Europe throughout the ages has been almost uninterrupted, and each has reacted upon the other in a remarkable fashion. India has never been entirely isolated. Before the dawn of history, as recent archaeological investigations have shown, an extensive chalcolithic culture existed in the plains of the lower Indus, which was closely connected with contemporary cultures in Mesopotamia and Asia Minor. Commerce between the mouth of the Indus and the Persian Gulf was unbroken down to Buddhist times, while we have direct evidence of early trade by sea between the Phoenicians of the Levant and western India as early as 975 B.C., when Hiram, king of Tyre, sent his fleet of 'Ships of Tarshish' from Ezion Geber, at the head of the Gulf of Akaba in the Red Sea, to fetch 'ivory, apes and peacocks' from the port of Ophir to decorate the palaces and the Temple of King Solomon. Whether Ophir is the ancient port of Supāra, not far from Bombay, or an unidentified harbour on the southeast coast of Arabia, there is no doubt that the objects imported came from India. And with merchandise there invariably comes an exchange, not only of *motifs* in pottery, jewellery, and woven materials, but of language and ideas. The Phoenicians were the earliest connecting link between the Indian and Mediterranean cultures, and this link goes back to very early times.

We next turn to the Greeks. The language of the Āryan invaders of the Punjab, their culture, and their social and

religious traditions, have sufficient similarity to those of the
Indo-Germanic peoples of early Europe to warrant the conclusion
that at some early period they must have been in close contact,
though it is scarcely necessary to warn the modern reader that
identity of language and culture do not necessarily indicate
community of race. But there can be no doubt about the similarity between the society depicted in the Homeric and Vedic
poems. In both we find a fair, stalwart folk descending from the
north upon a more advanced but unwarlike and decadent people,
conquering them, intermarrying, and absorbing their culture.
Both worship the gods of the 'upper air', Father Heaven (Ζεὺς
πατήρ, Jupiter, Dyaus pitar), Mother Earth, the wide expanse
of Heaven (Οὐρανός, Varuna), the Dawn (Aurora, Ushas), the
Sun (Ἥλιος, Sūrya). Society in both is patriarchal and tribal. It
consists of a number of loosely knit clans, in each of which the
king is the father of the tribe. The resemblance between the
Epic Age as depicted in Homer and the *Mahābhārata* is very
striking. In both, for instance, the warriors fight from a chariot,
and not, like the later Greeks or the Rājpūts, on horseback.
Neither the Hellenes nor the Āryans of the Punjab, however,
retained any recollection of the time when they had been
united, and, when they once more met, it was as strangers.

They were brought into touch through Persia. The mighty
Persian Empire, ruled over by Iranians who were themselves
kinsmen of the Vedic Āryans, stretched from the Mediterranean
to the Indus, and included both Greeks and Indians among its
subjects. The earliest contact between Greece and India was
made about 510 B.C., when Darius the Great, having advanced
as far as the head-waters of the Indus, sent a Greek mercenary
named Scylax of Caryanda to sail down the river to its mouth,
and make his way home by the Red Sea. Scylax took the old
route followed by the Phoenicians, and, after a voyage lasting
two and a half years, duly arrived at Arsinoe, the modern Suez.
His account of his adventures was probably utilized by Hero-

dotus, who was born at Halicarnassus, not far from Caryanda, in 484 B.C., the year before the death of Gautama Buddha.[1] Hero-dotus has a good deal to tell us about India: he knows that there were two races, the dark aboriginals and the fair Āryans ('white like the Egyptians', as a later writer calls them). He talks of the crocodiles of the Indus, the extremes of heat and cold in the Punjab, and the cotton, superior to sheep's wool, of which the Indians made their clothes. He is the first to recount the famous legend of the gigantic ants which guarded the Indian gold, and several of the stories which occur in his narrative, for instance, that of the foolish Hippocleides, who 'didn't care' when he danced away his wife, have been traced to the Buddhist *Jātakas* or Birth-Stories. More important, perhaps, is his description of a religious sect which ate nothing which had life and lived on a grain like millet, for this seems to be a reference to the Buddhists or Jains. A later Greek traveller and writer about India who flourished about a century after this was Ctesias, who was for twenty years a resident at the court of Susa, where he was physician to Artaxerxes Mnemon, having been taken prisoner at the battle of Cunaxa (401 B.C.). Unfortunately Ctesias has none of the sobriety of Herodotus. He is quite un-critical, and overlays a kernel of historical fact with a mass of picturesque fable. At this time India was fully aware of the existence of the Greeks or Ionians (*Yavana, Yona*), who are also mentioned in the inscriptions of Darius. Pānini, who is usually assigned to the seventh century B.C., mentions the *Yavanāni lipi*, or Greek script. During the whole of this period Persia was the link between Greece and India. Indian troops took part in the invasion of Greece in 480 B.C., while Greek officials and mercenaries served in various parts of the Empire, including India. 'At no time', it has been said, 'were means of communication by land more open, or the conditions

---

[1] This is the traditional date. Some authorities place it much earlier—543 B.C.

more favourable for the interchange of ideas between India and the West.'[1]

This may account for the influence of Indian ideas upon the development of Greek philosophy. One of the most marked features of the period preceding the Persian Wars was the revolt against the simple eschatology of Homer, and the search for a deeper explanation of the meaning of life. These speculations, it must be observed, originated with the Ionian Greeks of Asia Minor, who were in touch with Persia. The father of Greek philosophy was Thales of Miletus, but the foundations of Greek metaphysics were laid by the Eleatic school, Xenophanes, Parmenides, and Zeno, who sought for the One Reality underlying material phenomena in very much the same spirit as the authors of some of the later Vedic hymns and the *Upanishads*. Then came the Orphic movement. On the ultimate origin of the complex esoteric doctrines which we may conveniently group together under the title of Orphism we are quite in the dark, but we know that its chief features were a more or less explicit pantheism, a depreciation of the body in comparison with the soul, and the belief that the soul is imprisoned in the body, from which she seeks release. Orphism appears to have originated with Pherecydes of Syros (*c.* 600 B.C.), and his disciple Pythagoras.

Pythagoras was born about 580 B.C. at the cosmopolitan island of Samos, and, according to his biographer Iamblichus, travelled widely, studying the esoteric teaching of the Egyptians, Assyrians, and even the Brāhmans.

'It is not too much', says Gompertz, 'to assume that the curious Greek, who was a contemporary of Buddha, and it may be of Zoroaster too, would have acquired a more or less exact knowledge of the East, in that age of intellectual fermentation, through the medium of Persia. It must be remembered in this connexion, that the Asiatic Greeks, at the time when Pythagoras still dwelt in his Ionian home, were under the single sway of Cyrus, the founder of the Persian Empire.'[2]

[1] Rapson, *Ancient India*, pp. 87-8.   [2] Gompertz, *Greek Thinkers*, i. 127.

The most startling of the theories of Pythagoras was that of the
transmigration of the soul from body to body. Herodotus
traces this to Egypt.

'The Egyptians', he says, 'were the first to broach the opinion that
the soul is immortal, and that, when the body dies, it enters into the
form of an animal which is born at the moment, thence passing on from
one animal to another, until it has circled through the forms of all the
creatures which tenant the land, the water and the air, after which it
enters again into a human frame, and is born anew. The whole period
of the transmigration is (they say) three thousand years. There are
Greek writers, some of an earlier, some of a later date, who have borrowed this doctrine from the Egyptians, and put it forward as their
own.'[1]

Herodotus, like Plato and others, attributes all wisdom to
Egyptian sources, as was only natural. The Greeks were deeply
impressed by the great antiquity of Egyptian civilization, its
lofty temples, and its closely guarded religious mysteries. *Omne
ignotum pro magnifico.* Unfortunately, it is extremely doubtful
whether the Egyptians did actually believe in transmigration, and it is probable that the Greeks were misled by the
paintings on the tombs depicting the tribunal of Osiris, which
they did not properly understand. It is more likely that Pythagoras was influenced by India than by Egypt. Almost all the
theories, religious, philosophical, and mathematical, taught by
the Pythagoreans, were known in India in the sixth century B.C.,
and the Pythagoreans, like the Jains and Buddhists, refrained
from the destruction of life and eating meat, and regarded certain vegetables, such as beans, as taboo.

The theory of metempsychosis plays almost as great a part in
Greek as in Indian religious thought. Both Pythagoras and
Empedocles claimed to possess the power of recollecting their
past births.[2] Metempsychosis is referred to in many passages in

---

[1] Herodotus, book ii, chap. 123. Compare Cicero, *Tusc. Disp.* i. 16.
[2] Pythagoras remembered having fought, as Euphorbus, in the Trojan

Pindar, and, with the complementary doctrine of *Karmā*, it is
the keystone of the philosophy of Plato. The soul is for ever
travelling through a 'cycle of necessity': the evil it does in one
semicircle of its pilgrimage is expiated in the other. 'Each soul',
we are told in the *Phaedrus*, 'returning to the election of a second
life, shall receive one agreeable to his desire.' But most striking
of all is the famous apologue of Er the Pamphylian, with which
Plato appropriately ends the *Republic*. Er sees the disembodied
souls choosing their next incarnations at the hands of 'Lachesis,
daughter of Necessity' (*karmā* personified). Orpheus chooses
the body of a swan, Thersites that of an ape, Agamemnon that
of an eagle. 'In like manner, some of the animals passed into
men, and into one another, the unjust passing into the wild, and
the just into the tame.'[1]

It is interesting to note that India was passing through a
parallel stage of development about the same time or somewhat
earlier (700–500 B.C.). Men were no longer content with the
pursuit of earthly happiness, to be followed by an endless life
of bliss in the halls of Yama. They wanted to achieve the release
of the soul by correct knowledge. Transmigration first appears
in the *Brāhmanas* and *Upanishads*, the most ancient prose commentaries on the *Vedas*. The essence of their teaching is that
the individual soul is an emanation of the World Soul, which,
entering on a cycle of terrestrial incarnations, passes from body
to body in a seemingly endless round, now as a god, now as a
man, now as an animal or even a plant, finding no relief from
pain and suffering until it is finally absorbed, 'as the dewdrop
is absorbed in the Ocean'. This is 'deliverance' (*moksha, mukti,*
λύσις). To this the Indian thinker added the doctrine of *karmā*
or action. He whose actions in a former life were pure will be

War. Empedocles had been, in past incarnations, 'a boy, a girl, a bush, a bird,
and a scaly fish in the ocean' (*Frag.* 117, Diels).
[1] For the parallels between Platonism and Indian philosophy, see B. J.
Urwick, *The Message of Plato*.

reborn as a Brāhman or Kshatriya, while the evil-doer will be reborn as 'a dog, a hog, or a Chandāla'. As in Orphism, the soul during its earthly pilgrimage is regarded as a fallen angel, doing penance for her sins: only when the wheel of births and deaths comes full circle can she regain her lost inheritance. Orphism and its later developments and Indian transcendental philosophy abound in parallels. Hindu philosophy attributes rebirth to ignorance (*avidyā*): this is the Socratic doctrine that 'no one sins willingly'. The well-known simile of the Cave, with which the seventh book of Plato's *Republic* opens, reminds us of the Vedānta doctrine of *Māyā* or Illusion. The soul, imprisoned in matter, thirsts after objects of desire as the hart pants for the mirage-water of the desert. The noble prayer of the oldest *Upanishad,*

> From the Unreal lead me to the Real,
> From Darkness to the Light,
> From Death to Immortality,

finds many an echo in Plato's Dialogues. The resemblances are so numerous that it would be tedious to enumerate them, and one or two examples must suffice. The most remarkable is the Orphic legend that the Universe was formed in the body of Zeus, after he had swallowed Phanes, the offspring of the great 'World Egg', in whom all the seeds of things are present. Thus the world is the body of God: the heavens are his head, the sun and moon his eyes, and the ether his mind. In the same way, we are told in the tenth book of the Institutes of Manu how the Supreme Soul produced by a thought a Golden Egg (*Brahmānda*) from which he was born as Brahma. The resemblance between the two legends is too close to be accidental. The doctrine of Xenophanes (570 B.C.), that God is the eternal Unity, permeating the universal and governing it by His thought, occurs time after time in post-Vedic Hindu literature. Empedocles, besides believing in transmigration, holds a number of tenets which are curiously like those of Kapila, the author of

the Sāmkhya system. Kapila traces the evolution of the material
world to primeval matter, which is acted upon by the three
'qualities' or *gunas*, *sattva*, *rajas*, and *tamas*, lightness, activity,
and heaviness. Empedocles looks on matter as consisting of
the four elements, earth, water, air, and fire, acted upon by the
motive forces of love and hate.

Attention has been called to the resemblance between the
Hindu Varnas or Castes, Brāhmans, Kshatriyas or warriors,
Vaisyas or townsfolk, and Sūdras, and the division of the ideal
polity in Plato's *Republic* into Guardians, Auxiliaries, and Craftsmen.[1] The story that Socrates proposes to tell about their
divine origin, in order that the system may be perpetuated,
'otherwise the state will certainly perish', is curiously like the
Vedic myth about the origin of the four castes from the mouth,
arms, thighs, and feet of Purusha, the Primeval Man.[2] Are
these mere coincidences? Eusebius preserves a tradition, which
he attributes to a contemporary, the well-known writer on har-
monics Aristoxenus, that certain learned Indians actually visited
Athens and conversed with Socrates. They asked him to explain
the object of his philosophy, and when he replied, 'an inquiry
into human affairs', one of the Indians burst out laughing.
'How', he asked, 'could a man grasp human things without first
mastering the Divine?' (Φησὶ δὲ Ἀριστόξενος ὁ μουσικὸς Ἰνδῶν
εἶναι τὸν λόγον τοῦτον. Ἀθήνησι γὰρ ἐντυχεῖν Σωκράτει τῶν
ἀνδρῶν ἐκείνων ἕνα τινά, κἄπειτα αὐτοῦ πυνθάνεσθαι τί ποιῶν
φιλοσοφοίη. τοῦ δ' εἰπόντος ὅτι ζητῶν περὶ τοῦ ἀνθρωπίνου β ου,
καταγελάσαι τὸν Ἰνδόν, λέγοντα μὴ δύνασθαί τινα τὰ ἀνθρώπινα
καταλαβεῖν, ἀγνοοῦντά γε τὰ θεῖα).[3] If Eusebius is to be believed,
we must revise many of our preconceived notions about early
intercourse between the two countries.

Greece and India, however, were destined to be brought into

---

[1] B. J. Urwick, *The Message of Plato*.
[2] *Republic*, book iii; *Rig Veda*, x. 90.
[3] Eusebius, *Praep. Evang.* xi. 3.

yet closer and more direct contact. The older Greek States were exclusive in their outlook. To them, all non-Greeks were barbarians, and it needed some great shock to break down the barriers dividing them from the outer world. This was provided by Alexander the Great, himself only half Greek, but wholly inspired by the Greek spirit of inquiry. When he set out on his famous expedition to the East it was as an explorer as well as a conqueror: on his staff were a number of trained historians and scientists. In the spring of 326 B.C., the Macedonian hoplites, having marched half across Asia, entered the defiles of the Hindu Kush and found themselves in the fertile plains of the Punjab. Alexander's first halt was at the great city of Taxila, where, for the first time, the civilizations of East and West found themselves directly confronted. Taxila was of special interest for the scientists in Alexander's train, as being one of the leading seats of Hindu learning, where crowds of pupils, sons of princes and wealthy Brāhmans, resorted to study 'the three Vedas and eighteen accomplishments'. After defeating the Hindu prince Porus on the banks of the Hydaspes, Alexander travelled down the Indus to its mouth, establishing fortified posts or 'colonies' at strategic points, and turned his face westwards in October 325 B.C. In June 323 he died of fever at Babylon.

The actual effect of Alexander's invasion of India was negligible, and no mention of the event occurs in contemporary literature. After his death, the empire which he had founded quickly dissolved, and by 317 B.C. nearly all traces of Greek rule had vanished. But Alexander had broken down the wall of separation between East and West, and the contact thus made was never again totally lost. About the time of Alexander's death, a new ruler, Chandragupta Maurya, had established himself in the Ganges valley, and he quickly extended his empire to the Punjab. He was so successful that when, in 305 B.C., Seleucus Nicator tried to repeat his predecessor's exploits, he was defeated and glad to come to terms.

An alliance was formed and cemented by a marriage between the Indian king and a Greek princess. This was the beginning of a long, intimate, and fruitful intercourse between the Greek and Indian courts, which was continued by Chandragupta's son and grandson, Bindusāra and Aśoka. Ambassadors from the Greek monarchs of the West resided at Pātaliputra, the Mauryan capital. The most important of these was Megasthenes, who wrote a detailed account of Chandragupta's empire, much of which has been preserved. Megasthenes was greatly impressed by the resemblance between Greek and Indian philosophy.

'In many points', he says, 'their teaching agrees with that of the Greeks —for instance, that the world has a beginning and an end in time, that its shape is spherical; that the Deity, who is its Governor and Maker, interpenetrates the whole. . . . About generation and the soul their teaching shews parallels to the Greek doctrines, and on many other matters. Like Plato, too, they interweave fables about the immortality of the soul and the judgements inflicted in the other world, and so on.'[1]

The account written by Megasthenes, supplementing as it did the earlier works of Alexander's companions, gave the Greek world a vivid impression of the great and opulent civilization of contemporary India. The intercourse between the Indian and Syrian courts was not confined to the interchange of occasional courtesies. Megasthenes repeatedly visited Pātaliputra. Bindusāra maintained an amusing correspondence with Antiochus I. He asked him to buy and send him samples of Greek wine, raisins, and a Sophist to teach him how to argue. Antiochus writes in reply, saying that he has pleasure in sending the wine and raisins as desired, but regrets that 'it isn't good form among the Greeks to trade in Sophists!' Megasthenes was apparently succeeded at Pātaliputra by Daïmachus of Plataea, who went on a series of missions from Antiochus I to Bindusāra. Nor was Syria the only Greek state to depute ambassadors to the Mauryan

[1] See the passages quoted in the *Cambridge History of India*, i. 419–20.

PLATE I

INDO-GREEK AND PERSIAN COINS

1. Persian daric struck in India, *c.* 337 B.C.
2. Athenian *owl*, struck in India.
3. Coin of Sophytes, king of the Salt Range, *c.* 327 B.C.
4. Coin of Eucratides, king of Bactria, *c.* 175 B.C.
5. Coin of Demetrius, king of Bactria, *c.* 190 B.C.
6. Coin of Menander, Greek king of the Punjab, *c.* 165 B.C.

Court: Pliny tells us of a certain Dionysius who was sent from Alexandria by Ptolemy Philadelphus (285–247 B.C.). When Aśoka became a convert to Buddhism his first thought was for the dispatch of a mission for the conversion of his neighbours, 'the King of the Greeks named Antiochus', and the four other Greek kings, Ptolemy Philadelphus of Egypt, Antigonus Gonatas of Macedonia, Magas of Cyrene, Ptolemy's half-brother, and Alexander of Epirus. Whether the yellow-robed messengers of the Law of Piety ever actually reached Macedonia or Epirus may be regarded as doubtful, but there is no reason to suppose that they did not get as far as Alexandria and Antioch. Aśoka's object was not merely to promulgate Buddhism, but to establish a 'world peace', and prevent the repetition of tragedies like the Kalinga massacre, which had led to his conversion.[1] At the same time a flourishing trade was being carried on between Syria and India. Strabo tells us that Indian goods were borne down the Oxus to Europe by way of the Caspian and the Black Sea. No doubt they travelled along the Royal Road from Pātaliputra to Taxila, and by the old route from Taxila to Balkh. This was made easier by the fact that Aśoka's empire stretched far west of Kābul, and the passage of merchandise through this wild country was comparatively safe. The evidence of the coins shows that during the period when history is silent a busy life was throbbing on both sides of the frontier, and Greek and Indian merchants were constantly coming and going, buying and selling.[2]

With the death of Aśoka in 232 B.C. the close connexion with Pātaliputra appears to have been broken off, but in the meantime the Greek descendants of Alexander's colonists in Bactria, who had declared themselves independent in 250 B.C., had crossed the Hindu Kush, and established themselves in the Punjab. The greatest of the Indo-Bactrian rulers was Menander

[1] For the Edict see V. A. Smith, *Asoka*, pp. 185 ff.
[2] *Cambridge History of India*, i. 432 ff.

(*c.* 150 B.C.). Menander's capital was at Sāgala (Sialkot), and
he conquered for a time a considerable portion of the Mauryan
Empire. The Bactrian Greeks have been called 'the Goanese
of antiquity'. By this time they had become thoroughly
Indianized, and Menander was converted to the fashionable
creed of Buddhism. His conversion is recorded in that famous
work, the *Milinda-pañha*, or *Questions of Milinda*, a kind of
Platonic dialogue in Pāli, in which the sage Nāgasena plays the
part of Socrates. The history of the Bactrian Greek rulers of
the Punjab has been reconstructed from their coins. The earlier
issues are of great beauty, but they rapidly degenerate, and the
appearance of bilingual superscriptions tells its own tale. Curiously enough, the Greeks have left no other memorial in India
except a column erected at Besnagar in Gwālior State, by
Heliodorus of Taxila, an ambassador from the Mahārājā Antial-
cidas to King Bhāgabadra. This column records the fact that
Heliodorus was a devotee of Vishnu, and shows how rapidly
the Greeks were adopting the religions of their neighbours.[1]
The Bactrian Greeks were succeeded by a number of Śaka and
Parthian princes, and it was at the court of one of these that the
Apostle Thomas is said to have suffered martyrdom. The *Acts of
Judas Thomas*, which exists in Syriac, Greek, and Latin versions,
is apparently based on a kernel of historical fact, and the proper
names, both of persons and places, have been identified. Gondophernes has been recognized as Gaspar, the first of the Magi.[2]

About A.D. 48 these tribes were replaced by the Yueh-Chi
or Kushān horde from Central Asia. The Kushān Empire
reached its zenith under Kanishka, who seems to have succeeded
to the throne about A.D. 120. His capital was at Peshāwar, but

[1] Rapson, *Ancient India*, pp. 134, 156.
[2] A full bibliography of the Thomas and Gondophernes legend is given in
the *Cambridge History of India*, i. 687. See also V. A. Smith, *Early History
of India*, 4th edn., p. 260, and J. F. Farquhar in *Bulletin of the John Rylands
Library*, 1926–7.

his far-flung empire extended as far west as Kābul and as far
north as Kashgar. Kanishka was a convert to Buddhism, but
his coins, with their curious medley of deities, Zoroastrian,
Hindu, Greek, and Buddhist, indicate the cosmopolitan nature
of his territories, a veritable *colluvies gentium*, at the meeting-
place of the Central Asian trade-routes. Among the deities depicted are *ΗΛΙΟΣ, ΣΕΛΗΝΗ*, and *ΒΟΔΔΟ*, the latter in Greek
dress. Kanishka employed Greek workmen and silversmiths,
and the relic-casket discovered at the Shāhjī-kī-Dherī mound
near Peshāwar bears a Kharoshthi inscription to the effect that
it was the work of 'Agesilas, overseer of Kanishka's *vihāra*'.
Excavations at Taxila have revealed a wealth of beautiful *objets
d'art* of the Śaka and Kushān periods, showing how strong was
Greek influence there. Some of the friezes are decorated with
Corinthian pillars. Under the Kushāns that curious hybrid
product, the so-called Gandhāra school of sculpture, flourished.
It is a mistake, perhaps, to apply the term 'school' to a number
of artists of different nationalities, working in a variety of
materials over a long period. Their most striking achievement,
however, was the application of Hellenistic methods to the por-
trayal of scenes in the life of the Buddha, and, more especially,
to the delineation of the Master himself. Hitherto, Buddhists
had been content to represent him by conventional symbols:
it was probably the Indo-Greek artists of Gandhāra who evolved
the Buddha figure which is accepted as canonical all over the
Buddhist world to-day.[1] A cosmopolitan culture, borrowed
from Iranian, Hellenistic, Indian, and Chinese sources, sprang
up along the Central Asian trade-route, with its centre in what
is now the desert between the Tarim and Khotan rivers.

Meanwhile, the *Pax Romana* was promoting the growth of
a cosmopolitan culture in the Near and Middle East, where the
old racial and linguistic prejudices were fast melting away.

---

[1] This is disputed. Dr. A. K. Coomaraswamy contends that the Buddha
figure originated at Mathurā, quite independently of Gandhāra.

'Videtis gentes populosque mutasse sedes,' says Seneca. 'Quid sibi volunt in mediis barbarorum regionibus Graecae artes? Quid inter Indos Persasque Macedonicus sermo? Athenienis in Asia turba est.'[1] In Antioch, Palmyra, and Alexandria, Indian and Greek merchants and men of letters met freely to exchange ideas. Antioch, the old Seleucid capital, was the great meeting-place of caravans (συνοδίαι) from the Gulf of Suez on the one hand and from the headwaters of the Euphrates on the other, and its bazaars and market-places were thronged with a cosmopolitan crowd, second only to that of Alexandria. Travellers from Barygaza (Broach),[2] at the mouth of the Narbādā, would probably follow the overland route up the Euphrates and then cross the desert to Antioch, while those from South India and Ceylon would preferably go via Aden and the Red Sea. Palmyra, Solomon's Tadmor in the Wilderness, on the oasis which lies midway on the desert route between the great Red Sea port of Berenice and Thapsacus on the Euphrates, enjoyed a short but brilliant period of prosperity between the time when it ousted its rival, Petra, and its destruction by the Romans (A.D. 130–273).

The Kushāns were particularly anxious to be on good terms with Rome, whose eastern boundary was the Euphrates, less than 600 miles from their western border. The closeness of their intercourse is illustrated in a striking manner by the Kushān coinage, which imitates that of contemporary Roman emperors. The Kushān gold coins are of the same weight and fineness as the Roman *aurei*. It appears probable from an inscription that the Kushān king Kanishka used the title of Caesar.

The friendly and intimate nature of the relations between Rome and India is shown by the number of embassies dispatched by various Indian rājās from time to time. One of these, from an Indian king whom Strabo calls Pandion (probably one of the Pāndya kings of the south), left Barygaza in 25 B.C. and

[1] *De Cons. ad Helv. c.* vi.   [2] Sanskrit Bhrigukaccha.

encountered Augustus at Samos four years later. The time
occupied by the journey seems less strange when we study the
Elizabethan travellers' itineraries: people had to wait for prolonged periods at stopping-places until caravans were formed
and escorts arranged for. The ambassadors brought Augustus
a variety of queer presents, including tigers, a python, and an
armless boy who discharged arrows from a bow with his toes.
The leader of the embassy was a monk named Zarmanochegas
(*Śrāmanāchārya*), who brought a letter, written on vellum in
Greek, offering the Emperor an alliance and a free passage for
Roman subjects through his dominions. Like Kalanos, the
monk who accompanied Alexander the Great to Babylon, Zarmanochegas committed suicide by burning himself to death on
a funeral pyre. From this it is perhaps permissible to conclude
that he was a Jain, as Jainism looks upon voluntary immolation
as a laudable act. According to Strabo, his epitaph was 'Here
lies Zarmanochegas, an Indian from Bargosa, who rendered
himself immortal according to the customs of the country.'[1]
Another Indian embassy, probably from the Kushān king
Kadphises II, went to Rome in A.D. 99 to congratulate Trajan
on his accession. Trajan treated his Indian visitors with distinction, giving them senators' seats at the theatre. From the
time of Mark Antony to that of Justinian, i.e. from 30 B.C. to
A.D. 550, their political importance as allies against the Parthians
and Sassanians, and their commercial importance as controllers
of one of the main trade routes between the East and the West,
made the friendship of the Kushāns and other dynasties who held
the Indus valley and Gandhāra of the highest value to Rome.

Meanwhile, a brisk trade was springing up between the great
mart at Alexandria and the coast of Malabar. The products of
southern India had, as we have seen, been in demand in the
Mediterranean from time immemorial, and Alexandria had
replaced the old Phoenician ports of Tyre and Sidon as the

---

[1] Strabo, *Geography*, xv. 73.

clearing-house for Oriental goods. Owing to the discovery about
A.D. 50 of the existence of the monsoon winds, it was now possible for vessels to run directly across the Indian Ocean, from
Aden to the great Malabar port of Muziris (Cranganore),
instead of hugging the coast. This so shortened the distance
that the journey from Italy to India could be accomplished in
sixteen weeks.[1] The importance of this fact will be realized
when we recollect that, up to the opening of the overland
route in 1838, it took travellers from five to eight months to
reach India. India was nearer to Europe in the first century A.D.
than at any time up to the middle of the nineteenth. An interesting little book, called *The Periplus of the Erythraean Sea*, written
by an Alexandrian sea-captain about the time of Nero, gives an
account of a voyage down the Red Sea and round the Indian
coast from the mouth of the Indus to that of the Ganges. Pliny,
who complains of the 'drain' of eastern luxuries upon Rome,
which he estimates at over a million pounds sterling, deplores
the fact that the two countries had been 'brought nearer by lust
for gain', and, from the enormous number of Roman coins found
in southern India and references in Tamil writers, it is highly
probable that there were actually Roman colonies at Cranganore
or Muziris (where there seems to have been a Roman temple),
Madura, Pukar at the mouth of the Cauvery, and other places.
A Tamil poet sings of 'the thriving town of Muchiri, where the
beautiful large ships of the Yavanas, bringing gold, come splash-
ing the waters of the Periyār, and return laden with pepper'.
These colonies doubtless resembled the European factories at
Surat and other places along the Indian coast in the seventeenth
and eighteenth centuries. The colonists were probably natives
of Syria and Egypt, with Roman officers in charge. It also

---

[1] Pliny (*Natural History*, vi. 22) tells us of a revenue-ship of Annius
Plocamus, in the reign of Claudius, which was caught in the monsoon and
covered the distance between Aden and Ceylon in fifteen days. The usual
time was about forty days.

appears that Roman mercenaries, 'dumb *Mlecchas*' or barbarians, were employed by some of the Tamil kings. The *Periplus* mentions the import of Greek girls for the Indian harems, and Chandragupta's guard of Amazons may well have been Greeks. It was not unusual for Indian sovereigns to employ a foreign bodyguard as a protection from assassination.

Alexandria, in the first century A.D., was the second city in the Empire. In the height of her glory she must have resembled Venice in the full tide of her prosperity. The mercantile shipping of half of the ancient world tied up at her quay-sides, and scholars from the four quarters of the earth met and disputed in the Museum, and made use of the vast stores of literature in her great libraries. The Alexandrians were essentially cosmopolitan. They had none of the contempt for the 'barbarian' of the old Greek city-states, and a large proportion of the population, like the Athenians, 'spent their life in nothing else, but either to tell or hear some new thing'. A Buddhist monk from Barygaza would receive the same attentive hearing as did Saint Paul at the hands of the Areopagus, and the medium was Hellenistic Greek, the lingua franca (κοινή) from the Levant to the Indus. The *Milinda-pañha* mentions Alexandria as one of the places to which Indian merchants regularly resorted, and Dio Chrysostom, lecturing to an Alexandrian audience in the reign of Trajan, says: 'I see among you, not only Greeks and Italians, Syrians, Libyans, and Cilicians, and men who dwell more remotely, Ethiopians and Arabs, but also Bactrians, Scythians, Persians, and some of the Indians, who are among the spectators, and are always residing there.'[1] These Indian residents must have come to Alexandria from one of the numerous seaports on the western coast, probably Barygaza or Muziris. Barygaza was the chief port of call for vessels from the Persian Gulf. A road ran from Barygaza to Ujjain, a place where several routes converged, and from Ujjain through Vidisā, Barhut, Kausāmbī,

---

[1] McCrindle, *Ancient India*, pp. 174–8.

and Prayāga to Pātaliputra. Pātaliputra was linked up with
Champā, the port on the Ganges for trading-vessels going to
Ceylon, the Golden Chersonese, and the Far East. The traders
who settled at Alexandria must have been either Jains or Buddhists, as caste-rules forbade orthodox Hindus to cross the
black water. The *Jātakas* are full of references to Buddhist merchants and their adventures on voyages to distant countries.
For this reason Alexandrian writers are generally better acquainted with the Buddhists than with any other Indian sect.

Indian philosophy was acquiring a growing reputation in the
Hellenistic schools of Asia Minor and Egypt. That famous
miracle-monger, Apollonius of Tyana (*c.* A.D. 50), went to Taxila
to study under Brāhman preceptors. Bardesanes the Babylonian,
the well-known Gnostic teacher, learnt many curious facts about
India from an Indian embassy which came to Syria in the reign
of Elagabalus (A.D. 218–22). The lost work of Bardesanes is
freely quoted by later writers, and was evidently held in great
esteem. Bardesanes knew a great deal about the Brāhmans and
Buddhists and their discipline and mode of life. He describes,
in accurate detail, life in a Buddhist monastery, and a visit to a
cave-temple in western India, containing an androgynous image
of the god Śiva.[1] Plotinus, the founder of the Neoplatonic
school, was so anxious to be instructed in Indian philosophy that
he accompanied the expedition of Gordian against Sapor, king
of Persia, in A.D. 242, in the hope that this might bring him into
personal contact with some one who could help him. The
resemblances between Neoplatonism and the Vedānta and Yoga
systems are very close. The absorption of the individual into
the World Soul is described by Plotinus in words which have
a typically Indian ring:

> Souls which are pure and have lost their attraction to the corporal
> will cease to be dependent on the body. So detached they will pass
> into the world of Being and Reality.

[1] McCrindle, op. cit.

PLATE **2**

Bronze statuette of Harpocrates from Taxila

GREEK INTAGLIO GEMS FROM NORTH-WEST INDIA

Neoplatonism has many points of contact with Buddhism, especially in enjoining the abstention from sacrifices and animal food.

Buddhism was well known to Clement of Alexandria (A.D. 150–218). He repeatedly refers to the presence of Buddhists in Alexandria, and declares that 'the Greeks stole their philosophy from the barbarians'. He is the first Greek writer to mention Buddha by name. 'There are', he says, 'some Indians who follow the precepts of Boutta, whom by an excessive reverence they have exalted into a god.'[1] He knows that Buddhists believe in transmigration (παλιγγενεσία) and 'worship a kind of pyramid (*stūpa*) beneath which they think the bones of some divinity lie buried'. Perhaps these facts throw some light on the curious resemblances between the Gospel story and the life of Buddha as told in late Buddhist works like the *Lalita Vistara*. Some of those are the Buddha's miraculous conception and birth; the star over his birthplace; the prophecy of the aged Asita, the Buddhist Simeon; the temptation by Māra; the twelve disciples with the 'beloved disciple', Ānanda; and the miracles, coupled with the Buddha's disapproval of these as proofs of his Buddhahood.

More startling still are the points of similarity between the Buddhist and Christian parables and miracles. Thus in *Jātaka 190* we read of the pious disciple who walks on the water while he is full of faith in the Buddha, but begins to sink when his ecstasy subsides. On his arrival the Master inquires how he has fared. 'Oh, Sir,' he replies, 'I was so absorbed in thoughts of the Buddha, that I walked over the water of the river as though it

---

[1] Εἰσὶ δὲ τῶν Ἰνδῶν οἱ τοῖς Βούττα πειθόμενοι παραγγέλμασι· τὸν δὲ δι' ὑπερβολὴν σεμνότητος εἰς θεὸν τετιμήκασιν (*Stromata*, i. 15). McCrindle quotes other passages from other Alexandrian divines referring to Buddha, which show that Alexandrians must have been well acquainted with him and his teaching by the third century A.D. (*Ancient India*, pp. 184 ff.). They were greatly impressed with the story of the Immaculate Conception of Queen Māyā.

had been dry ground!' As Max Müller remarks,[1] mere walking
upon the water is not an uncommon story; but walking by faith,
and sinking for want of it, can only be accounted for by
some historical contact and transference, and the *Jātakas* are
centuries older than the Gospels. In *Jātaka 78* the Buddha
feeds his five hundred brethren with a single cake which has
been put into his begging-bowl, and there is so much over that
what is left has to be thrown away. In a late Buddhist work,
the *Saddharma Pundarīka*, there is a parable which bears a close
resemblance to that of the Prodigal Son.

During this period,

'nascent Christianity met full-grown Buddhism in the Academies and
markets of Asia and Egypt, while both religions were exposed to the
influences of surrounding Paganism in many forms, and of the countless works of art which gave expression to the forms of polytheism. The
ancient religion of Persia contributed to the ferment of human thought,
excited by improved facilities for international communication, and by
the incessant clash of rival civilizations.'[2]

It is possible that the rosary, the veneration of relics, and the
exaggerated forms of asceticism which were such a striking
feature of Alexandrian Christianity, may be traced to Indian
sources. When the French missionary travellers, Huc and Gabet,
visited Lhassa in 1842, they were deeply shocked at the close
resemblance between Catholic and Llamaistic ritual.

'The crozier, the mitre, and chasuble, the cardinal's robe . . . the
double choir at the Divine Office, the chants, the exorcism, the censer
with five chains, the blessing which the Llamas impart by extending
the right hand over the heads of the faithful, the rosary, the celibacy
of the clergy, their separation from the world, the worship of saints,
the fasts, processions, litanies, holy water—these are the points of
contact which the Buddhists have with us.'

---

[1] 'Coincidences', in *Last Essays*, 1st series (1901), p. 250. Gifford Lectures
(1890), ii. 390.

[2] V. A. Smith, *Oxford History of India*, p. 134.

Max Müller traces these to the contact between Tibetan and Nestorian monks in China between A.D. 635 and 841, when both were suppressed. At the famous monastery of Hsian-Fu they actually collaborated.

Gnosticism was a deliberate effort to fuse Christian, Platonic, and Oriental ideas at a time when syncretism was particularly fashionable at Alexandria. Gnosticism has been described as 'Orientalism in a Hellenic mask'. The great Gnostic teacher Basilides, a Hellenized Egyptian who was a contemporary of Hadrian (A.D. 117–38), definitely borrowed his philosophy from the wisdom of the East, which he interweaves in an ingenious fashion into the framework of Christianity. Like Buddha, he is a pessimist. 'Pain and fear are inherent in human affairs.' He has a remarkable explanation of the reason why God permits His saints to suffer marytrdom, which is evidently based on the Buddhist doctrine of *karmā*. 'The theory of Basilides', says Clement, 'is that the soul has previously sinned in another life (πρὸ τῆσδε τῆς ἐνσωματώσεως), and endures its punishment here, the elect with the honour of martyrdom, and the rest purified by appropriate punishment.' Basilides was a firm believer in transmigration, and cited texts such as St. John ix. 2 and Romans vii. 9 in support. Basilides' theory of personality has strong Buddhist affinities. The Soul is without qualities, but the passions, like the Buddhist *skandhas*, attach themselves to it as appendages or 'parasites' (προσαρτήματα). God is unpredicable, almost non-existent (οὐκ ὢν θεός), and the divine entity of Jesus at death alone passed into Nirvāna (ὑπερκοσμία).[1]

After many vicissitudes Alexandria as a centre of learning came to an end in A.D. 642, when the famous library was destroyed by the Caliph Omar, and, according to the well-known story, the manuscripts for six months supplied fuel to the public baths. But the Arabs were far from being mere vandals, and schools arose in Baghdad, Cairo, and Cordova, which rivalled the glories

---

[1] 'Buddhist Gnosticism,' by J. Kennedy, *J.R.A.S.*, 1902.

of the civilization which they superseded. Baghdad, founded in
A.D. 762, occupied a commanding position on the overland route
between India and Europe. It was frequented by Greek and
Hindu merchants. The Abbasides, like the Sassanians, were
great patrons of literature, and had foreign works translated into
Arabic. Baghdad remained the great clearing-house for Eastern
and Western culture until its destruction by the Mongols in
A.D. 1258. During the Dark Ages it was the Arabs who kept
the torch of learning alight, when Rome had perished and Europe
was still plunged in barbarism. The Arabs had little indigenous
culture, and much of their learning was borrowed from Hindu
or Greek sources. The widespread diffusion of the Arabic
language, however, made it an excellent medium for the transmission of ideas from Asia to Europe. Arabic travellers and
scholars like Alberūnī were strongly attracted by Hindu civilization, and transmitted it to the West. Alberūnī is particularly
important in this respect. Born in A.D. 973, he accompanied
Sultan Mahmūd of Ghaznī to India, learnt Sanskrit, and read
the Hindu classics, the *Purānas* and the *Bhagavad-gītā*. He
was acquainted, we are told, with 'astronomy, mathematics,
chronology, mathematical geography, physics, chemistry, and
mineralogy'. One curious result was that many ideas, which
were originally borrowed by India from the West, found their
way back to Europe in an Arabic guise. Three typical examples
are provided by Arabian astronomy, mathematics, and medicine.[1]
Hindu astronomers freely acknowledge their indebtedness to
Alexandria. One of the principal Sanskrit astronomical treatises
is the *Romaka Siddhānta* or Roman manual. Another, the *Pauliśa
Siddhānta*, is based on the works of Paul of Alexandria (A.D. 378).
The Sanskrit names for the signs of the Zodiac, and other
astronomical terms, are of Greek origin. These Sanskrit treatises
were later translated into Arabic, and from Arabic into Latin.
Much the same happened in the case of Hindu mathematics,

[1] See Macdonell, *India's Past*, pp. 175–93.

though the question is too technical to be discussed here. The medical works of Charaka and Suśruta borrow largely from Hippocrates and Galen, and if, as is usually stated, Charaka was court-physician to Kanishka, this is easily explicable. They had a marked influence on Arabic medical writers like Avicenna, whose works, in Latin translations, were the standard authorities in medieval Europe. The game of chess found its way from India to Europe through the Arabs, perhaps at the time of the Crusaders. It is first mentioned by the Sanskrit novelist Bāna, about A.D. 625: its Sanskrit name is *chaturanga*, the 'four arms' of the Hindu army. In Persian this becomes *shatranj*. Many of its terms, such as 'checkmate' (*shāh māt*, the king is dead), and 'rook' (*rukh*) are of Persian origin.

The East is the home of fables, and some of the oldest folk-stories, which are woven into the very web of European litera-ture, may be traced to those great Indian collections of tales, the Buddhist *Jātakas* or Birth-stories, the *Pañchatantra*, and the *Hitopadeśa* or Book of Useful Counsels.[1] Some of these tales reached the West at a very early date. The story of the Judge-ment of Solomon is an excellent example. In the Buddhist version the two women are ordered to try to pull the child away from one another by main force. The child cries out, and one of the women at once lets go, whereupon the wise judge awards him to her, as the true mother.[2] It is impossible not to wonder whether this story may not have reached Judaea along with the ivory, apes, and peacocks from Ophir. Many of these folk-stories are tales of talking beasts, and appear on Buddhist sculpture at Bharhut and Sanchi, and later in Gandhāra. They began to find their way to Asia Minor as far back as the sixth century B.C., and the earliest Greek version was attributed to Aesop, who was said to have lived at the court of Croesus of

---

[1] See Max Müller, 'On the Migration of Fables', in *Chips from a German Workshop*, iv. 412. *Selected Essays*, i. 500.

[2] Rhys Davids, *Buddhist Birth Stories*, i. xiii, xliv.

Lydia. Some of them, as we have seen, appear in Herodotus. There is a reference to the fable of the ass in the lion's skin in Plato's *Cratylus* (411 A). A collection of 'Aesop's' fables was made in Latin by Phaedrus in the time of Tiberius, and by Babrius in Greek at Alexandria about A.D. 200. One of the most famous of all the old Indian story-books is the 'Seventy Tales of a Parrot' (*Śuka Saptati*). This was several times translated into Persian under the name of *Tutināmeh*, and through it many Indian stories found their way into Europe, the best known, perhaps, being the tale of the fraudulent ordeal, made famous in Gottfried von Strassburg's *Tristan und Isolde*.[1] Another source through which many Indian *motifs* reached medieval Europe was the *Arabian Nights*. Masʿūdī, the 'Arabian Herodotus', writing at Basra about A.D. 950, says that this great collection contains Persian, Greek, and Hindu tales, and it was no doubt put together in the first instance at Baghdad, perhaps shortly after the reign of Harun al Rashid, to whom so many of the tales allude. The best known of the stories, that of Sindbad the Sailor, is of Hindu origin, and contains many Indian references.[2] One of the best known of the stories which found its way from the *Arabian Nights* to Europe is that of the Ebony Horse, which appears in Chaucer's Squire's Tale.[3] Another collection of Indian fables was made and rendered into Pehlevi in the sixth century A.D., by order of the Sassanian King Anushīrvān, and from Pehlevi into Arabic by the Caliph Al-Mansūr (A.D. 753–84). Their Arabic and Syriac title, *Kalīlah wa Dimnah*, is apparently derived from the two jackals, Karataka and Damnaka, who play a leading part in them. These stories were

---

[1] Macdonell, *India's Past*, p. 128.

[2] Id. p. 129. Macdonell is confident that the *Arabian Nights* was originally composed by a Persian poet imitating Indian originals. The framework, as well as a large number of the stories, is of Indian origin.

[3] Burton says that the story of the Ebony Horse originated in a Hindu story of a wooden *Garūda*. It came from India via Persia, Egypt, and Spain to France (*Le Cheval de Fust*) and thence to Chaucer's ears.

translated into Persian, Syriac, Latin, Hebrew, and Spanish. A German version, made in 1481, was one of the earliest printed books. In the next century they were turned into Italian, and from Italian into English by Sir Thomas North, the translator of Plutarch, and in this guise were probably known to Shakespeare. In Europe they were known as the Fables of Pilpay, Pilpay being probably a corruption of Bidyāpat or Vidyāpati, 'Master of Wisdom', a wise Brāhman who plays a leading part in them. La Fontaine made use of the fables of the 'Indian sage Pilpay'.

That the migration of fables was originally from East to West, and not vice versa, is shown by the fact that the animals and birds who play the leading parts, the lion, the jackal, the elephant, and the peacock, are mostly Indian ones. In the European versions the jackal becomes the fox: the relation between the lion and the jackal is a natural one, whereas that between the lion and fox is not. This change in the species of the animals in the course of the wandering of the fables is very instructive. Take, for instance, the well-known Welsh story of Llewellyn and Gelert. The father comes home and is greeted by his hound, which he had left to guard his infant daughter. Its jaws are covered with blood, and thinking it has killed the child, he slays it. Then he finds the child asleep in her cradle, safe and sound, a dead wolf by her side. In the original tale in the *Pañchatantra*, a mongoose and a cobra play the part of dog and wolf. Again, in La Fontaine's fable, a girl carrying a pail of milk (in some versions, a basket of eggs) on her head, builds 'castles in the air' about what she is going to do with the proceeds of selling it. She becomes so absorbed that she drops her burden. In the original, a Brāhman whose begging-bowl has been filled with boiled rice dreams of the profits he will make when a famine breaks out and he sells it. In his sleep he kicks the bowl over and the contents are spilt. In modern days the 'beast-story' has been revived in a delightful manner in Rudyard Kipling's Jungle Books.

Numerous European fairy-stories, to be found in Grimm or Hans Andersen, including the magic mirror, the seven-leagued boots, Jack and the beanstalk, and the purse of Fortunatus, have been traced to Indian sources. Many of them are found in the *Gesta Romanorum*, the *Decameron*, and Chaucer's *Canterbury Tales*. The Pardoner's Tale is derived ultimately from a story in the *Vedabbha Jātaka*. One of the most interesting examples of the migration of a tale is provided by the famous history of Barlaam and Josaphat.[1] This is the edifying history of the young Christian prince Josaphat, who is so moved by various distressing sights which he encounters, that he renounces the world and becomes an ascetic. It was written in Greek by John of Damascus in the eighth century A.D. From Greek it was translated into Arabic at the court of the Caliph Al-Mansūr, and from Arabic into a number of European languages. In the Middle Ages it was immensely popular, and in the sixteenth century Josaphat actually became a Christian saint! This is extremely interesting, as it is now evident that Josaphat is the Bodhisat or Bodhisattva, and the story is nothing more or less than that of the Great Renunciation of Gautama Buddha, as narrated in the *Lalita Vistara*. It is adorned with numerous apologues. One of them is the story of the Three Caskets, which was utilized by Shakespeare in the *Merchant of Venice*. Another story in the *Merchant of Venice*, that of the Pound of Flesh, is also of Buddhist origin, though it does not appear to be clear by what channel it came to Shakespeare's knowledge.

During the Middle Ages, however, there was little or no direct intercourse between India and the West. Direct contact was established for the first time since the fall of the Roman Empire on the eventful day, May 20th, 1498, when Vasco da Gama sailed into the harbour of Calicut. In answer to the astonished Zamorin's inquiry as to the cause of his coming,

---

[1] The text and translation are in the Loëb Classics. See Max Müller, *Selected Essays*, i. 500, F. Jacobs, *Barlaam and Josaphat* (1896).

the Portuguese captain briefly and characteristically replied, 'Christians and spices.' The English appeared on the field much later. The first Englishman (if we except the rather mythical Sighelmus, sent in the reign of Alfred on a pilgrimage to the shrine of St. Thomas at Mailāpur) to visit India was Father Thomas Stevens, a Jesuit who went out to Goa in 1579. He was one of the earliest Europeans to take an interest in Oriental languages; he published a grammar of the Konkani dialect, and in 1615 he wrote a remarkable poem, entitled the *Kristana Purāna*, in Konkani. This covers the whole Bible story from the Creation to the Resurrection, and was intended to be used by Indian converts in the place of the Hindu *purānas*, or popular poems about the gods. It contains many beautiful passages, and from its wealth of classical allusions and the polish of the style and metre it appears probable that Father Stevens knew Sanskrit. For the Marāthī language he has the highest admiration:

'Like a jewel among pebbles, like a sapphire among jewels, is the excellence of the Marāthī tongue. Like the jasmine among blossoms, the musk among perfumes, the peacock among birds, the Zodiac among the stars, is Marathī among languages.'

Another distinguished visitor to Goa at the same time was Jan Huyghen van Linschoten, who was the guest of the Archbishop of Goa from 1583 to 1589. His *Itineratio*, published in 1595–6, is one of the earliest and best European books of its day on India, and was translated into English and other languages.

In 1583 a party of English merchants, armed with a letter from Queen Elizabeth to the Emperor Akbar, set out to India by the overland route through Asia Minor. They went to Tripolis in the *Tyger*, a fact which is alluded to in *Macbeth*, when the witch says:

'Her husband's to Aleppo gone, master o' the Tyger.'

From Aleppo they followed the old caravan route to the Euphrates, and made their way down-stream to Basra. From

here they went to Ormuz, where they were arrested by the
Portuguese and sent to Goa. Eventually, however, they
escaped, and, after many adventures, three of them, Ralph
Fitch, John Newbery, and William Leedes, reached the Imperial
Court at Agra in 1585, but only the first-named returned alive
to England. Fitch describes Agra as 'a very great city and
populous, built with stone, having fair and large streets, with a
fair river running by it, which falleth into the gulf of Bengala.
It hath a fair castle and a strong, with a very fair ditch.' In 1608
the East India Company received permission from the Emperor
Jahāngīr to hire a house to serve as a factory on the banks of the
Tapti at Surat, and this was the cradle of the British Empire
in India.

But the English came to India as merchants, not as anti-
quarians or explorers, and were little interested in the religion
or culture of the country. An exception may be made in the
case of the two chaplains, Lord and Ovington. Henry Lord's
Display of Two forraigne Sects in the East Indies (1630) is the
first English account of the Hindus and Parsis of Surat, and
Ovington's *Voyage to Surat in the year 1689* also contains a
number of lively and interesting observations. There was,
however, a steady stream of travel-literature relating to India
in the seventeenth century, and upon one great poet the magic
of the 'Silken East' reacted powerfully. John Milton, sitting in
blind solitude, 'by darkness and by dangers compassed round',
must have been deeply impressed by the accounts of the Mogul
Empire given by travellers like Sir Thomas Roe, and it is probable that he heard more than one of them at first-hand. When
we read how

> High on a throne of royal state, which far
> Outshone the wealth of Ormuz or of Ind,
> Or where the gorgeous East with richest hand
> Showers on her kings barbaric pearl and gold
> Satan exalted sat.

our minds instinctively go back, as Milton's must have gone back, to Roe's dramatic first interview with the Emperor Jahāngīr, when 'high on a gallery, with a canopy over him and a carpet before him, sat in great and barbarous state the Great Mogul'. References to India in Milton's epic are almost too numerous to be quoted, but few can forget the wonderful description of the fig-tree, beneath the branches of which Adam and Eve take refuge after eating the forbidden fruit:

> They chose
> The figtree, not that kind for fruit renowned,
> But such as, at this day to Indians known,
> In Malabar or Deccan spreads her arms,
> Branching so broad and long, that in the ground
> The bended twigs take root, and daughters grow
> About the mother tree, a pillared shade,
> High over-arched, with echoing walks between;
> There oft the Indian herdsman, shunning heat,
> Shelters in cool, and tends his pasturing herds
> At loop-holes, cut through thickest shade.'[1]

The flying Fiend, winging his way through the air, suggests to him a fleet of East Indiamen under full sail

> By equinoctial winds
> Close sailing from Bengala, or the isles
> Of Ternate and Tidore, whence merchants bring
> Their spicy drugs.

Asiatic proper names had a peculiar attraction for Milton, and he uses them with magnificent effect in the Vision of Adam, where he beholds

> the destined walls
> Of Cambalu, seat of Cathaian Can,
> And Samarchand by Oxus, Temir's throne,
> To Paquin of Sinaean kings, and thence,

---

[1] For other references to the Indian fig-tree in English literature see the article on 'Banyan Tree' in Yule's *Hobson-Jobson*.

> To Agra and Lahore of Great Mogul. . . .
> Mombaza and Quiloa and Melind
> And Sofala thought Ophir.

Nor, lastly, can we omit the beautiful and arresting little pen-picture of

> The utmost Indian isle, Taprobane,
> Dusk faces with white silken turbans wreathed.

To seventeenth-century England, India was the India of the Great Mogul, whose court was so dramatically, if fantastically, portrayed in Dryden's popular drama *Aurengzebe* in 1675. This impression was strengthened by the narratives of the two famous French travellers, Tavernier and Bernier, which were translated into English in 1684, and give a vivid picture of the Mogul Empire. European travellers in India in the seventeenth and eighteenth centuries usually took the Muhammadan point of view about the Hindus. They looked upon them as degraded and superstitious, and this attitude was strengthened by the publication of works by missionaries like the Abbé Dubois,[1] who saw only the darker side of Hinduism. If Europeans studied any Oriental language, it was Persian. The poetry of Persia has certain affinities with classical literature, and the rendering of the stanzas of Sā'di or Hāfiz into English verse was an elegant exercise almost as diverting as making renderings of Horace. Curiously enough, it was through Persian sources that the West first became acquainted with the language and literature of the Hindus. In the eighteenth century missionaries like Hexlenden and Pons had managed to gather materials for a Sanskrit grammar, and a Dutchman named Abraham Roger had made a translation of the Hindu poet Bhartrihari, but these had excited little attention. Voltaire's praise of the lore of the *Ezour Vedam* created some interest, though it was proved afterwards to be

[1] *Hindu Manners, Customs, and Ceremonies* (1817). The Abbé wandered about South India from 1792 to 1823, and had unique opportunities for observation, which he utilized to the full.

founded on a worthless forgery. But the great Emperor Akbar, and after him that brilliant but ill-fated prince, Dārā Shikoh, were both keenly interested in Hinduism, and the traveller Bernier brought home to France a manuscript translation into Persian of those ancient Sanskrit works, the *Upanishads*, made by order of the latter. This fell into the hands of another famous French traveller and scholar, Anquetil Duperron, who in 1771 had discovered the Avesta. Duperron translated it into a queer jargon of Latin, Greek, and Persian in 1801, and this caught the attention of the German philosopher Schopenhauer.

Meanwhile, in British India, Warren Hastings was encouraging the study of Sanskrit for purely utilitarian reasons. He was engaged in drawing up a code of laws for the Company's Hindu subjects, and for this purpose it was necessary to obtain an accurate knowledge of the ancient Sanskrit law-books. In 1785 Charles Wilkins published a translation of the *Bhagavad-gītā*, the first rendering of a Sanskrit work into English, and a few years later Sir William Jones (1746–94), the real pioneer of Sanskrit studies and the founder of the Asiatic Society of Bengal, produced his famous version of the Code of Manu, the greatest of the Hindu lawbooks. In 1789 a Brāhman pundit told him of the existence of the Sanskrit drama, and in that year he astonished the Western world by a translation of Kālidāsa's famous masterpiece *Śakuntalā*. Scholars now prosecuted the search for Sanskrit manuscripts with the avidity of explorers seeking for Australian goldfields, and the study of Sanskrit was put upon a scientific footing by H. T. Colebrooke (1765–1837), the greatest of all the early Sanskrit scholars.

Sanskrit was introduced into Europe by a curious accident. One of the Company's servants, Alexander Hamilton, was detained in Paris during the Napoleonic Wars. He spent his time in teaching his fellow prisoners Sanskrit, and among his pupils was the German poet and philosopher Schlegel. Schlegel, on his return to Germany, published his work *On the Language and*

Wisdom of the Indians (1808). This sudden discovery of a vast literature, which had remained unknown for so many centuries to the Western world, was the most important event of its kind since the rediscovery of the treasures of classical Greek literature at the Renaissance, and luckily it coincided with the German Romantic Revival. The *Upanishads* came to Schopenhauer as a new *Gnosis* or revelation.

'That incomparable book', he says, 'stirs the spirit to the very depths of the soul. From every sentence deep, original, and sublime thoughts arise, and the whole is pervaded by a high and holy and earnest spirit. Indian air surrounds us, and original thoughts of kindred spirits. And oh, how thoroughly is the mind here washed clean of all early engrafted Jewish superstitions, and of all philosophy that cringes before these superstitions! In the whole world there is no study, except that of the originals, so beneficial and so elevating as that of the *Oupnekhat*. It has been the solace of my life, it will be the solace of my death.'[1]

Through Schopenhauer and von Hartmann, Sanskrit philosophy profoundly affected German transcendentalism. Kant's great central doctrine, that things of experience are only phenomena of the thing-in-itself, is essentially that of the *Upanishads*. Kālidāsa's *Meghadūta*, 'The Cloud Messenger', that beautiful lyric in which the banished Yaksha sends a message by the monsoon-clouds, hurrying northwards, to his wife in the distant Himālayas, inspired the passage in Schiller's *Maria Stuart*, where the exiled queen calls on the clouds, as they fly southwards, to greet the land of her youth. Two of Heine's finest poems, *Die Lotusblume* and *Auf Flügeln des Gesanges*, breathe the very spirit of Hindu lyrical poetry.

Śakuntalā was translated into German by Forster in 1791, and was welcomed by Goethe with the same enthusiasm that

[1] *Welt als Wille und Vorstellung*, 1st ed., p. xiii; *Parerga*, 3rd ed., i. 59, ii. 425–6. Schopenhauer, curiously enough, preferred Duperron's barbarous translation to later and more readable versions. Paul Deussen spoke of the Vedānta as 'the strongest support of pure morality, the greatest consolation in the sufferings of life and death'. *Elements of Metaphysics*, p. 337.

Schopenhauer had shown for the *Upanishads*. His epigram on the drama is well known:

Willst Du die Blüte des frühen, die Früchte des späteren Jahres,
Willst Du was reizt und entzückt, willst du was sättigt und nährt,
Willst Du den Himmel, die Erde, mit Einem Namen begreifen;
Nenn' ich Sakontala, Dich, und so ist Alles gesagt.

Wouldst thou the young year's blossoms and the fruits of its decline,
And all by which the soul is charmed, enraptured, feasted, fed,
Wouldst thou the earth and Heaven itself in one sole name combine?
I name thee, O Sakontala! and all at once is said.

The Prologue of *Faust*, where the author, stage-manager, and Merry-Andrew converse, is modelled on the prologue of the Sanskrit drama, which consists of a dialogue between the stage-manager and one or two of the actors, including the Jester or Fool (*vidūshaka*). Goethe had at one time formed a plan for adapting *Śakuntalā* for the German stage. He toyed with the idea of metempsychosis, and used to explain his attachment to Frau von Stein by the hypothesis that they were man and wife in a previous existence.

It is interesting to speculate to what extent Indian philosophy influenced Coleridge, Carlyle, and the pioneers of the English Romantic Movement through the medium of Germany. Shelley and Wordsworth looked to France rather than Germany for inspiration, but their pantheism is full of unconscious reminiscences of Hindu thought, which reached them through the medium of Neoplatonism. Nowhere is the Vedāntic doctrine of *Māyā* more magnificently propounded than in *Adonais:*

> The One remains, the many change and pass,
> Heaven's light for ever shines, Earth's shadows fly,
> Life, like a dome of many-coloured glass,
> Stains the white radiance of Eternity,
> Until Death tramples it to fragments.

Even more striking is Shelley's passionate conviction that Adonais has found that final absorption which in Hindu philosophy is the end of the Quest. He is not dead: he has 'awakened from the dream of Life'. He is 'made one with Nature':

> He is a portion of the loveliness
> Which once he made more lovely: he doth bear
> His part, while the one Spirit's plastic stress
> Sweeps through the dull dense world, compelling there
> All new successions to the forms they wear.

The Vedāntist would feel that Wordsworth was speaking in his own language when he writes of

> Something far more deeply interfused,
> Whose dwelling is the light of setting suns,
> And the round Ocean and the living air,
> And the blue sky and in the mind of man:
> A motion and a spirit, that impels
> All thinking things, all objects of all thought,
> And rolls through all things,

or when he declares,

> To every natural form, rock, fruit or flower,
> Even the loose stones that cover the highway,
> I gave a moral life: I saw them feel,
> Or linked them to some feeling: the great mass
> Lay bedded in a quickening soul, and all
> That I beheld respired with inward meaning.

Typically Vedāntist, too, is his view of the soul, 'here in this body pent,' as a fugitive and sojourner upon earth, φυγὰς θεόθεν καὶ ἀλήτης, as Empedocles finely puts it:

> Our birth is but a sleep and a forgetting ;
> The Soul that rises with us, our life's Star,
> Hath had elsewhere its setting,
> And cometh from afar.

Hindu philosophy played an important part in the American Transcendentalist movement, which was a strange compound of Plato and Swedenborg, German idealism, Coleridge, Carlyle, and Wordsworth. Emerson, one of the leading spirits in the movement, though he was no Orientalist, had read Sanskrit, Pāli, and Persian literature in translations. Ideas which he had imbibed in this way emerge from time to time in his essays, especially those on The Oversoul and Circles, and in his poetry. Human personality presented itself to him as a passing phase of universal Being. Born of the Infinite, to the Infinite it returns. Nowhere does Emerson's transcendentalism find more complete expression than in his remarkable poem *Brahma:*

> If the red slayer think he slays,
> Or if the slain think he is slain,
> They know not well the subtle ways
> I keep, and pass, and turn again.

> Far or forgot to me is near ;
> Shadow and sunlight are the same ;
> The vanished gods to me appear ;
> And one to me are shame and fame.

> They reckon ill who leave me out;
> When me they fly, I am the wings;
> I am the doubter and the doubt,
> And I the hymn the Brahmin sings.

Meanwhile, the two brothers Schlegel had been working upon the lines indicated by Sir William Jones in his presidential address to the Asiatic Society of Bengal in 1786, when he declared that Sanskrit, Greek, Latin, and probably the Celtic and Teutonic languages, sprang from a common source, no longer existing, and this led to the foundation of the Science of Comparative Philology by Franz Bopp in 1816. 'If I were asked', says Max Müller, 'what I considered the most important discovery of the nineteenth century with respect to the ancient history of mankind, I should answer by the following short line: Sanskrit *Dyaus Pitar* = Greek $Z\epsilon\grave{v}s$ $\Pi\alpha\tau\acute{\eta}\rho$ = Latin Juppiter = Old Norse Tyr.'

So far, scholars had been mainly confined to classical Sanskrit, though Jones and Colebrooke had both seen some *Vedas*.

Gradually, however, manuscripts were obtained, and in 1838 Rosen published the first edition of some of the hymns of the *Rig-Veda*. This work was carried on by Burnouf, Roth, and Max Müller, and from their patient researches sprang the study of Comparative Religion, which has had an effect upon modern thought only comparable to that of Darwin's *Origin of Species*. Max Müller said that the two great formative influences in his life were the *Rig-Veda* and the *Critique of Pure Reason*. The publication, in 1875, of the first of the great series of the Sacred Books of the East, under the editorship of Max Müller, made the Hindu scriptures available for the first time to the ordinary reader; and here, perhaps, is the proper place to pay homage to the great scholar who did so much not only to popularize Sanskrit learning, but to break down the barriers of prejudice and misconception between East and West. Sanskrit led to Pāli, and the study of the Buddhist scriptures revealed for the first time to the West the life and teachings of the greatest of all Indian religious reformers, Gautama Buddha. Pioneers in Buddhist studies were Burnouf, Lassen, and Trenckner.

It would be out of place here to make more than a passing reference to the work of the Archaeological Department. Generations of devoted scholars, from Horace Hayman Wilson and Alexander Cunningham down to Sir John Marshall, have wrested from oblivion, brick by brick and stone by stone, the long-buried secrets of India's glorious past. In 1834 James Prinsep, by discovering the clue to the Kharoshtī alphabet from the bilingual Bactrian coins, enabled scholars for the first time to read the early inscriptions, the contents of which had hitherto baffled interpretation, and so to reconstruct the pre-Muhammadan history of the country.

India, it has been said, suffers to-day, in the estimation of the world, more through the world's ignorance of her achievements than the absence or insignificance of those achievements. The work of three generations of scholars has done much to dispel the clouds of prejudice which prevent the West from appreciating the true greatness of Indian culture, but much remains to be done. Even the greatest of Indian rulers are still scarcely known by name to the general reader, and Indian art and architecture are regarded as grotesque and unfamiliar. More and more, however, we are beginning to realize the innumerable contacts, throughout the course of history, between East and West, and their mutual indebtedness in language, literature, art, and philosophy. As time goes on it will be increasingly realized that a knowledge of the history and culture of India is essential to the foundation of a proper understanding of the origin and growth of Western civilization. The intellectual debt of Europe to Sanskrit literature, already great, may well become greater in the course of years.

H. G. RAWLINSON.

LANGUAGE AND EARLY LITERATURE

Linguistically India is not, upon a superficial comparison, more complex than the area with which it is usually compared, namely Europe exclusive of Russia. If we set over against the Sanskrit and Indo-Āryan the Classical and Romance languages, against the Munda and Dravidian the Celtic and Teutonic, against the Iranian the Baltic and Slav, against the Tibeto-Burman the Finno-Ugrian and Turkish, we have not much left on either side, say the Albanian and Basque in Europe, the Austriac, Burushaski, and Thai in India. As the original and predominant vehicle of culture and religion, the Greek and Latin together may approach the position of Sanskrit, Pāli, and Prākrit. In both cases we have now, as regards a portion of the area, evidence of an earlier speech and civilization, the Mohenjodāro-Hārappa-Punjab culture in India, the Cretan and other early culture of Hellas, both obliterated and consigned to oblivion through the indifference or hostility of ruder conquerors, Indo-European in speech.

This slight comparison may serve as a basis for noting the outstanding differences in the two cases. The most general of these lies in the fact that most of the European languages named above belong to a single family, the Indo-European, and nearly all are of an inflectional, or quasi-inflectional, type; whereas the Indian languages represent five or six different families and morphology varying from monosyllabism through various grades of agglutination to high inflexion. A second notable difference consists in the extraordinary number and variety of the languages of the Tibeto-Burman family, located for the most part in the Himālayan districts, in Assam, and on the frontier of Burma: many of them belong to tribes having only a primitive culture. Most of the Munda-speaking peoples and some of the Dravidian occupy isolated or intermediate

areas of mountain or jungle, and they too have preserved conditions more elementary than any surviving in Europe. In the
western Himālaya and on the north-west frontier there is perhaps no area which has not passed through a period of literary
civilization, Brahmanic, Buddhist, Hindu, Iranian, or Musalman, reaching back in most cases beyond the commencement of
the Christian era.

Detailed investigation of the linguistic history of India has
hitherto been confined to the Indo-European, which is intrusive, having appeared first at a date subsequent to 2000 B.C.
At that time the south was in all probability mainly Dravidian,
as at present. How far Dravidian or Munda elements prevailed
in Hindustan, and whether Tibeto-Burman tribes were already
in occupation of the Himalayan districts, is wholly uncertain.
The discovery of the pre-Indo-European civilization of the
Punjab and the Indus valley introduces a further problem: it
is not ascertained whether the language concealed in its script
belonged to one of the families known in India or had connexions
with the West (Elam? Sumeria?) or with Central Asia. The
stages of Dravidian languages are—except for some phrases,
supposed to be Kanarese, contained in a Greek play of the second
century A.D., found in Egypt—not known prior to the third
(? Tamil) to tenth century A.D.; the Tibeto-Burman dialects,
except the Tibetan itself (from the seventh century A.D.), the
Newārī of Nepal (from the fourteenth?), the Lepcha of Sikkim
(from the seventeenth?) are all modern discoveries, as is also the
Munda. Thus the linguistic history of India, so far as at present
ascertained, is the history of the spread of Indo-European speech,
its internal developments, its modification through substrata,
and its influence upon those languages which it did not obliterate.
A minor feature is the influence of later intrusive elements,
Persian and Arabic (from the eleventh century A.D.), now succeeded, with much greater effect, by the English.

Upon the languages pre-existent in India the influence of the

Indo-European, or, as we shall henceforward particularize it, the Indo-Āryan, seems to have been mainly matter of vocabulary. As the source, or vehicle, of higher culture, it has at all periods been furnishing those languages with names for new objects and conceptions and then, as the effects consolidated, even replacing familiar native terms by its own. The Dravidian languages are as much affected by Sanskrit and its derivatives as is the English by the classical languages, in the case of the Malayālam perhaps even more. Structurally, however, these languages have internal developments in the main independent of Indo-Āryan.

The latter, on the other hand, has undergone continuous transformation. The language of the tribes whom at the earliest stage we find immigrant or settled in the Punjab was in its general features more or less on a level with the earliest Greek. With the expansion of the people eastwards and partly southwards and with the formation of large states in the Delhi region, in the Doab, in Oudh and North and South Bihār, as well as in Mālwā, it developed in the course of about a thousand years into the Sanskrit, chiefly through loss of a part of its grammatical forms. At the end of what may be termed the Āryan period, conveniently demarked by the rise of the empire of Magadha in the fourth century B.C., this Sanskrit was perhaps recognizable in three slightly differing forms. There was, first, the strict Sanskrit of the Brāhman schools, rendered precise by generations of refined and scrupulous study of texts and of pronunciation, the *bhāshā* proper, finally fixed in the fourth century B.C. by the Grammar of Pānini. Secondly, there was the language of the poets, court bards or others, known to us from the great Epics, the *Mahābhārata* and *Rāmāyana*, and distinguished by some irregularities. And, thirdly, there was a less literary Sanskrit, more akin, no doubt, to the normal speech of educated persons, and marked by further laxities: it may be seen in the more commonplace parts of the later Vedic literature, in supplementary works such as *Pariśish-tas*, and perhaps it was employed in such treatises as there were on practical sciences, such as politics and law, and practical arts, such as architecture. Each of these forms of Sanskrit has had a long subsequent history. The strict Pāninean norm, maintained by a succession of grammatical schools and a rigid training, was naturally dominant in learned works, commentaries, and philosophical discussions; but in such literature its complexity was greatly economized through employment of compounds (a means of evading syntax) and stereotyped forms of expression. It penetrated more and more into the poetical and narrative literature, which in the Classical period became grammatically faultless, except for a few particular irregularities, which the poets wilfully displayed as a residue of their old tradition: as early as the first century A.D. we find the Buddhist poet Aśvaghosha paying tribute to the new discipline by grammatical niceties, and the later poets all indulge occasionally in references to grammar and dictionary. Classical correctness is the rule for all Sanskrit works of literature composed in later and in modern times. The somewhat freer Sanskrit of the Epics also had an abundant progeny during later periods, in the more popular religious writings, such as *Purānas*, and in various kinds of pedestrian disquisitions in verse. The irregular oral Sanskrit was adopted by some Buddhist sects for their canonical writings, in some cases mixed with the actual vernacular, which had passed beyond the Sanskrit stage; but in the later Buddhist Sanskrit works correctness, indispensable in controversy with Brahmanical and other opponents, became the rule. The Jains also, when they took to Sanskrit, followed the established norm of grammar. Possibly a lineal descendant of the old oral Sanskrit may be seen in the extremely irregular language of such works as the *Māna-sāra*, the leading treatise on architecture and sculpture. But Sanskrit has always been in oral use among the more or less learned, naturally with limited range and slipshod expressions; and probably there has always been a vast amount of mundane composition, of genealogies and horoscopes for instance, which made no pretence of correctness.

In a millenary process of expansion from the Indus to the borders of Bengal and in adaptation to partly alien populations the speech of the Indo-Āryan tribes could not escape dialectical variety. Even in the literary usage some slight peculiarities are noted by Pānini and his commentators, as distinctive of easterners or westerners. The first emergence of actual vernacular, employed as official medium in the royal Edicts of Aśoka (middle of the third century B.C.), reveals what it called a Prākrit stage of development in at least three areas, in Magadha, or Bihār, the seat of the Maurya Empire, in the Punjab and the north-west, and in western India. Varieties intermediate between the first two of these would have appeared, if the Edicts found in the interspace had been composed in local dialect. The dialects are distinguished from Sanskrit and from one another chiefly by pronunciation, modifications of vowels, simplification of consonant groups, and by losses and confusions of forms in declension and conjugation. A slightly later stage is represented by the Pāli of the Buddhist canon, a dialect of undetermined local provenance, but preserved and developed in Ceylon; still later in recorded form is the Ardha-Māgadhī of the Jain canon, which must have originated in the eastern half of Hindustan. A sectarian, anti-Brahmanic, or popular feeling may indeed have favoured the official use of vernaculars, since both the Buddhists and the Jains betrayed at an early period a tendency to belittle the Brāhmans, and the Maurya Empire, wherein they flourished, was a novelty in Indian history; but perhaps a more material factor was the extended practical use of writing, which was slow in penetrating the Brahmanic schools. The Pāli and the Ardha-Māgadhī have been preserved down to the present time in the respective communities, and the more learned Buddhist priests of Ceylon and

Burma can still write and speak Pāli. There is no evidence of Prākrit in Brahmanical or general literature before the Christian era: Sanskrit was still customary in the higher society, as is shown by the division of dialects in the earliest known plays (Aśvaghosha, first century A.D.), and it was adopted as a medium even by some early Buddhist sects. In the first century A.D. it begins to show itself in epigraphic records. After about A.D. 300 Prākrit became rare in official and monumental employment.

The literary Prākrits, known chiefly as used by various classes of persons in the drama and, in much greater number, from descriptions and statements in special grammatical works, represent a stage of phonetic decay and grammatical transformation somewhat more advanced than is seen in the Aśokan dialects or the Pali. Several of them have territorial appellations, and they may reasonably be regarded as originally local varieties of speech, which, like the Doric and Aeolic in ancient Greece, the Braj and Maithilī in medieval India, the Mārwārī in modern times, became characteristic of occupations monopolized by natives of those districts, or won celebrity in certain genres of literature. The latter would be the case with the *Mahārāshtrī*, the chief medium of lyric verse, and the Paiśācī, in which was composed a very famous collection of tales, the *Brihat-kathā* of Gunādhya: whereas the use of Śauraseni prose by respectable women and of Māgadhī by policemen and others can have originated only in the alternative manner.

We are now approaching the threshold of the modern Indo-Āryan languages; but a stage has yet to be interposed. It seems probable that the literary Prākrits had attained a fixed norm by the end of the third century A.D.: henceforward they were a learned form of speech, no less artificial, but infinitely more restricted in use, than the Sanskrit, which in general structure they resembled. In the Apabhramśas, or 'degenerate' popular dialects, which may have attained maturity by the end of the fifth to the seventh century, and which in their turn acquired a literary use—we have some specimens which go back to the tenth century—the inflectional system has been reduced nearly to the stage of the modern languages, though it lacks the addition of post-positions, which is a marked characteristic of these.

If now we look round upon the actually existent Indo-Āryan languages, we may distinguish first of all those which probably never underwent Brahmanization or experienced seriously the influence of Sanskrit. These would include most of the 'Dard' dialects outside the north-west frontier, but not the Kāshmīrī, since Kashmir at an early period became a centre of Buddhism, later of Hinduism. These have become known only in modern times, and they are without literature, except folk-songs and stories collected orally. The Indus countries, to which belong the Sindhī and Lahndā, or western Punjābī, were also, it seems, never extensively Brahmanized. The Sindhī was probably the source of one dialect of Apabhramśa; but otherwise the literature of these countries, which has *motifs* either Persian or Sikh, does not go back beyond a late Sikh period. The Pahārī dialects of the Himālayan countries from Nepal to Kashmir are akin to those of Rājasthān. They have passed through the vicissitudes of Hindu civilization, and are without independent literature. In the old Indo-Āryan language of Nepal, which was akin to the Maithilī of Bihār, some literary works exist.

The chief languages have a continuous literary history reaching back to the fourteenth or fifteenth century, in the case of western Hindī and Maithilī-Bihārī even to the twelfth or further. They are thus somewhat younger than the chief modern European languages. In almost all cases their early literature consists exclusively of ballads or religious songs, and prose is relatively modern. The most obvious common features of these languages are the use of declinable post-positions to help out the old declension of nouns, which had been reduced to a minimum of forms, and a preference for passive constructions in the case of transitive verbs. In the old poetry the post-positions are often wanting, and this renders the grammatical construction vague. The origin of the two tendencies, which have not much precedent in earlier forms of Indo-Āryan, and which are shared by extra-Indian languages, such as Pashtū, Tibetan, Turkī, &c., is an interesting problem.

The main Indo-Āryan languages have thus their older periods, attested by some poetical literature. But until modern times they were not used, except in so far as they were adopted in the religious poetry of sects, for higher intellectual purposes. This region was appropriated by the Sanskrit or, in the case of Musalmans, by the Arabic and Persian. It may even be said that the languages did not exist. The poems were originally in dialects, and only occasionally did some dialect, like the Brajbhāshā of Hindī, become a standard for certain purposes. For the lack of a common standard there was no correct 'Hindī', &c., in general use: the learned were often unable to write grammatically the language supposed to be theirs and used only a patois. In modern times these languages have been called upon to take a place in general education, to be media of journalism, and to develop all forms of literature on European lines, in which process they have had to contend with difficulties of terminology and language-mixture.

Mixture of dialect has been manifold and complex. The absence of real frontiers in Hindustan has caused each local form of speech to be a transition stage between its neighbours. The partiality to journeyings and pilgrimages has introduced extraneous terms or forms of words. Intrusions from an officially adopted dialect are apparent even in the Edicts of Aśoka; and linguistic peculiarities have been domesticated outside their original areas by the activity of classes, such as the Mārwārī business men in modern times, and by religious movements, such as that of the Sikhs. Thus all periods of the derivate

Indo-Āryan languages have been affected by mutual 'borrow-ings'. But the chief and constant infusion has been, and is, from the classical language, the Sanskrit. A terminology exists for the discrimination of such loans according to the degree of altera-tion (i.e. on an average, the antiquity and degree of acclimatiza-tion) of the expressions; but the process has been even more continuous and general than the absorption of Latin and French phraseology into English.

Prior to the English only one foreign tongue had seriously invaded the speech of India. That is the Persian (with some Turkī elements): as the normal official language of the Musal-man courts and kingdoms, it was current wherever there was Musalman rule; and at least until the end of the eighteenth century English administrators had to be conversant with it, and it was familiar in the Durbars of states such as Jaipur, Nepal, and Kashmir. In this way most of the languages came to adopt a considerable number of political, legal, and business terms, some of which are among the most familiar Indianisms in English. The Urdū, or 'Hindustani', current during the nineteenth century among British administrators, soldiers, and visitors, developed, on the basis of a Hindī dialect, as a lingua franca in the region of the Mughal capital: it was characterized by a free use of Persian expressions, which in high literary Urdū overshadow the Indian element. In the sixteenth century it developed a poetical literature (the Rekhtā literature of Walī and other Deccan poets), and owing to its relations with Per-sian it was earlier than most of the Indo-Āryan languages in attaining to literary prose.

The other culture languages which at one time or another have contributed strands to 'the web of Indian life', the Syriac, and later the Latin, of Christian churches, the Zend and Pah-lavī of the Pārsīs, the Arabic, the Armenian of bankers, and so forth have not exercised serious linguistic influence. But some-thing may be said concerning the great multiformity of the modern Indian book product, when we shall have interpolated some brief explanations concerning the use of writing. About fifteen alphabets are commonly used in connexion with particular languages in India: in the south Tamil, Telugu, Kanarese, Malayālam, for the corresponding languages and for Tulu; elsewhere Bergālī, for that language and Assamese, Devanāgarī for Hindī, Marāthī, and Nepālī, Gurumukhī for Punjābī and Sindhī, Gujarātī for that language, Oriya for the language of Orissa, the Persian character for Urdū, but also for Punjābī, Kashmīrī, and Sindhī, Tibetan for that language in various dialects. Note also the Singhalese of Ceylon and the Burmese, Siamese, &c., of Further India, and, for completeness, the Javanese of Java. This is only the beginning of the complication. There are various minor local scripts which are rarely seen in print, such as the Sindhī, Multānī, Savara, Thakrī, Lepcha, and some which are widely used for business purposes, but rarely for printing literary compositions, e.g. the Kaithī and Mahājanī of northern India and the Mōdī of the Marātha country. Some older alphabets, for example the Śāradā of Kashmir and the Grantha of the Tamil country, are employed only for Sanskrit. Next, the combinations and alternatives: Sanskrit is printed preponderatingly in its own Devanāgarī, but also in all the chief alphabets, including the very inadequate Tamil and Persian; hence a Devanāgarī text is often seen accompanied by translation or comment in a different script and language, or in more than one, especially when English is a second. Periodicals in modern languages often insert articles in Sanskrit or English. The Pārsīs usually print their Pahlavī in Gujarātī characters, with exegesis in that language; but sometimes they retain the old writing. Muhammadans prefer their Hindī, Punjābī, Sindhī, Kāshmīrī, and even Tamil in the Persian writing; whereas the Musalman dialect of Bengālī is usually represented by the alphabet of that province. Tamil is occasionally printed in Telugu characters; and there are also many other sporadically occurring combinations of languages and scripts. Thus, even if we disregard the Roman writing, which besides its employment for English and other European languages (French in Chandernagore and Pondichery, Portuguese in Goa, Latin in Roman ecclesiastical works) is also the usual script for previously unwritten dialects and is occasionally, or on principle, substituted for other writings, the present alphabetic picture of India is elaborate indeed. The ideal of 'a single script for India' is involved in certain controversies, and for the present is Utopian. An historical view, though it reveals many stages of development, tends to clarity. For all the alphabets native to India are descended from a single form of writing, the Brāhmī, worked out in the Āryan period: for the most part they have preserved its excellent system and modified only (but beyond inexpert recognition) the actual shapes of the characters. The system, an outcome of the remarkable philological and phonological precision wherein the early Indians surpassed all ancient peoples, has been of priceless service: it has provided all the languages with an exact reflex of their pronunciation, and it furnishes the philologist with a measure whereby to estimate their history. Nor has this alphabetic legacy from Āryan India confined its benefits to the languages of the sub-continent. Ceylon and the Malay islands, Further India, Tibet, and Central Asia were equipped with exact notations, which record their pronunciation at the time: if China had consented to adopt a similar philologic equipment, many troublesome obscurities in its linguistic history would have been precluded, and its written character would have lost its terror.

With these alphabetic resources the Indian presses print each year in the chief languages, and also in English, (1) compositions of modern types, newspapers, college, university, and general magazines, scientific and technical periodicals and journals, Proceedings and Bulletins of Societies and Institutions, poetry (very numerous publications, but generally short or collections

of short poems), fiction (still restrained in amount, but including the detective novel), history, records, reports, philology,
archaeology, anthropology, natural science and mathematics,
economics, politics, philosophy, school and college text-books.
Any periodical in English may contain occasional articles in the
vernacular or in Sanskrit, and any periodical in a vernacular
occasional articles in English or Sanskrit. (2) Old texts in
classical languages (Sanskrit, Prākrit, Pāli, Zend, Pahlavī, Persian, Arabic, Tibetan), often accompanied by commentaries and
translations in the same or in a modern language or in both.
(3) Texts in old forms of the modern languages (Hindī, Tamil,
Bengālī, Gujarātī, Kanarese, &c.). (4) Occasional items in
Latin (Roman Catholic), French (at Pondichery), Portuguese (at
Goa), and even Dutch; and a number in Nepālī, Pashtū, and
Turkī. The total number of items in an annual 'Indian Catalogue
of Books' would probably exceed the figure for Great Britain,
while the multifariousness, as we see, would be much greater.
But, naturally, not all the publications on scientific, or even on
philological, subjects would lay claim to the maturity and cir-
cumspection of the best European work.

Probably the most spontaneous forms of literature in the pre-
newspaper age—the ballad, the song, the folk-story, the proverb—
have always been abundant in India. There are districts where
even within living memory every occurrence of local note—a
fight, a calamity, a romantic incident, the conduct of an adminis-
trator—was apt to become to the people at work in the field or
in village gatherings a theme of song. Such effusions are now
often evidenced in a printed form, for instance in the Punjab,
in Orissa, in the Kanarese and Tamil countries. The folk-story
would seem to be the most natural growth: the song, since the
community does not itself compose, implies a literary background
somewhere or a class of quasi-professional purveyors of such
things and an occasion for their production.

Vast quantities of folk-tales have been collected orally in

India, both from tribes of primitive culture and from among the civilized peoples. Examples of the former would be such extensive works as the *Santal Folk Tales* (2 vols., Oslo, 1925-7) of P. O. Bodding; but there are many other collections contained in ethnographical works, and a specimen for each dialect is given in the volumes of the Linguistic Survey. The second class, which includes tales of ultimately literary origin, is exemplified by many books, some of them endeared to generations of Europeans in India: let us cite only Frere's *Old Deccan Days*, *Legends of the Punjab* by Temple and Steel, *The Tales of Guru Paramartan* from the Tamil, *Romantic Tales from the Punjab* by Charles Swynnerton, and *The Folk-Literature of Bengal* and other writings by Dinesh Chandra Sen.

The great gifts which the Indians possess for story-telling, their humour, terseness, and entire objectivity, are in the case of the animal fable, with its criticism of life, too famous for any disquisition. The *Pañchatantra* in its various derivates, 'The Fables of Pilpay', &c., became in the middle ages known throughout Europe, and the Pāli *Jātaka* also seems likely to win a world-wide audience. Proverbs and gnomic utterances, of which there are numerous published collections in many Indian languages, are an outcome of kindred faculties of observation and reflection.

Among the poetic genres the love-lyric is perhaps that which comes closest to nature: a slight touch of art, and the emotional-aesthetic utterance becomes rhythmic. But, though perhaps primitive everywhere, and in India, as in Greece, fairly early as a literary form, it was preceded in both countries by poetry having a more functional character, the ballad and the religious hymn, implying a professional author and a more or less public occasion. In the earliest Indo-Āryan times the profession and the occasions already existed, and naturally they have never been lacking since.

In a measure, therefore, the formal literature of India may be viewed as having roots in the common life. Though the principle of its growth has been in the main innate, it has from time to time incorporated independent products of the same soil; and, like the banyan, it has sent down branches which have themselves there taken root. It is, in fact, not so much a literature as a complex of literatures. As we have pointed out, the several Indo-Āryan languages have their old poetry, which in some cases has still an oral life and which scholars and societies are engaged in editing; of the Dravidian languages, the Tamil especially has its classical form, the Sen Tamil, with an abundance of old religious writings ranking as masterpieces. The divergent faiths of the Jains and the Buddhists (the latter no longer surviving in India proper) have their ancient canonical writings in Prākrit and Pāli. But all these are at one point or another adjusted into a general frame of which the vehicle is Sanskrit. This is not to say that the other literatures have not, or have not had, an independent vitality; on the contrary the Sanskrit has been enriched by their inheritance or inspiration: how great has been, for example, the contribution of the Dravidian intellect to the philosophies, the religions, and all parts of the Sanskrit literature itself. But neither is the Sanskrit an external vestment which literature has tended to assume when it reached a certain level or when its original dialects lost their first popular appeal. The fact is rather that the Sanskrit literature has been a great stream, whose sources are all in the early Indo-Āryan region and which, while it has received a number of independent affluents, has also generally been their feeder from its upper reaches. No Indian literature approaches it in antiquity, and none can compare with it in multifariousness or volume or in its status as the representative of Indian mentality in its whole domain.

The customary distinction of Vedic Sanskrit and Classical Sanskrit, or of a Vedic period and a Classical period, is not meant to be taken literally. Study of the Veda commenced at least as early as the first compilation of the *Rig-Veda* and was pursued at all stages in the development of the language down to recent times. And, if we distinguish periods, there is a gap of five or six centuries between the Vedic and what is properly Classical Sanskrit. As time is an important general factor, we may recognize periods; but preferably they may be styled the Āryan and the Hindu. The former, which at its outset found the Āryans as a group of tribes in the land of the Five, or Seven, Rivers and which ended with the overthrow of the kingdoms established during their advance to the borders of Assam and Bengal, is conveniently demarked by the rise of the Nanda and Maurya empires in the fourth century B.C., the Grammar of Pānini, and the invasion of Alexander. It comprises the full development of the Vedic religion, with its ritual, grammatical, and other sciences; also the beginnings of other systematic studies, law, politics, architecture, medicine; the organization of the Brāhman caste and the caste system associated with the ideas of *dharma*, or religious and social duty, *karma*, retribution of acts, and transmigration; the rise of Brahmanic theism and tritheism and asceticism, but also of special semi-orthodox movements, such as the Krishnaic devotionalism (*bhakti*) and the psychic mysticism (*yoga*); metaphysical speculation and, towards the close of the period, an orgy of sophistic 'free thought'. All that is most characteristic and dynamic in Hindu mentality has its roots in this period, to which furthermore belong, both essentially and chronologically, the origins of the Jaina and Buddhist religions. The second period, much interrupted by foreign invasion and domination, commenced as an age of systematization in regard to philosophies and sciences and of expansion and organization in the Buddhist and Jain communities, whose scriptural canons took shape: there were huge compilations of narrative literature in verse and in prose, and the drama and art of the theatre were fully developed. From about A.D. 300 it becomes the Classical period, characterized by mature refinement in art, literature, and life. But from about A.D. 700 new races begin to play a part in Hindustan, and there is decline of vitality in the Sanskrit literature. At the close of the period, which may be marked by the stages of the Muhammadan conquest, the conflicts of these races and the wars with the Musalmans revived the Epic spirit, which found expression in vernacular ballad poetry. Under Musalman rule the learning and literature of the Hindus became more and more reduced to scholasticism. But in the fourteenth and fifteenth centuries vernacular poetry emerges in religious and devotional or mystic song, which leads up to the formation of new religious sects, Lallā Devī in Kashmir, Kabīr and the Kabīr Panth, Nānak, and Sikhism.

In the sixteenth century the Chaitanya movement in Bengal furnished fresh inspiration also for sensitive religious poetry in exquisite Sanskrit verse; and in the seventeenth, at the court of the Mughal Dārā Shikoh, lived Jagannātha Pandita, the last of the original Sanskrit lyricists and rhetoricians.

The Āryan Period

The *Rig-Veda*, the inspired utterance of the ancient Rishis, and doubtless the earliest literary monument of Indo-European speech, is in fact a hymn-book, apparently in a second edition. The main subdivisions, according to author-families, reveal its nature as an assemblage of collections; and the interior arrangement, according to the divinities invoked, the number of verses in the hymns, &c., shows the compilation to have been systematic, both in its original form and in the amplified edition which we have. What authority prevailed upon the poet-families to pool their collections? Was it royalty in an early kingdom centred in Brahmāvarta, the holy land of Brahmanism (the Delhi region)? or was it an independent council of Rishis, holding religious session 'in the Naimisha forest'? Like the Greek Homeridae, the Rishis were professionals, not (except in the case of the *purohita*, or family priest) officials, and their remuneration took the form of presents (*dakshinā*). Their repertoires consisted of old and new hymns: they were conscious of their art, comparing it to that of the chariot-builder, but also of inspiration; there is great sameness of idea and expression, the later hymns exhibiting many clichés from the earlier. So far as actually appears from references to successive generations of kings or poets, the collections did not cover a very long period. But mention of 'old poets' and legendary persons and regions west of the Indies, as well as development in the mythology and pantheon, show that the tradition of the hymn-makers had a remote beginning. A long interval separated the old Indo-Iranian divinity *Apām Napāt*, 'son of the waters', from the cosmological and agnostic speculations included in the late tenth book of the compilation.

In the great majority of cases the hymns are functional, composed for ritual use: the chief normal occasions are the worship of the household fire, the pressing of the soma fermentation, dawn and evening worship. Most frequently we are unable to specify the rite, which in general was at least semi-public, a celebration, say, in the house of a chief or in a village hall, since the communal 'we' is frequent, as in Pindar's odes. But seasonal or astronomic observances may be suspected in case of hymns to Indra or the storm gods or the wind which portray the weather or mythologize concerning it: in others, which refer to battles or sacking of the towns and winning of the kine of the black, flat-nosed aborigines, we may have ceremonial preparation for battle and foray or thanksgiving after these. The contrition for sin which appears in hymns to Varuna and the deprecation of disease which appears in those to Rudra may also have been topical or institutional, while the wedding and funeral hymns in the tenth book declare their employment. But it would be unreasonable to suppose that the poet-craftsmen did not at times yield to spontaneous inspiration or that no effusions of that nature had found a way into the collection. There are, in fact, hymns which resemble ballads in dramatic dialogue or embody reflection.

The *Rig-Veda* is an old, old book in somewhat hieratic language, and very difficult of interpretation. In respect of verbal translation a fairly advanced position has now been reached. But the point of many allusions to legend and mythology and the psychological 'value' of many observations still escapes. In this regard much remains to be dug out of the text. But the tone is manly, sane, unexcited, and unperturbed: the god of the household fire (*Agni*) is addressed with affectionate confidence; the exuberant storm and battle god, the 'fort-breaking' Indra, with vigorous, unsophisticating admiration; the dawn-goddess (*Ushas*), the forest-goddess (*Aranyānī*), and the god of homing cattle and the safety of roads (*Pūshan*) in the dusk, the sun in his golden car and the starry heavens, with real poetic feeling; even the contrition for sin against the eternal laws of Varuna is frank, and the lament of the luckless gambler practically says 'I am a fool, but I can't help it'. The prayer is for wealth in sons and kine, for victory and inspiration. The verse, in several metres not rigidly fixed syllable by syllable, is rather effectively managed by the old poets, who know how to work an antithesis, a cadence, a refrain, and to adapt the vigour of expression to the sense.

The *Atharva-Veda*, considerably later in linguistic form, in date of codification, and in recognition, take precedence, as regards originality of matter, over the two other constituents of the 'Triple Veda', namely the *Sāma-Veda* and the *Yajus*. It represents the domestic and personal side, and the lower levels, of the Vedic religion: the bulk consists of spells, exorcisms, charms against disease, poison, wild animals, snakes, and insect pests; but there are also marriage and funeral hymns, others relating to tools and occupations, and several containing philosophical reflections. In the end the prophylactic and remedial purposes of the hymns won for the Atharvan priests a supervisory status in the public rituals, as repairing errors and omissions, and a claim to the office of high priest (*purohita*) in the state.

In this essay it is impracticable to give quotations from a boundless literature. But, since the *Rig-Veda* must in any case be exemplified, we may select from its more than one thousand hymns one of those which have no normal ritual application, and from the *Atharva-Veda* a late popular piece, apparently a contemporary *gāthā*, or song, in praise of an ancient king who is celebrated in the Epics. The first has the form of a dialogue between the famous Rishi and *purohita*, Viśvāmitra, and the rivers Vipāśā and Śutudrī (Beas and Sutlej), whom he entreats to allow passage to his migrating tribe of Bharatas.

Rig-Veda iii. 33

Eagerly forward from the womb of mountains
Racing, as 'twere a pair of mares untethered,
Lapping, as 'twere two mother kine resplendent,
Hasten Vipāś and Śutudrī their waters.

Viśvāmitra. Indra-besped, asking for incitation,
On to the main flood charioteering, go ye:
Swelling with billows, when you're come together,
Each into other entering, O bright ones!
I have approached the stream, the best of mothers;
Unto Vipāś we're come, the broad, the blessed:
Lapping, like two mother kine a calf together,
Down a joint channel fare they on united.

The Rivers. Even so are we, with full flood swelling,
Faring along the channel god-created:
Not to be stemmed is our onset speeded;
What would the Seer, calling to the rivers?

Viśvāmitra. Stay for my speech mellifluous; a moment
Make, ever-gliding ones, pause in your going.
Out to the river I with loud entreaty,
Kuśika's son, have shouted, needing succour.

The Rivers. Indra raked out our passage, thunderbolt-arm:
Vritra he dashed aside, who girt the waters.

God of the light hand, Savitar us guided;
    His force impelling, move we widened onwards.
Viśvāmitra. Lauded eternally be that act heroic,
    Exploit of Indra, when he clove the dragon:
    Through the encirclement with thunderbolt smashed he:
    On moved the waters; their desire was motion.
The Rivers. Never forgotten be this saying, herald!
    Thine, that shall later generations echo:
    Kindly be thou to us in hymns, O Singer!
    Make us not lowly in man's world, prithee!
Viśvāmitra. Fairly give heed, O sisters, to the poet,
    Come from afar to you with wain, with war-car:
    Fairly bend down; be of passage easy;
    Be with your currents, rivers, axle-under.
The Rivers. Heed will we pay to thy words, O poet!
    Come from afar art thou with wain, with war-car:
    Down will I bend me, like a full-breast woman;
    Like maid to bridegroom, will I yield me to thee.
Viśvāmitra. Soon as the Bharatas be passed across thee (*sic*),
    Foraying band in haste at Indra's urging,
    Forthwith let start away thine onset speeded;
    Favour I crave of you (*sic*), so meet for worship.
    Now have the foraying Bharatas passed over;
    Gained had the Seer the favour of the rivers:
    Swell up the more, life-giving, in fair bounty;
    Fill full your udders: onward go ye swiftly!

Atharva-Veda xx. 127, 3

King of the folk united, a god all men beyond,
Every one's king Parikshit, to his good praise give ear!
'Weal has Parikshit wrought us, in highest seat enthroned',
So with his wife conversing, his cot the Kuru builds.
'What shall I set before you, curds, porridge, malted meal?'
Asks of her lord the goodwife in king Parikshit's realm.
Sunlight above seems spreading; ripe corn o'ertops the bin:
Finely the people prospers in king Parikshit's realm.

The two remaining *Vedās*, the Sāma, merely a book of tunes
for verses taken in nearly all cases from the *Rig-Veda*, and the
Yajur-Veda, manual of the officiating priest (*adhvaryu*), with
verses largely from the *Rig* and prose directions and ejacula-
tions of its own, have an affinity to the special ritual literature
of the next period, the *Brāhmaṇas*. Obviously tune and ritual
have a tradition not less ancient than the hymns themselves,
which in fact make mention of the special functionaries. But
it is really only in the *Brāhmaṇas* that the *Vedas* become Veda;
and these arid treatises, wherein was elaborated the full doctrine of the rituals, are of capital importance in the history of
Indian mentality. Prescribing in remorseless detail every action
and utterance in the elaborate rituals, which often extend over
several days or even much longer, their chief preoccupation
at each point is the significance, the thing symbolized; for 'he
who so knows' (*ya evam veda*) enjoys the fruit of the rite. The
fixed accruing of the result, which exalts the rite into a cosmic
force and mechanizes the action of the participant divinities,
may attest a reversion to a pre-Āryan mode of thought, exemplified elsewhere. The prayer-energy (*brahma*) becomes a sort of
mana, the hidden power which pervades the universe, and its
personified form (Brahmā) is the Creator. At the same time
the old conception of the universe as the body of a Great Person
led to analysis of the parts and functions of the body on the one
hand, and the constituent parts of the world and their divine
regents on the other; and psychological discriminations were
stimulated also by the idea of building up for the sacrificer a
spiritual body. Preoccupation with the significance of names
gave rise to etymologies and the notion of essence—thus
'pole-hood' is the essential nature of the sacrificial pole, because it was with a pole that the gods obstructed the way to
heaven.[1] Here and in some standing forms of explanation, which

[1] A romantic interest attaches to this expression. It terminated the Sanskrit
studies of a European scholar, who, having adopted the rendering 'they *yuped*

represent particular facts as instances of general truths, we have
the beginnings of grammatical theory, which also appears in
certain technical terms, and of logic. The meticulous requirements of exactness in ritual pronunciations and intonations
developed a refined observation and scientific understanding of
phonetics, which elsewhere was not attained until the end of the
eighteenth century A.D.

The *Brāhmanas* are discussions among priests, or instructions to pupils, concerning the procedures and significances of
their operations: the theoretical refinements led to an enormous elaboration in practice. The feeble analogies and inane
(often numerical) symbolisms and tireless repetitions, which one
scholar has attributed to actual dementia, may be regarded as
a nemesis of experts riding a theory to death. The training,
which, as we have seen, contains the germs of the Brahmanic
philosophies and sciences (we may add the 'Veda-supplements'
(*vedāngas*) relating to astronomy and metrics), must have
greatly helped to consolidate the order of priests into a caste;
but certainly this was not all; for the practice of austerities and
asceticisms (*tapas*), perhaps a primitive attribute of the order,
was an unfailing constituent of Brahmanic purity or brilliance
(*bahma-varcasa*). Towards outsiders, royal and other patrons,
the *Brāhmanas* exhibit no settled hostility or contempt; but
the rituals afforded opportunities for malignant treacheries,
which are occasionally noted as possibilities, and there is a
notable appreciation of large fees. In general the ethic is
honourable and human, and there is a good deal of common
sense. The rare literary gleams are seen in stories, such as that
of the boy Nachiketas, who won from the god of death the secret
of immortality (*Taittirīya-Brāhmana*, iii. 11. 8, the subject,
later, of the *Katha-Upanishad*), or, in the *Aitareya-Brāhmana*
(vii. 13 seqq.), the long narrative concerning the sacrifice of the

the *yūpa* with a *yūpa*: hence the *yūpa*-ness of the *yūpa*', confined himself to
other fields of learning, wherein he attained distinction.

boy Śunahśepha, which became the coronation legend of Indian kings.

The *Āranyaka*, 'Forest', portions of *Brāhmanas* and the *Upanishads*, originally attached to *Āranyakas*, introduce us to the subject of 'forest-dwelling', which at a later period was the third of the four stages (*āśrama*) of a Brāhman's life—student, householder, forest-dweller, homeless wanderer. The origin of the practice, which must have been early, and its development (perhaps not unconnected with the gradual spread of Āryans eastward along the then densely wooded Ganges valley) demand a special research. But in all contemporary literature, in the Epics, and at a far later period, the typical abode of the Brahman is the forest settlement; there reside his students, and thence he issues upon invitation to participate in rites, to join in tourneys of discussion at royal courts and so forth, or as a travelling scholar. The Greek accounts describe the Brāhmans as forest-living and state that kings consulted them by messenger: in later times the Buddhist monasteries usually grew up in parks and woodlands outside the city. Neither temples, which in the late Vedic period existed in the towns and which perhaps encouraged the worship of the great sectarian gods, nor service in temples had attraction for the genuine Brāhman, whose duty was study and teaching and maintaining the sacred fires. It is intelligible that the forest settlements should have been the scene of ascetic practices, elaborate rituals, and deeper professional discussions intended for Brāhmans alone.

It seems that the *Āranyakas* were connected with certain solstitial rites (*mahā-vrata*), which originally may have had the character of a popular festival. The popular character had slipped away, and the ritual, which contained some elements of atonement, was for Brāhmans exclusively. The texts, whose designation is stated to mean 'proper for study in the forests', but may originally have meant rites 'practised in the forest', are quite similar to the *Brāhmanas*, to which they are an appendix.

But the rite, which concluded a ceremonial 'extending over the year and symbolic of the year', was of deep significance, and 'they obtain immortality who observe this day'. It therefore led naturally to the *Upanishad*, or session of intimate discussion concerning the more general and profounder topics. The topics are rather miscellaneous, the origin and constitution of the universe, its regent powers, the development of living species, the bodily and psychical powers of man, sleep and dream, death and rebirth, the essence of the material and the spiritual. But the pervasive subject of inquiry was an ultimate 'Self' (*ātman*); and the decisive moments in Indian philosophy were reached when the Śāndilya doctrine (*tat tvam asi*, 'that art thou') declared its identity with the world-essence (*brahman*), and when (*Brihad-Āranyaka Upanishad*, ii. 4. 14, iii. 4. 2, etc.) it was pronounced to be beyond speech and cognition—for who can know the knower?— and only to be indicated negatively as 'not so, not so' (*neti neti*). A further stage, anticipating the future Buddhism, is attained in the *Brhad-Āranyaka Upanishad* (iii. 2. 13), when Yājnavalkya, pressed by the last question of Ārtabhāga:

' "O Yājnavalkya, when at death the man's voice passes into fire, his breath into air, his eye into the sun, his mind into the moon, his ear into space, his body into earth, his self into ether, his body hairs into the plants, his locks into the trees, his blood and seed into the waters, where then is the man?" '

replies:

'Ārtabhāga, take my hand: we two alone must know these things; in public none of that.'

'Then they went away and conferred. As to what they spoke of, it was *karma* (action) that they spoke of; and, as to what they commended, it was action that they commended: "good one becomes through good action, bad through bad". And Ārtabhāga, son of Jaratkāru, held his peace.'

The *Upanishads* are anything but systematic philosophy: they are to Indian philosophy what the *Rig-Veda* is to its religion. They are accumulations of anecdotes, experiences, and theorems. Their transitions from subject to subject, from terse narrative to parable and dialogue, render them more akin to the gospels of other religions than to their systematic expositions. The profundity of their ideas and the processes of deduction thereof lend them great importance in the history of early thought. But what gives to the *Upanishads* their unique quality and unfailing human appeal is an earnest sincerity of tone, as of friends conferring upon matters of deep concern. The somewhat later, metrical, *Upanishads* have a touch more of 'literature'.

Here would be the place, in a history of Indian Literature, for an account of the technical studies of the Brāhmans supplementary to their business of performing, expounding, and sublimating rituals, i.e. of the *Vedāngas* (Vedic supplements) concerning the phonetics, text, metre, etymology, grammar, astronomy; also of the works which were composed in extremely brief, elliptical aphorisms, containing systematic expositions of rituals, public and domestic, and of the sacred law. These works in mnemonic aphorism form, *sūtra*, which subsequently became a norm for enunciations of philosophies and sciences, have perhaps this interest, that they were probably the first to be committed to writing, a circumstance which may explain both their brevity and their name. The early mastery of grammatic science in all its branches, culminating in the work of Pānini, is one of the most signal triumphs of Indian intellect: it gave precision to their mental life, and it contributed greatly to the expansion of Indian culture through a method of study and through translation of their literature into foreign tongues. But we must omit the whole of this technical literature in preparation for still more wholesale omissions in the next period.

It would be strange if outside the priestly studies which we have exemplified the life of Āryan India had been without entertainment in the form of story, poetry, or dramatic show. Stories, in fact, are mentioned, under the designation *ākhyāna*, in the liturgical literature; and in the ritual there were occasions for narrating such, and some, as we have seen, are related in the *Brāhmanas*. Late Vedic texts seem to refer to an actual book, *purāna* or *itihāsa*, or at least a class of compositions which may have contained narratives both mythological and legendary and historical; and of the first of these kinds an example is preserved in a poetical text, *Suparnādhyāya*, of late Vedic times, whereof a version was afterwards incorporated in the *Mahābhārata*. The *gāthā* or song or *narāśamsa-gāthā*, song in praise of a person, is perhaps exemplified in the poem cited above. The *vākovākya*, or dialogue, may denote debates, such as are represented in the *Upanishads*, themselves for the most part in the form of reported conversations; but scenic dialogue of some kind occurs in certain rituals, and elementary drama with religious themes is indicated by references in the grammar of Pānini and his commentators. The oldest Buddhist texts are in the form of dialogues. Of all this narrative and poetic, not priestly, literature we can derive a conception only from the two great epics, the *Mahābhārata* and the *Rāmāyana*.

These two very extensive poems, mainly in the ordinary narrative metre, the *śloka*, but with occasional use of other metres, and in the case of the *Mahābhārata* even of prose, belong essentially, and also, as regards their main contents, chronologically, to the Aryan period. They both breathe the air of the old Kshatriya kingdoms of northern India, prior to the Nanda-Maurya Empire: the *Rāmāyana*, a product of the very region (Eastern Hindustan) where that Empire arose, betrays, even in its added Book I, no knowledge of the existence of the Empire or of its famous capital, Pātaliputra (Patna), and has no inkling of Buddhism. Not quite identical conditions, however, are reflected in the two poems. In the *Mahābhārata*, whereof the main theme is a war of succession in the old Kuru kingdom of the Delhi region and the victor in which became founder of the city of Hastināpur, there are features suggesting that the struggle was partly one between Church and State. In the legend of the Brāhman Paraśu-Rāma, 'Rāma with the Axe', who twice and thrice cleared the earth of Kshatriya blood, we may perhaps recognize a culmination of an opposition between the royal and the priestly orders, due to a growing consolidation of the latter and betrayed by some indications in its literature. The somewhat peculiar customs and proceedings of the Pāndu victors in the great war and the singular position of Krishna, a leading person, but not primarily a combatant, in the epic, suggest that the priestly power, in a struggle with the old royalties, patronized new semi-Āryan races and a new religious movement. It seems likely that the conflict, which involved, as allies on one side or other, all the kingdoms of middle and northern Hindustan, permanently impaired the ancient Āryan states of the centre and prepared the situation which existed at the time of Alexander's invasion, with powerful tribes in the Punjab and a Magadha Empire adjoining them on their eastern frontier. Of all this there is in the *Rāmāyana* no sign: in that poem Paraśu-Rāma makes a perfunctory appearance and is, so to speak, politely bowed out, as if in its sphere there were no work for him to do. There is nothing but cordiality between the royal and priestly orders, and the social superiority of the former is attested by several indications in the Buddhist and Jain writings. Further differences suggest that in the countries east of the Jamna-Ganges Doab the population, less Āryan in composition, and in a Vedic text noted as not yet Brahmanically pure, had a somewhat different ethos from that of the middle country. The spirit of the *Mahābhārata*, in its original undidactic portion, mingles with its vigorous chivalry an element of rough barbarity. In the *Rāmāyana*, where the flawless 'nobility' of the chief characters has made them a perpetual ideal for India, the sentiments of compassion (to which the poem is said to have owed its origin), generosity, and dutiful-

ness seem to prognosticate the future Buddhism with its pre-
dilection for the milder virtues, universal compassion (*karunā*),
and friendliness (*maitrī*). This difference in natural ethos had
been little, it appears, affected by intercourse between the two
regions. The western horizon of the *Rāmāyana* is remarkably
limited. Except for the north-western nationality of the queen
Kaikeyī, it is bounded by Kanyākubya (Kanauj) on the Ganges
and Kausāmbī (a little west of Allahabad) on the Jamna.
Nothing is known of the old kingdoms of the Delhi region, of
the Doab, or of Avanti-Ujjain, or of the personages or events
of the *Mahābhārata* story. On the other hand, its royal dynasty
of Ayodhyā, the Ikshvākus, has a name belonging to ancient Vedic
times, and its Brahmanical sages, Viśvāmitra, Vasishtha, Gautama, are the original founders of Rishi families. All this suggests
that the eastern parts of Hindustan, the kingdoms of Kośala,
Videha, and so forth, had in a comparatively early age received
an Āryan culture and had acclimatized some prominent figures
in its legends—just as subsequently the legends of Buddhism
found new homes in the trans-Indus province of Gandhāra and
elsewhere—but had, perhaps for centuries, lived their own life,
having little intercourse, other than Brahmanic, with the 'middle
country'. Its Brāhmans may have been relatively few and un-
ambitious, and the social and political situation unaffected by the
struggles of the central region.

Other factors also distinguish the two epics. While both
have been constructed with materials in the form of bardic
lays, the *Mahābhārata* seems to embody the tradition of the
court poets (*sūta*) of kings and nobles, who sang mainly of war
and adventure; it may be doubted whether the same classes
of minstrels existed in the domain of the *Rāmāyana*, whose
reciters (*kuśīlava*) are depicted as singing the story of Rama
'in gatherings of Rishis and assemblages of royal sages and of
respectable people'. Hence the *Mahābhārata* has a more historical background, an actual war; whereas the *Rāmāyana* story

has large mythological elements; southern India is a land of great forests peopled by monkeys, bears, and monsters, and Ceylon, its other chief scene, an island of demons, vaguely located. In manner also the *Mahābhārata* is closer to its material, retaining the bardic practice of stating everything as reported (like the messengers' narratives in Greek plays and Vergil's account of the fall of Troy, through the mouth of Aeneas): the *Rāmāyana* presents itself as the composition of a single great sage, who relates in his own person and circulates the poem through the mouths of his pupils. In point of fact the evidence of a single authorship and a poetic aim have given to the figure of Vālmīki a definiteness far greater than could attach to the diasceuast (*Vyāsa*) of the *Mahābhārata* and have secured for him the title 'Founder of Poetry' (*Ādi-kavi*). With him begins the conscious poetic art, which was to culminate in the classical *mahā-kāvyas*, whereas the *Mahābhārata* has bequeathed its style to masses of verse compositions, *purānas*, &c., more solicitous of matter than of form.

In other respects the two poems have much similarity. They employ predominantly the same (*śloka*) metre, with passages in other metres and, in the case of the *Mahābhārata*, a few in prose. They take the same slight grammatical and metrical liberties. They both share that amiable garrulity which a critic attributed to Homer: emphatically they are the work of poets 'on whose lips the goddess of speech sits unexhausted even at the end of their "Fits" (breaths)', a sustained quality, incorporating perhaps the vigour and invention of generations of predecessors, which, joined to a ripe wisdom of tone, sustains the interest of the reader also. In description of combats and battles both poems are brobdingnagian and unconvincing, a feature recurring in all the later poetry and derived, as has been ingeniously suggested, from mythological accounts of warring divinities.

The *Mahābhārata*, in its developed form four times as long as the *Rāmāyana*, is infinitely richer in characters and incidents, in old legends and other episodical narrations, including a summary version of the *Rāmāyana* story itself. Here we find the famous episodes of Nala, Sāvitrī, and Śakuntalā. It has amply justified its own boast that:

> Independent of this story no tale is known on earth,
> Like support of life without dependence upon food.
> This story affords maintenance to all the best poets,
> Like a noble prince to servants looking for promotion.

Jointly the two epics, in the form of oral reading or recitation, have been until modern times the main literary sustenance of the Indian masses. Their chief characters and incidents are familiar to both sexes from childhood, furnishing the ideals and wisdom of common life. They have supplied the themes of, we may say, the greatest part of the epic and dramatic literature in Sanskrit and its derivatives; and translations or adaptations of them are in several of the latter, such as Bengālī and Assamese, and also in Dravidian languages, Kanarese and Telugu, among the chief ornaments of their early periods.

What of dates? For the *Rāmāyana* a date in, say, the fifth century B.C., suggested, as we have seen, by its geographical, political, and social outlook, encounters opposition, due in the first place to lack of external attestation, for example in Buddhist books; the general regularity of the language and metre, in comparison with what is seen in Pāli writings, tends to strengthen such reluctance. The atmosphere of the original narratives may be supposed to have been instinctively preserved, as would be done in a modern version of the story of the *Iliad* or that of King Arthur: and the great poet who gave to the *Rāmāyana* its present form might then be assigned to, say, the second century B.C.—not later, since in the *Buddha-charita* of Aśvaghosha, who wrote in the first century A.D., the narrative style is far more artificial. There is, however, little plausibility in such a view, which implies an almost superhuman consistency in a poem of 24,000 couplets. A higher metrical accomplishment was to be expected from classes of professional poets than from the amateur or popular verse of moralists and monks: versification not markedly irregular is found even in much older works, such as the *Aitareya Brāhmana*, and regularity of language was certainly in the fifth century B.C. a conception very familiar among the learned.

The *Mahābhārata* in its present dimensions, as a work of 100,000 couplets, existed as early, it seems, as, say, the fifth century A.D., in all probability considerably earlier, since it set, no doubt, the fashion in respect of that size. The vast accretions of didactic matter, due to Brahmanic *remaniements*, which have been tacked on to the original story, may belong to the same period (say 100 B.C.–A.D. 200) as the foreign race-names, Yavana, Saka, Pahlava, which have elsewhere also found entrance. But the original *Bhārata* and *Mahābhārata* poem, mentioned in the Vedic Sūtra literature, is probably far older even than the *Rāmāyana*; and beginnings of its tradition, in the form of bardic lays, will naturally have been not greatly posterior to the actual conflict.

It is not possible to omit here a mention of a portion of the *Mahābhārata*, the most celebrated of all, which in India enjoys an ever-growing religious authority and which is fast becoming a world-Classic. If the position of Krishna is an essential feature in the story as it finally took shape, then the *Bhagavad-gītā*, 'The Song of the Holy One', is the core of the whole epic. It is one of those ambiguous compositions, wherein a fusion of poetical and religious inspiration presents obstacles to a clear critical judgement. Nothing, however, can blur the sublime poetical quality of its first conception. In the pause preceding the outbreak of battle Krishna, acting as charioteer to Arjuna, the Achilles of the conflict, drives out between the two armies to survey the scene; and, when Arjuna quails at the thought of the coming orgy of slaughter and fratricide, he revives the hero's spirit by a long discourse, in eighteen cantos, on the issues of life and death, on selfless performance of a warrior's duty and all duties, and on absolute devotion to Krishna himself, as the supreme divinity. The imaginative use of a situation, such as the *Iliad* represents in the discourse between Priam and Helen on the walls of Troy, shows that the germ of the poem, afterwards expanded to its present dimensions, was contained in the original lay—it was a product of the old bardic art, not of theological or philosophic reflection. But the theme was a splendid one; and some successor with theological and philosophic culture, but clearly no precise thinker, developed it into the most powerful expression of Indian religious sentiment. The beauty of the verse and of some of the ideas (borrowed in certain instances from the earlier literature), and the impressiveness of a discourse by the Supreme Being, inculcating devotion to 'Me', give to the work an unrivalled effectiveness. But the philosophical notions are confused; and when, in the eleventh canto, Krishna bids his interlocutor behold in his person the whole manifold universe, the feeling of the original poet might perhaps have recoiled, were it not that, as many literatures can attest, the religious sentiment has power to dominate the aesthetic. Concerning so famous a work, with its hundreds of editions or translations, no more need be said. The Bhāgavata religion—the religion of devotion to a personal divinity—whereof it is the earliest document, originated beyond question in the Āryan period. But the poem, as we have it, breathes the spirit of a dogmatic and propaganda age which under the Maurya Empire succeeded the intellectual and ethical 'sophistic' of Buddha's time. As we read in the *Mahābhārata* itself:

> Vedas in disaccord, still warring creeds;
> Doctrine of sage from sage's doctrine secedes:
> Thought in the deep attains not truth's abode;
> Where passed a great one's steps,[1] there lies the road.

F. W. Thomas.

---

[1] The translation 'the steps of the bulk or mass of mankind' (*mahā-jana*) seems, as was remarked by the late Professor E. B. Cowell, highly un-Indian.

INDIAN ART AND ARCHAEOLOGY

It is generally held that the study of Indian antiquities received its first impulse from Sir William Jones and that it was initiated by the foundation of the Asiatic Society of Bengal in 1784. In point of fact, Jones was one among many, including the Governor-General, Warren Hastings. The latter proved himself quick to realize the importance of this new field of interest; without interest there can be no understanding and without understanding administration is built on sand. It must be clearly understood that he was strictly practical in his appreciation of the possibilities inherent in Indian studies. Above all, it was desirable that India should be governed by her own laws. With regard to the Muhammadans of India, as people of the Book, they transcended nationality; for law is implicit in Islam. Hinduism remained to be learned and defined. A commission of Pandits was, therefore, set up and it was their work, couched in the native Sanskrit, which was translated into official Persian, before being rendered into English by Halhead and published in London in 1776. The method was roundabout but well established historically in post-Mughal India, where the records of many Hindu states are still kept in Persian. In spite of this step forward, it was clear that the practice of the courts was bound to provoke appeals to the original Sanskrit; hence the official consciousness of the need for Sanskrit learning. To administrative necessity, literary interest was added. Sir William Jones himself translated the Sanskrit drama *Śakuntalā*, as well as the *Institutes of Manu*, and so, within a few years, Indian literature was made accessible to European scholars and found a warm welcome, especially among the German Romanticists. In 1785 Wilkins published his translation of the *Bhagavadgītā* and two years later opened that treasury of romance and fable, the *Hitopadeśa*, to English readers. More significantly

still, he cut with his own hands the first Devanāgarī and Bengālī types, initiating a new era in the literary history of India
itself. So, in 1792, the lyrical Sanskrit poem, *Ritusamhāra,* was
published under Jones's editorship, the first Sanskrit text ever
to be printed.

Colebrooke may be said to stand at the head of the generations of professional Sanskritists, but it is worth noting that
his interests, far from being professionally circumscribed, were
enviably wide. The mere titles of his contributions to the
early volumes of the famous *Asiatic Researches* indicate the
comprehensive range of these pioneers in the exploration of
Indian culture. It is evident that for them, not only was Sanskrit the key to the understanding of India's past, but that
nothing Indian, past or present, lacked interest. It was left
to later generations of grammarians to allow the study of Sanskrit to lapse into the self-sufficient specialism of the schools,
and to forget the living interest of the India that exists outside books.

During these significant years India became known to the
world historically as well as geographically. Jones had already
identified the Sandrocottus of the classical historians with
Chandragupta Maurya and the site of his capital Palibothra
with the modern Patna. Under Wilkins the study of Indian
epigraphy was initiated; Colebrooke translated the *Vīsala Deva*
inscription on the Delhi pillar. In 1800 Dr. Buchanan, who
later took the name of Hamilton, was deputed by the Marquis
of Wellesley to make an agricultural survey of the recently
settled territories of Mysore. The practical results were so
valuable that in 1811 Buchanan was appointed by the Court of
Directors to make a statistical survey of Bengal. His work is the
monument of his genius and understanding, radically influencing
the compilation of the District Gazetteers of a later generation,
which so magnificently transcend their immediate administrative purpose and achieve monumental scholarship. Buchanan

was not alone: work on a lesser scale was being carried out all over India, by Salt at Kanheri, Erskine at Elephanta, Sykes at Bijapur, and Mackenzie in the south. In this way, step by step, the abstract place-names of the dispatches and official reports were correlated and established. Rennell's small scale mapping was supplemented by 'Itineraries', the first official routebook; finally, in 1825, appeared the earliest practicable map of all India, published by Kingsbury, Parbury, and Allen. In England, Daniell's drawings, the result of an intrepid journey round and across India, served to extend the field of interest. Engravings and aquatints of Indian subjects became popular and, indeed, had something of a vogue, finding a prominent place in the boudoir *Keepsake* Annuals.

After the settlement of the complex federations of middle India at the beginning of the nineteenth century, the focus of interest shifted to the north-west frontier. Lahore, the Sikh capital, was the centre of diplomacy, and farther west, beyond the reach of its sway, new and important factors had made themselves evident. Napoleon had advertised the trans-continental route and Russia was fast becoming a bugbear. The presence of European mercenary leaders, such as Ventura and Court, at Lahore and elsewhere, provided a channel for scientific information. Official missions played their part and the gentleman adventurer did not miss his opportunity. Foremost amongst these, firstly as adventurer and only secondarily as an intelligence officer of the Government, was Masson, whose admirable energy and dominating personality provided the first survey of the debatable lands that lie between India and Afghanistan. Not only was he gifted with the keen eyes of the born observer, but his sense of significance was infallible. His reports read as if they had been written yesterday. The treasures he brought to notice, Greek coins and Greekish sculpture, as Curtius later observed, opened 'a new page in the history of Greek art'. European scholars, imbued with the classical tradition, could not but turn their attention to this new and exciting body of material. It is, therefore, evident that Indian art came to be studied as exemplifying the extent of Greek influence in the East, not as being worthy of consideration and appreciation in itself. The interest was not in India, but in what light India had to throw upon the legacy of Greece, with which the academic mind proved itself preoccupied.

The material being to hand, the genius to handle it was not wanting. Masson's finds fell into the able hands of Prinsep, by profession an official of the Mint in Calcutta, by character the most charming of men, by genius the founder of Indian archaeology. He had already worked successfully upon Gupta epigraphy and now turned his attention to the bilingual coins of the so-called Bactrian kings. Masson himself had already identified the *Kharoshthi* repetitions of certain of the Greek names and titles, such as *Basileus, Soteros,* Menander, and Apollodotos; Prinsep was immediately able to extend the series of parallel letters. In 1837 he was working upon the Surāshtra *Kshatrapa* coins and, once more, within a few days, arrived at a complete solution. Later he turned to the Asokan rock-inscriptions and was able to demonstrate, in the XIIIth Edict, Aśoka's acquaintance with the names of his contemporaries, the Greek kings Antiochus, Ptolemy, Antigonus, Magas, and Alexander, thus providing concrete evidence from which the date of the inscription may be deduced as being *c.* 258–257 B.C.

Prinsep died in 1840. His mantle fell upon his young friend and disciple Cunningham, then a junior officer of the Engineers. He had from the beginning of his Indian service devoted his leisure to the study of the Indian monuments, travelling widely in the pursuit of his hobby. He lived to see the creation of the Archaeological Survey of India, with himself at its head as first Director-General. The twenty-three volumes of reports published under his guidance, each the record of a tour of exploration, remain the chief source books of the subject. As scientific records they are outstanding, being distinguished not only for accuracy of observation, but for that enduring quality which only personal experience and consideration can give to archaeology. Like Buchanan, he set an example which deeply influenced the methods used and the ideals incorporated in the District Gazetteers.

In 1845 Fergusson published an account of the rock-temples of India, the first of a series of books on Indian architecture culminating in his *History of Indian and Eastern Architecture*, published in 1875. He himself has recorded the purpose he had in view when he undertook this great work. He writes: 'What I have attempted to do during the last forty years has been to apply to Indian architecture the same principles of archaeological science which are universally adopted not only in England, but in every country in Europe.' His pioneer survey, re-edited by Burgess in 1910, survives unchallenged as the text-book of the subject. It will be noted that not only was Fergusson a professional architect and archaeologist, but that his conclusions (again in his own words)

'were based upon the examination of the actual buildings throughout the three Presidencies of India . . . during ten years' residence in the East. . . . My authorities . . . have been mainly the imperishable records on the rocks or on sculptures and carvings, which necessarily represented at the time the faith and feeling of those who executed them, and which retain their original impress to this day. . . .'

Since Fergusson's day archaeology has been granted the status of a science. Yet, though he did without the technical jargon of *corpora*, *culture*, and *distribution*, subsequent work has not altered the general trend of his exposition; new epigraphical evidence has in most cases merely added precision. A further quotation will, perhaps, indicate the source of his success. He writes:

'Greece and Rome are dead and have passed away, and we are living so completely in the midst of modern Europe, that we cannot get out-side to contemplate it as a whole. But India is a cosmos in itself. . . . Every problem of anthropology or ethnography can be studied here more easily than anywhere else; every art has its living representative, and often of the most pleasing form; every science has its illustration, and many on a scale not easily matched elsewhere.'

As with Cunningham, it was the width of his experience that made him what he was. He lived before the days of tourist-bureaux, and travelled to learn, at first hand painfully, in bullock-cart and on foot. Unfortunately his following words still apply.

'Notwithstanding', he continues, 'in nine cases out of ten, India and Indian matters fail to interest, because they are to most people new and unfamiliar. The rudiments have not been mastered when young, and, when grown up, few men have the leisure or the inclination to set to work to learn the forms of a new world. . . .'

Meanwhile, the practical interest typical of the nineteenth century bore fruit. The great exhibitions in London, Paris, and Vienna advertised Indian arts and crafts. Manchester was, of course, deeply interested in Indian textiles, a commercial but valid interest which led to various official publications, including Forbes Watson's magnificent series of volumes setting forth the textile products of India from north to south. The India Museum came into being in London, and in 1880 Birdwood wrote, also under official patronage, his *Industrial Arts of India*. Ironically the interest so aroused marked a new era; industrializa-tion was already abroad in India; the crude tones of the early aniline dyes were already slowly but inexorably dominating the soft but fugitive beauty of the old colours in the streets of the cities and where the women gathered with their water-pots at the village well. . . .

It will be seen that throughout the nineteenth century the study of Indian art and archaeology had steadily progressed. Everywhere the academic field was slowly widening. It was left to Lord Curzon to initiate a new era in the organization of the study of Indian culture. Addressing the Asiatic Society of Bengal in 1900, he said:

'I hope to assert more definitely during my time the Imperial responsibility of Government in respect of Indian antiquities, to inaugurate or to persuade a more liberal attitude on the part of those with whom it rests to provide the means, and to be a faithful guardian of the priceless treasure-house of art and learning that has, for a few years at any rate, been committed to my charge.'

Thus was created the Archaeological Survey of India as it exists to-day, with its triple obligation of conservancy, exploration, and publication. Under Sir John Marshall's guidance site after site was excavated, including the key sites of Sānchī, Taxilā, Sārnāth, and Bhītā. Finally, India won academic attention from the archaeological world as the result of the discoveries at the ancient sites of Hārappa and Mohenjodāro.

Apart from their intrinsic interest, such sites as Hārappa and Mohenjodāro are of great significance as indicating the antiquity of great cities in India. As a basis for the discussion of both Indian archaeology and ethnology, it may be suggested that there is not one India, but, at least, three Indias. On the one hand, there is the India of the large cities, which are, however, few in the land, the India of politics and commerce, once upon a time the India of artistic patronage. On the other hand, there is the India of the hill and forest peoples. Between them lies the India of the villages, in touch with both, differentiated by local traditions of great antiquity, but possessing a certain unity born of kindred interests and occupations, the interests and occupations of those whose livelihood is the soil. In view of this, it is perhaps as well to question the validity of certain generalizations, such as Dr. Coomaraswamy's statement that 'all India can offer to the world proceeds from her philosophy', or Mr. Havell's allegation that 'the main types of Indian art have been derived from the Yoga philosophy'—one system in a country that acknowledges many.

The doctrinaire's condemnation of a literary approach to any art, just because it is literary, is not justifiable. The formulae of the academic aesthetician or the inspired selectiveness of the dilettanti, both of them so certain of the purity of their appreciation, are too static to reach the heart of the matter and too small to take in actual experience. For instance, the direct function of patronage in the arts is too often forgotten. Of Western art, at least of the art of the great periods, it is probably correct to say that art is the artist's account of his reactions to his environment, as conceived by the particular scale of values, often transitory, which dominates his personality at the moment. Indian art is almost entirely anonymous and it is, also, strangely consistent. Though we are relieved of the artistic personality, it must be confessed that we do not know very much about the organization of the profession, except that it was on guild lines. Guild life, local and professional, was an integral part of ancient Indian polity and is prominent in the early Buddhist literature. The seals of these bodies survive in archaeology and there is, also, at Sānchī, a relief which is inscribed as the gift of the Ivory-workers of the nearby city of Bhīlsā. At Pattadkal, too, the name of the guild of the *Sarva Siddhi Āchāryas* is inscribed.

Fergusson, in his great history of Indian architecture, classified his material under religions, Jain, Buddhist, &c., and inasmuch as the purpose of a religious building, that is to say, cult, must have a great bearing on its architecture, he was right. However, unjustifiable references are often made to the first and second centuries B.C., when Indian sculpture came into being as we know it, as being specifically Buddhist, to 'the Buddhist period'. Early Buddhism was actually somewhat puritanical about the arts. Music and dancing, for instance, are classed with cock-fighting as examples of minor foolishness,

unprofitable to the wise. Though almost nothing of the wood
and sundried brick architecture of the early centuries has survived, except as depicted on the bas-reliefs and in literary
descriptions, we know that it was enlivened with painted
decoration. The names of the patterns are mentioned in the
texts; and there were figures of *yakshas*, godlings, painted on
the doorways as guardians of the entrance. At Bharhut, in the
second century B.C., the figure of the Buddha nowhere appears,
its place being taken by a simple, quite straightforward, un-
esoteric symbology. The *stūpa*, or relic-mound, however, is
surrounded by a multitude of lesser beings of very distinct
personality, who have found their way, as it were, in spite of
themselves, into the service of Buddhism. Buddhism adopted
them because it had to, admitted them, grudgingly no doubt, but
with full sanction. And there were sculptors ready to portray
them in stone and to inscribe their names. Among them are
Kuvera, guardian of the north; *Srī*, or *Sirimā* as she is called at
Bharhut, the goddess of fortune; *Virūpāksha*, guardian of the
west, whose name was given in the eighth century to a famous
temple at Pattadkal, and *Sudarśana*, guardian of still waters,
the embankment of one of whose haunts Chakrapālita, agent
of the governor Pūrnadatta, repaired in A.D. 457. Not only are
these beings not Buddhist, but they might with equal justice
be described as Brahmanical, for all four have found a place in
classical Sanskrit literature. Actually they are neither, but
belong to village India, where their descendants still survive,
ritually and psychologically.

At Sānchī, a century later, these godlings have lost their
names, but persist under the generic title of *yaksha* or *yakshī*,
guardians of the four gateways of the great *stūpa*. Swinging
from the branches of trees, *yakshīs* form brackets to the architraves, while on the uprights on either side are *yakshas*, standing
beneath flowering trees, *bignonia*, *kadamba*, or *mango*, holding
auspicious flowers or garlands in their hands. Between them

passed each one of the thousands of pilgrims who attended the great festivals (the archetypes of the *mēlās* or fairs of modern India), on their way to the acquisition of merit by the circumambulation of the relic-mound, which was the climax of the pilgrimage.

The inside of the North Gateway is typical of the subject-matter of the reliefs. Here is to be seen the *stūpa*, representing the death of the Buddha, just as the Wheel represents his first sermon, the pipal-tree his attainment of enlightenment, and the rose-and-lotuses his birth. Here, on the lower architrave, is also a *jātaka*-story, that of the former life of the Buddha, when he lived as Prince Vessantara and attained the perfection of charity, giving away his wealth, his kingdom, his royal elephant, chariot and horses, and even his children and his wife. Such unparalleled piety leads to the intervention of Indra, king of gods, and everything ends happily. These stories come straight from the lips of the people, although adapted to the ends of Buddhist morality. Such is the inspiration of the work of the early period. Buddhism uses the popular, but uses it to submerge it as a foreign element. Just as the godlings of Bharhut lose their names and individuality at Sānchī, within the space of two hundred years, so this ancient and delightful story-telling tradition is eclipsed by the growth of the canonical literature of orthodox Buddhism. Over thirty *jātakas* are to be seen at Bharhut; there are only half a dozen at Sānchī, and still less at Mathurā.

At Mathurā, at the end of the first century A.D., a foreign dynasty, that of the Kushāns, invaders from Central Asia, established itself, and it was under their rule that the city earned Ptolemy's title ἡ Μόδουρα τῶν Θεῶν.

Its fame as a religious and artistic centre is witnessed to by the fact that Mathurā sculptures are found far afield in India. Here were, also, Buddhist *stūpas*, complete with railings and gateways, as well as Jain and Brahmanical shrines. Here, indeed,

Indian iconography was created. The *yakshas* and *yakshīs* of the railing-pillars, cut in the local, mottled red sandstone, are of the old tradition; but two innovations are visible. The subject-matter, or story, at Bharhut and Sānchī is treated peripatetically, the persons of the protagonists being repeated, according to the necessities of the plot, within the borders of the panel or medallion devoted to it. In the Kushān reliefs the story is displayed in separately empanelled scenes. Secondly, the Buddha figure is everywhere.

References are often made to the 'Mathurā school' of sculpture; but it is to be observed that Kushān art, and, indeed, Indian art in general, is seldom purely local. Styles change in successive periods and certain well-demarcated areas preserve likenesses. In this case, the sculpture of the screen of the contemporary Assembly Cave at Kanhērī in Salsette, near Bombay, is in the Mathurā style, though at the other end of India.

The creation of iconography, Buddhist, Jain, and Brahmanical, coincides, significantly enough, with the first evidences of foreign influence, of the kind that produced the so-called Graeco-Buddhist work of Gandhāra, stretching across the Indus from Taxilā to Kabul, Hadda, and Bāmīyān. It is clear that the numismatic tradition set up by the successors of Alexander had already sunk into decadence. At Sirkap and at numerous frontier sites, such as Sari Deri and Shāhjī-kī-Dērī, near Peshawar, minor antiquities are plentiful, exhibiting classical influence of a quality and period distinct from the coins. In the west lay Parthia, the meeting-place of East and West, where the arts of both mingled and were transformed. Later, from this conflict of cultures, emerged Sassanian art, with its definite values, and, in the Indian border-lands, a hybrid concoction, usually spoken of as 'Graeco-Buddhist', but which is clearly Roman and not at all Greek. The influence under which Gandharan sculpture was brought into being is, again, clearly distinct from the earlier influence which produced the Harpocrates and Dionysos of Sirkap, and the almost unaltered classical terra-cotta figurines of the other sites mentioned above. Working in the soft talcose-schist of the frontier-hills Gandharan sculpture impinged upon the Kushān work of the early first and second centuries at Mathurā. Later, in Central Asia and in Afghanistan, where good stone was wanting, lime composition was adopted as a medium, the faces being cast in moulds and the bodies worked up on the stick-and-rag principle. It is significant that the pre-Gandharan figurines from the frontier are the earliest examples of the technique of moulding known in India. That Gandharan sculpture as a whole is hybrid is declared by the maltreatment accorded to such familiar Indian motives as the lotus. Its decadent influence may be traced in Kashmiri sculpture of the eighth century and in the architecture of the unique temples in the Salt Range.

As for the process by which Indian iconography came into being, there are some indications that the Buddhists followed the Jains. Every future Buddha or Bodhisattva, according to the tradition, is born with certain distinguishing marks, among them *ushnisha* or skull-protuberance. The problem of representing this was obviously a matter of some difficulty. In one of the earliest of the Kushān representations of the Buddha the *ushnisha* is in the form of a snail-shell. Finally, the difficulty was disguised by means of the adaptation of the conventionally close-curled hair of the Buddha-type. One minor figure at Sānchī fore-shadows this convention, which became universal in Gandhāra and thence was carried to China. Conversely, the Kushān and Gandharan Buddha-figure wears the orthodox monk's robes, though later in Gandhāra the treatment of the drapery is reminiscent, as Vincent Smith pointed out, of the Lateran *Zeus*. The Mathura 'Buddha' of the snail-shell *ushnisha* demonstrates an even deeper lying iconographical indecisiveness. It wears the orthodox robes, and is in every way a Buddha, in spite of the fact that the dedicatory inscription describes it as a Bodhisattva.

Artistically, the creation of these cult-images led to a break-away from the bas-relief tradition of the ancient railing-pillars and gateways, a change already foretold by the Sānchī bracket-figures, which are in the round. The most famous of Kushān sculptures is the standing royal figure, unfortunately headless, which is identified by an inscription as being that of the great king, Kanishka, himself.

Of all Indian sculptures, the bas-reliefs of Amarāvatī should be the most familiar, for they decorate the main staircase of the British Museum. They clearly belong to more than one period, but demonstrate a consistent development. Here appears in Indian sculpture, for the first time, a new sense of line that is akin to draughtsmanship, a quick-moving sureness concerted with a lightness of touch that is entrancing. Gesture has always been appreciated in India, but at Amarāvatī a certain poised movement or dynamic balance is discernible, the suggestion of timeless rhythm that is, perhaps, essential to all great art, a rhythm which might well be typified by the flow of the loose edge of the peplos in certain archaic Greek sculptures, notably the torso from Xanthos in the British Museum. Sculpture in the round is used at Amarāvatī, but the interest is concentrated upon the small-scale bas-relief medallions and panelled friezes that decorate the drum of the *stūpa*. In these the treatment of women is especially vivid, suggesting a parallel in the epithets and similes of classical Sanskrit, at this period approaching formulation. The epic heroes, like most heroes, are a little wooden; but Damayantī is 'like the flower that twines in the mango's dark branches, with slender arms, her lips like flowers, like buds rather, youth's rareness in her form.' The quality suggested is not so much a sentimental tenderness, as that which Professor Beazley notes in Greek vase-painting and describes as a 'devilish elegance'.

At Amarāvatī the old symbols are preserved side by side with the Buddha-figure, just as the old peripatatic method of story-telling is found side by side with the more sophisticated method of displaying scenes separately. Apart from this innovation, there is discernible a marked tendency to concentrate the drama of the plot into a single scene. It is noteworthy that the old method did not die out; it is the method of the Ajanta frescoes, where, however, the drama of the single scene or incident is dwarfed by the great cult figures of later Buddhism, and by the drama of the personalities they represent. Apart from these questions of subject-matter and mythos, it is obvious that the development of the cult-icon at Mathurā radically altered the function of Indian sculpture. It was not merely that a distinction was drawn between the object of worship and its setting, as it were between the mercy-seat and the bells and pomegranates of the *décor*, but that a difference was created in Indian sculpture, which it never quite loses. Henceforward, there is a grand style and a lesser, decorative style, the grand style of the formal image and the lesser style of the friezes and minor sculptures which give form to Indian architecture. In this lesser style the Amarāvatī manner lives, a delicate quality that might be called sentimental, if it were not so happy.

The third and the fourth centuries remain lacunae in the history of Indian sculpture; indeed, archaeological evidence is almost entirely wanting. The fifth century, the climax of the supremacy of the Gupta dynasty in northern India, has been acclaimed as a period of supreme accomplishment in all the arts. It was the period of what the literary historians call 'the revival of Sanskrit', to which Kālidāsa is attributed. This, perhaps, explains the common use of the epithet 'classical' for Gupta sculpture; but the word is not just. Most of the outstanding examples are cult-icons, by function demanding isolation. Only around the wide haloes is the delightful lesser style allowed to appear in wreaths of lotuses and foliage that are always fresh, and never merely fantastic. As a laudatory period name Gupta has been a little overdone. The trouble is that the work never quite escapes the period. The Buddhist iconographical tradition, which provides the bulk of Gupta sculpture, was drawing to its close in India proper. Buddhism had lost at this period what Brahmanism has always had, the ear of the people.

Schism came early to primitive Buddhism. Certain adherents, as always and everywhere, professed great concern as to the preservation of what they conceived the original doctrine to have been. The interests of these were ethical and disciplinary—and wholly personal. Their opponents, following metaphysical inclinations, rejected the limited intentions of the primitive tradition as being concerned only with individual experience and wanting in humanity. Its goal was *Arhatship* leading to *Nirvana*, a negative state of emancipation from the evils of transmigration, where, the flame extinguished, there is nothing left to be reborn. Other goal, or god, there was none, for self is a mere bundle of tendencies finding its only possible expression in works. Furthermore, release was hard to attain. For some few it might come intuitively. Some could preach, but not reach, emancipation. For some the teaching of one Buddha was not sufficient; these must await a doctrine yet unpreached to obtain release. Such, in outline, was the doctrine, later contemptuously known as *Hinayana*, the Lesser Vehicle. The followers of the opposing *Mahayana*, the Great Vehicle, formed a body of catholic persuasion. For them, not only was *Arhatship* attainable, but Buddhahood—and, therefore, the community and mankind in general were not without grace. The misfortune of man is not merely that he is what he is, but that he is not all that he might be. According to the *Hinayana*, the Buddha is a teacher. According to the *Mahayana*, he is a being, eternal and divine, proceeding from the infinite, who comes to sojourn among men on a mission that knows both compassion and the means of salvation. Looking upwards humanity may cry *felix culpa*—

So, according to the *Mahayana*, the community of the faithful transcends itself, for all bear the seeds of Buddhahood in them and may attain the highest heaven of the Divine Buddhas. These are innovations, necessitated by the doctrine of grace. They are the unmoved prime movers. From them emanate the Divine Bodhisattvas who create and rule, and are accessible to intercession. Moreover, these have their feminine counterparts, the Taras.

So scholasticism refines upon itself, soaring into the impalpable. . . .

The architecture of the period was still of wood and sun-dried bricks and is only known to us from the Ajanta frescoes, a magnificent architecture, spacious and colourful, set about with walled gardens, full of the contrast and change of light and shade. Building in ashlar had just begun. The little Gupta shrine at Sānchī is typical; by comparison with the sculptural details of the Chandragupta Cave at Udayagiri near by, it may be dated early fifth century. Distinctive and important details are the veranda and the intercolumniation of its pillars, the heavy eave-moulding, and the details of the sculptured doorway. Another example is to be found at Tigowa. It is important to note that comparisons can be drawn between these structural shrines in India proper and certain shrines in the Gandharan area.

It was in these small shrines that the images of the growing *Mahayana* pantheon were lodged, to be circumambulated without the walls, for there was no room within, and to be seen dimly by worshippers. In Brahmanism the dramatic possibilities of the cult were also emerging, in distinction to the mere ritual of the Brāhman household. The Divine Bodhisattvas of the *Mahayana* must have prepared the way, though like ideas had long been latent in the worship of Vishnu, who as *Vasudeva* in the abstract, and in certain of his *avatars* in actuality, was both god and man, and demanded devotion from his followers. The conception of the *ishta devata*, or personally selected or, rather, intuitively acknowledged personal deity, was also developing.

The Ajanta Caves are cut in the bent arm of the Vagha River, where it makes its way through the broken hills of the northern scarp of the Deccan, into Berar and the levels of the Tapti valley. Even in the hot weather there are pools in the river-bed, while a few minutes' rain will send the river into spate for hours, filling the gorge and the caves with noise of waters.

It is an ancient site, the earliest caves having been chiselled from the virgin rock by the primitive communities of the first and second centuries B.C. Architecturally these early caves are rock-cut replicas of the wooden architecture of the day, which has been preserved to us only in the bas-reliefs, but with astonishing accuracy. The great *chaitya-* or assembly-caves, of which Caves Nos. IX and X at Ajanta are examples, were not originally ecclesiastical forms, but were undoubtedly derived from the apsidal halls of the secular communities and guilds which play so prominent a part in early Buddhist literature. Although the great *stūpas* at Bharhut and Sānchī and Mathurā had their sculptured gateways and railings, none of these early caves is decorated with figure-sculpture. This fact has been over-stressed by Western scholars in whose minds the tenets of the Western protestant schism loom large. Actually they were freely decorated with fresco-paintings, as the surviving *Chadanta Jātaka* fresco in Cave X shows. The fresco tradition, indeed, dominated the whole conception. It is hard to realize that, as with ancient Greek sculpture, this beautifully chiselled, finely finished work was brought into being only to be plastered and polychromed. Here, as at the great sites in the holy land of Buddhism, the *stūpa* is the central object of worship. Later, in the sixth century, in Cave No. XIX its symbology is obscured by the colossal Buddha sculptured upon it. The living-caves or *viharas* are cut in imitation of the four-sided structural monasteries, universal from Sarnath to Gandhāra. Simple cells, provided with a stone bed and a lamp-niche, are on either side. Earlier all worship seems to have been centred in the *chaitya*-caves. Later, each *vihara* has its own private chapel, cut in the centre of the back wall, where the light from the entrance strikes full upon the figure of the Buddha. The later *chaityas* must have been designed for public use during the great festivals, which were without a doubt the main source of the brethren's income.

Ajanta is a world in itself, aloof and shut in. In the spring, when the rains have broken and everything is green, its beauty is surpassing. To the north are the two fine hill-forts of Baithalwadi and Abasgarh dominating strategic points, undoubtedly ancient. But there is no sign of a town or village of any size near by. The old pilgrims must have made their camp on the green bank at the turn of the river below the caves, where there is now a car-park. Four miles away is the Ajanta *ghat*, the ancient highway to Asirgarh and the north. Southward lie Aurangābād, Paithan, Junnar, Thāna, and the ports of Salsette, once thronged with the shipping of the African and Arabian trade.

Elura is more accessible and more human. The Elura *ghat*, a branch of the same arterial highway, actually cuts the scarp in which the caves are cut. Above lies the towering fortress-hill of Daulatābād, the 'city of wealth' of its Muhammadan conquerors, the 'city of god' of the older Hindu dynasty. Nearer still is Roza Khuldābād, the burial-place of Aurangzīb. Below is the modern village, where an eighteenth-century temple still preserves the traditions of sanctity, though the caves are delivered over to the sightseer. As at Ajanta, an annual fair has persisted in spite of all changes, and the stream that leaps the scarp into the pool below the water-gate of the *Dhumar Lena* (No. XXIII) is officially known as the Elura-Ganges. The place is, indeed, still one of the great Saiva places of pilgrimage. If Ajanta is to be seen at its best during the rainy season, Elura is the place to see the rains break; the green flows visibly over the hills in the wake of the clouds.

The scarp runs north and south, facing west. The Buddhist caves, which are the earliest, lie to the south. Then follow the Brahmanical caves, centred upon the great pile of the *Kailasa*, upon the very verge of which the road winds. The Jain caves lie apart to the north. A comparison of the pillar-forms of the first five caves at Elura with the latest caves at Ajanta makes it clear that the rise of Elura coincided with the decline of benefaction at Ajanta; the identity of the work is especially clear in Ajanta No. XXIV and Elura No. II. As the earlier Buddhist caves were derived from structural architecture in wood, so these later medieval caves are closely related to the little Gupta structural temples in stone. When it became necessary to provide each *vihara* with its own private chapel, it was only natural that structural models should be followed. The veranda with its four pillars (in the caves, two pillars and two pilasters), the decoration of the doorway and the plain, square sanctum are all reproduced in detail. In the earlier caves of this series the image of the Buddha is cut in high relief from the living rock that forms the back wall of the shrine; later it was cut in the round, allowing of circumambulation within the shrine by the officiant, but not the congregation. Later still a circumambulation passage was cut round the shrine, which then stands four-square and is an exact replica of the structural shrines. In the Brahmanical caves the same process is followed. These take over the form of the Buddhist *vihara*-cave, but have no dwelling-cells, for there was no community to house. There is only the sanctum in which the central object of worship is at Elura, and until the late eighth century everywhere, the phallus, the *Saivalingam*.

The doorways are particularly interesting. On either side of the architraves of the earlier medieval caves at Ajanta stand small female figures upon mythical water-beasts, the *makaras* of the ancient tradition. Elsewhere, in the Brahmanical caves

PLATE 3

ŚIVA AND UMĀ. KAILĀSA CLOISTERS, ELURA
8th century A.D.

PLATE 4

ŚIVA. KAILĀSA CLOISTERS, ELURA

8th century A.D.

and temples, they are identified as the river-goddesses, Ganga
and Yamuna. By nature and origin they are own sisters to the
Bharhut *yakshas* and the Sānchī bracket-figures. Even in these
later days they are distinguished by the trees under which they
stand, mango on the one hand, kadamba on the other. In the
later Buddhist caves, such as Cave No. VI at Elura, the place
of the door-guardians is taken by the towering figures of the
divine Bodhisattvas, Padmapani, 'he who bears the lotus', and
Vajrapani, 'he who bears the thunderbolt'. The magnified
scale is significant of the dramatic tendencies of the newer
Buddhism. Over them still hang the pendent branches of the
mango- and kadamba-trees of the vanished goddesses, whose
place they usurp as guardians of the shrine. On either side
of the shrine-door in Cave No. I at Ajanta, Bodhisattvas appear
in fresco, exactly as we read *Yakshas* were painted in the ancient
architecture. Here the left-hand figure holds the rosary and is
probably to be identified with Avalokita, whose personality
somewhat overlaps that of Padmapani, but who is above all
the Bodhisattva of intercession. A fourth Bodhisattva, Man-
jusri, is also found, a little later, at Elura. It is worth noting
that there is a certain degree of uncertainty in the representation of the attributes that identify these personages. It seems
that we are actually watching their evolution, at least artistically,
in stone. Inside the shrines they guard, the cult-image is always
that of the historical Buddha, Gautama. It is evident that the
earthly Teacher had already been transmuted, a transmutation
known to Clement of Alexandria as an historical fact, the result
of a process of sophistication parallel to the docetic heresy of
Basilides and Valentinus.

There is only one *chaitya*-cave at Elura, the last of its kind.
It maintains the apsidal plan of the old assembly-halls; but, as
in the Ajanta medieval *chaityas*, the older symbology of the
stūpa is dominated by the colossal figure of the Buddha it
serves to shrine or frame. In this cave the large-scale icons are

still of the Ajanta type, but the hosts of dancing dwarfs are facsimiles from Bādāmi, where Cave No. III is inscribed in the third quarter of the sixth century. The Elura *chaitya* may, therefore, be dated mid-sixth century. The Bādāmi dwarfs and certain details of the pillar-sculpture are also found in the earliest Brahmanical cave at Elura, the Rameshvara, though in a slightly more advanced stage; this cave, therefore, is probably late sixth century.

Historically, the medieval caves at Ajanta and the Buddhist caves at Aurangābād and Elura are to be associated with the influential Vakataka dynasty of Berar, who were allies of and intermarried with the Guptas. At the end of the sixth century a new dynasty arose in the Deccan, that of the Chalukyas, whose seat of power was fixed for two centuries in the Canarese country, first at Bādāmi, then at Aihole and Pattadkal, both the latter on the banks of the Malprabha river, a tributary of the Kistna. Southward they challenged the supremacy of the great Pallava dynasty, their hereditary and not unsuccessful enemies.

Bādāmi is a natural stronghold. Two great bastions of rock, indurated sandstone, meet there to enclose a re-entrant valley, which has been converted by means of an embankment into a lake. Below this embankment the houses huddle under the crumbling protection of double walls and a moat. Both bastions have been strongly fortified and the fort, as Tīpū Sahib's commanders left it, survived to see action in the nineteenth century. In the north face of the southernmost bastion are cut three Brahmanical caves and a single Jain cave, Cave No. III being dedicated to Vishnu, 'a shrine beyond the dreams of men and gods', by Mangalesa in the year A.D. 570. It is especially interesting that, though this cave is specifically dedicated to Vishnu, and its sculpture, as in the other caves, is large Vaishnava, the central object of worship is the *Saivalingam*. Again, with reference to the fine image of *Varahamurti*, the Boar incarnation of Vishnu, lifting up the earth from the waters, in

PLATE 5

MAHISHASURAMARDINI. KAILĀSA ELURA

8th century A.D.

Cave No. II, it is worth recalling the fact that the *Ramayana* and certain *puranas* credit Brahma with this deed. Furthermore, in the relief on the cross-beams of Cave No. III, which display the story of the Churning of the Ocean, Śiva, Brahmā, and Vishnu are represented where in the orthodox texts Vishnu alone should appear. It is, therefore, probable that the Brahmanical trinity was conceived as more in unity then than now, a reading which explains the extraordinary apposition of the Vaishnava dedication and iconography with the *lingam* as the central object of worship.

On the right of the veranda of Cave No. III is a figure of Vishnu seated upon *Ananta*, the serpent of eternity, which is one of many icons of this period which are not satisfactorily accounted for in the *sastras*. Sanskrit has never been the language of India and, in any case, the supposition that these sculptors worked book in hand is improbable. The outstanding quality of Indian sculpture is its dynamic speed. Furthermore, the existence of a host of works which do not follow the *sastras* disproves the allegation. It is obvious that iconography presupposes the existence of icons.

The light streams through the veranda pillars, sharply defining their bas-relief medallions and brackets. Only its reflection from the floor passes within. Looking back towards the veranda from the shrine door two worlds lie before one, the green quiet of the temple and the brilliant sunlight of the courtyard, filled with the chatter of monkeys pelting each other with figs. Midway, caught between dark and daylight, where the brackets of the capitals of the veranda-pillars half catch the light, jewelled and garlanded figures sport beneath flowering trees. . . . It is obvious that our ideas are strangely and strictly conditioned by the very vocabulary we inherit. So difficult is penetration into the minds of others that we never doubt ourselves as being acceptable examples of the human norm. Yet any one with comparative experience knows that what may be

construed as obsession to the one, is the natural idiom of the
other. Indian philosophy, or rather the basic quality of the
many Indian philosophies, seems a little cold to us, arid and
even hopeless. In India the life everlasting is dreaded. We
fight for continuation with oxygen and other means. The Indian
fears what he knows too well; the European fears the unknown
darkness which lies beyond consciousness. We have set mind
over body; with our bright intelligence goes everything. In
India, spirit and flesh are not antithetical, even when, as in
Jainism, the latter is for a working end to be cast aside. There
is no dualism, but rather a hierarchy of functions with many
and changing values, each valid in its own time and place.
Sensation and understanding, the delightful and the moral,
image and imagination are not opposed, but one, in so much
as they are the expression of life in the liver, in any case, a matter
of a few short moments. We, of course, object to bracketing
divinity with the fugitive. Protestants at heart, too often we
shut the doors of our religion against delight. In India loves
decorate the temple and the fact is worthy of deeper consideration than the writers of academic theses upon *erotische Kunst*
gave it. Of this class of Indian sculpture no more lovely examples
exist than the little couples of figures that adorn the Bādāmi
pillar-capitals.

At Bādāmi there are, also, many examples of structural temples,
of which the *Malegitta Sivalaya*, 'the temple of the garland-
maker', on the northern hill is typical. It is early seventh
century and very simple in form. In its simplicity, it illustrates
the basic truth that it is sculpture that gives Indian architecture
its form. Medieval Indian temples from the smallest to the
greatest are built, and then sculptured, the final form deriving
directly from the sculptor's chisel. On one side of this little
shrine the base-moulding with its frieze of dancing dwarfs,
the dominant motive of early Chalukyan sculpture, is unfinished,
and the sculptor's first esquisse in sure and rapid line can still

PLATE 6

INTERIOR OF CAVE II, BĀDĀMI
6th century A.D.

be seen. The development of seventh-century architecture is clearly demonstrated by the magnificent temples of the now decayed village of Aihole, some twelve miles away from Bādāmi. Pattadkal, eight miles higher up the Malprabha, is also a city of temples, of which only one, the Virupaksha temple already mentioned, is still in worship. Although its everyday name is of the greatest antiquity, its proper dedication is to *Lokesvara* and it was built about the year 730 by Lokamahadevi, senior queen of the Chālukyan king, Vikramaditya II, to celebrate her husband's conquest of Kanchi, the modern Conjeeveram, the capital of the Pallavas. Here the conqueror left his mark in the form of an inscription upon the *Rajasimhesvara* shrine. In fact the *Rajasimhesvara* is the original of the *Lokesvara*, in proof of which there is here an inscription which names the architect as famed in the southern country and master of the guild of *Sarva Siddhi Acharyas*.

The temple has three porches and is, therefore, cruciform, at the head of the cross being the shrine, enclosed by its circumambulation passage. Its pierced windows are very striking and, also, the setting of the images, which are on a medium scale, but magnificently placed under florid *makara*-arches. The iconography is very varied, but, as at Bādāmi, difficult to identify from the *Sastras*. In the south-east re-entrant corner is *Siva Lingodbhava*, perhaps the earliest definitely sectarian icon. Brahmā is represented as trying vainly to soar above, and Vishnu, in his Boar incarnation, to undermine the all-embracing *Sivalingam*. Near by a number of images of Siva with the goddess in the form of Gauri or Uma, of the type known as *Alingana*, forerunners of the many sculptures in which the god and goddess are shown together with Siva's vehicle, the bull, *Nandi*, and their off-spring, *Skanda*. Goddesses, female figures, are particularly beautifully rendered at Pattadkal, an inheritance in the direct line from Pallava sculpture. Notably so are the small figures, two-armed, without attributes, which stand enshrined between miniature pilasters beneath the dripstone moulding (Tamil, *Kabodam*). This proliferation of iconography, in conjunction with the very personal quality of the cutting, is evidence of the new spirit. The phallus of the great god remains the central object of worship, wrapped in shadows in the dark shrine, but, for every one of the devotees who penetrates to the steps of the sanctum, thousand remain outside. The growth of a complicated temple ritual is paralleled by the demand for the *ishta devata*. Both were undoubtedly important factors in the growth of Indian iconography.

Lokamahadevi's triumph in her consort's exploits was short lived. By the middle of the eighth century a new dynasty had arisen in the Deccan, that of the Rashtrakutas. Within a few years of the building of the *Lokesvara*, the Chālukyas had suffered severely at their hands. The so-called *Das Avatara*, Cave No. XV, at Elura is inscribed by the Rashtrakuta king, Dantidurga, who in another inscription is boasted of as the founder and patron of a Siva temple cut by heavenly powers from the rock at Elura. This is the great Elura *Kailasa*, Cave No. XVI, and, embodying the triumph of the Rashtrakutas, it is almost a copy of the Pattadkal *Lokesvara*. So that which was carried away from Pallava Kanchi to Chālukya Pattadkal appears in Rashtrakuta Elura. Indian historians too often forget the magnitude of these ancient empires, under-estimating the far-reaching shock of their conflicts. In the discussion of Indian polity, our talk is all of kingship and caste. We forget the nations of India.

The *Kailasa* is not merely a cave; it stands four-square in a courtyard hewn from the solid rock, complete with gateway, *nandi*-pavilion, right and left staircases, pavilions, porches, and subsidiary shrines, formed by the chisel, sculptured from top to bottom, without fault.

As at Ajanta the Buddhism of the day may be read from the frescoed walls, here is displayed the Hinduism of the day, figure

PLATE 7

VERANDA PILLARS. CAVE III, BĀDĀMI
6th century A.D.

PLATE 8

PILLAR MEDALLION. CAVE III, BĀDĀMI
6th century A.D.

upon figure crowding in upon one, as one passes into the courtyard. To the left of the entrance is Durga slaying the buffalo-demon; next to Durga, Krishna is lifting up the hill of Govardhan to protect the cowherds and their flocks from Indra's wrath. On the right is Vishnu on *garuda*, his man-bird vehicle; next to Vishnu, Kama, god of love, with his sugar-cane, *makara* standard, and his consort, Rati, desire. On the gate-posts, hewn from the living stone, are guardian figures in company with *Nagas*. Above towers the magnificent pile, its highest point marking the shrine, dedicated to Siva, Lord of the Sacred Mountain; no dedication could be more fitting. The main sculptures on the *Nandi*-pavilion are empanelled between severely cut pilasters, supporting floridly elaborated *makara*-arches. On the north side is a particularly magnificent figure of Siva, cut with daring simplicity in spite of the exaggerated flexure of the pose and the decorative wealth of the arch above. In Europe pseudo-classicism, an echo that will not die, has set limits upon sculpture. The white ghosts of Greece, stripped of their strange polychromy, haunt our criticism. We refine upon ourselves and in our subtlety end by questioning the intentionally, bravely decorative; or damn it by treating it as 'amusing', under the period title of Baroque.

To the right of the main upper porch is a figure of *Siva Andhakasura*, Siva slaying the demon of darkness, in which task he was assisted by the mother-goddesses, the *saptamatrikas*, who in orthodox Brahmanism are the consorts of the gods, but are actually the native deities of village India, absorbed into Brahmanism, as Buddhism absorbed the *yakshis*. It is obvious that the medieval expansion of Brahmanism owes much to its return to a popular tradition, neglected by esoteric Buddhism, the living diction of India major. This popular revival preceded the growth of the sectarianism upon which modern Hinduism is founded. The *Varaha Purana*, for instance, which is a Vaishnava work, claims that the *matrikas*, who are essentially *Saiva*, are to be considered as representing mental qualities which are morally bad, such as desire, covetousness, and anger; yet, in modern India, every village knows them. The origins of this academic partisanship may be seen at Elura. Surrounding the *Kailasa*, in the face of the quarry from which it is hewn, is a three-sided cloister. It is not by chance that the iconography of the left wing is *Saiva* and that of the right *Vaishnava*. Many of these sculptures are not identifiable in the Sanskrit texts, *puranas* and *agamas*. Some of them are repetitive. For instance, among the *Saiva* sculptures are several showing the god and the goddess together, obviously forerunners of the *Uma-sahita* type of later days. The cliché to apply to Indian art is 'complicated', but these *Kailasa* cloister-sculptures are almost severe, though theirs is a severity full of charm.

Our taste is so much a matter of what has been collected, of things in museums or in our own possession. We like everything to be labelled and easily recognizable. It is not easy to label Indian sculpture. Its range is so wide and its manner so varied. These *Kailasa* sculptures have a strange sense of the contemporary. There is a present imagination in them, wide in experience, and as profound as wide. Masterly as the cutting is, it is not a matter of mere technical ability, but of dominant keys or moods, which one comes, in time, to recognize. The single figures are especially memorable. The classical tradition has made much of the presentation of the single figure in sculpture. Like all limiting predispositions, this dogma defeats itself. The development of art to-day hangs upon our willingness to admit that simplicity is not necessarily good in itself. It is to be found here, and with no trace of the pomposity with which the Italianate tradition has so closely associated itself.

So much for the grand style at the *Kailasa*. The lesser work is, also, perfect. High up on the walls of the shrine, flying figures hover; the pilasters are picked out with creeper-work in the most delicate relief; while along the plinths of the north cloister is a miniature frieze of little figures, some of them clearly based upon metal-casting types, all of them delightful. The shrine itself displays two periods of fresco-painting and it would seem that all this carefully finished sculpture was originally all poly-chromed.

The later cave-temples attain large dimensions. The *lingam*-shrine is thrust forward into an immense pillared hall, that all may see and hear. The Elura *Dhumar Lena*, Cave No. XXII, which is late seventh century, is, perhaps, the most dramatically placed of these great caves. Its water gate is provided with steps down into the pool, into which the Vel-Ganga plunges from two hundred feet above. Up these the worshippers passed in clean clothes, after bathing in the pool, to make their offerings at the shrine.

The great temple at Elephanta or Garapuri, a green island opposite Bombay, is cut on the same plan. The shrine, which is isolated in the centre of the cave, has four doorways, each doorway guarded by its gigantic *dvarapalas*. Behind it is the great trinity, the *Trimurti*, or rather *Mahesamurti*, in which the qualities of Brāhma, the creator, and Vishnu, the preserver, are portrayed as being absorbed by and comprehended in the dominating personality of Siva, *Lingesvara*. At Elura, in the later caves which are cut in the bank of the nullah above the main scarp, the *Trimurti* is used as a reredos, that is to say, it is cut in the back wall of the shrine behind the *lingam*. In the south in many Pallava shrines the *Trimurti* is replaced by a group of the *Uma-sahita* type, consisting of Siva, the god-dess, and Skanda, or Karttikeya, the son. It is interesting to note that it was in the south and approximately at this time that Sankaracharya taught. It would not be untrue to say that, when Ramanuja followed Sankaracharya, modern orthodox Hin-duism was created. The literature upon which it is based is admittedly scholastic and the point of view is basically sectarian. As such it hardly influences the religious life of the villages at all. Here the *Gita* is still repeated and tales from the great epics told, and religious songs of absolute simplicity, but great beauty, are heard everywhere. . . .

The common approach to the study of Indian art, especially sculpture, is through the numerous *sastras* or iconographical passages of the *puranic* literature. These works are late, and their descriptions do not tally with the sculptures of the early medieval period. From the tenth century onwards iconography undoubtedly became standardized, but even then it is evident that the sculptures vary geographically and that the nomenclature of the various texts differs. The intentions of this literature are largely mnemonic, the passages serving as *dhyana-shlokas*, instructing the worshipper as to how he should visualize the god.

As such they obviously must post-date the sculpture and can have no bearing upon its origins. In certain cases, however, it is possible that echoes of what may be described as the memoria technica of the craft have been preserved. As for symbology, it is obvious that in Indian sculpture symbols serve to identify icons, while only in certain cases may the origin of the symbol be traced to the legend. To the orthodox Hindu, who devoutly follows his guru's teaching, these things, as sculpture or symbol, merely serve to fix the mind in contemplation. To the villager who has travelled weary miles on foot or on bullock-cart to make his little offering at the famous shrine, each icon is an embodiment of the songs and stories he has known since he was a child. It is a truism in India that the value is not in the object, but in the eyes that look at it. In many cases the esoteric merely disguises the story. It is, perhaps, just as well to point out that lotuses are not primarily symbols, but real flowers, not less common in India than wild violets in Devonshire. Taken as a whole, Indian iconography is a medieval accretion, derived from a folk-idiom, eventually crystallizing out in literary form under the influence of scholasticism.

In point of fact, a common icon, which portrays the personalities of Siva and Vishnu combined as *Hari-Hara*, is described in the *sastras* and is found repeatedly at Bādāmi, Elura, and Pattadkal. In early days it seems that the worship of Siva was somewhat suspect, in spite of the universality of the *lingam* as the central object of worship. Passages, such as that in the *Vasishtadharma-shastra*, an undoubtedly early work, which assert that Brahmanhood is incompatible with the worship of any other god but Vishnu, are obvious partisan interpolations. The fact remains that images of Vishnu did supplant the *Saivalingam* as the cult object in temples. The commonest Vaishnava icon during the formative period under discussion is that which displays the god as *Trivikrama*, he of the three strides. The medieval story is typical. It tells how a certain demon-king waxed mighty and overwhelming, so that the gods, threatened by him, were forced to come to Vishnu for redress. The great god took upon himself the form of a Brāhman student, a misshapen dwarf, and appeared before the king. Having ingratiated himself, he obtained the asking of a boon, and all he asked was as much space as he could cover in three steps. When the boon was granted and the water of contract poured, then Vishnu, manifest god, displayed himself, covering all the earth in one stride and all heaven in a second.

This story, however, has ancient origins. Sanskrit has never been the language of India and, therefore, such poetic amplifications were necessary. Actually the myth derives from Vishnu's primeval titles in the Veda *trivikrama*, he of the three strides, *urukrama*, the wide-strider. The epithets of the ancient hymn have played no small part in giving Vishnu pre-eminence: Vishnu, the all-knowing protector, and preserver, 'within whose three strides is contained the bliss of existence of all living things'.

K. DE B. CODRINGTON.

PHILOSOPHY

ONE may divide the philosophical development of India into three stages, pre-logical up to the beginning of the Christian era, logical up to the Muhammadan domination of India, A.D. 1000 or 1100, ultra-logical, A.D. 1100–1700. The philosophical contribution of the first period is to be found in the philosophical hymns of the *Vedas*, in the more mature *Upanishads*, in the *Gītā*, which is something like a metrical commentary on the *Upanishads* working out their ideals in their practical bearing to life; and in the rise and growth of Buddhism and the Sāmkhya and the Vaiśeshika philosophy. From about the beginning of the first or second century B.C. we have the various systems of Indian philosophy, the Yoga-sūtras, the Sāmkhya treatises, the Mīmāmsā-sūtras, the Brāhma-sūtras, and the Nyāya-sūtras and their numerous commentaries and subcommentaries. In the logical period we have keen logical discussions and dialectics of an extremely subtle character such as had never developed in Europe, and which are in part so difficult that no occidental scholar has been able to master them.

In the philosophical hymns of the *Vedas* we come across men who were weary of seeking mere economic welfare through religious rituals of a magical character. They wished to know something greater than their ordinary religion and sought to delve into the secret mystery of the Universe—the highest and the greatest truth. They formed the conception of a being who is the depository and the source of all powers and forces of nature, from whom nature with its manifold living creatures has emanated and by whom it is sustained and maintained. In spite of all the diversity in the world there is one fundamental reality in which all duality ceases. The highest truth is thus the highest being, who is both immanent in the world and transcendent. He holds the world within him and yet does not exhaust himself in the world. The ordinary polytheism and henotheism of Vedic worship thus slowly pass away, sometimes into monotheism and sometimes into pantheism; and in this way the Vedic hymns declare the spirituality of the world and denounce the common-sense view of things. This view is developed in the *Upanishads*, which may be regarded as a continuation of the philosophical hymns of the *Rig-Veda* and the *Atharva-Veda*. In the *Kenopanishad* we are told the story how all the presiding gods of the powers of nature, such as fire and wind, tried their best to compete with Brāhman, but the fire could not burn a piece of straw and the wind could not blow it away against the wishes of Brāhman, for they all derived their powers from him. We have a vivid description in the *Mundaka* of how the world has emanated from Brāhman, like sparks from fire or like the spider's web from the spider. But the *Upanishads* advance the thought a little farther. They do not merely speculate on the nature of Brāhman externally as the immanent-transcendent cause of the world, but they also try to demonstrate its reality in experience. Neither the *Upanishads*, nor the philosophical hymns of the *Vedas*, give us any reasons in demonstration of their philosophical conception of the ultimate being. They do not raise any question, nor give any premiss from which they drew their conclusions. Their opinions are only dogmatically asserted with the forceful faith of a man who is sure of his own belief. But, after all, it is only a belief, and not a reasoned statement, and there naturally arises the question as to its validity.

The *Upanishads* are driven by their inner thought to give some grounds for such assertions. Yet there is no attempt at logical speculations and demonstrative reasonings. The intuitive affirmations surge forth with the reality of the living faith of one describing an experience which he himself has had. They affirm that this ultimate reality cannot be grasped by learning or reasoning. It reveals itself only in our heart through

sublime purity, absolute self-control, self-abnegation, and cessation of mundane desires. Man not only becomes moral in
his relations to his fellow beings, but becomes super-moral, as
it were, by an easy control of the conflicts of his lower instincts
and desires, and by superior excellence of character. It becomes
possible for him to merge himself in an intuitive contact with
the transcendental spiritual essence with which he can immediately identify himself. The *Upanishads* again and again
reiterate the fact that this spiritual essence is incognizable by
any of the sense-organs—by eye or by touch—that it is beyond
the reasoning faculties of man and is therefore unattainable
by logic, and that it is indescribable in speech and unthinkable by thought. The apperception of it is not of an ordinary
cognitive nature, but is an apperception of the essence of our
beings; and, just as external nature was regarded as being
held and maintained in Brāhman, so the totality of our being,
our sense-functions, and thought-functions were regarded as
having come out, being held and sustained in this inner being.
It was also regarded as the Antar-yāmin or the inner controller
of our personality—the spiritual entity which was its root and
in which lie sustained and controlled all our vital activities and
cognitive and conative functions. We could have an apperception of it only when we transcended the outer spheres of ordinary
life and penetrated into the cavern on which neither the physical luminaries nor the luminaries of thought and sense shed
any light. Yet it was a light in itself, from which all other lights
drew their illumination. It was subtle and deep, and revealed
itself to those who attained that high spiritual perfection by
which they transcended the limits of ordinary personality.

We find anticipations of doubt as to the possibility of such a
subtle essence, which was our inmost being, becoming identical
with the highest reality of the universe from which everything
else emanated. Various parables are related, in which attempts
are made to prove the existence of a subtle essence which is

unperceived by the eye. In the parable of the banyan tree we are told how the big banyan tree can reside inside a grain-like seed. In the parable of the salt-water it is shown that the salt which is invisible to the eye can be tasted in saline water. The parable of the honey shows how honey from different flowers are so blended together in the honey of the honeycomb that they cannot be distinguished. We have also the parable by which Prajāpati instructed Virochana and Indra how two different states of the self can be distinguished from the corporeal body, the dream self and the dreamless self, and it was the self of the deep dreamless sleep that displayed the nature of the eternal unthinkable within us. The deep dreamless sleep brings us into daily contact with the eternal self within us, which is dissociated from all changes and forms the essence of our whole being. In the dialogue between Yama and Nachiketa, when the latter seeks instruction regarding the fate of men at death, he is told that when inquiry is earnestly made the true self in man is discovered to be eternally abiding, and can be grasped only through spiritual contact and spiritual union. Taken in this sense, death is a mere illusion which appears to those who cannot grasp the one absolute reality. There are other passages in which this absolute reality is regarded as one which is undetermined in itself, but from which all our faculties and experiences emanate in concrete determinations. We have thus in ourselves an epitome of the emergence of the world from Brāhman. From the subtle state of indifference in deep dreamless sleep one suddenly awakes to the varied experiences of ordinary life. Similarly, concrete varieties of objects have emerged into being from the pure subtle being of Brāhman, in which they existed in an undivided and undifferentiated state. Since that which emerges into manifold variety may ultimately lose itself in the being of the transcendent cause, and since the transcendent cause alone remains unchanged through all the processes of emergence and dissolution, that alone is the truth. The multiplicity of things is false, for the truth in them is the one abiding essence.

The *Upanishads* are not philosophy, if we mean by the word philosophy a reasoned account or a rationalization of experiences; yet they contain suggestions of rationalization as to the nature of reality from concrete experience of dreamless sleep and from ineffable mystical experience. Though ineffable, the mystical experience is not regarded as an ecstatic communion with the divine: it is a revelation of the subtlest essence of our being, which lies far below the depth of the common animal man. It is only when we transcend the limits of the ordinary biological man that we can come in contact with the pure personality which the *Upanishads* call the Ātman or the self. This pure self is one in all and is identical with the highest reality of the universe. It is pure spirituality and pure experience (*Jñāna*) and, as such, the absolute concrete truth which is immanent and transcendent at the same time in all our experiences and in all objects denoted by it. It is infinite reality, limitless and illimitable. The *Upanishads* thus lay the foundation of all later Hindu philosophy. All Hindu thinkers accept in more or less modified form the fundamental tenet of the *Upanishads* that self is the ultimate reality, and all experiences are extraneous to it.

The Sāmkhya is regarded as the earliest systematic attempt at philosophy. The word Sāmkhya has two meanings: (i) philosophic knowledge of wisdom, (ii) pertaining to numerals or numbers. The Sāmkhya philosophy admits twenty-five categories. It is called by this name both for these reasons and in consideration of the fact that it is regarded as the earliest formulation of rationalization of experience. The Sāmkhya philosophy is attributed to Kapila, who is said to have written the original work *Shashti-tantra* in sixty chapters. This work is now lost, and we know only the names of those chapters. We find the elements of Sāmkhya even in the earliest *Upanishads*, and we have reason to believe that the system was probably not originally written, but underwent a course of development at different stages and under different influences; though it is possible that at some particular stage Kapila may have contributed so much towards its systematization as to be generally regarded as the original expounder of the system. It is generally accepted that the Sāmkhya has two principal schools, the Atheistic and the Theistic. But there are differences of opinion as to whether the original Sāmkhya of Kapila was Atheistic. The Theistic Sāmkhya is now associated with Patañjali and is otherwise called the Yoga System. The Atheistic or non-theistic School of Sāmkhya in its generally accepted form is now available in a compendium of Iśvara Krishna (third century A.D.). Patañjali is supposed to have flourished somewhere about the middle of the second century B.C. As these two schools of thought gradually grew in prominence, other schools have been more or less forgotten in later times and can only be discovered by a critical examination of the older literature. The Sāmkhya and Yoga, however, in their various forms have profoundly influenced Hindu culture and religion in all their varied aspects.

The word Prakriti means the original substance, which in Sāmkhya consists of three classes of neutral entities—Sattva, Rajas, and Tamas. These are continually associating with one another for the fullest expression of their inner potentialities. They form themselves into groups or wholes, and not only are the inner constituents of each of the groups working in union with one another for the manifestation of the groups as wholes, but the wholes themselves are also working in union with one another for the self-expression of the individual whole and of the community of wholes for the manifestation of more and more developed forms. Causation is thus viewed as the actualization of the potentials. The order of all cosmic operations is deduced from the inherent inner order and relations of the neutral *reals*. Relations are conceived as the functions of these reals, with which they are metaphysically identical. Prakriti is regarded as the hypothetical state of the pure potential condition of these reals. It is supposed that this pure potential state breaks up into a state which may be regarded as the stuff of cosmic mind. This partly individuates itself as individual minds, and partly develops itself into space, from that into potential matter, and later on into actual gross matter as atoms. The individuated minds evolve out of themselves the various sensory and conative functions and the synthetic and analytic functions called *manas*. The individuated minds also reveal themselves in the psychical planes or psychoses of the different individuals. It is evident that the complexes formed from the neutral reals derive their meaning and functioning through a reference to the other or the others for the manifestation of which they are co-operating together. This other-reference of the reals (*gunas*) is their inherent teleology. But such other-references must have a limit, if the vicious infinite has to be avoided. In a general manner it may be said that the two broad groups, the psychical and the physical, are working together in mutual reference. But the total mutual reference must have a further reference. It is therefore assumed that there is an unrelational element, called *Purusha*, as pure consciousness which presides over every individuated mind. By a reference to this the non-conscious psychic phenomena attain their final meaning as conscious phenomena. The whole history of conscious phenomena again attains its last metaphysical purpose in self-annulment, by an ultimate retroversion of reference from *purusha* towards the ultimate principle of consciousness, by which the final other-reference to the *purusha* ceases. There must be a stage in which the positive other-references must end themselves in self-reference whereby the ultimate bond of the psychic manifestation or the psychosis with the *purusha* will cease. This cessation in the history of any individual psychic

plane marks its culmination and is regarded as a final metaphysical liberation of the *purusha* associated with that individual
psychic plane. There are as many *purushas* as there are psychic
planes. The *purusha* is regarded as the principle of consciousness and as unrelated to its fellow *purushas* and also to any
of the complexes of the neutral reals. According to the Sāmkhya
analysis a state of awareness can be looked at from two points
of view. From one point of view it may be regarded as a relational system which holds the many separate events or constituents in an integrated whole. Any such whole is related to
other psychical wholes or states of awareness. And even any
relational constituent inside the whole may be related with
other psychical entities or wholes; but from another point of
view no state of awareness, so far as it is merely awareness, can
go beyond itself. An awareness is a final fact which rests in
itself and does not depend upon anything else for the manifestation or the elaboration of its nature. It is only with reference
to the content of consciousness that other references exist. But
consciousness *qua* consciousness is independent as regards both
its origin and self-revelation. A content of consciousness is
related to other contents of consciousness, but an awareness
by itself as self-revelation is not connected with anything else.
It is a final fact. It is even difficult, nay, impossible to expound
any relation between the awareness and the content. The contents group together and express themselves in a unified form
in awareness, but the awareness does not in its turn depend on
anything else for manifesting its nature. It is not the additive
results of the contents, but a final emergent which is self-sufficient and self-sustained and different in nature from the content
of consciousness or from anything else of which we may speak.
A psychical structure is a relational complex. Like other
relational complexes, physical or biological, it consists of parts
which are mentally separable and which can be regrouped in
various relations; but awareness is homogeneous and has no

parts. It is absolutely structureless and therefore unlimited and non-relational. It is therefore called the principle of consciousness. With reference to the history of psychic development interpreted as personal experience, it may be regarded as the principle which runs through the psychic history and gives it meaning. It is an aspiration of the mental history. Regarded from the point of view of an analysis of any mental state, it is the principle of infinitude which is the point of reference that indirectly helps the aggregation of mental constituents for the formation of complexes and the revelation of their meaning as awareness. Though the constituents of any mental complex have a relational *nisus* towards it, it has no such relational *nisus* itself: it is complete in itself.

It has already been said that space is derived as a modification of the reals. Time is to be regarded as having a transcendental and a phenomenal aspect. Under the former, time is identical with the movement inherent in the *guna* reals and as such it is even prior to space. In the latter aspect, that is time as measurable, and as before and after, it is mental construction in which the ultimate unit of measure is regarded as the time taken by an atom to traverse its own dimension of space. Since all conceivable objects in the world are products of the *guna* reals, and since there is no other agent, the *guna* reals hold within themselves in a potential manner all things of the world, which are manifested first in the emergent categories of cosmic psychosis, ego, the eleven senses, five kinds of potential matter and five kinds of actual matter. These together form the twenty-five categories from the enumeration of which the Sāmkhya is supposed to have drawn its name. In the field of actual matter and the individuated mind (*chitta*), as an integration of the ego, the senses and the individuated psychosis, they are continually suffering changes and manifesting qualities which constitute the phenomenal world. The ultimate neutral nature of the *gunas* cannot be known. All that we can know is their phenomenal manifestation. It has been suggested above that all the evolutionary manifestations of the reals take place in consonance with the ultimate teleological necessity inherent in them, that these manifestations should be so directed as to be in harmony with the possibility of the psychic manifestation securing psychic experience and their ultimate disintegration at emancipation.

It is held by the Sāmkhya that psychical experience is possible only through a negative failure on the part of the psychic complexes to represent in the content the distinction that exists between the *guna* complexes and the non-relational transcendent *purusha*. If this distinction were comprehended in the psychic complexes there would not have been any *nisus* in them as one-sided other-reference towards the transcendent *purusha*. The Yoga, which is in general agreement with the entire metaphysical position of the Sāmkhya, thinks that the elements leading to a positive misconception or misidentification of the *purusha* as being of the same nature as the *guna* complexes are responsible for the possibility of the *nisus* and the resulting experience. This is technically called ignorance or *avidyā*. Yoga further holds that this *avidyā* manifests itself or grows into the various cementing principles of the mind, emotional and volitional, such as ego-consciousness, attachment, antipathy, and the self-preservative tendency. As a result of the operation of these principles, as grounded in the *avidyā*, the mind behaves as a whole and acquires experience and determines itself in the objective environment. According to both Sāmkhya and Yoga, the individuated mind has a beginningless history of emotional and volitional tendencies integrated or inwoven, as it were, in its very structure as it passes from one cycle of life to another. The determination of the mind in pursuance of its end as desire, will, or action is called *karma*. It is further held that all such determinations create potential energies which must fructify as diverse kinds of pleasurable or painful experiences, environments, conditions, and the periods of particular lives in which these experiences are realized.

The self-determining movement of the mind for the attainment of liberation can only start when one begins to discover that all experiences are painful. As a result thereof the young saint becomes disinclined towards all the so-called joys of the world and ceases to have any interest in the propagation of the life-cycle. Such a cessation cannot be by death. For death means further rebirth. The cessation of the life-cycles must necessarily be sought in the extinction of the conditions determining the mind-structure. For this, he adopts means by which he can invert the process of operation—that is, fundamental to the formation of the mind-structure, which is built up out of the integration and co-relation of experiences. He must destroy the working of all the laws of operation that make mind what it is. Such a disruption of mind will be ultimately effected with the destruction of the *avidyā* determining the *nisus* of the mind towards the *purusha*. The mind-structure consists of the integrated content of images, concepts, and their emotional and volitional associates, of various kinds, below the surface. These are immediately absorbed below the conscious level as the subconscious, semi-conscious, and unconscious. The various elements of the psychic structure in the different levels are held together to a great extent by ties of emotion and volition referring to the enjoyment of worldly objects. It is these that are continually attracting our minds. The follower of Yoga should in the first instance practise a definite system of moral and religious restraint, such as non-injury, truthfulness, purity, sincerity, sex-control, self-contentment and the like, called *yamas* and *niyamas*, for the external purification of mind. Ordinarily all activities associated with mental life are of the nature of continual relationing and movement. The Yogin who wishes to invert the processes underlying the maintenance of psychic structure arrests his mind statically on a particular object to the exclusion of all others, so that on the focal point of consciousness there may be only one state, which does not move, and all relationing process of the mind is at complete arrest. Yoga is defined as a partial or complete arrest or cessation of the mental states. As an accessory process the Yogin learns to steady himself in a particular posture (*āsana*) and gradually to arrest the processes of breathing (*prānāyāma*). His efforts to exclude other objects and to intensify the selected mental state which is to be kept steady on the focal point are called *dhāranā* and *dhyāna* respectively. As a result of his progressive success in arresting the mental states, there arise new types of wisdom (*prajñā*) and the subconscious potencies gradually wear out; ultimately all the subconscious and unconscious potencies of the structural relations are destroyed, and, as a result thereof, the *avidyā* which was determining the *nisus* of the mind is destroyed, and the whole fabric of the mind is disintegrated, leaving the pure *purusha* in his transcendent loneliness (*Kaivalya*), which is regarded as the ultimate aspiration of the human mind. In the Yoga process supreme ethical purity in thought, word, and deed is the first desideratum. When the mental field is so prepared the Yogin attacks the more difficult bondage of its psychological nature, consisting of the subconscious and unconscious forces which may drive him to sense-objects and sense-gratifications. At each stage of meditative concentration he has a supra-consciousness which destroys the roots of the conserved experiences and the fundamental passions, and yet does not build any psychological structure. This leads to the ultimate destruction of mind and self-illumination of the transcendent *purusha* in an utterly non-phenomenal and non-psychological manner.

The Yoga believes in the existence of God, who is associated with an absolutely pure mind. With such a mind He exerts a will such that the evolution of the *prakriti* or the *guna* reals may take the course that it has actually taken in consonance with the possible fruition of the mundane and supra-mundane or spiritual needs of the individual persons. The Yoga thinks that had it not been for the will of God, the potentialities of the *gunas* might not have manifested themselves in the present order. The Sāmkhya, however, thinks that the necessity inherent in the potentialities is sufficient to explain the present order, and the existence of God is both unwarrantable and unnecessary.

The *Gītā*, which I believe can be shown to be of pre-Buddhistic origin, is a metrical interpretation of the instructions of the *Upanishads* in their bearing on social life. The *Gītā* accepts the four types of duties fixed for the four castes, Brāhmana, Kshatriya, Vaiśya, and Śūdra, respectively, as study and sacrifice; fighting and the royal task of protecting subjects; looking after economic welfare, agriculture and trade; and service and the menial duties. It also accepts the final instruction of the *Upanishads* regarding the nature of the self as the ultimate reality, and the means of the highest moral perfection as leading to it. But at the same time it enjoins on all persons that the moral and social duties should be strictly followed. It argues, therefore, that having attained the highest moral perfection by cleansing oneself of all impurities of passion, such as greed, antipathy, self-love, and the like, having filled the mind with a spirit of universal friendship, compassion, and charity, and having attained perfect stability of mind, so as to be entirely unaffected by pleasures and afflictions of any kind, and being attached to God through bonds of love which unite him with his fellow beings, the true seer should continue to perform the normal duties that are allotted to his station of life in society. Even if he has no self-interest in the performance of his duties, no end to realize, no purpose to fulfil, no fruition of desire to be attained, he must yet continue to perform all normal duties, just as an ordinary man in his station of life would. The difference between the seer and the ordinary man in the sphere of performance of actions is that the former through the attainment of wisdom, the conquest of passions, the wasting

PLATE 9

GHĀT AT BENARES

away of all inner impurities, through the bonds of love with God and fellow beings and through the philosophical knowledge of the ultimate nature of the self, though dissociated and detached from everything else, yet takes his stand in the common place of humanity as represented in society and continues to perform his duties from a pure sense of duty in an absolutely unflinching manner. The latter, however, being engrossed with passions and bound down with ties of all kinds, cannot take a true perspective of life, and while performing his duties can only do them from motives of self-interest. His performance of duties is thus bound to be imperfect, and vitiated by self-seeking tendencies and the promptings of lower passions.

The aim of transcendent philosophy is thus not merely theoretical, but is intensely practical. However high a man may soar, to whatsoever higher perspective of things he may open his eyes, he is ultimately bound in ties of social duties to his fellow beings on earth in every station of life. A high and transcendent philosophy, which can only open itself through the attainment of the highest moral perfection and which leads one through the region beyond good and evil, again draws him down to the sharing of common duties with the other members of society. The attainment of the highest wisdom, which makes one transcend all others, is only half of the circle. The other half must be completed by his being on an equal footing with his fellow beings. The philosophy of 'beyond good and evil' does not leave a man in the air, but makes him efficient in the highest degree in the discharge of duties within 'good and evil'. The illusoriness of good and evil has to be perceived only for the purpose of more adequately obeying the demands of duties in the common social sphere. Almost all systems of Indian philosophy, excepting the followers of the Śaṃkara School of Vedānta, agree in enjoining the perfect performance of normal duties on the part of a seer.

There is a heretical school of thought which is associated

with the name of Chārvāka, supposed to be its founder. It is also known by the name Lokāyata (popular). The literature of the system is now practically lost, and we have to depend on the accounts of others to learn its main contents. The system had many schools, but the fundamental tenets seem to be the same. This school denied the existence of any soul or pure consciousness, which is admitted by all schools of Hindu thought. It also denied the possibility of liberation in any form, the infallible nature of the *Vedas*, and the doctrine of *karma* and rebirth. All Hindu schools of thought assume as their fundamental postulates the above doctrines, and it is on account of their denial that this system is regarded as heretical (*nāstika*). It holds that consciousness is an emergent function of matter complexes, just as the mixture of white and yellow may produce red, or fermented starch become an intoxicant. Consciousness being thus an epiphenomenon, nothing remains of the man after death. According to the Dhūrta Chārvākas, in the state of life some sort of a soul is developed which is destroyed at death; but, according to the other adherents of the Chārvāka school, no such soul is formed and the behaviour of a man is guided in responses by physico-physiological stimuli. Thus Chārvākas do not believe in the law of *karma* or of rebirth and they have also no faith in any religious creed or ritual of any sort. In the field of logic they think that since there is no way of proving the unconditional validity of inductive propositions all inferences have only a probable value: perceptions are all that we can depend upon.

Side by side with the doctrine of the Chārvāka materialists we are reminded of the Ājīvaka school of Makkhali Gosāla, the sophistical school of Ajita Keśakambali, and we read also of the doctrines of Pañchaśikha, Sulabhā, and others which were also intensely heretical. Thus Gosāla believed in a thorough-going determinism and denied the free will and moral responsibility of man. According to him, everything was determined by conditions and environments. Keśakambali also denied the law of *karma* and insisted on the futility of all moral efforts. In the specific details, there is a great divergence of views in the different systems of Indian philosophy regarding the concept of the law of *karma*. Stated in a general manner, the theory supposes that the unseen potency of action generally required some time before it could be effective and bestow on the agent merited enjoyment or punishment. Through the beginningless series of past lives, through which every one passes, the mysterious potency of the action accumulated and only became partially mature from time to time. The period of life, the nature of enjoyment and suffering in a particular life, and the environments were determined by the nature of the *karma* which had ripened for giving fruit. The unripe store of accumulated *karma* may be annulled by the destruction of ignorance, rise of true wisdom, devotion, or grace of God. But there is a difference of opinion as to whether the inevitable fruits of the ripened actions can be annulled. The theory of *karma* is the foundation-stone of all Indian systems of thought, except the aforesaid heresies.

The system of thought that began with the Buddha and was developed by his followers was regarded by the Hindus as heretical, as it did not accept the infallibility of the *Vedas* and the existence of an eternal and immortal soul. Gautama the Buddha was born in or about the year 560 B.C. He made his 'Great Renunciation' to solve the enigma of disease and death when he was twenty-nine years old. The main problem before him was how to escape from the misery of decay and death. Then it occurred to him to ask why there are decay and death, i.e. on what they depend. The reply that occurred to him was that decay and death could not be if there was no birth. Birth was conditioned by the accumulated *karma* (deeds) of past lives; this was conditioned by desires, and these were conditioned by ignorance (*avidyā*) of the true nature of all things. The early Buddhist philosophy did not accept any fixed entity as determining all reality; the only things it recognized were the unsubstantial phenomena, and these were called *Dharmas*. The question arises, if there is no substance or reality, how are we to account for the phenomena? But the phenomena are happening and passing away, and the main point of interest with the Buddha was to find out 'what being, what else is', 'what happening, what else happens', and 'what not being, what else is not'. The phenomena are happening in a series. We see that, there being certain phenomena, there become certain others; by the happening of some events, others also are produced. This is called dependent origination (Pali *paticca sampuppāda* = Sanskrit *pratītya-samutpāda*). Everywhere we have an assemblage of concomitant conditions making up the appearance of a whole. The moment such an assemblage is formed it is destroyed and is followed by another assemblage, which comes into being conditioned by the destruction of the previous assemblage. It is the law of all phenomena that units assemble together and give the appearance of a whole which seems to the ignorant mind an indivisible entity. There is no indivisible permanent entity anywhere; we have only the complex wholes coming into being and ceasing to exist at the same moment and thereby conditioning the being of another complex whole; and that also ceases the same moment that it comes into being, and thereby conditions the coming into being of another complex whole. Our notion of an ego, self, or person as a homogeneous permanent entity is thus an illusory one. The essence of ignorance (*avidyā*) is the notion of oneness in the complex and permanence in the momentary. 'When one says "I", what he does is to refer either to all the mental constituents, conational, emotional, and rational, or to any of them, and he deludes himself that that was "I". Just as the fragrance of the lotus belonged to the petals, the colour or the pollen, so one could not say that the sensation was "I" or that the feeling was "I" or any of the other mental constituents was "I".

There are nowhere to be found in the mental constituents "I am".'

Ignorance is beginningless, for we can never point to a period when it first started; the desire for continuity of existence and the sorrow and suffering that come in its train are also thus beginningless, and the mutual determination among them can only take place in and through the changing series of dependent phenomena; for there is nothing which can be said to have absolute priority in time. Our false perspective, by which we are habitually inclined to regard things as permanently existing or ourselves as permanently existing, is the cause of all our attachments and desires and consequently our bondage to the world of experience. If we could realize that there is no self, no 'I', there would be no basis on which desires and attachments may be formed. All the moral discipline involving non-injury to all living beings, and self-control of diverse kinds, Yogic concentration and meditation are directed to one end, namely, to induce cessation of *avidyā* through the cessation of desires. Since each phenomenon, mental or extra-mental, is nothing but a composite complex which dies the moment it comes into being, we have death and birth at every moment; for our life is nothing but a series of successive momentary mental complexes. At death we have a new series, which can be distinguished from the previous one by its association of an entirely new series of body complexes. According to Buddhism, there is thus no such entity as self that transmigrates from one life to another, but there is the birth of a mental complex in the succeeding life, as determined by the last mental complex of the previous life. Each mental or extra-mental complex by its very destruction determined the coming into being of another complex, either similar, partly similar, or else entirely dissimilar. From one life to another we have thus series of complexes following one another in continual succession—the history of the previous series determining the history of the later series; the procession of the series of mental complexes is kept going through the dynamic of desires and *karma*. With the cessation of desires and the destruction of ignorance the determinative function of the complexes ceases, and this leads to the cessation of the flowing series, which is regarded as the state of ultimate extinction or *nirvāna*. There is a difference of opinion as to whether *nirvāna* is a negative or a positive state, or whether it is a positive ultimate bliss, or a state of mere indifference.

As Buddhism spread and secured new converts from the Hindu circle, who wished to interpret Buddhism in the light of the teachings of the *Upanishads*, and as the logical presuppositions of the system began to be discussed, it began to be formulated in different ways, and this led to the rise of different schools which go by the name Mahā-yāna as distinguished from the original school called the Hīna-yāna. Thus Aśvaghosha (A.D. 100) tried to work out a metaphysics of the indefinite from the ante-metaphysical Buddhism of the older school. From the soulless Buddhism he extracts the theory of the soul having two aspects in it, as pure 'thatness' and as undergoing the cycle of birth and death. The soul in its reality means the oneness of the totality of all things. Things appear in their individuated form owing to the presence of the beginningless traces of incipient and unconscious memory of our past experiences of previous lives. Nāgārjuna, on the other hand, works out a theory of pure phenomenalism or nihilism. He holds that there is no truth, no essence in any phenomena that appear. As the phenomena have no essence they are neither produced nor destroyed. They are merely appearance. Everything is in relation to some kind of position, but nothing has an absolute position by itself. Nāgārjuna enters into elaborate dialectical discussion to show that all our concepts are relative and self-contradictory and therefore false. His conclusion, therefore, is the absolute denial of all reality. It is on account of the negative nature of his conclusion that he is called a nihilist (*śūnya-vādin*). The philosophy of the Laṅkāvatāra-sūtra is also of the same type as that of Nāgārjuna though it has a decided leaning towards idealism (*vijñāna-vāda*). The dialectical criticisms that deny the reality of all relations, as introduced by Nāgārjuna and the Laṅkāvatāra-sūtra, are of the same nature as those of Bradley in his *Appearance and Reality*, though more thorough and trenchant. The Laṅkāvatāra-sūtra, however, takes an entirely subjectivistic attitude towards the phenomenal world and its relations, and urges that all sensations and perceptions and their relations are created from within our minds and have no objective existence.

The philosophy of idealistic absolutism that was started by Maitreya and Asaṅga and elaborated by Vasubandhu denies the existence of the eternal objective world and ends in the affirmation of oneness of all things. The difference of perception and memory is also explained on a subjective basis, and the difficulty of intercommunication and uniformity of experiences is solved by the theory of direct action of one subject upon another. The evolution of the subjective and objective categories, the individual perceivers and the objects perceived, are held to be the self-creation of one thought-principle. The transformation of the self-evolving thought is regarded as real by Vasubandhu, as opposed to Aśvaghosha, who believed such transformation to be illusory appearance. The mode of causation allowed by Vasubandhu is that of *pratītya-samutpāda*, which holds that the effect is a novel phenomenon distinct from the cause, which comes into being independently of an external excitant cause. It is entirely different from the *pariṇāma* (transformation) theory of the Sāmkhya school, which means that the effects produced are but transformations which were already existent in a latent form in the causal substance. Vasubandhu, who flourished in the fifth century A.D., anticipated and laid the foundation of a scheme of philosophy which was later on expounded by Śaṁkara as the Vedānta philosophy of the *Upanishads*.

Buddhism, divided into various schools of logical speculations, manifests diverse shades of conflicting thought; but there is one fundamental essence which must be regarded as unflinchingly true of all its various forms. This consists in the fact that the highest wisdom or enlightenment, which is the goal of our life, can be attained only through the highest moral perfection and contemplation. Though this highest enlightenment may awaken in man the view that everything in the world is phenomenal or mental, that there is not even a persistent self, but that what we call self is a momentary congeries of thoughts, ideas, emotions, and volitions, yet the imperative character of the performance of the moral duties and the execution of all our acts in consonance with the principles of universal friendship, compassion, and charity is absolutely maintained. The example of the Buddhist king Aśoka, who reigned as both a king and a monk, sending edicts through the whole of India and his missions through Asia, amply demonstrates the Buddhist view of life, that we should all work for the spiritual welfare of all our fellow beings, and the general welfare of all existent beings. Chandragupta, who established the Maurya Empire, is said to have died as a recluse in the hermitage of Bhadrabāhu, a Jain saint; Harsha, the great conqueror and king of mighty fame in the sixth century, lived a life of self-abnegation and charity. The spiritual message of India thus fulfilled itself through the lives of the three greatest emperors of Hindu India. Nāgārjuna, the great Buddhist preacher of Nihilism, who denied all kinds of reality, yet drew from his philosophy the imperative character of high morality. Thus he says,

'Exhibit morality faultless and sublime, unmixed and spotless, for morality is the supporting ground of all eminence. View as enemies avarice, deceit, duplicity, lust, indolence, pride, greed and hatred. Nothing is so difficult to attain as patience. Open no door for anger. Of him who has conquered the unstable, ever-moving objects of the six senses, and of him who has overcome the mass of his enemies in battle, the wise praise the first as the greater hero. Thou, who knowest the world, be indifferent to all the worldly conditions of gain and loss—happiness and suffering, fame and dishonour and blame and praise. If a fire were to seize your hand or your dress, you would extinguish it and subdue it. Even thus endeavour to eliminate desire, for there is no higher necessity than this.'

It will thus be seen that, though the Gītā and the Nihilistic Buddhism are based on two fundamentally different types of metaphysical opinion, yet in practical life they are completely unanimous in their instructions. A Buddhist saint when he attains his highest enlightenment through moral endeavour has to devote his life to the welfare of all beings.

Though the chief emphasis of the Vaiśeshika and Nyāya systems of thought may ordinarily appear to be placed elsewhere, yet keener analysis would show that in their case also the ultimate aim is fundamentally the same—the attainment of salvation through moral perfection. A large number of sub-schools associated with various religious sects developed in India through a form of eclectic admixture of Vedānta, Sāmkhya, and Yoga together with the Bhāgavata theory of love. But in all these systems the central idea is the same, viz. the attainment of transcendent moral perfection and of the perfect social behaviour induced by it.

There is another vein of thought which runs through Indian minds, probably from pre-Buddhistic times, and which may be regarded as being in some sense a corollary and in another sense a supplementary to the attitude and perspective of life described above. This attitude consists in the lowering of emphasis on one's limited self-sense as egoism or selfishness in the consequent experience of equality with all men and the development of a spirit of love towards them and towards God, who manifests himself in the persons of all men. The cultivation of love of humanity was one of the dominant characteristics not only of the Gītā and Buddhism and Jainism, but also of Yoga and most systems

of Indian theism, such as those of Rāmānuja, Madhva, Nim-
bārka, and others. The Vishnu-Purāna says that to look upon
all beings as equal to one's self and to love them all as one would
love one's own self is the service of God; for God has incarnated
himself in the form of all living beings. The Christian principle
of love and equality is anticipated in Buddhism and Bhāgavatism,
which flourished in India long before Christ; but the force of
innate sin is not emphasized in it as it is in Christianity.

Limitations of space forbid me to enter into the various
logical concepts and philosophical creeds, criticisms of thought
and dialectic developed in the semilogical and logical epochs of
the evolution of history of philosophy in India, which could
be demonstrated as anticipating similar doctrines and modes
of thought in medieval and modern philosophy. Philosophy
developed in India continuously for about three thousand years
over a wide tract of the country, and a large part of it still
remains unexplored and unexplained in any modern language.
A careful reader of Indian philosophy who is fully acquainted
with Western philosophy is naturally agreeably surprised to see
how philosophic minds everywhere have traversed more or less
the same path and how the same philosophical concepts which
developed in later times in Europe were so closely anticipated
in India. An illustration of this may be found in the address
delivered by the present writer before the 6th International
Congress of Philosophy in 1924, in which anticipations of
the dominant ideas of Croce's philosophy were shown from
Dharmakīrti and Dharmottara, the Buddhist writers of the
ninth century. But it is impossible to dilate on this here. I
have therefore made no attempt to trace in any detail the
philosophical legacy of India. My chief effort in this chapter
has been to show the Indian conception of the bearing of
philosophy to life, which has been almost uniformly the same
in almost all systems of Indian philosophy and which has always
inspired all philosophy and all religion. That philosophy should

not remain merely a theoretic science, but should mould our entire personality and should drive us through the hard struggles of moral and spiritual strife on the onward path of self-realization and should ultimately bring us back again to the level of other men and make us share the common duties of social life in a perfected form and bind us with ties of sympathy and love to all humanity—this is the final wisdom of Indian thought.

S. N. DAS GUPTA.

CASTE AND THE STRUCTURE OF SOCIETY

THE division of mankind into groups based on fundamental differences in disposition, capacity, and character is a common feature of society all over the world. Such groups have a tendency to isolate themselves into separate classes holding intercourse chiefly among themselves; but the evolution of a caste system postulating hereditary orders functioning within rigidly circumscribed spheres of social intercourse and yet sharing the large life of the community is a phenomenon peculiar to the organization of Hindu society; including as it does an elaborate code of ceremonial purity and defilement, unapproachability and untouchability, commensal restrictions and connubial prohibitions, penance and excommunication.

In other communities the principal factors determining class and status are wealth, pedigree, or profession. In the case of Hindus, however, membership of a caste is determined by birth. Whereas in other countries social barriers separating class from class are being swept away by rapidly changing conditions in the social, industrial, and political order of society, in India many of these remain impregnable. The hereditary classes into which the Hindu community is divided still refrain from eating or intermarrying with those not of their caste. Their differences are taken to be innate, such as cannot be annulled. No one hopes to raise his or her caste in this life, but every one stands in danger of lowering it by neglect of ceremonial, or by intercourse with unclean people. Hence the elaborate code of pollution, penance, and purification; hence also the penalty of loss of caste for infringement of regulations and established usages.

How important a part caste plays in the social life of the people is vividly brought out in the conversation which the author of *The Peoples of India* had with Chandra Sen, a Bengali poet.

Asked if he would attempt a definition of what a Hindu was, the poet, after many suggestions, all of which had to be abandoned, on closer examination, came to the conclusion that a Hindu was one who was born in India of Indian parents on both sides and who accepted and obeyed the rules of his caste.[1]

At the head of the hierarchy stands the *Brāhman* (priest); at the bottom the *Śūdra* (serf). Between the two there stood, according to the original four-fold division, the *Kshatriya* (warrior) and the *Vaiśya* (husbandman or trader). At the present time instead of these four classes we find a multiplicity of castes and sub-castes. Food and water offered by a member of a caste inferior to one's own is taboo. So is marriage outside one's own caste. Even sitting, or travelling, with a member of a lower caste was once sternly forbidden, but the injunction is no longer generally observed. The idea that persons belonging to certain groups were, without exception, impure and caused pollution by their touch and even by their look, or presence, has exercised a powerful influence, and still materially influences the social relations of the different groups. Even now members of the privileged orders indulge in punctilios about ceremonial defilement, rendering the task of social and political reform exceedingly difficult. The most extraordinary characteristic of the Indian institution of caste is, however, the denial of certain civil and religious rights to a large number of people. Born to slave for the superior orders, the Śūdra has, for centuries, carried on his forehead the mark of inferiority, while some castes remain 'untouchable'.

It was not so in the ancient times when the first picture of the life of the Indo-Āryans was drawn in the *Rig-Veda*, the earliest record of the Vedic period which ended about 600 B.C. These hymns introduce us to a united people led by their priests and kings, knit together in a bond of common brotherhood. There is nothing in the earlier portion of the *Rig-Veda* about

[1] J. D. Anderson, *The Peoples of India*, p. 33.

hereditary status or occupation, no exaltation or degradation, no taboo on breaking bread, no ban on intermarriage, no penalty of interdiction. It marked an epoch when the Āryans stood united as one community. There was, no doubt, the broad division of society into classes: Brāhman (priest), Kshatriya (noble), and Vaiśya (husbandman). Later we are introduced to Śūdras or serfs, but this division marked merely orders socially distinct yet not isolated.

How, then, did the Brāhmans come to be exalted as the gods of the earth, and the Śūdras looked down upon as the confirmed serfs of the privileged classes? Whence originated social inequalities and social segregation, and what made the law-givers set up barriers of untouchability? Numerous theories have been put forward by Indian and European scholars. Some have stressed ethnological distinctions; others have traced the origin of the system to the racial struggle during the Vedic age between the fair-complexioned Āryan conquerors and the dark-skinned aborigines; others again have emphasized common occupation or division of labour as the chief, if not the sole, basis of caste; some insist on excluding all influence of race and religion from the factors determining the origin and growth of the system, while others point to the influence of tribal differences, especially among the non-Āryans, upon Hindu culture and social organization, an influence which survived the diffusion of a common Āryan culture. An attempt will be made to solve this sociological problem by a joint appeal to history and tradition.

Early Beginnings

Far back in the dim ages there lived somewhere in Central Asia, or in southern Russia as some authorities surmise, a number of human families called Āryans. Man then lived with nature. Upon the physical forces around him he depended for food and shelter. To him these hidden powers appeared to be pulsating with life; and he appeased and adored them with prayers and sacrifices.

In course of time, either because there was a great increase in their population, or because their homeland was rendered uninhabitable by extreme cold, they migrated southwards. Society was still unsettled. There were constant migrations in search of new lands. One of these entered India by the passes of the north-west. At the time of their arrival they lived a simple life. The father of the family was its head; his sons and grandsons lived with their wives and children under the same roof. Their wealth consisted of their cattle. Milk and butter with grain constituted their staple food, although animals were sacrificed and eaten. The father of the family acted as priest of his own household. He lighted the sacred fire and offered sacrifices to the gods. On his death the duty devolved on his son. Even during those early days considerable importance was attached to ceremonial purity and ritual, the subsequent elaboration of which during the later Vedic period gave rise to notions of defilement, which were largely responsible for a long process of differentiation and the ultimate ramification of the divers groups into castes. Before that there was only a broad division into classes; there were the priests who performed sacrifices; there were the chieftains who fought; there were the rest, representing the mass of the people, who were husbandmen; but there were no castes.

Clash of Cultures

Then commenced an era of conquest. Crossing the Sutlej, the Indo-Āryans marched eastwards towards the Gangetic valley, in which developed civilized Hindu kingdoms. With the expansion of territory and growth of numbers, the once simple organization of society became complex and intricate. This was a period of constant struggles with the aborigines and between different racial elements and types of culture. The dusky natives of the soil are referred to in the hymns as flat-nosed, of unintelligible speech, worshipping no god, offering no sacrifice, and following strange and repulsive customs. Long after they were subdued, the distinction between the conquerors and the conquered endured. A certain admixture of blood was, however, inevitable. Year after year witnessed a confusion in the social order calling for safeguards for the maintenance of the purity of the race and the preservation of the ancient tradition. However ridiculous the conceptions of that 'aristocracy of eugenics' may appear to be to the opponents of the theory of organic inequality, the sages of the Vedic age considered it imperative to view every social question in the light of its effect upon race purity. Of still greater importance, however, was the maintenance of the integrity of their faith and the observance of its ritual.

Rise of the Priestly Class

On the performance of the elaborate religious rites and on the perpetuation of the time-honoured traditions hung the prosperity, and even the very existence, of the commonwealth. The mystic and miraculous hymns and liturgies had to be preserved and handed down from father to son by word of mouth. Their sanctity depended not merely on their words or general sense, but also on every accent rightly placed. There was a need for men who could specialize in the study of the texts, comprehend the symbolic meaning of the ritual, and assist in the perpetuation of this textual tradition.

Members of the priestly families devoted themselves to this task. It required laborious study and detachment from worldly pursuits. The word was holy; holy also should be the earthly repositories of such treasure. This ideal was constantly before the eyes of the Brāhman. Self-control and self-culture enabled him to uphold the standard of purity and renunciation essential for the manifestation of *brahma*, or the divine within him.

Brahmanhood was thus a matter of personal qualities and attainments rather than of descent; but, as priestly functions gradually became the monopoly of a single class, it closed its door against the intrusion of others.

The literature of the time shows that the Brāhman advanced claim after claim to the sacrosanct privileges of his caste. Without his help even a monarch's offerings were not acceptable to the gods; nor was a ruler's safety on the battle-field assured without his prayers. He added, moreover, to the king's *punya*, or merit. It was believed that the sixth part of the *punya* accumulated by a Brāhman by sacrifices and good deeds went to the credit of the ruler of the land. It was even suggested that the king ruled by the authority delegated to him by the Brāhman. Such ascendancy of the sacerdotal class must have been due to the Hindu's concern for personal salvation; and his conviction that such salvation could not be secured without the performance of religious rites and recital of the Vedic formulae by the Brāhman.

Rise of the Kshatriyas

In the earlier days royal families owned land and cattle, just like ordinary people. There is nothing in the *Rig-Veda* to indicate the existence of a separate noble, or warrior, class. Indeed, no special military order was then called for, as it was still a custom for freemen to take up arms, whenever necessary, in defence of the State. However, with the expansion of territory, a line of demarcation came to be drawn between the ruling classes, including the nobles who had led the tribes to conquest, and the commons. The king's retainers, many of whom were probably connected with him by blood, received large shares of the conquered territory. It was neither possible nor necessary for them to cultivate such lands with their own hands. That work was relegated to others. Thus grew up a separate class of warriors. Originally applied to those who were guardians of the king's person, the term *Kshatriya* came to denote protectors of the entire kingdom and the established order of things.

The Norman Conquest of England shows the manner in which subjugation of a nation by foreigners creates a royal caste. The Kshatriyas afford another illustration. They included not only the members of the royal houses and their kinsmen and nobles, but also the royal military vassals and feudal chiefs corresponding practically to the *barones* of early English history.[1] 'Had the Moghuls or the present Englishman been without an organized priesthood,' says one of the authorities on the subject, 'and had they accepted the Brāhmans as their spiritual guides and taken pains to adopt elevating sacraments, they also could have formed one of the Kshatriya castes.'[2]

The Vaiśyas

The mass of the people retained their ancient name of *Viś* or *Vaiśya* (people) and formed a separate class, the Vaiśyas. They were, however, a unit merely in name, a conglomeration of different groups with different functions. Pastoral pursuits and agriculture were their normal occupations, but trade and industry also claimed a large number of them. The Vaiśya was advised to learn the values of precious stones and metals and other commodities, to acquire a knowledge of different languages, and to be conversant with the conditions obtaining in different countries and the prospects of business. There were also various other professional classes in the Rigvedic society, such as *rathakāra* (chariot-maker), *takshan* (carpenter), *kulāla* (potter), and *karmāra* (blacksmith). They all enjoyed the status of respectable citizens. As yet there were no hard-and-fast rules prescribing their specific functions.

[1] *Vedic Index*, vol. ii, p. 203.
[2] Shridhar V. Ketkar, *History of Caste in India*, p. 94.

The Śūdras

Below these three orders were the Śūdras, or serfs. In the early portion of the *Rig-Veda* there is no mention of this class. Instead, we are introduced to *Dasyu*, or *Dāsa*, both as aborigines independent of Āryan control and as subjugated slaves. Only in the later portion, the *Purushasūkta* (hymn of the *Primordial Male*) the Śūdra appears for the first time. In this hymn also we find the earliest reference to the origin of the four orders in which society was then divided, an origin which suggested the idea of specific creation of each order: 'The *Brāhman* was his (Creator's) mouth; the *Rājanya* was made his arms; the being (called) the *Vaiśya*, he was his thighs; the *Śūdra* sprang from his feet.'

The last order embraced not only the subjugated serfs, but also all those who were beyond the pale of the Āryan state. The ruling tribes that neglected religious rites and ceremonial were also drawn into the orbit of this caste. Thus the line of demarcation which separated the Śūdras from the rest was not one of race, but of sacrament.

Such social gradation was the inevitable result of expansion and progress. It marked merely the normal evolution of the constitution of the family. Every individual had his own place and value in the organization. The different classes represented merely the different phases of its development and culture. While contributing its service to society within the sphere assigned to it, each participated in the larger life of the confederacy of the different groups.

Organization in Iran

Evidence of such functional differentiation of men thrown upon the collaboration of others and made dependent on them is found also in the sacerdotal literature of ancient Iran. In the earliest Iranian society known to us there were three classes, namely, *Ātharvan*, *Rathaeshtar*, and *Vāstriya*, priests, warriors, and agriculturists. Later we are introduced to the complete group of four orders, the last one being *Huiti*, or artisans. When two such advanced parallel organizations of society are found in two different societies in two different countries, their origin might well be ascribed to the common heritage of ideas and civilization inherited from their ancestors who lived together during the early period of Indo-Iranian unity. In fact, if we accept the account, given in the *Shāhnāma* of Firdausi, of the early organization of society in Persia, the origin of the fourfold division according to profession can be traced to the initiative of King Yima, in whose reign the Āryan people lived as one family in their ancient homeland. There was then such an enormous increase in mankind, as well as flocks and herds, that *Airyana Vaejah* could no longer contain them. Thrice the illustrious king led his overflowing subjects southwards, 'in the way of the sun'.[1] The Avestan texts represent the prophet Zarathushstra, not Yima, as the originator of these social divisions, but later tradition associates Yima's name with their foundation, and Firdausi adopts this view in his *Shāhnāma*.[2] If this be correct, it would appear that such an organization of society was one of the ancient institutions of civilization which the early Aryan settlers took with them and developed in India.

The seers of the early Vedic period knew nothing of caste. Delve as much as one may into the literature of the period, one discovers only classes, not castes. The elements which go to form castes were, however, there, so that gradually a gulf was created between one order and another. For a long time, however, the conception of social segregation and untouchability was repugnant to the genius of the people, who sought unity in variety and dissolved variety in unity. Each class was regarded as an integral part of the whole fabric of society. Each submitted

[1] *Vendidād*, 2. 19–19.
[2] Vide *Zoroastrian Civilization*, by M. N. Dhalla.

cheerfully to the special functions and duties assigned to it. Even the Śūdra appears to have been content with his mission in life; and there were no agitators abroad to sow in the minds of the proletariat the seeds of discontent. There appeared to have been a tacit understanding that different classes of individuals stood at different stages of evolution and that, therefore, the duties, modes of life, and rules of conduct applicable and helpful to each must necessarily differ. The differentiation was, however, regarded only as a means to an end, not an end in itself. It assigned to each individual his due position in the social order; it regulated his relations with other members of the community, and provided means for his orderly development, eliminating possibilities of a clash of interests between master and servant, landlord and tenant, capital and labour, state and subject.

The four classes are mentioned in later Vedic literature as *varnas*. Since *varna*, which means colour, is also used as an equivalent of caste, many a scholar has been led to ascribe the origin of caste to the fair-skinned conquering Āryans' pride of blood. But in the *Rig-veda* the term *varna* is never applied to any one of the classes. There it is used in its literal sense and the entire *Āryavarna*, or the Āryan population, is shown to differ from the *Dāsavarna*, or the population of the aborigines, not only in colour, but also in physical features, speech, religious usages, and customs. The distinction of class, therefore, rested not on colour (*varna*), but on innate tendencies.

According to Hindu philosophy divine energy manifests itself in different degrees according to the preponderance in each person of one or other of the three *gunas*, or fundamental qualities, which make up the *prākriti*, or nature, of an individual. These *gunas* are (1) *sattva*, or light, which fully reveals *brahma* or the divine element within, and stands for purity; (2) *rajas*, or passion, which partially veils the *brahma* within, and promotes activity; (3) *tamas*, or darkness, which obscures the *brahma* within, and produces stolidity. In everything that springs from nature there are these three *gunas* striving for mastery.[1] The temperament of an individual is determined according to the predominance in him of one or other of these three constituent principles. If *sattva* is not allowed to be overcome by 'passion' or 'darkness', one secures the blessing of serenity; from this springs concentration, which in its turn leads to subjugation of the organs of sense and, finally, to *ātmadarśanayogyatā*, fitness for beholding the Self.

It follows, therefore, that for his own salvation as well as for social efficiency an individual should be allowed to develop along the lines best suited to his natural endowments and that he on his part should perform the duties assigned to him in accordance with the predominant quality of the strand in his nature. The well-known episode of Arjuna in the *Bhagavad-gītā* is a typical illustration of this philosophy of life. Dismayed, he refuses to fight; but Krishna, the preacher, prevails upon him to discharge the duty proper to his Kshatriya caste.

There is nothing, however, in the whole body of Sanskrit literature to show that the caste system was deliberately devised as a means to attain the coveted end of realizing the divine within man. The doctrine of the *gunas* merely helped to give a rational explanation of the phenomenon, when the original fourfold classification hardened into a rigid system, and when the rapidly multiplying castes attached undue importance to outward form. A remarkable and almost unique feature of Hindu culture is the process of minute analysis and synthesis to which it subjects from time to time the phenomena which leave their impress upon the senses and the mind and the unchangeable soul. Such an exposition has helped succeeding generations to grasp the significance of the philosophic doctrines underlying the social and religious systems of a race excelling in spiritual

[1] *Patanjali*, iv. 15.

speculation and metaphysical subtleties. The same process was visible in the attempts made to create a new philosophy of caste. It would scarcely be fair to describe such analysis and synthesis as an artificial rationalization composed centuries after the origin which it professes to explain. The doctrine of the three *gunas*, elaborated by Kapila, who probably preceded Buddha by about a century and founded the earliest or the Sāmkhya school of Hindu philosophy, appears to have been foreshadowed in Vedic literature. In the tenth book of the *Atharva-Veda* we read: 'Men versed in sacred knowledge know that living Being that abides in the nine-petalled Lotus Flower (i.e. the human body) enclosed with triple bands (or three strands) and bonds which the three qualities (or *gunas*) enclose.' It is possible, as suggested by Muir, that there may be here the very first reference to the three *gunas* afterwards expounded in Indian philosophical speculations.[1]

The learned authors of *Vedic Index of Names and Subjects* have characterized the relation between the later and the earlier periods of the Vedic history of caste 'as the hardening of a system already formed by the time of the *Rig-Veda*'. Whether the system had 'already been formed', or whether it was merely in the process of formation in the Rigvedic age, we have no authentic evidence to prove or disprove; but it is beyond dispute that by the end of the Vedic period each of the four original orders had evolved into a caste, and had come to constitute its own special and exclusive social world. Each was distinguished by its origin and its sacraments.

The Vaiśya formed the basis of the organization of state and society. On this basis the two superior orders, the Brāhman and the Kshatriya, rested; while all the three groups were superior to the Śūdras. The ecclesiastical order claimed pre-eminence as constituting the spiritual power of the land; but

[1] *Man in India* (article on 'Caste, Race, and Religion in India', by Sarat Chandra Roy), vol. xiv, no. 2, pp. 193–4.

the wealth and martial prowess of the temporal power also demanded recognition. There were terrible feuds between the two forces. At last, however, a policy of give and take appears to have composed their differences. It was realized that only the union of the two could uphold the order of society. The association of the Brāhman and the Kshatriya in the sacred hymns shows that the gulf separating the two classes was not so wide as that which severed the commoners from the spiritual lords of the earth. It was declared that the Kshatriyas could prosper only with the assistance of the Brāhmans and that only the combination of the two could uphold the moral order of society. In such an alliance, however, the dominating partner was necessarily the Brāhman. Gautama laid down that when a king and a Brāhman passed along the same road, precedence on the road should belong to the Brāhman, not to the king.

For the privilege conceded to him the Brāhman had to pay a stiff price. The Code of Manu demanded of him a life of study, sanctity, and austerity. Even for his daily food and raiment he was made dependent on the devotion of the other classes. He was to 'shun worldly honour as he would shun poison'. If he erred in this respect, he was no more than a Śūdra.

Though ranked higher, the Kshatriyas did not draw a sharp line between themselves and the commoners. They were warriors and administrators by profession, but the hand that stretched the bow and wield.d the sword could also use the scythe. Nor did those aristocrats of India regard commerce with aversion, as did their compeers in ancient Iran, who looked upon the market-place as a breeding-ground of falsehood and deceit and who took pride in affirming that they did not soil their fingers with coins in the process of buying and selling. As the divisions of caste hardened, the Vaiśyas were relegated to a position distinctly inferior to that of the first two orders. 'The Vaiśya', declared the *Aitareya Brāhmana*, 'is tributary to another', 'to be lived on by another', and 'to be oppressed at will'.[1]

Degradation of the Śūdras

The Śūdra fared still worse. He was relegated to the lowest stratum of humanity. He was described as 'the servant of another to be expelled at will' and to be 'slain at will'.[2] According to the *Śatapatha Brāhmana*, the Śūdra was untruth itself. He was unfit for the ceremony of initiation (*Upanayana*), the importance of which may be gauged from the fact that, when invested with the sacred thread, the symbol and badge of the Aryan tribe, the newly initiated is said to be born again. This constituted the main difference between the Śūdra and the Vaiśya; one was a *dvija* (twice-born); and the other was not. A Śūdra could neither listen to, nor recite, the Vedic texts. Denied the right of initiation, he was also deprived of the study of the *Veda* and the kindling of the sacred fire. 'A Śūdra attempting to hear the sacred texts', says Āpastamba, 'shall have his ears filled with molten tin or lac; if he recites the *Veda*, his tongue shall be cut off; and if he remembers it, he shall be dismembered. If he affects a position of equality with twice-born men, either in sitting, conversing, or going along the road, he shall receive corporal punishment.'[3] Even to this day, while all ceremonies of the three higher castes are performed by reciting sacred formulas, those of the Śūdras are performed in silence.

It seems, however, that the position of those down-trodden people was not so desperate as the later texts would indicate. The code of Manu, written after class distinctions had assumed the rigidity of caste exclusiveness, recognizes the personal liberty of the Śūdra and gives him licence to emigrate in case of distress even beyond the bounds of the Āryan dominion. Many a Śūdra

[1] vii. 29. 3.   [2] vii. 29. 4.
[3] Āpastamba, ii. 10. 23.

rose to the highest position in the state and even to the rank of royalty. Śālivāhana and Chandragupta are two of the most conspicuous examples of such elevation. The family of Holkar, one of the prominent modern dynasties of Indian rulers, is also of Śūdra origin.

Gradually, however, the Śūdra was pushed more and more into the abyss of degradation. He was held to have been doomed to serfdom. He must not acquire wealth, lest he should thereby cause pain to the Brāhman. So physically unclean was he believed to be, so prone to defile objects by his touch, that a householder was warned not to sip water brought by him for purification. Members of the superior castes were not to travel in his company. So morally depraved was he taken to be that, while the twice-born castes were exhorted to shun spirituous liquors, he was left severely alone. Doomed as he was to irrevocable decadence, what use attempting to make 'white' virtue enter into the 'black' body of the Śūdra! Even when ways and means of allowing him access to the gods by prayer and sacrifice were subsequently devised, a distinction was drawn between the *Sat*-Śūdra, who merited emancipation by the observance of his caste duties and good conduct, and the *Asat*-Śūdra, who was past all hope of redemption. Only to the good ones was allowed the privilege of Brahmanic rites and sacraments, but even in their case the recital of the *mantras*, or the Vedic formulae, was forbidden.[1]

Theory of the Divine Origin of Caste

How could myriads of people be made to resign themselves to a system under which such disabilities were attached to them? How could they be expected to tolerate perpetually the stigma of impurity and infamy ruthlessly fastened upon them? Was there anything in the sacred books to make man respect such dispensations of Providence? According to that late *Rig-Veda*

[1] G. S. Ghurye, *Caste and Race in India.*

hymn, the different classes sprang from the four limbs of the Creator. It was meant to show that the four classes stood in relation to the social organization in the same relation as the different organs of the Primordial Man to his body. Together they had to function to give vitality to the body politic. There was nothing in that account to warrant the assumption that the order in which the four groups were mentioned, or that the particular limbs specified as their origin, marked their social status. In the Brāhmana literature, the *Dharmaśāstras*, and the *Purānas*, however, such an interpretation was definitely put upon this text; and the creation myth, which exalted the first two orders of priests and warriors, was made the basis of an elaborate code of rules demarcating the functions and status and regulating the interrelations of each group.

Philosophy of Caste

Even the theory of divine origin does not appear to have carried conviction to the people. A philosophy of caste was, therefore, evolved, providing a rational sanction for the apparently arbitrary distinctions of caste and guaranteeing salvation to each individual through the performance of duties. The status of every individual in life, according to such philosophy, was determined by the *karma*, or actions, of his former birth. Similarly, his salvation depended on the due observance of the doctrine of *dharma*, which has been variously translated as duty, virtue, order and law, and ideal of life, but which includes all these and a good deal more. It is that which holds the people together; and its scope is defined in the *Mahābhārata* as concerned with the duties of kings and subjects, of the four orders, and of the four modes of life. *Dharma*, in short, lays on every man the obligation to do his duty to himself and to society in that station of life in which it has pleased Providence to place him. It is the law of development, making human progress dependent on the practice of virtues and performance of duties

which are rightly one's own at a particular stage of evolution.[1]
Dharma may be compared with *daena*, which literally means
religion, but signifies the ethical law governing the life of a
Zoroastrian. The character of a man is moulded by the ethical
law which he observes in his daily life. *Daena*, therefore, stands
also for character, or the active self, of a person. Similarly, a
man's *dharma* makes him what he is, and stands for his active
self.

A person's worth is determined by his knowledge and capacity
and the inherent qualities which mark his conduct in life. 'The
fourfold division of castes,' says the Creator in the *Bhagavad-
gītā*, 'was created by me according to the apportionment of
qualities and duties'. 'Not birth, not sacrament, not learning,
makes one *dvija* (twice-born), but righteous conduct alone
causes it.' 'Be he a Śūdra or a member of any other class,'
says the Lord in the same epic, 'he that serves as a raft on a
raftless current, or helps to ford the unfordable, deserves respect
in every way.'

How at the dawn of creation individuals came to be endowed
with different qualities and capabilities is nowhere explained,
but this theory of divine dispensation according to one's qualifications appears to have succeeded in securing the resignation of the people to their lot. It induced the belief that caste
was a question of capacity and character and that observance
of caste duties (*svadharma*) in the spirit of true renunciation,
as one's humble offering to God, led to perfection and final
emancipation. Gautama Buddha, who raised the standard of
revolt against the tyranny of caste and preached the doctrine
of equality of man, raised millions from the slough of despair

[1] In his thesis *On the Vaishnavas of Gujarat* Dr. N. A. Thoothi gives a lucid
exposition of *dharma* in this sense. It equals, he says, 'certain conditions of
the inner nature within each one of us in accordance with which the individual
is called upon to evolve towards perfection in terms of action and behaviour
that mould his relations with the outside world.' Pp. 42–3.

by his cheering message that members of the different orders who lived according to their *dharma*, and performed the duties proper to their *varna*, enjoyed after death the rewards for such devotion to their duties. If they were men of lower castes, they were reborn in excellent countries, castes, and families, endowed with beauty, knowledge of the *Vedas*, virtuous conduct, health, wealth, happiness, and wisdom. Those who failed to live according to their *dharma* were born again in degrading conditions. Āpastamba went even so far as to affirm sententiously that sinful persons were reborn not only as members of low castes, but even as animals.

According to the same theory, no work in itself is evil, impure, or sinful. It is only the manner in which one's allotted work is done that determines its worth. 'Better is one's own duty, though defective', the disciple is told, 'than another's well performed. In performing the duty prescribed by nature one does not incur sin.' Lest the individual belonging to a particular caste, who desires to follow the vocation of another for which he is ill fitted, be a burden to himself and society, the same authority warns him that 'death in (performing) one's own duty is preferable; (performance of the) duty of others is dangerous'.[1]

Division of Functions

Society, it was held, could not function efficiently and harmoniously without a division of labour. If the different castes neglected their respective avocations and encroached on the preserves of others, the entire social order would be thrown into a chaotic condition; 'the dog and the crow would devour the sacrifices, the gods would withdraw their favour, the commonwealth would hasten to ruin.'[2] Trades and crafts thus came to be organized on an hereditary basis and sons took to the industry of their fathers. The advantages of such specialization are

[1] *Bhagavad-gītā*, xviii.   [2] *Manu*, vii.

obvious; for exquisite delicacy of workmanship and blending of colours the arts and manufactures of India acquired world fame.

In an ever-changing order of society it could, however, hardly be expected that social divisions should invariably coincide with economic functions or that members of a caste could, or would, always confine themselves to the pursuits traditionally assigned to them. Realizing this difficulty, the law-givers authorized the twice-born castes, in special cases, to betake themselves, subject to limitations, to an occupation of a caste inferior to their own. Vasishtha laid down that in times of distress one might resort to an avocation prescribed for the lower orders, preferably that prescribed for the caste next in status to one's own, but never that intended for the higher order. Gautama allowed a Brāhman to take to agriculture and trade, with this proviso, however, that, if he engaged in agriculture, he must not plough after breakfast, nor yoke to his plough bullocks whose noses were pierced. For this work, which entailed cruelty to animals, he should employ Śūdra labour. In the *Jātaka* litera-ture we find instances of Brāhman physicians, Brāhman traders, Brāhman hunters and trappers, and of a Kshatriya prince as an archer, trader, labourer, and an idol-maker. Kuśa, a prince, became an apprentice by turn under a potter, basket-maker, florist, and cook.[1] Similarly, the Vaiśya got over his aversion to crafts involving manual labour prescribed for the lowest caste, while the Śūdra rose in the professional scale and became the Vaiśya's equal in trade, agriculture, and crafts.

There was thus no bar, in practice, to the free mobility of labour. An indelible stigma was, however, attached to certain trades and crafts. Butchers, meat-sellers, fowlers, hunters, trappers, trainers of animals, snake-catchers, leather-manu-facturers, cobblers, washermen, and even mechanics, makers of weapons, carpenters, carriage builders, basket-makers, weavers, dyers, and tailors, were held in disrepute. This list of 'low'

[1] *Jātaka*, iv. 361, 1, 356, 57, 11, 87.

trades was evidently drawn up and elaborated for the guidance of the highest caste.[1] Certain occupations were obnoxious because they necessitated the handling of articles deemed impure and involved processes offending against the Brāhman's austere ideals of ceremonial purity. It was not intended that the economic activity of the other orders of society should be thus rigidly restricted. Nārada, however, laid down the following absolute standard applicable to the entire society concerning the purity or impurity of a vocation: 'Sweeping the gateway, the privy, the road, and the place of rubbish; gathering and putting away the leavings of food, ordure, and urine; and, lastly, rubbing the master's limbs when desired; this should be regarded as impure work. All other work besides this is pure.'

Another reason for condemning certain occupations was the moral deficiency implied or involved in the pursuit thereof. Contempt for quackery, fraud, and the practice of the black arts is a feature of the literature on the subject. Manu condemns fencers, jesters, and mercenary temple-priests as persons belonging to the low class; Brihaspati abhors quacks, interpreters of evil omens, and practisers of propitiatory rites, as being no better than thieves; while Nārada declared that dancers, enemies of guilds, butchers, leather-manufacturers, and quacks were ineligible for giving evidence before law courts. Such offensive trades were shunned by most of the members of the superior orders, but they were freely resorted to, under stress of circumstances, by their more necessitous castemen. Disowned by their caste for such transgression, they formed new groups known as 'mixed castes'.

It will be seen that the caste regulations concerning the pursuit of occupations were based on principles not only of economics, but also of personal and social hygiene and morality. The most important consideration which the law-givers had in mind was the purity of the race, physical, moral, spiritual.

[1] Radhakumud Mookerji, *Local Government in Ancient India*, pp. 70–2.

Quaint though some of these regulations may appear to an out-
sider to be, they all rested on the sciences of 'eugenics, hygiene,
mental therapeutics, or metaphysics'.

Food Restrictions

The regulations about food were particularly stringent, because it was believed that it materially influenced for good or for
evil not only one's health and vigour, but also one's nature and
character. Foodstuffs were, accordingly, classified under three
heads, *sāttvika*, *rājasa*, and *tāmasa*. The food that is sweet and
agreeable to the taste and conducive to longevity, strength,
health, and equanimity, comes under the first category; it
brightens up the intellect and the spirit. That which is very
sour, pungent, saltish, and excites thirst, is classified as *rājasa*;
it makes one restless and fiery. Food that is stale, insipid, rotten,
and odorous, also food that is a remnant from another's portion, falls under the category of *tāmasa*; it makes one dull
and indolent.[1] Although meat and drink appear to have been
permitted in the early days on occasions of sacrifices, they were
interdicted in later times, and people who indulged in them
were regarded as filthy and polluting. It was the general belief
that certain persons defiled, while others sanctified, the company, if they sat down to dinner in the same row. Hence the
various inhibitions against interdining.

Food restrictions vary in different provinces in India.
Generally speaking, in Gujarat and southern India an orthodox
Brāhman does not accept water, or cooked food, from any caste
other than his own. Members of the other castes also refuse to
partake of cooked food from persons belonging to orders lower
than their own in the social scale. In the United Provinces a
distinction is made between food cooked in 'ghi' (*pakka*) without
the addition of water and that cooked with water (*kachha*). As
a rule, a man will never eat *kachha* food unless it is prepared

[1] *Bhagavad-gītā*, xvii. 8, 9, 10.

by a member of his own endogamous group, or by his Brāhman 'Guru', or spiritual guide.[1] In practice no objection is taken to *kachha* food being taken from a Brāhman, but the courtesy cannot be returned. Some of the Brāhmans, for instance the Kanaujiās, are so exacting in this respect that it has given rise to a proverb that three Kanaujiās require no less than thirteen hearths.[2] Strange customs these, and hard to reconcile with the traditions of the Vedic times when one of the duties definitely assigned to a Śūdra was to prepare food for the household of his master.

In Bengal the two main divisions are (1) the Brāhmans and (2) the Śūdras. The Śūdras are further divided into four sub-castes: the *Sat*-Śūdra, the *Jalacharniya*-Śūdra, the *Jalalbyabdharya*-Śūdra, and the *Aspriśya*-Śūdra. At the hands of the first two a Brahmin can take water, but not at the hands of the last two. The touch of the Aspriśya-Sudra is believed to be so impure that even the waters of the Ganges would be polluted thereby.

Rules of Marriage

Marriage among the Āryans was monogamic, but polygamy was not unknown, mainly among the ruling classes. In the *Aitareya Brāhmana* we read: 'one man may have more than one wife, but one woman has never more than one husband.'[3] In the domain of domestic life the husband was the master and the wife the mistress, although subservient to the lord of the household. The standard of morality among women was high; they enjoyed an honoured place in society. The *Rig-Veda* mentions cultured women who composed hymns and who are described as Rishis. There was no 'purdah', nor seclusion; the burning of widows on their husband's funeral pyre was un-

---

[1] U.P. Census 1911, p. 328, quoted in G. S. Ghurye's *Caste and Race in India*.   [2] U.P. Census 1901, p. 212.

[3] x. iii. 23.

known. The sacred tie of marriage was regarded as indissoluble by human action. The wife was believed to be part of her husband's body; therefore she could not by repudiation or divorce be released from her husband. Even after death they could not be separated. Remarriage in the case of a widow does not, therefore, appear to have been contemplated, although it is not definitely prohibited in the *Rig-Veda*. On the contrary, it was a general custom for a widow to marry the brother of her deceased husband in order to bear him children.

Marriage in one's own caste was the only sanctified union of man and woman acknowledged by the law-givers. The essence of the caste system is, as Westermarck remarks, endogamy. In the case of the Hindu castes and sub-castes endogamy was, however, a guiding principle rather than a rigid rule. Marriages among the three higher castes, particularly between the Brāhman and the Kshatriya, were not uncommon. Baudhāyana laid down the law that the offspring of a Brāhman by a Kshatriya woman was a Brāhman and that of a Kshatriya by a Vaiśya woman a Kshatriya. In course of time, however, the Vaiśyas came in closer and closer contact with the Śūdras in various fields of work; and marriage connexions between them increased to such an extent that the higher order was in danger of being merged in the submerged class. Hence the law-givers stressed more and more the desirability of marriage in one's own caste and condemned the union of a Brāhman or a Kshatriya with a woman from the Vaiśya community. Manu would not assign any definite name to the progeny of a Vaiśya by a Śūdra woman; and other authorities had no hesitation in classifying them as Śūdras. Vasishtha also prohibited a man of any one of the first three groups from marrying a Śūdra woman, as it led to the degradation of the family in this life and loss of happiness in the next. The child of a man of the Brāhman caste and a Śūdra woman was considered as impure as a corpse. In practice, however, men belonging to the higher orders formed matrimonial alliances irrespective of caste restrictions, although their children were not allowed equal rights with those born in wedlock within the endogamous group.

Marriage of men of lower castes with women of higher castes was regarded with even greater horror. The law-givers refused to recognize it, and placed the offspring of such union beyond the pale of the sacred law. For the preservation of the purity of the race the mother was regarded as the more important factor than the father. 'The Āchārya', we read in the *Vasishtha Smriti*, 'is ten times more honourable than an Upādhyāya; the father a hundred times more than the Āchārya, and the mother a thousand times more than the father.' The most heinous alliance was that of a Brāhman woman with a Śūdra. The indignant Solons of the day could not find words violent enough to denounce it. When a son was born to such an accursed pair, he was expelled from the village and compelled to live with the unclean *pariah* people outside. One of these so-called casteless castes was the *Chandāla*, an unclean savage tribe that lived in forests outside settled habitations. Hence the offspring of that most hated union became *Chandālas*, the untouchable and unapproachable class of the population.

It would appear from this that despite all barriers intermarriage among the different castes must have been very common and that even the most aristocratic caste was not free from contamination. All the evidence points, besides, to the prevalence of polygamy during the later period, which encouraged the mixture of superior castes with the inferior ones. People were warned, on pain of interdiction, not to marry outside the spheres specified in the law-books; but, prohibition or no prohibition, such alliances did take place, swelling the list of castes.

The Caste Balance Sheet

The original fourfold division, once considered universal and immutable, is now merely of historic interest. The process of disintegration had commenced during the later Vedic times. Subsequent differences of religion, occupation, language, and locality, on the one hand, and the increasing fusion of one sect with another, on the other, have led to a multiplication of castes, sub-castes, and mixed castes which defy all attempts by Census officers at accurate enumeration. It is estimated that there are at present more than 3,000 castes in the whole of India and that there are over 1,800 subdivisions among Brāhmans alone. Changing environment, contact with other nations. clash of cultures, new systems of faith and worship, economic contests, social struggles, political convulsions, have all modified the old order considerably. The old world values have not, however, yet lost their utility. They still influence the lives and character of the people and still the idea of caste distinction persists. Social reformers of one caste may dine together with members of other castes and contract marriages in defiance of caste regulations, but the orthodox yet cling tenaciously to the old ideas rooted in *dharma*.

Dharma sanctions incompletely understood, mechanically applied, and arbitrarily enforced thwart further progress. There is an incessant conflict between those who insist on old-world values and the preservation of ancient traditions, and those whose ideals of life are influenced by the current of modern tendencies, and who seek to interpret the doctrine of *dharma* in the light of these tendencies. Despite this prolonged conflict, and the gulf that still separates the various groups socially, they have all banded together, for centuries, in divers spheres of public usefulness. Together they have fought their social and political battles, together making the best possible use of their physical and mental endowments in satisfying their material and spiritual needs, as though they were close corporations constituted on a joint-stock basis.

Who can draw up, with any degree of accuracy, a general balance sheet evaluating the assets and liabilities and giving a

profit and loss account of the operations of these caste corporations, their interdependence and interrelations, their achievements and failures, for the period during which they have been
functioning ever since the dawn of history?

Critics of the system say that it contained within itself the
principles of its destruction; that it prevented the growth of
patriotic or national feeling by breaking up the people into so
many distinct blocks that it was hostile to modern democratic
notions; that it checked combination in social and public life
and excited sectional jealousies, and that the social organization
thus suffered from lack of integration and co-operation. They
believe that the old walls that kept the ancestors of Hindu race
safe within the enclosure of caste have been tumbling down and
that the entire structure of caste must collapse in surrender
to the relentless buffets of progress. Others claim that a tradition of common descent and racial purity generates consciousness of unity among a group of people; that such unity fosters
a sense of national feeling and solidarity; that uniformity of
manners and customs fostered such solidarity in the case of the
different castes of India, and that a realization of contrast,
separating like from unlike, intensified it. They claim further
that specialization in occupations and crafts secured the hereditary transmission of professional skill and knowledge of arts
and sciences from father to son and preserved their identity;
that caste-fellows hung together through thick and thin and
supported one another, while the sense of interdependence
of members of different groups induced a strong feeling of
democracy and fraternity, which held Hindu society together
and preserved the ancient tradition, despite all vicissitudes of
fortune. They maintain that *dharma* is still the pivot round
which Hindu society revolves; that it will and must continue
to be the pivot of the social order.

The good of caste is thus so inextricably mixed up with the
evil, and the philosophical ideas on which it rests are so dimly

understood that it is necessary to examine the system from the time of its inception. The *summum bonum* of the life of an individual, in those days, was recognition of one's self and attainment of spiritual bliss, while the ideal of the commonwealth was preservation of the purity and integrity of the race and the raising society as a whole through the improvement and elevation of its component parts. Herein lies the contrast between the past and the present. Modern individualistic tendencies make the good of the individual the goal of life; the Hindu ideal was the good of the body politic. Ever since the ancient elastic community-family in India assumed the rigidity of regular caste groups, the philosophy of life which permeated the social organization stressed the following four principles: (1) that a man's place in society is assigned to him by Providence; (2) that there are fundamental differences between man and man as regards nature, disposition, character, capacity, and educability; (3) that individual members of society have, therefore, distinct duties and responsibilities and distinct rights and status suited to their respective places in the social organization; (4) that co-operation of the various units is essential for the usefulness, happiness, and progress of society.

Sense of Solidarity and Fraternity

The end of all sciences, according to Hindu philosophy, is the realizing of the unity of everything that exists. The scheme of social polity, based on caste, recognized such unity; at the same time it took into account the diversity of temperaments and the complexity of the needs and processes of human life. The strong point in favour of such a system was that, while it took cognizance of the differences and inequalities between man and man, it did not regard them as immutable or irreducible. It made a distinction between the four basic functions for upholding human society, and assigned them, respectively, to four distinct groups best qualified for performing such functions. It sought to integrate differences of disposition and character. The system was a compromise between individualism and collectivism, between unrestrained competition and constrained co-operation. It has even been described as 'ancient, time-tested scientific socialism', maintaining the balance of power between the vocational classes.[1]

The concept of organic unity and interdependence ran through the whole system. Even when it was sought to deduce divine sanction for the ascendency of the superior orders on the hypothesis that the four castes had emanated from four different limbs of the Creator of the Universe, the underlying idea was not one of detachment but of union. Each unit formed part of the whole. Every one had, therefore, to perform his duty towards himself and society at large. While none was allowed to remain in want, each was under an obligation, as long as he was able, to contribute his share of labour, according to his capacity and calling, for the benefit of society. Such an attitude of mind brought all the castes, their beliefs, customs, and activities, under one common system. Every one found a place appointed for him; every one had his legacy of the common tradition, common creed, and common ethical code in addition to the special legacy of hereditary skill for the fulfilment of the part to which he was called. The system conduced to the solidarity of castes as distinct units of the social organization, it promoted effective association not only of the different members of each group but also of group and group. Thus was the ancient tradition preserved, social tranquillity safeguarded, civic and economic welfare secured, individual happiness and contentment promoted.

The most enduring tie that bound all members of society together was its sacred tradition. Although the *Vedas* were a sealed book to the lowest class, the boon of reading the *Purānas* and other sacred books, which were based on the *Vedas*, was not denied to them. All members of the society worshipped

[1] Vide *Ancient versus Modern Scientific Socialism*, by Bhagwan Das.

the same deities, shared the same common belief, and celebrated the same festivals. The forms of worship differed, no doubt, but all such differences were dissolved in the universal homage to the all-pervading Self. This cardinal principle of Unity in Variety, coupled with the exaltation of the principle of *dharma*, induced among the divers groups a sense of solidarity and fraternity that has held Hindu society together for centuries.

Neighbourliness and Co-operation

Ideas of rank and status are inseparable from a social structure based on a differentiation of classes and their functions. It might, therefore, be presumed that class rivalries would creep in and that a spirit of class interest would militate fatally against the cultivation of civic spirit, community of interests, and healthy co-operation. It must not be overlooked, however, that no society, whether caste-ridden or not, is free from class rivalries. Clashes of interests, such as they were, did not hamper neighbourliness and co-operation among the different Hindu castes. Based though their social organization was on differentiation of individuals and demarcation of their status, it was not the individualism which is developed on the basis of self-interest and which has for its goal wealth and power to command other people's service, but the individualism which coveted for every one nothing more than a position in the commonwealth in which he might be able to render the best possible service and to assist as best one can in the establishment of a static and satisfactory form of life.

Self-governing Institutions

Incessantly the various groups, working together, contributed their service to the common life of their cities and villages, and their team spirit led to a remarkable development of corporate life unparalleled in the contemporary annals of other countries. Caste-riven though the population was, these groups may be likened to the fingers of one's hand, perpetually separated, yet perpetually co-operating. Thus a system, which at first sight appears to be antagonistic to the elementary principles of democracy, was instrumental in creating a strong sense of democracy and in evolving a social-economic system on the basis of class collaboration and the rule of law. Under its influence the genius of the people for corporate action expressed itself in a variety of self-governing institutions with highly developed constitutions, rules of procedure, and machinery of administration which challenge comparison with modern parliamentary institutions. Reading the election rules of these bodies, the division of villages and districts into electoral units, their rules of debate and standing orders for the conduct of business and maintenance of order in debate, and their committee system, one might wonder whether many standing orders of the House of Commons and of the London County Council are not derived from the regulations of the ancient local bodies, ecclesiastical councils, and village assemblies of India!

Village Councils

Foremost among the self-governing institutions of the day were the village communities. These were compared by Megasthenes, who spent a long time at the Court of Chandragupta, to little independent republics. A village or a town had a council of elders chosen from *all* castes and representing *all* the interests concerned. This council had complete freedom in the management of internal affairs. It controlled taxation, maintained, with the co-operation of the different castes, order and peace, settled disputes, upheld individual rights, and preserved intact the internal economy of the country.

These village councils were still functioning when Sir Charles Metcalfe wrote his famous minute in 1830, protesting against the introduction of a system of collecting revenue directly from individual landholders instead of through the village organization. His observations, though often quoted, are so apposite as to bear repetition.

'In times of trouble they arm and fortify themselves: an hostile army passes through the country: the village communities collect their cattle within their walls, and let the enemy pass unprovoked. . . . If a country remains for a series of years the scene of continued pillage and massacre, so that the villages cannot be inhabited, the scattered villagers nevertheless return whenever the power of peaceable possession revives. A generation may pass away, but the succeeding generation will return. The sons will take the places of their fathers; the same site for the village, the same position for the houses, the same lands will be reoccupied by the descendants of those who were driven out when the village was depopulated; and it is not a trifling matter that will drive them out, for they will often maintain their post through times of disturbance and convulsion, and acquire strength sufficient to resist pillage and oppression with success . . . all acting in union with a common interest as regards the Government, and adjusting their own separate interests among themselves according to established usages.'[1]

Craft Guilds and Merchant Guilds

Equally efficient and equally strongly imbued with the sense of solidarity and spirit of co-operation were the craft-guilds and merchant-guilds. Vedic society was then sufficiently advanced to admit of an elaborate differentiation of occupations among the people. Considerable progress had been achieved in trade, manufactures, and arts; concerted action was necessary to protect and promote the individual and collective interests of the different units. The various guilds (*śreṇī*) and clubs (*pūga*), or associations of persons of different castes, with which the student of Indian history is familiar, were the natural outcome. These guilds safeguarded the professional interests of their members, regulated working hours and wages, enforced their decisions by fines, and generally controlled and supervised the activities

[1] *Minutes of Evidence taken before the Select Committee on the affairs of the East India Company*, vol. iii (Revenue), pp. 331–2 (Appendix 84).

PLATE 10

A GOLDSMITH AT WORK, DELHI

of the professional classes and artisans in the interests of the whole community. Sir William Hunter was not merely drawing a roseate picture when he observed: 'The trade guilds in the cities, and the village community in the country, act, together with caste, as mutual assurance societies, and under normal conditions allow none of their members to starve. Caste, and the trading or agricultural guilds concurrent with it, take the place of a poor-law in India.'[1] No wonder these trade guilds flourished throughout the country and attained a position of the utmost importance, socially, economically, as well as politically.

The guilds were governed by their own laws and the king was expected to recognize and respect these laws. 'A king who knows the sacred law', observes Manu, 'must inquire into the laws of castes, and districts, guild laws, and family laws. . . . What may have been practised by the virtuous, by such twice-born men who are devoted to the law, that he shall establish as law, if it be not opposed to the laws of countries, families and castes.'

The guilds merely represent a type of those self-governing bodies which flourished at one time all over the peninsula. Megasthenes records the tradition heard by him that sovereignty was dissolved and democratic governments set up in various places.[2] The greater portion of Āryan India—north, west, and south—was covered with republican constitutions. Only in the Doab, and from Delhi eastward to Allahabad, did monarchy still prevail. Farther east, in the Prachi, there was the Sāmarājya (literally, a combination of monarchies) or a federal imperialism around one dominant member; except the Doab and Magadha the whole country was republican.[3]

In the sphere of local government there were provincial and

---

[1] *Indian Empire*, p. 199.
[2] *Epitome of Megasthenes*, Diod. ii. 38.
[3] Vide *Hindu Polity*, by K. P. Jayaswal, Pt. I, pp. 137–8.

urban corporations, *Paura* and *Jānapada*, organized on lines beloved of the most ardent advocate of local self-government in modern times.[1] Here, too, the guilds of the city merchants played a prominent part. The *Paura*, in which was vested the municipal administration of the capital, was presided over by a leading citizen who was usually a merchant or a banker.

The question arises: How did the people of India develop the aptitude and obtain the necessary training for self-government at so early a date? For an answer to this question one has to turn to the system of caste rule of these people. Could we not trace such qualifications and discipline to the instinctive and implicit obedience of all the members of a caste to its rules? Could not continued practice in enforcing, and submitting in turn to those rules have developed traits of character and mental faculties essential for a system of popular government? Local government in the West owes far more to central government and represents a process of decentralization and devolution of power, but in India those local bodies were practically *sui generis*. They grew independently out of the conditions created by caste life, which set up a system of social self-government and autonomous village organization. That system lasted in one form or another throughout the long period of Hindu imperialism, Hun invasions, and Muhammadan despotism, and it was in existence when the British assumed territorial sovereignty. Under the centralizing policy of the new rulers, the more important communal institutions such as the *Samīti*, the *Sangha*, the *Sabhā*, the *Gana*, the *Nitaya*, the *Janpada*, and the *Paura* vanished; but the village panchāyats, which the British administrators freely used, but failed to preserve, have shown greater vitality and tenacity. If Hindu culture has persisted through the ages despite all political convulsions and social revolutions, if it has succeeded in combating destructive influences of changing environment to which other cultures and civilizations have

[1] Vide *Evolution of Local Self-Government in Bombay*, by R. P. Masani.

succumbed, it is due in no small measure to the institution of caste, which taught both high and low the art of governing, while being governed by the rigid rule of caste.

Lack of National Spirit

We have so far considered only the asset side of the balance sheet—that, too, only the balance sheet for the most glorious epoch in the history of the community. What about the subsequent depreciation in the value of the various items of assets and the growth of liabilities? What about the intensification of the caste feeling at the expense of national feeling, national discipline, and national solidarity? What about subordination of patriotic feeling and public spirit to the spirit of class interest and class exclusiveness, though not actual class war? What about caste prejudices, caste jealousies, caste hostilities and tyrannies, and what about that most disconcerting item of untouchability?

When the Brāhmans of the early times first imposed restrictions on the acceptance of food and intermarriage, they were not unconscious of the homogeneity of the first three orders. These restrictions reveal their instinct for race-preservation and their anxiety to save society from going off the rails. Since then the four orders have been multiplied a thousand times; and the original scheme of unification is practically forgotten. Every group has been obsessed with the idea of maintaining its own prestige and solidarity. As a result, caste consciousness in its most obnoxious form is the order of the day. The guiding principles of humanity and social service and social justice and the accepted criteria of nationality have been forgotten. Doubtless so-called nationalists and national organizations abound; but real national spirit and unity are lacking. A healthy, vigorous national life is still a dream. Caste feeling is not solely responsible for this state of affairs, but it has certainly failed to generate a robust sense of nationality. Caste consciousness is good, but when it kills national consciousness, it becomes a serious drawback. Caste patriotism is valuable as the first step to nationalism, but, when it degenerates into sectarianism and checks the growth of nationality, it is an unmitigated evil. Caste loyalty is a virtue, but, when it degenerates into passive disloyalty to the state, it is a positive crime. Caste restrictions on actions likely to undermine the foundations of the social structure are wholesome; but, when such restrictions lead to disabling inequalities and denial of social justice, as in the case of the untouchables, now mercifully called *harijans*, they are a curse. Happily, some of the undesirable features which crept into the caste system during later years, particularly after the Muhammadan conquest, have disappeared during the last few decades, mainly under the influence of English education; but not a few of such features still persist. Of these the most obnoxious is the doctrine of untouchability. The barriers between the higher orders have been fast disappearing under modern conditions; but the age-long scruples concerning personal and ceremonial purity and inviolability of religious rites, which detach the superior orders from the lowest, are still almost as strong as ever, vitiating the attitude of a large number of orthodox Hindus towards the depressed class. It is a problem that baffles all social reformers at present, and has given such a bad name to caste that it has come to be regarded as a godless system of social segregation and slavery, whereas exclusiveness is foreign to the original conception of caste. Untouchability is but an excrescence, a malignant outgrowth which can be and must be removed.

The Future of Caste

Had the caste system rested merely on a functional basis, modern economic development and the industrialization of the country would already have sealed its fate. But it rests on a philosophy of life that has not yet ceased to appeal to the human soul. *Dharma* is still the key-note of the Hindu's philosophy of life. Therefore the institution still exists—not quite a shadow of its former self—still influencing the lives of millions, and it bids fair to survive the shocks of the destructive forces that have been at work for some time. Those who speculated on its future, fifty years ago, thought they saw the order tottering and predicted its total disappearance, within a few years, as the result of the impact of Western education. All such critics of the caste system have turned out to be false prophets. It is not for us in this chapter to visualize or discuss the future of the institution. We are concerned only with the legacy of the past. In spite of embarrassing encumbrances, that legacy has proved a precious social heritage. The organization of society on a basis of caste has stood the test of centuries. The demarcation of the functions of individuals classified under certain groups, having regard to their innate qualities and qualifications, provided a closely knit economic fabric. It was, so to say, an insurance against that uncontrolled working of economic forces which has been, since the last war, the source of so much evil. It minimized class conflict and cut-throat competition. It enabled individuals to work out their salvation, according to their ideal of life, and provided a basis on which society as a whole might build a life of orderly progress. Such a basis did, in fact, promote class collaboration as well as corporate action and national development in several spheres of public activity. So long as people adhered to the ancient ideal of *dharma*, the caste system induced a moral cohesion of the different units and gave society a static form. It was only when that ideal was lost sight of that it developed fissiparous tendencies and evolved a code of inequalities and iniquities which have given it a bad name outside as well as inside India. Nevertheless, it still stands before the world as a marvellous attempt to develop a static social order.

Not a few Western thinkers, past as well as present, have been impressed by the synthetic unity of the four castes and the potentiality, elasticity, and vitality of such a system of social gradation. Nietzsche, for instance, advocates caste organization as a means to the evolution of a higher and more spiritual species of mankind. The three classes constituting his ideal society closely correspond to the first three orders of Hindu society, the first eminently spiritual, the second predominantly strong in muscle and temperament, and the remainder consisting of ordinary individuals. There is, however, a difference in the functions assigned to the three classes. For the priesthood there is no place in this scheme of social gradation. The first in rank are the supreme ruling class; the second are their instruments for governing; and in this category are included guardians of order and security, judges and soldiers, with the king as their head. The third class engages in manual labour, business, agriculture, science, and the ordinary forms of art. Nor is there any suggestion here of hereditary status or of taboos, but the doctrine of the three *gunas*, in a modified form, and the scheme of giving every individual a place in the social organization for which he is best fitted, are clearly discernible.

The huge experiment now being made in Soviet Russia is another illustration. Having demolished all deities and abolished all ritual, it can have nothing in common with a caste system rooted in worship. Nevertheless, stripped of the element of state-regulated co-operation, it stands before us as a conscious or unconscious adaptation of the functional classification of the population which for centuries gave society in India a stable, social equilibrium.

Another example of the trend of modern philosophical thought in the West in favour of reconstruction of society on the basis of caste has been given by Mr. H. G. Wells, who in his *Modern Utopia* favours a social structure in which men would be classified on a psychological basis. Four principal classes are distinguished, the Poietic, the Kinetic, the Dull, and the Base. Here is propounded a system of self-imposed government of scientific experts, in which there are the principal constituent elements of caste *minus* religion and the hereditary principle. As in the case of the Hindu system of caste, so in these idealistic theories in the West, the underlying idea is that of integration of the natural differences between individuals as a means to promote the advancement of society to the highest pitch of efficiency. Caste, in that sense, is not inconsistent with democracy. Not merely modern idealistic doctrines, but also the systems of government actually functioning in some of the principal countries in the world show the same tendency. Communism and Fascism both recognize certain features of the caste system. Whether judged by results or regarded in the light of modern philosophical thought, the survival utility of the caste system is assured, if only caste-fellows bear steadfastly in mind that it asks for free souls rather than free men, for moral rather than material strength; that the essential basis of the institution was the development of groups of individuals in consonance with their qualities and qualifications; that the keystone of the structure was not detachment, but union; that the element of exclusiveness and untouchability is repugnant to the social philosophy and tradition of the Aryan race; and that the main, if not the sole, object of the caste system should be to secure social efficiency on the democratic and socialistic principles of class collaboration and the rule of law.

R. P. MASANI.

BUDDHISM

An amazing number of popular or semi-popular books on Buddhism have been published during recent years. I am myself responsible for some of them. As a rule these books are built on the same pattern. They begin with an account of the religious and social life of eastern India before Śākyamuni, and then give a sketch of his life and work. Unfortunately the ideas, events, and men of this time can only be known by conjecture, and the reader is confronted, either by doubtful facts and questionable theories, or by a sceptical discussion about them. I shall dispense with some of those historical speculations and biographical accounts, which can be found in so many works, believing that it will be more useful to explain what we know about the internal constitution of Indian Buddhism, and about its changes during the eight or ten centuries of its early history.

The present work deals with the world's debt to India. In writing of Buddhism my first task will be to consider what that religion owes to the land in which Śākyamuni lived and taught.

Buddhism is not wholly original; it appears, during centuries, as a 'buddhification' of institutions, ideas, or feelings, which were simply Indian: the asceticism and the clerical institutions took a special character in Buddhism; the Buddha doctrine of transmigration, of the action and the reward of actions, was a recast of the parallel Hindu doctrines; the cult or worship of Buddhism evolved according to the general transformation of cult and worship; the belief in a God Saviour, prominent in later Buddhism and less developed in early times, reflects also the gradual growth of devotion (*bhakti*). In short, Buddhism is only the 'buddhized' aspect of contemporaneous Hinduism.

It cannot be said that the most notable features of the Buddhist speculation—its 'rationalism' (I mean its antipathy to every kind of ritualism and superstition), its atheism (i.e. its negation of a God creator and providence), its high morality, its pessimism, its anti-caste tendency, its mildness and humanity, and so on—are specifically Buddhist.

But, on the other hand, I believe that Buddhism, owing to the 'solidity' of the Brotherhood, owing to the dialectical strength of its schools, gave to the ideas and feelings it adopted or patronized a great strength and *rayonnement*. The common Indian belief in the reward of good and bad actions was enforced by the Buddhist propaganda. The common Indian feeling of the misery of life, and the general Indian compassion and benevolence, had in the noble figures of the Buddhist saints very suggestive and attractive representations. The early brahmanic literature shows that many sages disapproved or clearly condemned social distinctions; but the Buddhist order was a living example of equality and mutual esteem. And so on.

Owing to Buddhism (as also owing to Brahmanism) many old things have conserved life and even vigour. The Buddhist monastic institution of Ceylon of to-day is probably very like the Buddhist monastic institution of pristine days: and this last was probably very like the institutions of the sects of Buddha's epoch.

Prefatory

(*a*) In early India, before the rise of the Brāhman speculation which is embodied in the treatises called *Upanishads*, Hindus knew only of gods to be worshipped, of paradises to be obtained through worship, rites, and good works. But there was later a great change. Many men admitted that paradises are perishable; that the gods themselves die; that beings transmigrate from the beginning: at one time they may be men, at another animals, they may suffer in hell, or rise to be gods. There is something better than paradise, there is a *summum bonum*, a highest good, a supreme happiness, known later as Nirvāna or Brahma-nirvāna, an abode beyond transmigration, change, consciousness, or personality; technically an abode 'supramundane' (*lokottara*) in contrast with the 'world' (*loka*), which includes paradises and hells.

This abode is not to be reached through the worship of any god, the doing of any good work, the acquisition of any merit, but by austerity or meditation or wisdom, in short by the discipline later known as *yoga*.

Henceforth, from the times of the *Upanishads* (sixth century B.C.) down to our days, every branch of the Indian faith, be it Brahmanism, Buddhism, Jainism, Vishnuism, or Śivaism, has presented a twofold aspect. One is 'religious', or 'mundane' (*laukika*), and deals with paradises, happy rebirths, gods or God, worship, meritorious actions. The other is 'transcendent' (supramundane, *lokottara*), or 'mystic', and makes man's chief object the attainment, through gnosis and ecstasy, of an abode of everlasting, inconceivable happiness.[1]

The difference of the goal involves differences amongst the devotees. The men of mean aspirations, attached to sensual pleasures, wish for paradises. The 'few ones', the 'happy ones', wish for a 'better part' than paradises: they leave home and practise continence and religious life in order to achieve Nirvāna.

(*b*) The contrast between 'religion' and 'supramundane discipline' is a permanent feature of Buddhism. But both the 'religion' and the 'discipline' take a twofold aspect owing to the development of the Buddhology; that is, owing to the fundamental change that the doctrines concerning Buddha and Buddhahood underwent about the beginning of the Christian era.

Our knowledge of the feelings of the early Buddhist folk towards Śākyamuni, living or dead, is scanty.[2] But we feel sure

[1] The first aspect corresponds to what is called 'Lower Hinduism', the second to what is called 'Higher Hinduism'.

[2] I am inclined to believe that laymen and ordinary devotees never thought

that the general conviction of the monks was that Śākyamuni, no longer visible to gods or men, was lost in eternal quietude. A process of apotheosis began soon, both amongst the good folk and amongst some sections of the clergy. It resulted in a theory which constitutes the essential tenet of the later Buddhist faith (Mahāyāna): Buddhas, who are many in number, have been men, but their 'buddhification' is an event of a primitive age; they are now, as they have been for centuries and will be for ever, divine beings enthroned in the highest heavens. The real Śākyamuni has been reigning for many cosmical periods on the celestial 'Peak of the Vultures'. The historical Śākyamuni, who was born at Lumbinī, left his home, obtained Buddhahood, preached and reached Nirvāna, is only an image, a fiction, a 'created body' of the real Śākyamuni.

It will be easy to understand the profound modification which Buddhist religion and Buddhist mysticism must undergo when such Buddhology is admitted.

I. *Early Buddhist Religion*

A number of good *recoupements*—Asoka's edicts, a few books of popular inspiration, monastic texts relative to laymen, archaeology—give an approximate idea of the true nature of early extra-monastic Buddhism.

1. *Upāsakas or Laymen.* Śākyamuni came rather late into a world where ascetic institutions had long been flourishing. This explains why the rules of the monastic Buddhist discipline were rapidly fixed (not without variants and recasts), and why the congregation of the laymen—the Upāsakas or 'devotees'— rapidly took the form of a *tiers ordre*.

that the death of the Holy Man had deprived the world of a superhuman protector. But, to tell the truth, we have no information. It is difficult to understand the ideas which found their expression in the worship of relics and stūpas—we know that Asoka never speaks of a 'paradise of Śākyamuni' but only of *svargas*, paradises according to the ideas of Hindu mythology.

The reader of Kipling is well aware that a holy man (*sādhū*) easily finds food and a roof. But the religious orders, with their little village-convents, could not live without regular and organized assistance: they had official friends, 'bourgeois' and villagers, who gave alms, clothing, houses, and fields.

The 'official' position of the laymen is more important than is often admitted. First, they are really 'Buddhists', not only generous alms-givers, but members of the Church: a man becomes a Upāsaka by taking liturgically the 'triple refuge' (I take refuge in the Buddha, in his Doctrine, in his Brotherhood); by binding himself to the observation of the fivefold morality (I shall not kill, steal, &c.). Secondly, while laymen are under the guidance of the clergy, they exercise on the clergy a right of control (legend or history of the Council of Vaiśālī), and the clergy have to submit to 'public opinion'. Buddha often says to his monks: 'Will such behaviour please the people?'

2. One character of the lay-Buddhism is that Nirvāna is of little importance. It opens the way to paradises or to a happy rebirth as a man. It is sometimes styled *devayāna*, the vehicle of the gods.

By a sinless life, by perseverance in the practice of family and social duties, by benevolence and kindness, by alms to the monks, by the worship of the Buddha and his relics, by the fortnightly fast, a man earns merit (*punya*) and enjoys the reward of this merit in a future life, either as a god or as a happy man.

It must be remembered that paradises (*svarga*) are only places of pleasure and sensual enjoyment. They present no Buddhist features, and are simply the Hindu paradises adopted by Buddhism, but not adapted. The idea that a man might be reborn in the palace of a Buddha, and enjoy his presence, is absolutely foreign to Aśoka (third century B.C.).

3. *Buddhist elements in this early religion.* There is much in this religion which is properly Buddhist; its very pure morality, free from ritualism or superstition; the 'buddhification' of the

path of paradise, which consists in the strict observance of morality, not in sacrifices; the gods have been ethically improved, they have been 'converted' by the Buddha, and learnt to favour the good and hate sinners; the cult of the dead has been metamorphized by Buddhism—they are helped by good deeds accomplished for their welfare by their relatives; there is created a new and very white 'white magic': the best defence against evil spirits and serpents is to 'direct towards them the strength of benevolence'—'I am your friend, oh serpents' (as in Kipling's *Kim*).

The dogmatic basis of the system is the belief that man transmigrates, that good and evil deeds are rewarded and punished in a future life. We do not know exactly what stage of development the notions of reincarnation, transmigration, act, retribution, had reached in the Kośala-Magadha of the sixth century B.C. But we know that the Buddhist doctrines of transmigration and good works differ from the Brahmanic. Brāhmans have never conceived transmigration as the universal rule: they have always thought that the great gods at least are gods by nature. Buddhists say that the person who is actually Brahmā has obtained this 'place' by his good works; that, after centuries, when the merit of his good works will be exhausted by the very enjoyment of the reward, the actual Brahmā will die and be reborn as a man or as a citizen of hell. Brāhmans teach that the good man obtains a happy rebirth, and reversely; but they do not object to the doctrine of 'fate' and they attach great importance to sacrificial or ritual 'good work'. According to Buddhists, 'fate' is only the former actions of every one, and the only good work is the moral act, the act accomplished with the purpose of benefiting oneself in a future life, and one's neighbour in the present one. Brāhmans admit the retribution of works, but they believe that the great god Brahmā is the 'retributor' and places beings in a high or a low rebirth according to their merit. Buddhists strongly object to a God, to a Providence: they teach that actions, good or bad, bear their fruit, owing to their own (semi-magical) strength. As concerns deities, fairies, and spirits, Buddhism admits not only their existence, but also their power; they are very useful and must be properly worshipped: they care for a number of things too mean to attract the attention of the Buddhist Persons. But they nevertheless hold a very humble position in Buddhism.

It is very probable that these moral and rationalist views have exercised a notable influence on the old India.

Śākyamuni has often been described as a social reformer: 'He attacked the system of caste and conquered for the poor and the outcasts a place in his spiritual kingdom.' Oldenberg has said in so many words that this description is a misrepresentation. He observed that the man who has abandoned the worldly life in order to be a monk has no longer any interest in worldly or social affairs.

Let us observe that the Buddhist Brotherhood is open to men of low extraction. True, the Buddhists followed the example of other sects. But the fact remains that orthodox Brahmanism scarcely approved this contempt of the caste principle: it condemns the men 'who bear by imposture the dress of ascetics and are professional thieves'. The liberalism of the Brotherhood was clearly anti-caste.

Again, the Buddhist monks became the spiritual advisers of their lay supporters. The moral system they taught contradicts the Brahmanic tradition and the system of caste. Bloody sacrifices are murders; funeral ceremonies are of no use since the defunct is already reborn either in hell or in paradise. Brāhmans are conceived and born like other men, they do not differ from them in colour or physique. The best 'fields of merit' (the alms receivers who give efficacy to charities) are the Buddhist monks, not the Brāhmans.

4. *Buddhism owes much to its non-clerical elements.* According to tradition the worship of the relics was at first the business

of the laymen. Ascetics or monks who have in Nirvāna their goal and in the preparation for Nirvāna the rule of their religious life, consider Śākyamuni as the sage who has discovered the Way, no more. The worship of the relics and of the stūpas, all-important in historical Buddhism, has in itself no specially Buddhist character.

Scholars believe that the legend of Śākyamuni—his descent from the Tushita heaven into the womb of Māyā, his miraculous birth, the poetic and mythological features of his 'conquest of Buddhahood' under the Sacred Tree, and so on—is the work of popular speculation. When we are told that Śākyamuni in his former birth has been the good elephant, the patient bear, the generous King Sibi, &c., we feel sure that the history of the former Śākyamuni has been embellished with Hindu stories wherein the popular faith had embodied its conception of the good man; we are even justified when we admit that the chief characteristic of Śākyamuni, his universal benevolence, his pity for all creatures, has its origin in the kindly and generous feelings of the folk of Magadha, rather than in the speculation of the clerical part of the Church. For monks Śākyamuni is the 'great Ascetic' (*mahāśramana*); India has venerated and loved Śākyamuni as the 'Great Compassionate One' (*mahākārunika*). Of course the true personality and the psychological figure of Śākyamuni remain a riddle. His 'goodness' was probably fascinating; but India was prepared to worship an incarnation of goodness. The monkish ideal was quite different, an ideal of stoic tranquillity, and the clerical tradition is that Śākyamuni first decided to keep to himself the truths which he had discovered, in order to avoid the trouble of preaching.

5. *Buddhist lay-religion and brahmano-hinduism.* Buddhism was a *pūjā*, worship, also a *dharma*, code of ethics. But it had no rites for marriage, birth, death, or ceremonies for the welfare of the dead. Not that it did not enforce precepts for conjugal morality, for the preparation for death, for benefiting the dead

by gifts to the monks and by pious works; but the Brāhmans continued to officiate at marriage, birth, and death; they continued to be the guests at the funeral banquets.

As Buddhism did not impose or even propose any *substituta* for the traditional rites of the family life, it did not destroy these rites or jeopardize the position they assured to Brāhmans. To destroy them, it was not enough to preach that, 'although they might be useful for the present life, they are without utility for the next one' (Aśoka).

Brahmanism catered for happiness here below and hereafter. Buddhism professed to be and indeed was much more concerned with the future life; but as an established religion it was deficient in supernatural devices for the welfare of everyday life. Kings, merchants, villagers did not find in Buddhism the manifold contrivances of Brahmanism for victory, profit, or bringing rain. Of course Buddhist women implore Hāritī for children, villagers implore Serpents for rain: Hāritī and Serpents have been admitted into the Buddhist pantheon; but they are no more Buddhist for that. The consequence is that a lay Buddhist is not a Buddhist as concerns familiar life; as concerns all the needs of the daily life, he remains a Hindu.

II. *The Religion of Mahāyāna*

1. This Buddhist religion which until the present time is the religion of the Buddhists of the Far East (Churches of 'Pure Land') is generally styled Mahāyāna, 'Great Vehicle' (but this term means exactly the form of mysticism described in § IV); it is in short a hagiolatry with saints who possess all the power and all the benevolence of really godly persons.

From about the beginning of the Christian era Buddhism had gods of its own (celestial Buddhas, celestial Future Buddhas or Bodhisattvas)[1] and therefore paradises of its own. The devotee

---

[1] The Buddhas are not creators, but they are providences: Mahāyāna is a particular sort of theism. The Bodhisattvas often take the aspects of Saviours:

hopes and tries to be reborn in one of the paradises, which are no longer places of sensual pleasures, but abodes worthy of their kings: eternal abodes of music, light, worship, and contemplation.

Morality and worship continue to be the chief requirements from the candidate to a rebirth in paradise. But devotion (just as in Vishnuism) becomes more and more important. According to the 'low' section of Mahāyāna, a man, even a sinner, is saved and goes to paradise if he only has one unique thought for the Buddha (just as in the Pāñcharātra section of the Vishnuist Church).

Chinese translations give dates; religions of the Mahāyāna cannot be later than the first Christian century, and are probably earlier. The original places cannot be ascertained. But the definition of the Buddhas as true living gods is the natural development of the primitive belief in the supernatural character of Śākyamuni: therefore the theist Mahāyānist system probably took growth and importance at the same moment in all the provinces of Buddhist India. The literary testimonies do not indicate the real evolution of the religious ideas, but only the gradual admission by the clergy of ideas probably born outside its pale. It is probable that the Mahāsamghika sect was the first to give an official theology to the adorers of the Buddhas: namely the distinction between the true heavenly Buddha and his human substitute or avatar (see above, p. 165). But we remain in the dark concerning the place, the date, the diffusion, and the way by which religious ideas obtained literary and iconographic expression. Art is an important feature.

The problem is the more complex because there are several religions of the Mahāyāna. All have the same doctrine, but the Buddha-God is sometimes Maitreya, sometimes Śākyamuni,

---

at the beginning of their career they have practised self-sacrifice for the welfare of all beings; later they are occupied in benefiting creatures by every kind of boon. The descent of Avalokita into hell is a well-known topic.

sometimes Amitābha, sometimes Avalokiteśvara. Our knowledge of the origin of these Persons (Śākyamuni excepted) is less than scanty. There is some probability that many figures of the Buddhist hagiolatry have been adapted from non-Buddhist beliefs: many scholars observe that Amitābha, the most popular of the Buddhas of the Far East, bears the mark of Iranism and of the Solar religion.

Maitreya, Ajita Maitreya, Invictus Maitreya, is not a Buddha, but the Buddha who is to come. He reigns in the Tushita heaven, in the heaven which according to an early tradition Śākyamuni inhabited before incarnating himself in the womb of Māyā. Devotees either desire to be reborn in Tushita or make the 'resolve' to be reborn on earth when Maitreya will 'descend' and become a Buddha. Early Buddhism ignores this 'Messiah': he only appears in the latest part of the old Canon; but he is certainly an interesting figure.[1]

In early sources there are two disciples of Śākyamuni, of no particular importance, one named Ajita, the second Maitreya. Later Ajita, *invictus*, is the name or 'surname' of Maitreya. The idea that many Buddhas came before Śākyamuni is an old one; the idea that a new Buddha is to come is not early, although it is natural. When it developed the beneficiary was a person the name of whom is like the name of the Vedic Mitra ('Sun' and 'Friend') and the name of the Iranian Sun God.

III. *Buddhism as a 'supramundane' discipline; early form: the Vehicle to Nirvāna*

1. In early days the disciples of Śākyamuni who were 'men of ascetic or spiritual dispositions' aimed at Nirvāna, or 'end of misery', 'deliverance from rebirth', the state or the abode of eternal peace which after death will be the lot of the saint, the Arhat.

---

[1] Emil Abegg, *Der Messiasglaube in Indien und Iran*, 1928; J. Przyluski, 'La croyance au Messie', *Revue de l'Histoire des Religions*, juillet, 1929.

This form of Buddhism ought to be styled *nirvānayāna*, Vehicle leading to Nirvāna. It is generally named *Hīnayāna*, 'inferior or low vehicle', from the designation used by the adherents of the form of Buddhism described under § IV; because these new philosophers thought that Nirvāna (an unconscious beatitude) is not worthy to be sought for, or that the Arhat, an egoist saint, is not really a saint.

This form of Buddhism still survives in Ceylon, Burma, &c.; it has practically disappeared in the Far East.

We believe that it is early: the Buddhist Nirvāna is nothing else than a certain aspect of the 'deliverance' or of the 'supramundane abode' aimed at by a great number of ascetics or ecstatics; Śākyamuni is one of the doctors or saints who fixed the practical means of reaching Nirvāna.

In short, Nirvāna is to be reached by the suppression of passion, by ecstatic or hypnotic devices. Therefore a candidate for Nirvāna, according to Buddhist principles (which are marked by a high morality), must lead a continent and frugal life, he must be a monk or, more exactly, a 'beggar, son of Śākya'. The Brotherhood is one, since it has only one master and one goal; but owing to minutiae in monastic discipline (or to unknown circumstances) it was early divided into a number of sects. Their number is said to have been eighteen.

Śākyamuni's path to Nirvāna is known to us by the canonical texts, which are comparatively late. Scholars are confronted with the same difficulty as regards the disciplinary (or monastic) rules: there is little doubt that the early Brotherhood had fixed rules and was distinguished from the contemporaneous sects; but the disciplinary books we possess are the result of long growth and regularization.

We feel sure that the early Buddhist candidate for Nirvāna must be a monk, a good monk, must practise frugality, continence, meditation on the corpse, meditation on the transitoriness of pleasure, must concentrate his thought and wishes on the eternal peace of Nirvāna. But we also feel sure that the clerical (or scholastical) speculations on Nirvāna and the way thereof do not correspond exactly to the early state of Buddhist philosophy and mysticism. To give an example. A few early narrations certainly prove the habit of religious suicide. Many saints of the primitive Brotherhood 'took the knife' in order to reach Nirvāna. The orthodox theory and rule is that 'a saint does not wish for life or death', and patiently waits for his natural time. This detail shows that scholars who describe early Buddhism as a 'rationalismus' misrepresent Buddhism, and have an inexact (or incomplete) idea of the intellectual and moral 'climate' of old ascetic India.

2. It is probable that, even at an early date, there was a contrast between the monks who attached great importance to ecstasy (and to mystic experiences) and the monks who relied on 'wisdom'. There is a Buddhism centred on the 'true meditation', the meditation which destroys the opposition of 'subject' and 'object', knower and known; this meditation is the fruit of a transcendent agnosticism. There is a Buddhism which teaches that liberation from desire and existence is the fruit of the 'knowledge of the nature of things'. Both have a long history. We owe to the second a number of theories.

A. *Nihilism.* According to the teaching of many canonical texts there is not in man any permanent principle—what we style a soul—capable of going through successive existences and of reaching Nirvāna. Man, like a chariot, has not real unity: he is made of pieces (*skandha*): material atoms, spiritual or mental atoms (sensations, perceptions, actions, &c.).

Several theories have been concocted in order to explain how such a 'complex' can commit acts, eat the fruit of its acts, pass into a new existence where it enjoys the fruit of its acts. These theories cannot be early, nor indeed is the philosophy of the negation of a living and permanent and free soul. In early days Buddhists probably believed simply in transmigration and release.

Now this philosophy, according to the Canon, is the truth which must be meditated upon in order to eradicate desire. It is the 'corner-stone' of wisdom and holiness. By an irresistible progress it turned into a system of universal nihilism: the material or mental atoms have no more reality than the material or mental compounds. This is 'acosmism'.

It is well known that the great monist philosopher of Brahmanism, Śamkara, who taught the existence of the Brāhman only and the non-existence of the world, of souls, of God, has been criticized by theist Brahmans as a 'Buddhist in disguise'. And scholars agree that Śamkara's philosophy is the result of the synthesis of the old Brahmanic faith in an Absolute (Brāhman) and the Buddhist nihilism. Thus Śamkara appears as one of the heirs of Buddhism.

We shall see (p. 180) that Buddhist philosophers also adopted the notion of an Absolute.

B. *Nirvāna.* During the nineteenth century and the first decade of the twentieth European scholars believed that the early Buddhist Nirvāna was annihilation.

They now feel sure that early Nirvāna was not eternal death, but 'immortality', an imperishable abode of undefinable peace, above thought and consciousness. The Canon contains testimonies to this early view, for it describes Nirvāna as 'the unborn which is the refuge of what is born', also as the 'Immortal element' which is 'touched' during trances by the living saint.

But owing to the nihilistic theory (above, A), the Buddhist schools went very far in the way of negation, and sometimes proclaimed an annihilation-Nirvāna.

Some schools preserved the doctrine of the 'immortal element', the eternal entity, which is 'touched' by the living saint. But they believe that a saint is only a compound of transient atoms and therefore completely perishes at death. The Nirvāna of a saint is only the annihilation of this saint.

Some scholars wholly rejected the notion of the 'immortal element' and said in so many words that Nirvāna is only 'non-existence following existence'.

A third view is that Nirvāna is eternal happiness; the dead saint possesses beatitude (*sukha*) for he no longer suffers: but he has no feeling of beatitude (*sukhasamvedana*). This Nirvāna is, according to a school of Mahāyāna, the Nirvāna of the ordinary saints.

Lastly, according to the Mahāyāna, the Buddhas have a Nirvāna of their own: perfectly calm and free, they are in Nirvāna: but they are nevertheless compassionate and active. They do not abandon existence, and will continue for ever.

3. It has been said above that a monk is 'by definition' a candidate for Nirvāna. But, in fact, Nirvāna, when we consider the majority of the monks, is only the ideal of a distant future.

All the immediate disciples of the Master reached sainthood and Nirvāna. But already, at the time of the compilation of the Scriptures, the great object was not to reach Nirvāna, but to enter into the path leading to Nirvāna: a man who has entered into this path must be reborn eight times before attaining the goal. In fact the only candidate for Nirvāna is the ascetic who practises mortification and penances, and the faculty of *dhyāna* or ecstatic trance, more than are enjoined by the rules of his order, thus acquiring supernatural powers. To pretend falsely to have realized such spiritual progress is one of the four sins (together with murder, &c.) which are punished by expulsion from the Brotherhood: this shows that any pretence to holiness was looked upon with suspicion. We are told that in the early days saints were many and disciplinary rules few: later the position was reversed, and it was commonly admitted that sainthood had disappeared.

The conclusion is that we cannot give an absolute value to the opposition of the monk and the layman, in regard to the spiritual dignity or the goal which they try to reach. As a rule, a monk only wishes to 'earn merit' by the practice of his professional duties (abstinence, continence, preaching—the most excellent work of charity, receiving alms, or worship), just as a layman earns merit by the practice of his professional duties (abstention from murder, 'home-chastity'—that is, conjugal fidelity—giving alms, worship): in both cases the fruit of merit is rebirth as a god, or as a human being who is capable of entering into the Path that leads to Nirvāna.

IV. *Buddhism as a 'supramundane discipline'. Later Form: The Vehicle of Buddhahood*

1. From the beginning of the Christian era and probably earlier a number of Buddhist monks came to despise Nirvāna, and entered into the path which had been followed by the man who was to become Śākyamuni, the path leading to Buddhahood. The second form of 'supramundane Buddhism' is a *Bodhisattvayāna* or a *Buddhayāna*, the Vehicle of the future Buddhas, the Vehicle of the Buddhas, the path that leads to the possession of Buddhahood.

This Buddhism differs from the Buddhism of § III. The devotee no longer aims at Nirvāna but at Buddhahood; therefore his discipline is no longer the egoistical virtue and impassibility of the Arhat,[1] but the charitable practices of a future Buddha. The Arhat reaches Nirvāna by his own unique exertion: Buddhahood is obtained by personal exertion coupled with the help of the Buddhas and heavenly Bodhisattvas who are living gods.

This Buddhism may be considered as the 'learned', mystical branch of the Buddhism of § II. It differs: the candidate for

---

[1] Altruistic virtues have a place in the preparation for Nirvāna, for peace of soul presupposes the suppression of anger, the culture (*bhāvanā*) of feelings of universal benevolence; but this place is a small and a prefatory one, since the candidate for Nirvāna must destroy hate and love.

Buddhahood loves and worships the Buddhas and does not despise a rebirth in the paradise of a Buddha (as in § II); but such a rebirth is regarded by him as a temporary stage in his progress towards Buddhahood. The devotee of § II is only a *bhakta*, a *dévot*; he is not a future Buddha.

The vehicle of the Bodhisattvas is nothing new in Buddhism. Buddhist antiquity was well aware of the fact that Śākyamuni has obtained Buddhahood in his last existence because during many (552) previous existences he had followed the path of the future Buddhas, that is, because he had heaped up heroic deeds of virtue and self-sacrifice (narrated in the *Jātaka*).

But the general opinion was that Śākyamuni is 'exceptional', that Buddhas are very rare.

There was (before the compilation of the *Saddharmapundarīka*, Lotus of the true Law, perhaps about the beginning of the Christian era) a new departure: the discovery of a new truth, namely that all men can or must imitate Śākyamuni, can pronounce (as did Śākyamuni) the vow of becoming Buddha, in other words can become 'future Buddhas'.

2. At the time of Asanga (fourth century A.D.) a monk was always a member of one of the eighteen early sects. But a number of monks, not satisfied with the mystical goal (Nirvāna) and the moral ideal (impassibility of the *Arhat*) of these sects, added to the obligations of the traditionary clerical life (old disciplinary rules) the obligation of a future Buddha, heroic charity and self-sacrifice; they took the vow of Buddhahood. There was a ceremony, a private one, in the presence of a man (monk or layman) already equipped with this vow.

Later on, as the new spirit developed, as the candidates to Buddhahood became more numerous and influential, the adhesion to an early sect was no longer necessary. A special discipline for the Bodhisattva-monks had been delineated, and they had monasteries of their own.

The chief innovation, as concerns discipline, was probably

the prohibition of meat. The worship of the Buddhas, which from of old was admitted by some at least of the early sects, became more pompous and general. There was also a new or renewed spirit of charity and propaganda; a spiritual life more noble, intense, and profound. One cannot read without respect and admiration the formulas of the eightfold supreme worship (confession of sins, &c.) and the homilies on patience, love of one's neighbour, considering a neighbour as one's own self and one's own egoist self as an enemy to be humiliated and destroyed.[1]

There is sometimes much wisdom and moderation in Mahāyāna teaching. We are beginners in the path of self-sacrifice. To save others we must not jeopardize our own welfare: therefore we must first avoid sin and exert ourselves in the humble virtues of everyday life; such is the right way to prepare oneself for the heroic deeds of future rebirths.[2]

But this wisdom is not general. A future Buddha must imitate the habit of self-sacrifice which characterized the future Śākyamuni when he gave to beggars or to tigresses his eyes or his flesh. Hence an epidemic of religious suicides.[3] As the Church officially deprecates suicide, an orthodox method of self-sacrifice was created. The initiation into the Mahāyānist community (i.e. the solemn vow of Buddhahood) was accompanied by the 'burning of the skull' (China): a number of incense-sticks are fixed on the skull of the candidate and lighted: the candidate is looked upon as a man who has burned his body for the welfare of mankind.[4]

During all his former existences Śākyamuni was not a monk, but a layman. A future Buddha may be a layman. A consequence of this doctrine is that the clerical life lost its prestige

---

[1] L. D. Barnett, *The Path of Light* (Wisdom of the East Series) (John Murray, 1909).

[2] *Śāntideva's Śikshāsamuccaya*, tr. by W. H. D. Rouse (Indian Texts Series) (John Murray, 1922).

[3] I-tsing, *Records of the Buddhist Religion* (Clarendon Press, Oxford, 1896).

[4] De Groot, *Code du Mahāyāna en Chine* (Amsterdam, 1893).

and that Buddhism, hitherto essentially a clerical brotherhood, became more and more a popular religion. This religion was more and more open to Hindu (*Śivaist*) influences: this is one of the causes of the disintegration and disappearance of Indian Buddhism.

3. The popular and sincere belief in the divine power and providence of the Buddhas was not to satisfy the intellectual needs of the learned monks. The Mahāyāna has elaborated systems of metaphysics and Buddhology.

A. *Tathatā*. The first Buddhist speculation resulted in a nihilistic or quasi-nihilistic attitude (§ III); but, while admitting the conclusions of the Ancients—namely absence of a soul, unsubstantiality of all phenomena (or 'caused contingent things')—some of the eighteen early sects and the schools of the Mahāyānist Church recognized an 'absolute' which is probably derived from the absolute of the Brāhmans (*brāhman*). There is an immutable element (*dhātu*) below the changing flow of phenomena; more precisely a 'nature of things' (*dharmatā*) or 'true reality' (*tathatā*), which is a spiritual or meta-mental reality, a transcendent thought free from the opposition of 'subject' and 'object'.

All beings are metaphysically the *tathatā*. But only a few beings (the Buddhas) have attained knowledge of the *tathatā* by personal experience: they have attained the perfect 'equation' of their individual thought to the very nature of thought. This sort of identification is the cause of Buddhahood, is Buddhahood itself.

We are the *tathatā*; therefore we are Buddhas *en puissance*; we shall become actually Buddhas when we attain the consciousness of our identity with the *tathatā*. It is a long business: a long endeavour in self-sacrifice and contemplation, the career of a future Buddha: to conceive the vow of Buddhahood, to progress during many rebirths before entering upon the first of the ten stages of a future Buddha.[1]

[1] Such is the early and orthodox view; but the thesis that all living beings

PLATE II

BODHISATTVA
Gandhāra (Graeco-Buddhist)
2nd–5th century A.D.

B. *The four bodies.* Early Mahāyāna taught that Buddhas have two bodies: there is a quasi-eternal and divine Śākyamuni; there is a human Śākyamuni who is only a 'creation body', a magical contrivance managed in order to guide men towards happiness.

Later a Buddha is said to possess four bodies: (1) a transcendent one, the *tathatā*, the same, of course, for all the Buddhas; (2) the 'body of personal enjoyment', that is, the real thought and form which constitutes a certain Buddha, Amitābha, Śākyamuni, and so on: this body, which is the Buddha himself, will last for eternity; (3) the 'body of altruistic enjoyment': the form under which a Buddha manifests himself to saints in the heavens: this body of course is manifold, since saints differ in holiness and needs; (4) the 'creation-body', the form under which a Buddha manifests himself to very imperfect beings, men, devils, and so forth. The best creation-body is the human Buddha.

C. The Buddhology just described is a compromise between two notions: (1) the early dogma that Buddhahood is obtained through long exertion by beings who have been transmigrating 'since a time which has not begun'; (2) the metaphysical view of the universal and immutable *tathatā*, which is the transcendent body realized by each Buddha.

Mahāyāna sometimes abandoned the early dogma. According to many schools, some of which are certainly old (possibly fourth century A.D.) there is a primeval eternal Buddha—Vajrasattva, the 'diamond or the thunderbolt', Adibuddha, the 'Buddha of the beginning'—from which the Buddhas issue by a process of meditative emanation; the Bodhisattvas are no

have the nature of a Buddha could not but result in the hope of quickly actualizing this nature. Hence a number of magical or ecstatic devices in order to acquire the body, the voice, and the thought of a Buddha. See La Vallée Poussin, *Le dogme et la philosophie du Bouddhisme* (Paris, Beauchesne, 1930).

longer 'future Buddhas' but 'spiritual sons' of the Buddhas.
Tantric and Tibetan Buddhism illustrate this new aspect of the
religion of Śākyamuni.

Some remarks on the disappearance of Indian Buddhism

Scholars have given many explanations of the gradual decay
and final disappearance of Indian Buddhism. Of course, epigraphical and literary sources are not wanting, and it is not
impossible to follow, province by province, the process of decay:
this preliminary and necessary work has not been carefully done,
and the problem remains terribly obscure. Nevertheless a few
general observations may be useful.

(*a*) For centuries and almost everywhere Buddhism had
numbered its monks by thousands, enjoyed the most vigorous
life in devotional and philosophical directions, obtained the
patronage of kings and sometimes the advantages of being the
state religion. But, as we have seen, it had never and nowhere
taken the place of Brahmanism.

(*b*) The bonds which for a time strongly attached laymen to
Buddhism were the worship of the Buddhist saints and the
veneration of the monks—who were not 'priests' but moral
advisers and excellent 'fields of merit'.

Śākyamuni has been for centuries a most popular figure: the
history of his previous births, of his miracles and deeds, enjoyed
the favour of the people at large. Later on Śākyamuni was
superseded in learned and lay Buddhist circles by other Buddhas
or saints: Maitreya, Amitābha, Mañjuśrī, Avalokita, Tārā or
Tārās. These figures lacked the personal character of Śākyamuni, never possessed his prestige, or, again, had features which
established between them and Hindu gods an undeniable
likeness.

The presence of fairies and minor useful deities in the Buddhist
pantheon was not in itself a great danger, but, with centuries,
the Hindu infiltration took a new character. We know that the

monks of the conservative party accused their brethren of philo-śivaism (eighth century A.D.); in Bengal, after the Muhamma-dan destruction of the Buddhist monasteries, the Buddhists exchanged their worship of Buddhist figures for the worship of Vishnuist ones; the Buddhism of present-day Nepal is a mixture of Buddhism and Brāhmano-śivaism.

Buddhism admitted into its pantheon and worshipped under the title of Buddhas or Bodhisattvas or Vajradevatās figures deeply stamped with the Hindu (Vishnu-śivaite) mark. Its theology too had been penetrated by Hindu conceptions. One of the favourite deities of later Buddhism is Tārā, 'the Star' or 'the Saviouress', who owes all her 'Buddhism' to her kindness, to her title of 'future Buddha', or of wife of a Buddha.

(*c*) The strength of Buddhism is in its clergy, in the Brother-hood. For centuries the Brotherhood flourished in the East, in the Deccan; in the West, in the Konkan and the Telugu country. Buddhist pilgrims and archaeology show the gradual decay of the Buddhist communities almost everywhere.

One lesson of the Mahāyāna (see §§ II and IV) is that a layman has the same right to holiness and salvation as a monk: the Mahāyāna to some extent deprecates clerical life. Can we say that asceticism—at least this form of comfortable asceticism which characterized the Buddhist clergy—was losing its pres-tige and its hold on religious India?

Buddhist casuists have always admitted that a monk commits no sin when he officially declares that he is not capable of keep-ing his vows: he then becomes a Buddhist layman and can marry. With the Mahāyāna this casuistry turned into a historical feature: we have evidence of the growing habit of young men to take the monastic vows (a meritorious act), only to proclaim immediately after the ceremony that they renounce the vows of a monk in order to take the vows of a lay Bodhisattva. Kashmir and Nepal have had or have a married clergy.

Another cause of weakness in the Brotherhood was the

decline of intellectual activity (already visible during the sixth and the seventh centuries), and the development of the Tantric (or magic) form of Buddhism: pure Śivaism in disguise. The master or teacher (*guru*) who gives the initiation and shows the way to a rapid acquisition of Buddhahood or of worldly advantages is no longer a monk, but a *siddha*, a magician, a *vajrāchārya* (often of very low moral habits).

(*d*) The fate of Indian Buddhism must be explained by its own internal faults. At least this aspect of the problem deserves attention. But external circumstances also had no little effect.

The advantage of official or kingly patronage is great. Inversely, when kings were strongly 'Śivaizing' (like Śaśānka or the Cholas), or 'jainizing' (as in Malwa), or 'lingaïzing' (as in the Telugu country), or simply 'anticlerical' (as the Hun kings, some potentates of Kashmir, the Muhammedans), Buddhism suffered.

Greater importance than that of the occasional bias of the civil power in favour of non-Buddhist creeds and clergy must probably be attached to the change that Brahmanism underwent during the Middle Ages under the guidance of many religious reformers.

Formerly Brāhmans were domestic priests or held liturgical duties in the ceremonies of the temples; but they had no 'cure of souls', they were not preachers nor propagandists, as the Buddhists and Jains were of old. But with Śamkara, Rāmānuja, many other saints and their disciples, Śivaism and Vishnuism acquired an active clergy. While the vital energies of Buddhism were declining, the Brahmano-Hinduist religion enjoyed a sort of revival.

DE LA VALLÉE POUSSIN.

LANGUAGE AND LITERATURE

The Hindu Period

DURING the last age of the Aryan period the orthodox Brāhmans were engaged, as we have seen, in formulating their ritual, grammatical, and cosmological systems, and also in codifying their canonical law: they continued their *Upanishad* speculations and meditations on the Self as identical with the soul of the world. The triad of great gods, Brāhman the Creator, Vishnu the Sustainer, Śiva the Destroyer, had taken shape. There were very numerous divisions of sect and school (*śākhā* and *charana*) according to the Vedic text or *Sūtra* authority specially followed. In the common life were developing codes of law and theories of kingship and royal action in internal and in inter-state relations. Military science, fort and town-building, and architecture and painting were studied, and the minor arts and crafts multiplied. Temples and images had come into use. Religious movements and practices originally outside the range of orthodoxy had acquired recognition, the most important, perhaps, being the Krishnaic or Bhāgavata devotional religion and the practice of *yoga*, i.e. spiritual exercises of a psychologico-corporeal kind, a thing different from the old *tapas*, austerities, of the Brāhmans. World-renouncing (*pravrajita*) individuals or companies, perhaps an ancient feature of the easy life of India, wandered from place to place, eager to discuss some adopted tenet or rule of life. In the time when Buddhism arose the most active questioning related to matters cosmological and ethical: was the world a product of Time or Nature or Accident or Fate, or of physical elements only, or of a Person? Was there such a thing as action (*kriyā*) or moral action and retribution (*karma*), or was the sword-stroke of the slayer simply a severing of material particles, and were vital phenomena only a kind of fermentation? There were also

dialecticians who held that 'A is B' does not preclude 'A is not B'
—perhaps the Jain doctrine of 'aspects'. In this mêlée of sophistic, wherein the Jains reckon 353 possible views, the most
important contention, no doubt, was that between the partisans of action (*kriyā-vādins*) and the partisans of non-action
(*akriyā-vādins*). The *Upanishads* in their quest of the self had
come, as we have seen, upon the idea that what passes from one
life to another is simply acts. When Buddha, originally, as was
inevitable in his time, a thinker, worked out this notion in its
full consequence, the self, the thrice-refined gold of the Brāhman speculation, was seen as an otiose addition to the series of
acts, or rather, were it not nothing at all, an evil thing, associated with caprice, greed, and infatuation. This was a Buddhist
contribution to the process which indelibly engraved upon
Indian mentality the doctrine of *karma*.

The idea of a 'law' of moral retribution without a providence
is curiously, and perhaps not accidentally, analogous to the idea
of a religious retribution without a god, wherein the Brahmanic
ritualism, as a dogmatic system, culminated. This was the
Pūrva-Mīmāmsā philosophy. In the Vaiśeshika system was considered the topic of physical action, which was a functioning of
atoms and gave rise to conjunction and disjunction. Although
the three notions do not seem ever to have been welded by the
Indians into a whole, they show a special preoccupation with
the notion of action at the time when their thought was turned
to systems.

The second leading constituent in the Hindu conception of
life was the idea of *dharma*. *Dharma* is the mode or fashion in
which anything does behave. When stress is laid upon the
'does', the *nuance* of meaning may be in the direction of 'truth';
when it is on the 'behave', we may get the opposite idea of mere
phenomenon or aspect. But it is when the idea of obligation,
social, moral, or religious, is included that the term assumes its
great practical importance, as denoting the manner in which a

person *ought* to behave. In the earlier occurrences of the term the notion is the general idea of righteous conduct, or, when religion is involved, of religiously right conduct. With the growth of caste, regarded as a natural or divine institution, the socially most important kind of behaviour, after the greater moralities, was the observance of caste duties, though, of course, other associations, such as family, station (as king and so on), sect, locality, likewise carried with them their *dharmas*: it is in this wide, not strictly ethical, sense—since any custom was a *dharma*—that the doctrine of selfless performance of duty was preached in the *Bhagavad-gītā*.

The expression *varnāśrama-dharma*, i.e. *dharma* of *varnas*, or castes, and of *āśramas*, or stages of life—almost a synonym for Hinduism—introduces a further factor in the systematization of Hindu life, the theory of the four stages, pupilhood, life of the householder, retreat at the commencement of old age to forest seclusion, and all-renouncing, nothing-owning vagrancy. The recognition of the last-named stage incorporates in the completed Hindu system the originally unchartered practice of the vagrant sectaries whom we have mentioned.

These slight observations, wherein we have summarized a few of the leading ideas of the Hindu system, must lamely excuse us for leaping over some six centuries of literary activity, which, far from being unimportant or exiguous in quantity, was really the most prolific, imposing, and widely recognized of all. In this period the scheme of life which in Alexander's time was already beginning to mark off the Indian people from all others was completed. The philosophies and sciences were codified in dogmatic (*śāstra*) form. The *Mahābhārata* received those immense didactic accretions which gave it the character of a popular exposition of Hinduism as a whole; and versified treatises on usage, law, and politics (*dharma-smritis*), and on cosmology and history in connexion with the worship of the chief gods (early *Purānas*), the sacred books of Hinduism as distinct from Vedic Brahmanism, were multiplied. This mass of compositions would demand in a history of Indian literature a large space. What excuses us from surveying it here is, in addition to lack of even approximate dating, the fact that its great importance lies in the matter, not in the linguistic or literary form: only in regard to the śāstraic method of exposition in brief aphorisms (*sūtra*) accompanied by discussions (*bhāshya*), best exemplified by the grammatical work of Pāṇini and Patañjali and the *sūtras* of the Mīmāmsā philosophy, did any decisive novelty emerge.

But what is to be said of the new literature of the Jains and Buddhists, whose canonical writings were almost entirely constituted during these centuries? Both these are rather separate worlds of literature than departments. Certainly they are dominated by the purpose of edification, religious and moral. But that does not prevent them from comprising much of more ordinary interest in the form of striking observation or reflection, anecdote or narrative, or artistic verse. The earlier literature of the Jains has not yet been thoroughly studied, and it cannot be said that any entire work included in it has attained a special place in Indian literature as a whole. But much of it is of elaborate form, with descriptions obviously aiming at a literary effect; and there is no doubt that much has still to be learned from it in regard to developments both in language and in style. Like the early Buddhists, the Jains make great use of dialogue; but in their case, as well as in that of the Buddhists, an objection to public displays prevented any early use of the drama.

The Buddhist canon presents far more formidably the same impossibility of brief description. It has been stated that the canonical writings in Pālī are not more than twice as extensive as the Bible. The *Sutta* (*Sūtra*) section, consisting mainly of dialogues between the Buddha and various interlocutors, is literature in the same sense as are the dialogues of Plato, though the stiff Pālī style has not the grace of the Greek philosopher. The *Vinaya*, exposition of monastic rules, retails many socially interesting anecdotes concerning the occasions which dictated the rules, and is of the highest documentary value in regard to the constitution of a religious order. The *Abhidhamma*, or dogmatic statement of the psychologic and philosophic discriminations, is technical. But, fortunately, there are some treatises in this Pālī literature which can be appreciated by humanity in general: the *Milinda-pañha*, dialogues of the Buddhist monk Nāgasena with the Greek King Menander, ruler of northern India, for the acuteness and point of the discussions and the dramatic appeal of the situation; the *Dhamma-pada* and the *Sutta-nipāta*, ethical and religious verse, for their deep human wisdom, their touching goodness and magnanimity, and their artistic expression; the 'Songs of the Monks' and 'Songs of the Nuns' (*Thera-gātha* and *Therī-gātha*), the latter perhaps the most pusillanimous of all poetic compositions, for their autobiographical intimacies of spiritual experience; the 'Life' of Buddha, as related in the Introduction to the Pālī *Jātaka*, and his 'Great Decease', in the *Mahā-pari-nirvāna-sūtra*, as the 'Romantic Legend' and biography of Buddha, the highest poetical creation of Indian religion; and finally, the *Jātaka* book of 547 stories of Buddha's prior incarnations in various animal and human forms, stories so rich in homely observation of man and beast, in shrewd humour, and ideal conduct, that the book is sure to become in translations, if it is not already, a classic of world literature.

The problem of the Pālī books, which for the most part have not been translated into Oriental languages other than Chinese (far the oldest; a few also into Tibetan), Sinhalese, Burmese, and Siamese, is thus in outline not unmanageable. As regards the Sanskrit and other dialects, the complication is far greater. From an early period of the Buddhist Church several sects adopted for their versions of the canonical texts different dialects.

the Sanskrit being preferred by the important sect of the Sarvāsti-vādins. For the most part these versions, which in their linguistic form were perhaps later than the Pālī, have perished. But the *Vinaya* portion has in several cases been preserved in Chinese and Tibetan. The *Sūtras*, or dialogues, do not there appear grouped, as in Pālī, in five *Nikāyas*, but as separate works, and, so far as they coincide in title with the Pālī, they are widely different in style and matter. Few of them can be ascribed to a date preceding the Christian era, and many, including probably all Mahāyāna *sūtras*, are considerably later and represent new developments of Buddhism: some of them reflect rather Central Asian than Indian conditions and were composed, no doubt, in that region. A specially rich expansion of the 'Northern' Buddhism was the *Avadāna* literature, hagiographa describing the religious heroisms of saints or others, and some of this, including perhaps an *Aśoka-avadāna*, belongs to the pre-Christian era. The same applies to certain 'Questions' (*Pariprichchhā*) put to Buddha by various persons and 'Prophecies' (*Vyākarana*) concerning others.

It is perhaps hardly necessary to mention that the vast Sanskrit literature of Northern Buddhism, as translated into Chinese and collected in successive editions and catalogues, constitutes the scriptures of Chinese and Japanese Buddhism. In these two countries the religion has partly gone its own way and has given rise to sects, some of them distinguished by adherence to particular texts of the Canon. Thus some of these works stand out from the mass, and one, the 'Lotus of the Good Law' (*Sad-dharma-pundarīka*), has been styled the 'Bible of half Asia'. In the eighth century A.D. commenced the translation of scriptures into Tibetan; and eventually, in the fourteenth century, was constituted a Tibetan canon of vast dimensions, which under the influence of Mongol sovereigns was translated into Mongol, Manchu, and Kalmuck, and provided those peoples with the collections of great calligraphic volumes which fill the shelves of their monastic libraries. In the early centuries of the Christian era there were translations of some Sanskrit texts, and also original Buddhist compositions, in languages of Central Asia, which have been rediscovered only during the present century, and of eastern Turkey, which now for nearly a thousand years has been devoted solely to Islam.

As in the case of the Brahmanic and Jain literature, so in the case of the Buddhist, historical obscurity precludes any intelligible account of developments during about six centuries, say 350 B.C.–A.D. 250. Even were it otherwise, no doubt the religious and edifying character of the Buddhist and Jain writings would make them a 'side issue', so to speak, in the general current of Indian literature. It would be impossible to deny to the Buddhist and Jain scriptures, despite their wilful and remorseless tediousness, the literary qualities of definitely formed style and expression adequate to their subject. When they employ verse, they show accomplishment in metrics. The stock descriptions wherewith the Jains adorn their stories are of definitely artistic conception. In some of the Buddhist works, where the theme inspired to poetry—such is the *Lalita-Vistara*, 'Life of Buddha'—there is a flow of ideas and a swirl in the verse which give it a rich poetic quality; and perhaps this is one of the works which take a place in the general, as well as in the religious, literature. But literary art is a jealous principle; and, just as in the history of Greek and Latin literature the works of Christian religious inspiration are treated as something apart, so in the Sanskrit literature the Buddhist and Jain scriptures remained outside the general current. Had Buddhism succeeded in pervading the life-blood of the Indian spirit, its scriptures might have dominated the later literature as they have in Ceylon, Burma, Siam, Tibet, and pre-Islamic Central Asia, and in the Buddhist worlds of China and Japan. But they were both nonconformist movements, and they were forestalled by others, Krishnaism, Vishnuism, Śivaism, more rooted in Indian social usage and human nature. Buddhism ultimately expired in India through absorption of superstitions and magical practices, and through Muhammadan detestation of its superabundant idolatry. Jainism, never so widely influential even in India and probably never much subject to like corruptions, presented equal provocations to Islamic fervour, which seems to have been directed with special violence against its shrines: in southern India it was also a victim of religious reactions among the Hindus. But what the world in general, which has limited time for becoming acquainted with all its religious writings, will feel to be its best excuse for not penetrating far into the canonical texts of these two noble-hearted faiths is their intolerable and pedantic reiteration, which recalls, and possibly has some internal affinity with, the proceedings of primary schools. No wonder the Buddha often during some long-winded statement by one of his disciples fell into *samādhi* (the Pālī books, too modestly, fail to record such effects of their scriptures): the same blessed state must often have been attained by members of monastery congregations engaged in reciting (*sangīti*) the inspired texts.

There was, however, one early Buddhist writer, fortunately with an approximate date, whose lustre was seen both within and without the Buddhist mansion. This was Aśvaghosha, a converted Brāhman, who in the first century A.D. became a leader in the prevalent sect of the Sarvāsti-vādins and who is regarded as eleventh in the succession of patriarchs of the whole (Northern) church. He is the great literary figure, with only one rival, of Buddhism. He brought to the service of his new faith the strict linguistic training of the Brāhman schools and a technical artistry which had, no doubt, been steadily developing among the professional or quasi-professional poets—the Jain and Buddhist versifiers, with their predominantly religious intent, may be regarded as amateurs. Aśvaghosha, whose 'Life of Buddha' (*Buddha-charita*) is quoted in the Brahmanic anthologies, may be regarded as standing midway between Vālmīki and Kālidāsa. He has not the serenity of the old epic or the unrivalled delicacy and cleverness of the classical poet. But in comparison with the former he manifests a great advance in rhetorical and metrical technique, and in comparison with Kālidāsa he has the strength of an earnest ethical and religious conviction. The *Buddha-charita* is a poem which by reason of the substantiality of its matter and the poetical and ethical force of fresh expression and illustration can be enjoyed in translation, while the metrical and linguistic accomplishment are to the reader of the original a delight. The poem on the conversion of 'Nanda, the Handsome' (Sundara-Nanda) has an even stronger flush of poetical and human emotion and flow of verse, though with less firmness of texture and grandeur of theme. It is evident that Aśvaghosha's conversion brought into Buddhism a new literary power and that his poems were celebrated in all Buddhist lands. Whether he was author of the hymns attributed to a poet known as Mātricheta may perhaps not yet have been finally decided; but certainly what is stated concerning the latter is true of Aśvaghosha's works:

'These charming compositions are equal in beauty to the heavenly flowers; and the high principles which they contain rival in dignity the lofty peaks of a mountain. Consequently in India all who compose hymns imitate his style, considering him the father of literature.'

That he was also an 'ancestor', if not the progenitor, of the Sanskrit drama is proved by recovered fragments of certain plays, one of them allegorical or a religious 'Morality', composed by him.

We have now reached the end of what may be called the creative period of Indian literature. Archaic, but not unsophisticated, in its earliest stages, it developed in a priestly system of thought, with a portentous ritual system, ritual symbolism, and theory of ritual efficacy, with exact study of textual matters and a remarkably thorough understanding of phonetics and grammar, with expositions of religious law and usage, with cosmological speculations, physical and psychological, ending in the discovery of a 'self' identical with a universal spirit. In less professional milieux there began a systematization of practical law and discussions concerning royal authority and action, and some arts, such as architecture, painting, and medicine, began to have a theoretic side. In popular literature the heroic or laudatory ballads of the court poets or other professional singers and narrators were consolidated into two great epics, one, the *Mahābhārata*, centred upon a great war, the other, the *Rāmāyana*, relating the partly mythological exploits of a legendary king of eastern India. This period, which saw the rise of the Hindu Trinity of great gods and of Krishnaism, an originally unorthodox adoration of a tribal hero, ended in an outburst of sophistic free thought, wherein the historical Jainism and Buddhism arose.

The second age, historically somewhat less obscure than the first, has a commencement more or less demarked by the rise of the Nanda and Maurya Empire. It may be regarded as terminating about A.D. 300, at the beginning, more or less, of the Gupta period (A.D. 319). From a literary point of view this period may be considered one of organization: organization of the chief Brahmanical sciences and philosophies and of other sciences, such as politics, law, and medicine; organization of two great heretical sects with their church systems, scriptural canons, and other writings. The form which the *Mahābhārata* assumed, as a kind of encyclopaedia of Hindu life, itself now organized as a matter of four stages, fixed caste divisions, ruled by the law of *karma*, may likewise be considered an example of Brahmanic organization.

With the requisite allowances for time and place, such as are normally made in the case of other ancient literatures, Greek, Latin, &c., all this mass of writings, except the more technical parts, is appreciable by humanity in general: much of it, for example, some hymns of the *Rig-Veda*, some passages in the *Upanishads* and the *Mahābhārata*, the life legend of Buddha and some texts such as the *Dhamma-pada*, have begun to be familiar to the general reader in Europe. The acceptability of Buddhist literature in general as religious scripture is, as regards central and eastern Asia, at least, established in history. It inculcates universal friendliness and compassion, selflessness, self-sacrifice, and a stringent morality. In its propagation among civilized and uncivilized races there must have been plentiful examples of the heroic self-devotion which the literature so extravagantly conceives; and even in late writings corrupted by superstitions there are often to be found, beside the large professions of altruism, residues of ordinary goodness and good sense. The philosophy of Buddhism may, like other philosophies, not be true; but its principles are still alive in the metaphysical debate. In regard to the Brahmanic philosophies, all of which (and especially the Sāmkhya) contain some striking conception or intuition, a certain propaganda value in Vedānta and Yoga ideas is evidenced by modern facts.

From about A.D. 300 we may date the beginning of the Classical Sanskrit literature, which is, in fact, what is commonly known as Sanskrit literature. It may be distinguished as the literature which is dominated by aesthetic aim and theory. In most cases the themes, whether of drama or of narrative poems, are derived from the old period, 'slices from the great feasts of Homer', and only the treatment is new. This literature has been described as Alexandrine, an expression which invites reflection. Why is it that, whereas the Alexandrine poetry holds so inferior a place in Greek literature, the Indian 'Alexandrines' include in their number the most admired literary figures, Kālidāsa, Bhavabhūti, Amaru, Bāna, Bhāravi, Māgha, and others? The answer may partly be that behind the Alexandrine technicians in poetry there was no national feeling, and that soon the Roman literature with its solid interest began to command the general attention; whereas the Indian poets were neither out of touch with the interests of their contemporaries nor dependent upon any foreign model. Moreover, the Classical literature of India corresponds not simply to the Alexandrine literature of Greece, but also to the Classical Attic. The distinctive feature on the side of India is the fact that the Indian writers worked in the consciousness of a doctrine of literary aesthetic, developing in intimate relation to their dominant philosophic tendencies. Perhaps everywhere the literary movement is controlled by semi-professional groups, whose innovations the amateurs follow, while the great writers absorb them. The technical movement is not to be underrated: given a favourable conjunction, a device which may have been somewhat coldly contrived may in some connexion evoke a strong aesthetic response. The idea of the ocean as the earth's garment was in India probably conceived by one of the old bards; it became in quite early times a tag; but Fitzgerald's *Omar Khayyam* is credited with sublimity in the expression

> the seas that mourn
> In flowing purple, of their lord forlorn.

Any Indian poet would have been capable of hundreds of such imaginations, because that concentrated meditation (*dhyāna*) whence they spring is a racial characteristic, derived from age-long discipline. Perhaps the grandest simile ever contrived in flattery of a king is to be seen in a verse of a late versifier, who says that his king 'has the grandeur of an opposite shore with the mountain heads (sc. all other kings) seen (reflected in the water) at his feet'. Such imaginations, which, as we see, may be put to poor uses, seem cheap in Indian poetry, because the 'striking' (*chitra*) is only one element in the structure, which must have a total aim. This aim is the evocation of a savour (*rasa*) in the soul of the cultivated critic, who with the aid of his natural sentiments (*bhāva*) and of the feelings, actions, and characters represented in the poem or drama is enabled to realize it. This 'savour' is of a supramundane, selfless character, akin to the innermost bliss of the impersonal soul. Its object is an ideal creation issuing from the poet's thought; for the poet, no less than Brahmā, is a creator of universes by his meditation. No wonder that he must submit himself to discipline and study and must have regard to times and seasons favourable to calm contemplation. The plain substantial sense, the qualities which give it a poetic body, the ornaments of sound and sense (alliteration, &c., simile, &c.) which lend it grace, the subtleties and indirectnesses of expression which surprise and kindle the intellect, are means to the realization of an unexpressed, inner meaning, which is the final object of aesthetic delight.

It is evident that this conception, which differs from the 'pleasure' view of common thought, from the inductive theories of expert critics, and from Aristotle's *katharsis* of ordinary emotions, must give rise to elaborate kinds of composition. It has not escaped criticism by Indians, some of whom admit natural poetry and poetry devoid of inner meaning: theoretically, it might be said, even though impossible in practice, the same meaning, whether presented as inner or as outer, should yield the same delight. But that the end has sometimes been thought to have been attained may be gathered from verses such as:

What poetry is that which should not stir the heart, as if it had drunk
    much wine,
Should not by force of its sentiment thrill the hair even of those with
    minds befogged by envy,
Make the head tremble, the cheeks redden, the eyes fill with tears,
Prop the voice intent on chanting out the imagined theme?

Besides working in the light of a somewhat metaphysical aesthetic theory and with the consciousness of an audience of expert competitors and sensitive critics, aware of the existence of such theory, the Sanskrit poet had to satisfy the demands of refinement and culture. There might be occasions when violent or gross expressions would be appropriate, but they would be special occasions. As to culture it is said that:

Thorough knowledge of metre, grammar, arts, the world, words and
    meanings,
A discrimination of suitable and unsuitable, this is culture.
At large what is there that it is not? In this world no matter, no ex-
    pression,
But may be an element in poetry. Hence this (culture) is omniscience.

And again:

If from one content with describing merely the describable, a stranger
    to deduction,
Without a mind made delicate by pondering over ornament, bereft
    of training by connoisseurs of poesy,
Should come a savourous poem, charming altogether,
Then from a crow's blackness might be made a king's white palace.

In a culture thus widely defined it is not necessary to single out particular departments; but normally it would, no doubt, include a number of *śāstras*, such as grammar, logic, rhetoric, politics, *ars amoris*, some appreciation of *yoga*, and a core of Vedantic world-theory.

The Indians were not at all unaware that in the end it is faculty (*śakti*), inspiration or fancy (*pratibhā*) that counts. It may be fostered by culture, but:

That wherethrough there is constantly in the concentrated mind a
    flashing of ideas in divers ways,
And unlaboured words present themselves, is faculty.

and such is the poet's power that:

Imprisoned, coerced at the outset to make them hand over,
How should they not promptly deliver the things they are charged
    with?
Like thieves, a deal softened in usage of master poets,
Words hastily render moreover belongings of others.

The coruscations of associated or secondary meanings (*ślesha*),

'touches' in passing, do indeed lend to the elaborate Sanskrit
stanza an unrivalled brilliance. They add to the point of a saying and accompany the whole with a similitude. It is not as
with the ordinary casual pun. As in the verse last quoted, where
indeed the actual mention of 'thieves' might have been suppressed, they cohere into one conception, and they must be
faultless to the last letter. 'What a Brāhman has written must
work out.' Pity only that in the less inspired works the double
meaning becomes an obsession, so that one writer chose to
epitomize in the same words the substance of the *Mahābhārata*
and the *Rāmāyana*.

Burdened with aesthetic theory, intricate metres, culture,
and technique, the poet's inspiration might well fail to generate
a perceptible 'savour'; or the reader, after comprising all the
intimations in a single idea, might be too exhausted to relish it.
This would infallibly be the case if the sentiment itself had been
weak or artificial; and, of course, that sometimes is the case.
No doubt the complex stanza is unsuitable for narrative poetry,
and the defect is enhanced if each stanza contains a witticism or
other intellectual point. But in the main the sentiment of the
Indian poet is not artificial or complex in the sense of nineteenth-
or twentieth-century civilization. Even his aesthetic theory,
much more his philosophic mysticism, has deep emotional
potency; if he nourishes devotion (*bhakti*) towards a personal
divinity, that is a consuming passion; in regard to external
nature he has a refined sensibility and a feeling of communion;
and the charms, graces, and wiles of women, without deceiving,
entirely fascinate him. The 'savours' are not all sweet, like the
erotic, compassionate, heroic; and others, such as the frightful
and the loathsome (beauty in disgust) and comic, may be posi-
tively helped by artful harshness or discords of syllables. The
tumult of a throng, a storm, suits the style no less than its opposite: description is in fact its forte, and nothing is finer than
Kālidāsa's verses on the ocean in the thirteenth canto of the

Raghu-vaṃśa or on the ascetic Śiva in the third of the *Kumāra-sambhava*. In speeches where argument, terseness, irony, fierceness, or cajoling are in place its finished manner is telling: and here Bhāravi and Māgha are especially strong.

Probably no literature is richer than the Sanskrit in what may be called anthology verse, whether erotic, gnomic, or devotional. The *Rig-Veda* and *Atharva-Veda* themselves may be regarded as anthologies; and next in time would be the Pali *Dhamma-pada* and *Sutta-nipāta*, which are collections of verses on Buddhist religion and morality arranged under heads, and the 'Songs of the Brothers' and 'Songs of the Sisters'. Probably the next, belonging to perhaps the third century A.D., might be the 'Seven Hundred of Hāla', a collection of artistic love-stanzas in Prakrit, ascribed in a large proportion of instances to named authors, real or fictitious. The later anthologies are also sometimes devoted to particular subjects: one of the last, the *Padyāvalī* of Rūpa Gosvāmin (16th century), consists of about 400 verses of extreme delicacy and charm, and even excessively sentimental devotion, concerning all incidents in the legendary life of Krishna. But the large general anthologies, some of them containing thousands of verses, are rather minutely divided under headings, descriptions of seasons, of the charms of women—in great detail—of the stages of love, of animals, natural objects (mountains, seas, &c.), of the ways of good and bad men and of various classes of mankind, morals, fate, misfortune, worldly wisdom, and satiric themes. Many of the treatises on poetics in general or particular branches thereof are in fact anthologies, being very copiously illustrated by quoted stanzas: though in some cases all the illustrations are composed by the author of the treatise.

Akin to the anthologies, in so far as consisting of isolated stanzas, are the centos of verses by a single author upon a particular subject, such as Amaru's verses on love, Bhartrihari's centos on love, prudence, and resignation, Śilhana's cento on quietude,

Chānakya's on prudence. Then there are the 'messenger' poems, whereof the most famous and original is Kālidāsa's 'Cloud Messenger'. General reflection or philosophy is the subject of a number of poems, such as the *Ātma-bodha*, 'Awakening to the Self', and *Moha-mudgara*, 'Hammer of Delusion', ascribed to Śamkara, and a number of others. The *stotras*, or hymns to divinities, in various degree of artistic quality, are beyond counting, some of them, like the hymn to the sun by Mayūra, that to the Goddess Chandī by Bāna, the *Ānanda-laharī* ascribed to Śamkara, and the Buddhist hymn to Lokeśvara, being of a highly elaborate artistry. In the latest period of pre-Islamic Bengal, at the court of King Lakshmanasena, lived the poet Jayadēva, author of the *Gīta-govinda*, a long hymn of phenomenal metrical skill and melody in praise of Krishna.

Many of the gems of the anthologies are extracted from plays, where they are adroitly inserted to serve for the choice expression of a sentiment, the description of a scene, or a summary report of an incident. The same occurs in prose narratives; and there is indeed a form of narrative composition, called *Champū*, which is *ex professo* a mixture of prose and verse. The insertion of verses in prose writings is indeed a very ancient mode in Sanskrit, since it is exemplified in the oldest *Brāhmanas* and copiously exhibited in the canonical literature of the Jains and Buddhists, and to a certain extent in the Pāli *Jātaka* book and in the Buddhist Sanskrit hagiographies, and in collections of Hindu tales such as 'Vikrama's Adventures' and the 'Seventy Stories of a Parrot'. But the most famous example is the collection of (chiefly) animal stories with a moral, which in the Middle Ages found its way in various disguises, through the Pahlavī, Arabic, Hebrew, and Syriac, into all the chief European languages—it was also represented by versions in languages of southern India and the Malay Islands, Further India, and the Far East. This *Pañchatantra*, known in English as 'The Fables of Pilpay', is in its oldest recension the original and strongest form of the book. But a tenth-century recast of it, the *Hito-padeśa* or 'Friend's Counsel', has been more familiar in India, a preference which it merits by the perfect fitting of its prose style to the matter and the very rich addition of accomplished, sententious, and witty verse.

We have thus lightly indicated the chief occasions for employment of the Sanskrit artistic or artificial style of verse. It may be said that, wherever there is a point to be made, whether amatory, devotional, ethical, emotional, or reflective, there this characteristic Sanskrit form of composition is effective; and such is its intellectual charm that scholars too deeply imbued with it are apt to find all other verse inane or require to be recalled to the appreciation of the unrivalled clarity and dignity of the Greek, or the less schooled quality of modern European poetry. It may be said that in amount of 'cleverness per square inch' no poetry surpasses the Sanskrit *kāvya*; but of course some finenesses of atmosphere may escape. The Greek and Latin anthologies, if somewhat liberally furnished with double meanings and with similes, &c., explicit or implied, might convey a fair idea of the Sanskrit *kāvya*. But they would not furnish many examples to match the more trifling and (in most cases) rather late experiments such as the diagrammatic verses (known in Europe in the Middle Ages), specimens of which are found even in the 'great *kāvyas*' of Bhāravi (*Kirātārjunīya*, 6th century A.D.) and Māgha (*Śiśupāla-vadha*, 8th century); or the 'backwards poems', wherein each line can be read backwards, thus celebrating at once both Rāma and Krishna; or the rhyme (*yamaka*) poems, wherein each stanza may have four lines ending with the same four or five syllables taken in varying senses; or verses which can be read in more than one dialect (Sanskrit and Prakrit) or contain mixtures of dialect.

It should be added that the notion of *kāvya* extends to ornate prose, where double meanings are plentiful, and that here also we have examples of eccentric feats of language, as in the *Vāsavadatta* of Subandhu (6th century A.D.), where elaborate descriptions are strung upon a thin trickle of narrative with, as the author professes, double meaning in each syllable; or as in the seventh chapter of Dandin's 'Story of the Ten Princes' (7th century), wherein the narrator, whose lips have been cut off, evades the use of all labial consonants.

Most of the works to which we have been referring belong to the class of short or minor poems. Some of them may be regarded as lighter efforts or mere *tours de force*; but among them are some of the most exquisite products of Indian poetic observation and reflection. When we turn to the 'great *kāvyas*', there can be no doubt of the seriousness of the poet's intent. They are for the most part narrative, and their subjects may be either heroic, as in Kālidāsa's 'Story of the Raghu Lineage' (*Raghu-vamśa*), Bhāravi's 'Kirāta and Arjuna', and the Prakrit '[Rāma's] Bridge' (*Setu-bandha*, 6th century); or biographical, as Śri-Harsha's 'Story of Nala' (*Naiṣadha-charita*, 12th century, containing much poetry, though denounced for its 'faults'), and not a few others of far inferior celebrity: Kālidāsa's 'Birth of the War God' (*Kumāra-sambhava*) is a story of the dread god Śiva's austerities, and his wedding, nevertheless, to the daughter of the Himālaya. The incidents are descriptions of persons, cities, country scenes, battles and fights (miraculous and unconvincing), journeys, embassies, and well-pointed discussions and deliberations. As in the *Faerie Queene*, the stanza form is an impediment, and it encourages unrealistic conceits, as when in the *Raghu-vamśa* two warriors, mutually slain, are instantly transported to Paradise, where, unconscious of what has just happened to them, they mechanically essay to continue the combat. The subjects are usually taken from the old epics. In the poem of Bhāravi there is an energy and gravity which, joined to the classical perfection of its form, cannot fail to impress. In that of Māgha, said to have been composed with a definite intention of surpassing Bhāravi, there is less force, but even more technical skill; so that the Indian critics held that:

> For simile Kālidāsa; for weight of meaning Bhāravi;
> The Naiṣadha for lilt of words: in Māgha are all three qualities.

The ideal Sanskrit poet, however, is beyond question Kālidāsa (4th–5th century A.D.). Figuring rather early in the long relay competition of the poets and the theorists (he, too, is credited with the composition of an *Ars Poetica*), he is in style hardly more artificial than Virgil. He has not the penchant for over-elaborate expression, for assonances, plays on words and verse jingles. There are smartnesses indeed, such as that noticed above, and some references to linguistic and other sciences (the latter not out of place), and even some plays upon words, though imperfect, like those in European literature, in comparison with the exactness and completeness of the Indian. The qualities of delicacy, freshness, and ripeness of sentiment which Goethe recognized in the play *Śakuntalā*, when first made known by Sir William Jones's translation, are in part a general property of the Sanskrit drama, a matter of oriental courtesy and pithiness of speech. But in their degree they are characteristic of Kālidāsa. His superiority is in refinement, moderation, and reserve. Kālidāsa was a supreme literateur and probably of a highly critical sensitiveness; but his criticism takes the form of avoidance of faults into which others may have fallen. Indian stories ascribe to him, perhaps with true instinct, a certain roguishness and a touch of kindly malice. But the domestic sentiment in the *Megha-dūta* and the wide humanity of the *Śakuntalā* are equally of his essence. A degree of national outlook may be seen in the subjects of his *Raghu-vaṃśa*, 'History of India's Ancient Solar Race', and his *Megha-dūta*, a bird's-eye view of a flight over some of its most impressive or legendary scenes. In the 'Birth of the War God' the asceticism of Śiva is a sort of epic of the Indian spiritual philosophy and religion in its heroic struggle of intellect against passion: the fourth canto, the 'Lament of the lady Dalliance', when in place of her husband, the Flower-god, consumed by Śiva's glance of fire, she finds only a man-shaped heap of ashes, is among the most keenly appreciated expressions of Hindu sentiment. The story can be capped only by the sublime insouciance of a later poet, Rājaśekhara (9th century), akin in nature to Kālidāsa, but of a somewhat more flippant mood, who commences one of his plays with a choice invocatory couplet in these terms:

> In vain the grim god's odd-eyed glare
> Shot fire: Love's ashen frame,
> Maids! at your light glance debonair
> Lives. Ye my homage claim.

It is possible that the *Megha-dūta* may, despite the charming descriptions of sacred scenes and the happy domesticities of Part II, extort the European reader's admiration rather than touch his heart. He may not realize that the Indian poet looked out upon a world of nature which was not just nature or a creation of 'God', but a field of action of many divine powers approachable by human sympathies and thronged with associations which were not mere mythology. When Kālidāsa describes the Himālaya as the 'massed laughter' of Śiva, the reader may manage to imagine that stretch of great white teeth; but the full idea may still escape him, unless he has realized the figure of the grand Ascete, eternally enthroned in the towering mountain world, where the Ganges in her descent from heaven passes through his matted locks, with the moon their crest-jewel. The same grandiose imagination, well within the reach of other Sanskrit poets, appears in the opening verse of the *Kumāra-sambhava* referring to the Himālaya as 'standing with its extremities plunged in the eastern and western oceans, like a measuring rod over the earth'.

Chronologically somewhat posterior to Kālidāsa, the Prakrit 'Bridge-building' poem of Pravarasena displays much skill in poetic description and much metrical accomplishment. The same may be said of another poem relating to Rāma's conquest of Ceylon, the 'Rape of Janaka's Daughter' (*Jānakī-harana*, 6th century), by the Sinhalese king Kumāradāsa, which, however, is lacking in strength. Concerning the other *kāvya* epics mentioned above no more need be said, except that the 'Slaying of Rāvana' by Bhatti, though composed as a grammatical treatise for the confusion of the dullards, is also respectable poetry. One epic in Prakrit, the 'Slaying of the Gauda (Bengal King)' (*Gauda-vaho* by Vākpatirāja, 8th century), has a historical subject. There are numerous other *kāvya* epics of various dates, and some have been composed in this twentieth century.

Of the prose *kāvyas* the most outstanding are the 'Life of Harsha' (*Harsha-charita*) and the *Kādambarī* of Bāna (7th century), the greatest master of the Sanskrit language. In the case of this writer the punning Euphuistic style is combined with an originality of matter and a fertility of idea and truth of sentiment which reduce it to the status of an embellishment. The 'Life of Harsha' has great importance both as a historical document and also by reason of its vivid descriptions, which at many points light up the life and psychology of the time. Its avowed idea is to combine new matter, cultured style, vivid 'savour', and striking sound. The very long and complicated sentences give pause to the reader; but there is a feast for those who can linger over the rich texture of fancy and wit. In the *Kādambarī*, similar in style, but without historical limitations, the author, free to indulge in an ideal creation, has composed a divine story, left indeed by him unfinished, but by his son succinctly and not unadroitly wound up.

The *kāvya* style, which is proper to high poetry and has been employed in countless dedicatory and laudatory poems (*pra-śasti*) and in the more elaborate inscriptions and donative deeds, is not exclusively dominant in Sanskrit verse. The plain style, descended from the *Mahābhārata*, is usual in all verse composition where the main interest attaches to the matter; in the very numerous *Purānas*, containing the Hindu religious cosmologies, histories, tales, legends of sacred places, festivals, and so forth; in the associated *mahātmyas*, celebrating the virtues of particular districts, shrines, festivals, &c.; and in countless treatises on scientific and practical matters of all kinds. Perhaps the most important compositions of this kind are the astronomical work, *Brihat-samhitā* of Varāha-mihira (6th century); the dictionary, *Amara-kośa*, of Amara (7th century?); the 'Ocean of the Rivers of Stories' (*Kathā-sarit-sāgara*, 11th century) by Somadeva of Kashmir, a most deft narrator; the 'River of Kings' (*Rāja-tarangini*, 12th century), Kalhana's history of Kashmir; the chief architectural text, the *Māna-sāra*, in 'bad' Sanskrit; and numerous Jain and other religious biographies and tales. But the extent of such literature is beyond recounting: it only remains to add that some works of this kind, for example the epitomes of the *Mahābhārata* and *Rāmāyana* by Kshemendra (11th century) and parts of the *Bhāgavata-purāna* have a more ambitious style, with an infusion of *kāvya* ornament; while in works on logic and philosophy the verse becomes crabbed through a striving for extreme precision and terseness.

Of dramatic representations some elementary forms reach back into Vedic times. The literary drama, which is represented by hundreds of surviving plays, commences with some fragments of Buddhist dramas by the great poet Aśvaghosha, one of them, notably enough, a 'morality' with virtues and other abstractions for dramatis personae. Already there is distinction of dialect, only high personages using Sanskrit. When we come to the first treatise on the theatre and dramatic art, the *Nātya-śāstra* of Bhārata (2nd or 3rd century A.D.?), we find already a complete theory of the spectator's aesthetic experience and a classification of plays into the ten kinds (*daśa-rūpa*) usually recognized in later times, though with many sub-species. Several of these kinds are not represented by any known early example. Some are one-act plays, exhibiting, for instance,

an embassy at court or a combat. The differences are in part
dependent on the matter or are in other ways unessential. The
principal species (*nātaka*) is that which has some famous ancient
king as hero. There is no tragedy—in fact a real tragedy is
hardly, according to Indian ideas, possible; but there are species
which are professedly comedies or farces. Practically the chief
kinds are (1) those in which there is a royal amour involving some
political or dynastic matter—examples, Kālidāsa's *Śākuntala*,
Harsha-deva's *Vāsavadatta*, Bhavabhūti's *Uttara-Rāma-charita*;
(2) the purely political or warlike—examples, Visākhadatta's
Mudrā-Rākshasa (4th century?), Bhatta-Nārāyana's *Veṇī-sam-
hāra* (8th century); (3) the ordinary romantic drama with fictitious persons—examples, Śūdraka's *Mrichchhakatika*, Bhavabhūti's *Mālatī-Mādhava*, Rājaśekhara's *Karpūra-manjarī* and
Viddha-sālabhanjika; (4) allegorical plays with abstract or religious ideas for dramatis personae—examples, the above-noted
fragment by Aśvaghosha, Krishna-Miśra's *Prabodha-chandrodaya*
(11th century); (5) other plays dealing with philosophic or other
ideas—examples, Harsha-deva's *Nāgānanda*, Chandragomin's
Lokānanda (*c.* A.D. 600), Bodhāyana's *Bhagavad-Ajjukīya*; (6)
the farce (*prahasana*)—example, the *Lataka-melaka* of Śankha-
dhara (12th century); (7) the monologue (*bhāna*), generally
humorous, wherein a single person maintains a quasi-dialogue,
addressing others who do not appear and quoting their replies
after a 'What say you?' Special developments are (8) the pup-
pet-play and (9) the shadow play—example, the *Dūtāngada* of
Subhata (13th century); (10) the *Mahā-nātaka* (8th–9th century?), a very long play consisting solely of verses, many of them
being cited from other works, so that the *whole* is largely of the
nature of a cento and is exclusively in verse.

In the language of the plays the most obviously striking feature,
found even in the earliest, is the mixture of dialects. This
feature is partly analogous to the natural use of local or vulgar
forms of speech in the mouths of uncultured persons and partly

to that of Doric and Aeolic in certain parts of Greek plays: as in the latter case, certain dialects had become standard for certain literary forms—thus one of the Prakrit dialects was preferred to another for metrical use. The system of Indian society also favoured linguistic stratification in various ways. In the drama the main outcome is that Sanskrit is employed only by men of high status and by religious personages, while women, even queens, share one kind of Prakrit with ordinary characters and others are employed by inferior or special classes. There are, however, some late dramas which are wholly in Sanskrit, and certain kinds of plays are in Prakrit alone. A second notable feature, insertion of verse stanzas, has been already mentioned: here we need only add that in some instances the plays are rather richly bespangled with such verses, and the dramas have supplied some of the choicest and most famous gems in the anthologies. The prose is in most plays (but not in those of Bhavabhūti, for instance) of a clear and simple character, and the reader needs only to be reminded that it is economic and intended to be meaningful, the speech of a society quick to see points.

Scholarly drama is plentiful in Sanskrit literature, and such plays are still produced. Perhaps the best representative is the *Anargha-Rāghava* of Murāri (11th century?), a Rāma play of excellent style and force. Among those of outstanding general interest the first place belongs to Kālidāsa's famous *Śakuntalā*, of unrivalled naturalness, dignity, and delicacy, with touches of generous human feeling and deep reflection breaking through its finesse. Its many oft-quoted verses include that concerning the hermit's daughter which runs:

> The flower unsmelled, the leaf unplucked of hand,
> The gem unset, honeys that unsipped stand,
> The undiminished fruit of well done duty;
> Yea, even her stainless beauty:
> Ah! what enjoyer shall these joys demand?[1]

[1] Reproduced by kind permission from *Chosen Poems*, by Mr. Douglas Ainslie.

Second in rank among the dramatists is Bhavabhūti, a master of Sanskrit and a romanticist of gorgeous and exuberant (alas! too exuberant) imagination. The marvellous political astuteness of the *Mudrā-Rākshasa*, the varied social interest of the *Mrich-chhakatika*, the ethical and philosophic interest of the *Prabodhachandrodaya*, some early *bhānas*, with their stories of rakes, show that pre-Muhammadan India—like eighteenth-century Europe—could appreciate escapades of spirited youth. The poet Bāna's patron, Harsha-deva, most fortunate of emperors and most famous of royal authors, has to his name two plays of widely different success: the *Vāsavadatta*, a story of a royal amour with political implications, is unoriginal in subject, but remarkably neat in construction and dialogue and contains many familiar verses; in translations it is known on the European stage. It may be called the most workman-like Indian play: what it lacks is depth of feeling. The *Nāgānanda*, famous throughout the northern Buddhist world, is saved from that failing by the glow of Buddhist altruistic self-sacrifice. In southern India there has survived a class of professional actors, called *Chākyārs*, who have in their traditional repertoires a number of old plays or parts of plays; and to them probably is due the preservation of some dramas of remarkable freshness and force and of early style and language, with subjects largely taken from the *Mahābhārata*. One of them, the 'Dream Princess' (*Svapna-Vāsavadatta*), a play of considerable power, is certainly a recension of a famous work of Bhāsa, predecessor of Kālidāsa, and most of the others have features favourable to their recognition as 'plays of Bhāsa'. In Bengal a form of popular representation called *yātrā*, connected with the worship of Krishna and including representation of scenes and chorus singing, has continued into modern times.

Outside the drama the simpler prose style is found chiefly in collections of stories, which are either purely fictitious, such as Dandin's 'Story of the Ten Princes' (*Daśa-kumāra-charita*,

7th century?), 'The Twenty-five Stories of a Vampire' (*Vetāla-pancha-vimśatika*), 'The Seventy Tales of a Parrot' (*Śuka-saptati*), or anecdotes relating to celebrated persons, such as Merutunga's 'Wishing-stone of Narratives' (*Prabandha-chintā-mani*), or Ballāla's 'Court of [King] Bhoja' (*Bhoja-prabandha*). The vast literature of commentaries also, philological, legal, &c., is of fairly easy comprehension. The philosophic style is charac-terized by increasing rigidity, and concentrated attention is necessary in order to avoid missing the point. Hence few philoso-phical works in Sanskrit prose are suited, even in translation, for the non-technical reader, who has, however, in the *Vedānta-sāra* of Sadānanda an excellent introduction to the Vedānta system. Some philosophico-ethical compositions in verse, such as the 'Self's-awakening' (*Ātma-bodha*) and 'Delusion-hammer' (*Moha-mudgara*) ascribed to Śamkara, have a popular effectiveness.

The Indian Buddhist literature of the Classical period was at first mainly of a dogmatic, philosophical, and logical character, the Mahāyāna *sūtras* being for the most part earlier: to logical theory, in fact, very important contributions are associated with the names of the two divines, Dignāga and Dharmakīrti, and profound metaphysical doctrines are developed in the works of Ārya-Deva, Asanga, Vasubandhu, Chandrakīrti, and others. There are very numerous works of more general religious edifi-cation, especially *Avadānas* (Hagiographa in prose and verses) such as the *Divyāvadāna*. Some of these, however (e.g. the *Avadāna-śataka* and *Karma-śataka*) are of earlier date: a late work in rather ornate Sanskrit verse is the *Avadāna-kalpa-latā* of Kshemendra (11th century). A very pleasing work, full of quotations from the older literature, is the 'Compendium of Teachings' (*Śikshā-samuchchaya*) of Śāntideva. All these expound or illustrate the heroic self-sacrifice and noble altruistic ethics of Buddhism in a way which can be appreciated in translation. But the gem of all such literature is unquestionably the 'Jātaka-Garland' (*Jātaka-mālā*), an ornate rechauffé of thirty-four birth-stories, by Ārya-Śūra (3rd–4th century A.D.), a poet whose mastery of metre, combined with a rich flow of idea and sentiment, fully entitle him to be named in company with Aśvaghosha. The later Buddhist Sanskrit literature of India was a welter of Tantric and Yogic mysticism, which after its expiry (11th–12th century) in the country of its origin continued its existence in Nepal and Tibet.

Jainism, on the other hand, has preserved down to the present time its integrity as a separate world in the midst of Hinduism. In addition to a vast output of commentaries upon its canonical texts, of dogmatic exposition and works of edification, it has developed its own metaphysics, cosmology, logic, and grammar and also its own expositions of the several sciences. Dogmatic or controversial works on special matters of philosophy or conduct (often in verse) are extremely numerous. Hymnology and poetry of reflection or exhortation are also very abundant. There has been a certain tendency to appropriate the titles of famous Hindu works: there is a *Jaina-Mahābhārata*, a *Jaina-Rāmāyana*, a *Jaina-Purāna*; but the matter is independent or widely different, the Jains having their own perspective of early history. In narrative literature, both prose and verse, Jainism is extremely rich, and it has overflowed from Sanskrit and Prakrit into vernacular languages, especially Gujarātī and Kanarese: in the case of the latter language, indeed, it would appear as if the bulk of the old literature has been contributed by the Jains. The Jaina Sanskrit has some idiosyncrasies, especially in vocabulary, and its own tradition; but its styles are the same as those of the Classical Sanskrit, and some of its poetical biographies have the ornate quality of the *kāvya*. While thus the Jaina community has provided itself with a complete substitute for the literature of the Hindus, it has not altogether eschewed the study of the latter, and many commentaries on famous works, and editions of some of them, are the work of Jain authors. The great intellectual power and high ethic of the Jain literature as a whole would have a stronger appeal but for the unremitting earnestness of its dogmatic aim.

It is not possible here to give even the briefest account of the literatures in modern Indo-Āryan languages. The old war-ballads, songs, and legends, which are especially abundant in the Hindī-Rājputānī area, in Gujarātī and Panjābī (*Hīr and Ranjhā, Rājā Rasālu,* &c.), seem to have been purveyed mainly by professional classes, *chārans, bhats, yogis,* &c., descendants of the original creators of them, but no longer themselves productive. Most of the popularly known poetry consists of religious songs by celebrated authors, Chandīdās (14th century) in Bengal, Vidyāpati (15th century) in Mithilā, Kabīr (15th century), and Mīrā Bāī (15th century) in Hindi, Nāmdēv (13th century) and Tukārām (17th century) in Marāthī, Narsingh Mehta (15th century) in Gujarāt, Lallā (14th century) in Kashmir, all with many successors. Most of the languages boast of old versions of the *Mahābhārata* and *Rāmāyana*; and from about the fifteenth century they become more and more dominated by the Sanskrit and add more and more adaptations of Sanskrit works, generally in artificial style. The most important works of a more independent character are the Sikh bible, the *Granth* (parts of which are in Hindī and Marāthī, 16th–17th century), and the *Rāmāyana* of Tulasī Dās (16th–17th century), which has been described as 'the bible of modern India'. Collected 'Lives of Saints' (*Bhakta-mālā*), belonging to various sects and with various titles, exist in several languages. In the Punjab and Sindh Persian competes with Sanskrit for influence on the vernacular. Historical works (*buranjis*) exist in Assam from the fourteenth (?) century, and Marāthī has many unpublished prose *bakhars*, narratives of events belonging to the times of the Marātha wars and ruling houses.

Much of what has been said concerning the Indo-Āryan languages applies also to the Dravidian languages of southern India. They all abound in adaptations or translations of

Sanskrit works, and the literatures are also preponderatingly religious. Kanarese, Telugu, and Tamil probably all commenced with a Jain (in the case of Tamil also Buddhist) period; and in the first of them Jain influence was predominant until about the sixteenth century, being followed by the Lingayat (Śivaite) and Vaishnava. In the Tamil and Telugu country Jainism succumbed to persecution in the tenth and eleventh centuries, and it is little represented in the literatures. In all three languages there are important old adaptations of the *Mahābhārata* and *Rāmāyana*, and, later, of works of classical Sanskrit. A Telugu catalogue looks, indeed, like a list of Sanskrit books. Nevertheless the three Dravidian literatures are older and more important than the Indo-Āryan vernaculars. They have their classical and modern stages; the earliest Kanarese literary work, the 'Poets' Highway' (*Kavi-rāja-mārga*, 9th century) names many old poets, and the Telugu of the eleventh century has reminiscences of earlier, perhaps Buddhist, popular writings; while in the case of the Tamil it is a question whether such works as the *Nāladiyār* and the *Mani-mekhalai* go back to the second or the fifth or the seventh century. The languages have early prose—in Telugu and Kanarese the *champū* mixture of prose and verse is favoured—and also important works on grammar. Moreover, the adaptations of Sanskrit works are more fused with south-Indian materials. There is also in Telugu (cantos by Vemana, 15th century, and others) and Tamil (*Nāladiyār*, *Kural* of Tiru-Valluvar, and Manikka-Vachakar's works) an abundance of original ethico-religious gnomic poetry, and also a fair quantity of secular tales. The Tamil is undoubtedly, next to the Sanskrit, the greatest Indian literature. After the earliest works its pride is in its two great collections of the works of its Śaiva and Vaishnava devotees, the *Tiru-Murai* and *Nālāyira-prabandham* (11th century), and in the hagiographa concerning the authors. The note of this Tamil hymnology is all-renouncing, enthusiastic devotion to the chosen divinity, Śiva or Vishnu; the poetic style is more elaborate even than that of the Sanskrit. The Tamils are conscious of the value of their literary inheritance, and they maintain a tradition of its regulation from very remote periods by successive 'Academies' sitting in judgement at Madurā, which is still the great centre of Tamil studies.

It is hardly necessary to state that all the vernacular languages, being associated with an old culture, are rich in proverbs and maxims, whereof many collections have been published, and that they are all now engaged upon the task of creating a new literature, periodical and other, on modern lines, and elaborating the necessary lexicographical aids. In the former process the Bengālī, which, as is well known, has made great advances, serves in some degree as a model for the rest.

The intellectual heritage of India has been shared in part with other countries. As regards the west there are still obscure possibilities in the case of some Pythagorean doctrines. The acknowledged Indian ideas brought to Greece in consequence of Alexander's invasion and of the relations between the Seleucids and the Mauryan Empire comprise nothing precise. The distinction between Brāhmans and Sramanas, i.e. Jain, Buddhist, and other ascetics, is indeed clearly drawn; but the celebrated colloquy of Alexander with the ascetic Dandamis, though containing, no doubt, a core of fact, is in its expanded versions nothing but a sermon. The Greeks of Bactria, when (2nd century B.C.) their dominion extended over considerable parts of northern India (as far east as Mathurā), must have had an intimate knowledge of the country, as is implied in the 'Questions of King Milinda'. But in pagan writers we find no evidence of transmission of information bearing upon ideas. In Christian legend there are some items (Barlaam and Joasaph, St. Christopher, St. Eutychius, St. Hubert) of demonstrably Buddhist origin. Some ray from the East is visible in the reference by the Church writer Hippolytus to βραχμᾶνες who τὸν θεὸν φῶς εἶναι λέγουσιν and the tract of Palladius *Concerning the Races of India and the Brāhmans* adduces some new matters of fact. But the whole question of Buddhist contributions to the Christian atmosphere is still altogether obscure. Buddhist communications with the West were initiated by Aśoka about the middle of the third century B.C., Christian missions to India (the Indus region, Malabar, and the Coromandel) in the first century A.D.: in the sixth century A.D. there was a Christian bishop in Ceylon. Buddhism has not yet been traced in the Parthian Empire; but later, when there was a Christian bishop of Herat, and still later, when Transoxiana became largely Christian, and finally when, in the seventh century, Christianity crossed the Pāmīr and entered into competition with Buddhism (also with Zoroastrianism and Manichaeism) in Chinese Turkestan and China itself, the sharp separation of rival religions cannot have excluded mutual influences. Whether the Christian asceticism and gnosticism in Egypt owed anything to Buddhist inspiration is another matter. After the long interruption due to the rise of Islam in the Near East and its ultimate adoption by the Central Asian Turks the Mongol conquests reopened communications with middle Asia; but beyond the settlement of Buddhist Kalmucks in Europe they do not seem to have conveyed anything Indian. Through Islamic intervention came the 'Fables of Pilpay' and the Indian system of number-ciphers and the game of chess: if the Arabic work of Al-Bīrūnī had been known in Europe, it would have transmitted a large amount of accurate information. Some slight notices of Indian usages, beliefs, and languages are contained in the works of Marco Polo and other overland travellers from Europe; but a real acquaintance with languages, including even, to a slight extent, the Sanskrit, commenced with the Portuguese missionaries of the sixteenth century. In the last quarter of that century the English Jesuit, Thomas Stephens, possibly the first Englishman to visit India, wrote a grammar of the Konkanī-Marāthī language and composed a Christian poem under the title *Krista-Purāna*, which is a classic of that speech. Early in the seventeenth century Father Roberto de Nobili, an Italian Jesuit, with a view to conversions among the Brāhmans of Madurā, adopted the title and some of the usages of an Indian *sannyāsī*, for which proceeding he was indicted, but ultimately, on papal authority, exculpated. He acquired an intimate knowledge of the Tamil, Telugu, and Sanskrit languages and literatures and both conversed familiarly and composed in all three. The later stages of European knowledge of Indian literature having often been recorded, we need notice only the fact that a second European Jesuit, Father Beschi, has the distinction of having contributed to an Indian language, the Tamil, a Christian work, *Tembāvani*, which ranks as a classic.

Whether in Transoxiana and Persia during Parthian and Sassanian times Buddhism ever obtained a real foothold is (except as regard Seistan) wholly unknown: in the seventh century A.D. these countries seem to have been practically without Buddhist establishments. But in Afghanistan, Balkh, and all the Pāmīr countries the Buddhist religion prevailed at least until the coming of Islam in the eighth century A.D.

In Chinese Turkestan the state of Khotan is said to have been founded with a partly Indian population in the third century B.C. But the Buddhist Indian civilization, which, with little rivalry on the part of Zoroastrianism, Manichaeism, and Christianity, dominated that state and all its neighbours until about A.D. 1000, arrived perhaps about the beginning of the Christian era. The religion made its way later also among the Turks, who became overlords of the country at about the middle of the sixth century A.D.: the Uigur kingdom of the ninth and tenth centuries was officially Buddhist, and in the Turfan region the religion persisted into Mongol times.

In the countries which have been mentioned the presence of the Buddhist or Hindu religion implied, no doubt—in Ceylon,

Further India, the Malay Islands, and Chinese Turkestan certainly—a preponderance of Indian ideas in administration and
in the culture of the upper classes. In Tibet, which received
Buddhism in the seventh century A.D. and which in about the
thirteenth century became a mainly ecclesiastical state, the
intellectual and monastic life has been wholly Buddhist; but
the social usages, except in matter of diet, have not been greatly
influenced either by India or by China. The same may be said of
Mongolia, which in the fourteenth century derived its Buddhism
from Tibet. China itself, which had in the first century A.D.
its first contact with Buddhism and which in the course of centuries acquired some acquaintance with Indian ideas and literature not specially Buddhist, was too great an empire and too
deeply rooted in its ancient culture to be seriously affected even
by the masses of Buddhist literature which it acquired or the
millions of Buddhists included in its vast population, especially
on its western side: only by way of imperial patronage at certain
periods or in the vague general circulation of ideas has India at
all affected the Chinese system of life. Japan received in the
sixth and seventh centuries A.D. a Buddhism chiefly derived
from China; it has been, no doubt, far more affected by the
spirit of the Indian religion, which inspired its famous Bushido
chivalry: its scholars are now among the most competent in-
vestigators of early Indian Buddhist literature, and its missionaries in the Far East are the chief propagandists of the faith.
Thus a legacy of Indian thought and literature, extending in a
measure outside the limits of Buddhism itself, is still functioning
throughout the greatest part of Central Asia and the Far East,
though in certain areas where it was once active, namely in Java
and Sumatra, in Chinese Turkestan and the regions to the west
thereof, it has long been obliterated by Islam. When the
Buddhist scholarship of China, Tibet and Mongolia, Burma,
Siam, Ceylon shall have attained to the level of modern philological competence which has already been reached by Japan,

the interest in the ancient Indian origins and history of Buddhism will have an impressive momentum in the intellectual life of the civilized world.

India itself, where the Buddhist tradition has been since the twelfth century A.D. almost completely lost, has inherited many others. Those which at different periods entered its confines in a form already mature and have preserved their separate individuality, Christian, Zoroastrian, Islamic, Modern European, may be regarded as unessential, though to some of them (for instance, to Christianity in relation to south Indian monotheism and to Islam in relation to Kabīr and the origin of the Sikh religion) certain influences may be attributed. The remainder may be regarded as Indo-Āryan; for, though the Dravidians may have made very important contributions to developments in Indian literature, philosophy, and art, only in vague general terms would it be possible to indicate elements in them which are free from Indo-Āryan inspiration. Is there anything, apart from primitive culture, which is pre-Āryan? Until the last decade the question might have seemed fanciful. But it is now known that the Āryan immigrants (*c.* 2000 B.C. ?) found in the Punjab and Sindh at least a culture superior to their own. Accordingly the progress of Indo-Āryan civilization may have been conditioned not only by racial mixture with the aborigines, but also by cultural factors present from the beginning. Only the Vedic hymns, whose line of tradition comes into India with the Āryans, can be confidently regarded as practically unaffected by such fusion.

At the end of the eighteenth century the educated Hindus retained the tradition of the Classical Sanskrit literature. The poetry, the drama, the literary theories, and the six orthodox philosophies could still be appreciated by them, and manuals and commentaries continued to be produced. The Āyurvedic medicine and the procedures of the architect and image-maker, the designer of horoscopes and almanacs were based on literary works. The stories of the *Mahābhārata* and *Rāmāyana* and the chief Puranic and sectarian legends were familiar to the population in general through oral readings, festivals, and temple celebrations. The old poetry in the modern languages seems likewise to have been orally known, and Madurā seems to have still been a centre of Tamil as well as of Sanskrit learning. In various parts of the country there were seminaries or residences (*matha, pītha*), head-quarters of the traditions of sects or schools of Vedānta philosophy; and there were some famous centres of pandit learning, e.g. Benares for all studies and Nadiyā in Bengal predominantly for logic. For Vedic studies there remained numerous small endowments (land-grants, *agra-hāras*), survivals from the lavish donations of earlier centuries for maintenance of studies and rituals; but the studies were hardly more than memorizing of texts not understood and the rituals of no interest to any one except the professionals. Ram Mohun Rāy (1774–1833) and his friends rediscovered the *Upanishads*, usually known only by citations in Vedānta books: in the *Upanishads* they seemed to find a pure original inspiration which might redeem the corrupt Purānic Hinduism of their time. During the fourth quarter of the nineteenth century, when the older parts of the *Veda* had been brought into prominence by the work of scholars, Dayānanda Sarasvatī sought in the hymns evidence of an ideal Āryan society which had not yet endured the yoke of caste. At the end of the same century the Vedānta philosophy and the Yoga practices began to be subjects of propaganda even outside India. During the present century some portions of the old theoretical literature, the political conceptions, the aesthetic theories, and even the physical sciences have been recalled with an interest which is more than editorial; and the significance of Buddhism and the reputation of Indian philosophy are realized as matter of national concern.

Philological study of Sanskrit and other old Indian literature on modern lines is organized by professorships and curricula in the colleges and universities: many of the teachers have returned with degrees from European and American universities, or have been trained by those so equipped. The number of editions, treatises, and theses published in Indian by such scholars is probably greater than in all other countries together. An attempt is made in the chief universities also to maintain a bridge between this modern scholarship and the old pandit learning, which is on the wane. Sanskrit holds accordingly in Indian education a position similar to that of the Greek and Latin Classics in Europe. The chief vernacular languages also have acquired in periodical and other current literature a fixed form, and scholarship is applied to publication of their old texts.

Modern Europeanism in India is apt, with the young, to lack respect for the old literature, philosophies, and religion, and to join in a 'flight from the past'. The older men, it is said, not infrequently revert. The deep concern which India has in the literary record of its ideas and tastes is all the more pervading by reason of unbroken linguistic continuity. Unlike the peoples of Europe, whose cultural and religious origins have to be traced across great linguistic barriers to partly diverse sources, the Indo-Āryan finds most strands of speech and usage leading back to the Sanskrit and Vedic alone, as French, Italian, Spanish, and Portuguese lead back to Latin: even the Dravidian languages are as replete with Sanskrit elements of all periods as is the English with Latin and Greek. Hence all inherited prepossessions find their satisfaction in the Sanskrit, and a general continuity is likely to be maintained. But it seems doubtful whether, apart from aesthetic pleasure, historical enlightenment, acquaintance with particular striking ideas which may be found in all departments of the literature, and a justifiable pride in a great intellectual life continued during more than three thousand years, the India of the twentieth century will derive from that source conceptions more congenial than those with which it has been so long familiar, namely, *Vedānta*, doctrine of an impersonal self, *Yoga*, principle of spiritual exercise, *karma*, retribution of acts, *dharma*, principle of social and religious conformity, and *bhakti*, devotion to a personal god.

F. W. Thomas.

MUSLIM ARCHITECTURE IN INDIA

To any ordinary person the title of this chapter would seem to be above reproach and to describe its contents accurately. Indeed, it would be difficult to find any other precise and simple description to cover the admittedly various, styles of building produced in the vast area of India under the Muslim dominion that lasted from the year 1193 up to the eighteenth century. Mr. E. B. Havell, an enthusiastic and pugnacious champion of the Hindu genius, strongly objects to the term 'Indo-Saracenic' as 'an unscientific classification based on the fundamental error which vitiates the works of most European histories of Indian civilization'.[1] He is thinking primarily of James Fergusson's great book, the first really scholarly survey of the subject, but other and later historians come under his lash by adopting the same terminology. We may abandon the word 'Saracenic' nowadays, because it was never more than a picturesque nickname and has been discarded for many years by the learned, but it seems ridiculous to admit that the great influence and power of Islam, implied in the words 'Muslim' or 'Muhammadan', can be neglected in considering the long series of mosques, palaces, and other buildings erected during more than five centuries. On the other hand, Muslim architecture in India does differ radically from its works in other countries. As M. Saladin has well said:

'L'Inde est si éloignée du centre géographique de l'Islam que l'architecture musulmane y a subi l'influence de l'art florissant qui y était implanté depuis des siècles. Le continent indien, peuplé de races très diverses, dont les antagonismes assurèrent la servitude, constitue cependant un monde particulier. Une civilisation religieuse s'est étendue sur les races ennemies et a donné à l'art indou une vie puissante et originale.'[2]

[1] E. B. Havell, *Indian Architecture* (2nd ed., London, 1927), p. 121.
[2] H. Saladin, *Manuel d'art musulman* (Paris, 1907), vol. i, p. 545.

It was in 712 that the Muslim hosts first entered India and established themselves in Sind, but the colony there soon became detached from the Khalifat, eventually expired, and left no architectural remains of importance. In the tenth century, about 962, a former Turkish slave named Alptigīn entered Afghanistan from Turkestan and established a small independent principality at Ghaznī. His successor Sabuktigīn, another ex-slave, became Amir of Ghaznī in 977, raided the Punjab ten years later, and founded a dynasty. His son Mahmūd, who succeeded him in 997, assumed the title of Sultan and soon began to make his power felt beyond the Indus, capturing Kanauj, the capital city of northern India, in 1019. But it was only in Ghaznī itself that he became famous as a builder, and the sack of that city by a rival chieftain in *c.* 1150 destroyed all the buildings except Mahmud's tomb and two others.

Ghaznī lies in the modern kingdom of Afghanistan, not in India proper, and therefore does not strictly belong to our subject. But it must be recorded here that, in the days of its glory, it became a city of some importance. A contemporary chronicler, Ferishta, wrote that 'the capital was in a short time ornamented with mosques, porches, fountains, aqueducts, reservoirs, and cisterns, beyond any city in the East'.[1] Unfortunately, no systematic survey appears to have been made of the architectural remains of Ghaznī, which may eventually prove to have had considerable influence on the origin and development of Muslim architecture in India. Fergusson says that:

'Even the tomb of the great Mahmūd is unknown to us except by name', but that its gates, removed to India long ago, 'are of Deodar pine, and the carved ornaments on them are so similar to those found at Cairo, on the mosque of Ibn Tulun and other buildings of that age, as not only to prove that they are of the same date, but also to show how similar were the works of decoration at these two extremities of

[1] Quoted in Fergusson's *History of Indian and Eastern Architecture* (revised ed., London, 1910), vol. ii, p. 192.

the Muslim empire at the time of their execution. . . . At the same time there is nothing . . . Hindu . . . about them'.[1]

Mr. Robert Byron recently visited this tomb and described it as follows:

'The tomb resembles an inverted cradle of white marble, and bears a beautiful Kufic inscription whose high spots have grown translucent beneath the devotions of nine centuries. It was covered, when I entered, with a black pall, on which fresh rose-petals had been strewn, to show that the memory of the first great patron of Persian Islamic art is still revered among the people he once ruled.'[2]

Mr. Byron does not mention the Jāmi' Masjid ('Friday mosque'), which Fergusson expected to provide interesting information when it came to be examined, but he saw the two remarkable towers described and illustrated by Fergusson. Apparently only the lofty six-sided bases now remain, the tapered cylindrical superstructure having vanished. Mr. Byron speaks of them as 'minarets', but Fergusson says that they were pillars of victory, adding that 'neither of them was ever attached to a mosque'. Be this as it may, the form of these towers or minarets became important in the later history of Muslim architecture in India.

After Mahmūd's death in 1030 the power of Ghaznī began to decline, and it was occupied in 1173 by the rival prince of Ghūr. Twenty years later, Muhammad the Ghūri ruler of Ghaznī, with his generals Kutb-ud-dīn-Ibak and Bakhtiyār, conquered Hindustan and established the new Muslim capital at Delhi. This date, 1193, marks the real beginning of Muslim architecture in India itself. Except for the scattered and ruined fragments at Ghaznī in Afghanistan, no earlier buildings of any note survive which are due to Muslim influence or bear its characteristic features.

[1] Ibid., p. 193.
[2] In *The Times* for 28 December 1934, article entitled 'Middle Eastern Journey'.

Before describing the early architecture of Delhi and Ajmir it is necessary to indicate briefly the point of development to which Muslim building had attained in 1193 in Persia and the neighbouring countries whence its influence must have reached India, and then to study the nature of the existing indigenous architecture with which it became fused and on which, in spite of all statements to the contrary, it eventually impressed the unmistakable features of Islamic tradition.

The congregational mosque or 'Friday Mosque' (*Jāmi' Masjid*) had long attained its normal and almost standardized form, consisting of a large open rectangular court (*sahn* in Arabic) surrounded by arcades or colonnades (*līwānat* in Arabic) on all four sides. The *līwān* nearest to Mecca was usually made much deeper than the others and formed the sanctuary. In the centre of the back wall of the sanctuary, and on its inner side, stood the *mihrāb*, a niche with a pointed head, indicating the proper direction (*qiblah*) for prayer, i.e. the direction of Mecca. The call to worship (*adhan*) was chanted by a muezzin (*mu'adhdhin*) from a gallery near the top of a minaret (*ma'dhana*), a tall slender tower. Within the mosque the chief ritual furniture consisted of a pulpit (*mimbar*) and facilities for ceremonial ablution. A large mosque might have several minarets, their form being usually cylindrical or polygonal in Persia, though the first known example at Qayrawān near Tunis (8th century) is a massive square tower, slightly tapered. Arches were freely used in all parts of the mosque, their form being generally 'Persian' (i.e. somewhat depressed and struck from four centres like our 'Tudor' arch), or less frequently of ogee type. Cusping was occasionally used. Windows were often filled with plaster or stone lattices or *claire-voies* to break the force of the sun, but glazing does not appear to have been introduced before the thirteenth century. Enamelled tiles were certainly employed, also bands of decorative lettering and geometrical surface patterns ('arabesques') in profusion, while the famous 'stalactite' ornament, the hallmark of Muslim architecture in all countries, had made its appearance in the mosque of Al Aqmar at Cairo in 1125. Lastly, the masonry or brick dome had come into general use for tombs and tomb-mosques, though in ordinary congregational mosques it was normally of small size and placed over the space in front of the *mihrab*.[1]

The buildings which the Muslim conquerors found in India in 1193 were numerous and decidedly florid in character. Indeed, it is the profuseness of the decoration in early Hindu temples that tends to obscure their structural features and thus makes them difficult for a European critic to analyse dispassionately. Havell writes that 'it may seem to the Western eye, trained in the formula of the classical schoolmaster, that the Muhammadan prescription is more pleasing, just because it is more correct according to the canons called classical';[2] but the difference seems to be more fundamental than that. To an English student, at any rate, it seems to be a basic distinction between ordered and restrained architecture on the one hand, and mere profusion on the other. However, it should be possible in this brief survey to avoid unnecessary and futile comparisons between varying styles of building, concentrating rather on matters of ascertained fact in the story of architectural development. Havell contends that an honest view of the subject is difficult to obtain, because of the misleading though well-meant efforts of Fergusson, the first man to attempt a rational survey of the whole vast field. 'The history of Indian architecture', he writes, 'has therefore remained where Fergusson left it—not a history of Indian life, but a Museum of Antiquities wrongly labelled.'[3] Havell states 'the reasons for rejecting entirely Fergusson's classification of styles' in one of

[1] For a concise summary of the characteristics of Muslim architecture in general, see my chapter in *The Legacy of Islam* (Oxford, 1931), pp. 155–79.

[2] E. B. Havell, op. cit., p. 51.

[3] E. B. Havell, *Ancient and Medieval Architecture of India*, p. xxiv.

his books; in brief, they amount to a denial that there was any actual separation of style due to sectarian differences between Buddhism, Jainism, and Hinduism, all of which religions, he contends, 'had their common root in the life of the village and in the Vedic philosophy', finally concluding that 'the derivations of Indian temple architecture must be looked for in the simple shrines of the Indian village'.[1] Throughout his two interesting and thoughtful but highly controversial books on Indian architecture, he is concerned to stress its unbroken continuity. 'The vital creative impulse which inspired any period of Indian art' had its sole source 'in the traditional Indian culture planted in Indian soil by Aryan philosophy . . . and influenced the greatest works of the Muhammadan period as much as any other'.[2] He objects to the common delusion 'that everything really great in Indian art has been suggested or introduced by foreigners' and that 'between Hindu and Saracenic ideals there is a great gulf fixed', denying that 'the fundamental antagonism between Hindu and Musulman religious beliefs, which we so often assume, ever existed at any time'.[3] Havell, who is supported, in his claim for an intensely nationalist and a strictly continuous view of Indian architectural development, by Coomaraswamy, has established a case which is far from negligible, but we need not follow him in all his strictures on Fergusson and on Englishmen in general.

The story of architecture in India prior to the Muslim invasion in 1193 has already been extended backwards by three thousand years or more since the sensational discoveries made recently at Harappa and Mohenjodāro, and soon all our existing ideas may require revision. Until the full results of these researches are made available we can only accept the prevailing belief that the earliest surviving Indian buildings were constructed mainly of timber, but with sun-dried brick for founda-

[1] E. B. Havell, *Ancient and Medieval Architecture of India*, pp. 33–4.
[2] Id., *Indian Architecture*, pp. 1–2.   [3] Ibid., p. 3.

tions and plinths. In the prosperous reign of Aśoka (*c.* 272–232 B.C.), stone came into use, but the forms of timber members were often reproduced in stone. Aśoka, whose dominions included the whole of modern India except its southern extremity and part of Assam, became a devotee of Buddhism. Hence the monuments surviving from his day consist chiefly of great stone pillars (*lāts*) inscribed with his religious edicts; *stūpas*, i.e. structures or shrines enclosing relics of Buddhist saints, or marking places where Buddha lived or worked; temples; and various monasteries and chapels for Buddhist monks. In these buildings, which were scattered all over Aśoka's vast empire, there are many indications of foreign influence, even at this early date.

Thus the Aśoka pillars have capitals somewhat resembling the type used at Persepolis seven hundred years before, decorated with Persian mouldings, and crowned with lions or other beasts. Where these lions were disposed in pairs or in fours (as on the fine capital from the Sarnath pillar, which was 50 feet high from the ground), we find the prototype of the famous 'bracket-capital' which later played so important a structural part in Hindu architecture and came to be freely used in Muslim mosques. The *stūpas* are extremely interesting monuments, but do not appear to have influenced mosque-building to any marked extent. Where they assumed a domical form, as in the celebrated example at Sānchī, of which models exist in the Indian section of the Victoria and Albert Museum, the dome was a solid mass of brickwork, so had no structural significance. The *stūpa* was normally surrounded by a railed enclosure with gates at its four cardinal points; but, though these features again are interesting, there is nothing novel about such an enclosure to suggest that it formed the prototype of anything in later Muslim architecture. The magnificent gates of the enclosure at Sānchī are chiefly remarkable for the use of the bracket cap, and they have a Chinese appearance.

The monasteries (*vihāras*) were often placed near the shrines (*chaityas*). Some of them were hewn out of the solid rock, others were free-standing structures; some had columns, others were astylar. The monasteries of the Gandhāra district, on the present north-west frontier, have attracted much attention for the Hellenistic sculpture and architectural detail which they contain. The *chaitya* caves of Buddhist times form a long series covering a period of about a thousand years (*c.* 250 B.C.–*c.* A.D. 750), the best-known examples being at Bhaja, Nasik, Karli, Ellora, Ajanta, and Elephanta. All these are situated within 300 miles of Bombay and are carved out of the solid rock, with roofs in the form of a barrel-vault, often fashioned into ribs to resemble timber construction. At Karli and Bhaja, actual timber ribs are used though there is nothing for them to support. The typical plan of a *chaitya* is a long 'nave' or apartment, with an apsidal end in the centre of which stands the *stūpa* or shrine, the *chaitya* proper. The nave is normally flanked by aisles and separated from them by massive columns, generally octagonal, with (at Karli) great convex abaci surmounted by a pair of elephants ridden by female figures: these form the capitals. The effect of such a colonnade recalls the temples of Upper Egypt, massive and dignified; but the interior as a whole suggests a Christian basilica, and Fergusson has pointed out that the dimensions of the temple at Karli are almost identical with those of the choir at Norwich Cathedral. Light was admitted through a huge sun-window in the rock façade so that it fell upon the *stūpa* or *chaitya*, the focal point of worship. The sun-window almost invariably assumed the form of a horseshoe, and Havell has explained its symbolic purpose in some detail.[1] He takes great pains to prove that this horseshoe-arch, which eventually became a characteristic feature of Muslim architecture in certain countries, was invented in India a thousand years or so before the first mosque was erected. Another scholar, Rivoira, is equally concerned to show that its use in India at this early

[1] Havell, *Ancient and Medieval Architecture of India*, p. 55, &c.

a. KARLI: INTERIOR OF CHAITYA CAVE

c. 150 B.C.

b. NASIK: SUN-WINDOW AND HORSESHOE-ARCH

c. 150 B.C.

PLATE 12

date was merely decorative, not structural.[1] Havell also claims
that the pointed arch, the stilted arch, and the 'trefoil' or
foliated or cusped arch were Buddhist inventions; and, still
more important, that when the Muslims first saw the Buddha-
niches in the temples which they destroyed, they conceived the
idea of the *mihrāb* or prayer-niche which became the heart and
kernel of every mosque.[2] Many of these claims will not stand
critical examination, and in appraising the direct debt of Indian
Muslim architecture to ancient Indian art we may conclude that
it appears to be limited to the use of bracket-capitals (a Persian
heritage) and certain arch-forms, the latter being disputable.
Other details borrowed from Persia, Greece, and perhaps Rome
(e.g. the quasi-Doric capitals at Elephanta and the fluted pillars
of the temple at Mārtānd in Kashmīr and elsewhere), passed
out of use long before the Muslim invasion and so had no effect
on Muhammadan architecture.

But it must not be inferred that nothing of importance was
transmitted indirectly, and after considerable modification, from
the earlier period to the later. Certain features developed during
the ensuing centuries before 1193, and passed almost imperceptibly into the design of mosques after that date. Meanwhile
it must be admitted that Indian craftsmen were acquiring great
skill in all decorative details. Moreover, it is quite fallacious to
regard the rock-hewn *chaitya*-cave type as archaic or barbaric.
As Havell says, 'in India it represents a refinement of luxury for
the users, an exceptional trial of skill for the craftsmen, and a
special act of devotion and consecration on the part of the
individual or the community for whom the work is performed';[3]
and again, that 'the sculpturesque or architectonic quality which
is generally lacking in pure Arab buildings, belongs pre-eminently
to Hindu architectural design: the Hindu builder was a sculptor

[1] G. T. Rivoira, *Moslem Architecture* (1918), pp. 113, &c.
[2] Havell, *Indian Architecture*, pp. 5–6.
[3] Id., *Ancient and Medieval Architecture of India*, p. 69.

as well as a mason, having acquired his skill at Elephanta, Ellora, and Ajanta in many generations from dealing with great masses of living rock'.[1] This last claim must be borne in mind as we come to consider the fully developed Muslim architecture of India, later in this chapter.

Very little is known about Buddhism in India after the seventh century A.D. For nearly a thousand years it had been the state religion and now it was supplanted by Hinduism (or Brahmanism) and Jainism. For the sake of simplicity, and with a view to avoiding controversial questions, we may therefore consider the architecture of India from *c.* 750 to 1193 as a whole, ignoring Fergusson's division of it into the Jain, Hindu, Dravidian, and Chalukyan styles. It was, of course, in north and central India that this early architecture had its most direct influence on later Muslim building.

Although Fergusson states that from about 650 'the curtain drops on the drama of Indian history . . . and for three centuries we have only the faintest glimmerings of what took place within her boundaries',[2] subsequent research has rendered his statement no longer valid. During that period India was a chaotic mass of rival clans and small states. Brahmanical Hinduism replaced Buddhism as the State religion of the majority of the inhabitants, but Jainism—which was as old as Buddhism in its origin—continued to flourish abreast of it, and was responsible for the erection of many important temples. Havell writes that 'Jainism cannot be said to have created a special architecture of its own, for wherever they went the Jains adopted the local building tradition'.[3] The chief monuments remaining to-day from the middle of the eighth century to the close of the twelfth are temples and, whether Hindu or Jain, they differ from the Buddhist temples in being shrines for individual rather than

[1] Havell, *Indian Architecture*, p. 23.

[2] Fergusson, *Indian and Eastern Architecture*, vol. ii, p. 8.

[3] Havell, *Ancient and Medieval Architecture of India*, p. 175.

for congregational worship. Few monasteries or tombs were built. The typical Hindu temple of this period consists of two elements: a shrine-cell crowned by a curvilinear tower or steeple (*sikhara*) and an entrance porch or veranda. Havell considers that this type was directly derived from the primitive village shrine of a thousand years earlier, with its veranda giving shelter to 'the two guardians of the shrine, human or divine'.[1]

In South India, instead of the curved *sikhara* we find a more primitive structure, a *vimāna* or pyramidal tower with stepped sides, not unlike the Babylonian *ziggurat*. Otherwise, variations from the standard plan take the form of the addition of pillared halls (*mandapam*) and enclosures (*prakāra*) round the original shrine as a nucleus, with lofty gateways (*gopurams*) at the various entrances. It is only in the pillared halls that any noteworthy structural experiments are to be seen, and there one sometimes sees primitive stone domes on an octagonal arrangement of pillars, a system which found its way into Muslim architecture. Undoubtedly the most striking feature of all these early Hindu temples is the bold and picturesque massing of the *sikhara* or *vimāna* and the porch, with or without subsidiary buildings. In itself the *sikhara* has no structural interest or significance. Well described as a 'curvilinear pyramid', it is simply a square tower with curved sides, in form and construction not unlike a lime-kiln. The massive walls are built in thick horizontal courses of stone, and the whole structure is generally surmounted by an enormous feature—also built in stone courses—resembling a gigantic knob and known as an *amalaka*. This knob, Vishnu's emblem, is crowned with a finial in the form of a water-pot (*kalasha*). The whole exterior of the *sikhara* is usually carved with surface ornament from top to bottom. Fergusson writes of the *sikhara* of the great temple at Bhuvāneśwar in Orissa that 'It is, perhaps, not an exaggeration to say that if it would take a sum—say a lakh of rupees or pounds—to erect such a building

[1] Ibid., p. 37.

as this, it would take three lakhs to carve it as this one is carved'.[1] Thus, in spite of the immense solidity of their construction, these great towers, rising sometimes to nearly 200 feet in height, produce the effect of some nightmare tea-caddy or confectioner's *capolavoro*, a wedding cake for a royal marriage. This effect is in no way mitigated by the design of the porch, usually somewhat lightly built and betraying its timber origin; for one feels that the porch was intended to serve as a foil for the more important *śikhara* and not to compete with it. The roof of the porch is often pyramidal, constructed of stone and stepped in horizontal courses; and the substructure sometimes consists of rather squat columns, sometimes of solid walls. But in either case there is a tendency to cover every available inch of external masonry in the porch with profuse carving, and to confuse the main lines of the architecture with a multiplicity of horizontal plinths and mouldings. The same criticism applies almost equally to the interior of the shrine, generally square in plan, but often varied by recesses. These produced a multiplication of vertical lines, while horizontally the habitual use of an enormous plinth—often half the total height of the chamber—and the subdivision of the entablature mouldings into many members caused further confusion. Add to this a prodigal use of sculpture and the result leaves the Western mind bewildered.

If one can so far forget the overgrowth of ornament and the complexity of subdivision as to penetrate to the underlying structural forms and elements, it appears that the Hindu temples prior to 1193 were mainly of trabeated stone construction, based in large part on timber prototypes. Great stone lintels, beams, and purlins are freely used, and arches are almost if not entirely unknown, the tops of window openings and doorways being flat. Bracket-capitals are employed to reduce the span of openings. Pyramidal roofs are formed by successive projections of masonry courses, and domes of primitive type are constructed

[1] Fergusson, op. cit., vol. ii, p. 101.

in the same way on an octagonal base of stone lintels, themselves supported on stone columns in late examples (after the 10th century). The top or cap of such a structure, the *amalaka* already mentioned, sometimes appears to be carried on the slightly curvilinear piers or ribs forming the skeleton of the *sikhara*, where the walls of the *sikhara* are not entirely solid, and in this system Havell finds the origin of the later ribbed dome. Columns were seldom used in the architecture of Hindu temples in north India, but are frequently found in buildings erected further south. There is no doubt that the Muslims borrowed many of these structural features, notably lintels and bracket-capitals, from Hindu tradition; and it is equally certain that the domes they built in India showed similar influence. But their architecture was not based entirely on Hindu models, as extremists would have us believe.

The largest group of early Hindu temples in north India is to be found in the Orissa district, which escaped invasion by the Muslims until 1510. Fergusson observes, not very euphoniously, that 'the Orissan style is almost entirely astylar',[1] hardly a column being used. He adds that the towers have no stories or steps, that the crowning member is never a dome, and that the tower with its porch always forms the temple. The ancient city of Bhuvāneśwar, one of several 'temple-cities', once contained 7,000 shrines around its sacred lake, but now less than 500 remain. These date from *c.* 700 to the eleventh century A.D. The Great Temple, one of the finest of its kind, follows the type already described. It originally consisted of a *sikhara* and a porch, to which a dancing-hall and refectory were subsequently added. The height of the *sikhara* is over 180 ft., and the date is usually ascribed to the ninth century. The structure is covered with carving. The neighbouring temple of Mukteśvara resembles it but is much smaller. The so-called 'Black Pagoda' at Kanarak, not far away, is considered by Fergusson to be a

[1] Fergusson, op. cit., vol. ii, pp. 92–3.

work of *c*. 860, but that date is not accepted by scholars nowadays. The huge temple of Jagannāth ('Juggernaut') at Puri is also in the same district, but is of much later date (1174–98) than those already mentioned, to which it is artistically inferior. In the Bījāpur district, east of Goa and south of Bombay, there is another group of early Hindu temples, of which the most famous is the temple of Papanatha at Pattadakal (7th or 8th century) in the 'Dravidian' rather than the 'North Hindu' style; that is, it has stepped pyramidal *vimānas*, profusely carved. In the same area are some rock-cut temples. At Chandravati in Rajputana and at Baroli in central India are other examples, probably of the ninth century; and at Khajraho, about 150 miles south-east of Gwalior, is a remarkable group of about thirty temples built between *c*. 950 and 1050. The most important of these, the Kandarya Mahadeo temple, has a fine *śikhara* 116 feet high buttressed by tiers of smaller replicas of itself, each crowned with the typical *amalaka* and *kalasha*. It is a wonderful example of massing, spoilt by over-ornamentation and too great a multiplicity and repetition of features. The plan is magnificent. Other notable examples are at Sinnār near Nasik, and at Udayapur in the Gwalior territory.

The chief Jain temples were erected between *c*. 1000 and *c*. 1300, and are distinguished by the large number of cells provided for images, as many as 236 being found in one building, but architecturally they do not differ in character very much from the Hindu temples described. They are usually picturesquely situated, often on hill-tops. Some of them are rock-cut as at Ellora and in Orissa; others are free-standing structures, such as the temples at Lakkandi in Dharwar, at Palitana and Girnar in Gujarāt, at Somnāth south of Girnār, and at Vindhya-giri and Chandra-giri in Mysore. But the most famous examples are at Mount Ābu, about 400 miles from Bombay on the line to Delhi. Here the older temple, built in 1031 and illustrated by Fergusson, forms one of the finest architectural groups of the period. The shrine itself, with its pyramidal roof and porch, is surrounded by a closed courtyard 128 feet by 75 feet, lined with 52 cells.

When the Muslims under Muhammad of Ghūr invaded India in 1191, they encountered defeat at first from the Hindu raja who ruled over Delhi and Ājmīr. In the following year, however, they were successful, and in 1193 Delhi, Kanauj, and Benares were captured. The surrender of Gwalior occurred three years later, the conquest of Upper India being completed in 1203. It used to be customary to describe the new rulers as 'Pathan' (i.e. Afghan) kings right up to the time of Bābur, the first Mughal emperor, and their architecture was christened the 'Pathan style' by Fergusson. But most of them were of Turkish or Arab blood, and several of the early sultans of Delhi were Turkish slaves who, like the Mamelukes of Egypt including the famous Saladin himself, rose to the highest positions in the State from this lowly origin. The general in command of the army which conquered Delhi in 1193 was one such slave, by name Malik Kutb-ud-dīn Ībak, a native of Turkestan, and it was he who, even before he became the first sultan or king of Delhi on Muhammad's death in 1206, put in hand the building of two large 'congregational' or metropolitan mosques in Delhi and Ājmīr. Undoubtedly this step was intended as a symbol of conquest, as an evidence of the Muslims' belief in the faith of their fathers, and possibly also as a memorial of their triumph over idolatry.

The invaders were certainly soldiers, probably marching light and without any elaborate system of administration prepared in advance for the vanquished territories. But those writers who have assumed that no architects were brought into India from Persia or Turkestan have been rather rash: even if there is no record of such an importation, it seems conceivable that it may have happened. At all events the point is unimportant, because it is obvious that somebody—perhaps

Kutb-ud-dīn himself—must have given precise instructions to craftsmen and labourers for the building of the two mosques just mentioned. It may also be assumed that these workmen were mainly if not entirely Hindus: that fact is proved by the clumsy way in which they dealt with the few non-Hindu items of construction required by the conquerors. Moreover, this was the practice in all the countries subdued by the Arabs in the early days of Islam. The plan of the mosque, utilitarian as well as symbolical in its nature, was prescribed by tradition and was insisted upon by the Muslim governor or ruler; the materials employed, and the constructional methods used to achieve desired effects, were largely left to be determined by local circumstances and the particular skill of the native craftsmen. As we have seen, Hindu temple architecture had reached a high level; and sculpture had become almost too easy, as it was assuredly too common. Havell has rightly observed that the Hindus, at this period, had ceased to be borrowers of architectural forms; indeed, he claims that they had become lenders, and goes so far as to suggest that the only two countries where 'pure Saracenic' architecture is to be found, i.e. Egypt and Spain, owe all the main features of their Muslim buildings to India, Mesopotamia, Persia, and Central Asia.[1] This is too sweeping a claim, though it contains a measure of truth.

The first mosque at Delhi, dedicated to the Kuwwat-ul-Islām ('Might of Islam') is admirably situated on a slight eminence and was completed in 1198. It originally measured externally about 210 feet from east to west (that is, from front to back) and 150 feet from north to south, the measurements inside the colonnade being 142 by 108 feet. (In India, the *mihrab* is always at the west end.) It was erected on the site of a Hindu temple, but an Arabic inscription on the east wall states that the materials of 27 'idolatrous' temples were used in its construction. The sanctuary at the west (Mecca) end is now

[1] Havell, *Indian Architecture*, p. 10.

PLATE 13

a. ĀJMĪR: GREAT MOSQUE

c. A.D. 1200

b. DELHI: KUTB MINĀR

A.D. 1232

in ruins, only 22 of its numerous columns remaining, but the fine stone arcade or screen forming its frontage to the courtyard survives to show the magnificence of the original design, with a central arch of slightly ogee shape, 22 feet wide and 53 feet high. The low colonnaded sanctuary behind it, like the other colonnades surrounding the courtyard, appears to have survived from the earlier temple, so that Kutb-ud-dīn's work was mainly confined to the erection of this huge arcaded sanctuary-façade. The Hindu craftsmen employed were unaccustomed to the construction of arches; hence, instead of proper voussoirs, they used projecting courses of masonry such as were familiar to them in building *śikharas*. After Kutb-ud-dīn's death, his son-in-law and successor Altamsh proceeded in *c.* 1225 to extend this arcaded screen to treble its original width north and south, and also to erect a new east colonnade to the mosque, so that it now measured some 370 by 280 feet. Within the extended courtyard he built the great 'Kutb Minār', a detached tower or minaret 238 feet high, which may possibly have been commenced by Kutb-ud-dīn himself. There is some doubt as to the real purpose of this remarkable monument. An inscription, and a reference by the poet Amīr Khusrū, support the theory that it was a normal minaret used by a muezzin; but many authorities hold that it was a tower of victory, perhaps inspired by the 'pillars of victory' which still stand on the plain of Ghaznī. A detached minaret is not unknown, and there are very early examples at Samarra in Mesopotamia (846–52) and at the mosque of Ibn Tulūn in Cairo (868–969). The sharply tapered cylindrical form is found at Damghān in Persia (12th century), and the fluting of the surface is a Persian feature (as at Rayy) derived from older Mesopotamian prototypes. The 'stalactite' cornices under the tiers of galleries round the Kutb Minār recall one of the earliest uses of that feature on a twelfth-century minaret at Bostam in Persia. All things considered, there is no reason to doubt the statement that the Kutb Minār was designed by a Muhammadan architect and built by Hindu craftsmen.[1] It is absurd to say that it is 'a Saracenic modification of the Indian type'.[2]

The tomb of Altamsh, who died in 1235, lies near the mosque, and is a beautiful example of nearly pure Persian art, though there are certain features of its decoration—such as the design of the shafts and the cusped arches—that suggest Hindu taste, and much of the ornament betrays an inexperienced hand. The mosque at Ājmīr, already mentioned, was commenced *c.* 1200 and finished during the reign of Altamsh. It originally measured 264 by 172 feet and was erected on the site of a Jain temple or college built in 1153. As at Delhi, the chief alteration to the temple consisted in erecting a great screen or arcade of Persian arches in stone, bordered with characteristic Arabic decorative lettering, and as at Delhi the arches are quite unconstructional, having horizontal joints formed by projecting courses of masonry. But only a fragment of this beautiful building now remains, including the ruins of two small fluted minarets. The legend that it was built in 2½ days, repeated by nearly all historians, may be ignored as ridiculous—Oriental hyperbole carried to excess.

The Mongol wars which devastated Central Asia in the twelfth century, and the weak character of the rulers of Delhi after Altamsh, may account for the fact that no outstanding monument was erected for nearly a hundred years by the Muslims of India. Then in 1300 'Alā-ud-dīn, who had succeeded to the throne of Delhi in 1296 and had previously conquered part of south India, began to enlarge the Kuwwat-ul-Islām mosque and to build a *minār* which was intended to be more than double the height of the lofty Kutb Minar. 'Alā-ud-dīn was a megalomaniac, and his vast projects remained unfinished, but in the so-called 'Alāi Darwāza, a noble south gateway to the mosque

[1] Vincent Smith, *History of Fine Art in India and Ceylon*, p. 69.
[2] Havell, *Indian Architecture*, p. 49.

enclosure (1310), he has left us a very charming and delicate little building which may be considered to mark the culmination of early Indo-Muslim art. Its general character and its ornament are Persian, but the Hindu tradition may be seen in the same features as at the Tomb of Altamsh just described.

For the next period, corresponding with the duration of the Tughlak dynasty in Delhi (1321–1421), that city continued to be virtually the capital of Muslim India, though from time to time various principalities, such as Bengal, asserted their independence. Delhi, which may have been founded in 993 or centuries earlier, was certainly a flourishing place when the Muslims captured it in 1193. Its favourable strategical situation is considered to explain its continuance as a capital through a thousand years. The site of the old 'cities' of Delhi, reckoned at least seven in number without the pre-Muslim town, is spread over a triangular area measuring some ten or eleven miles from north to south, with the apex of the triangle at the junction of the 'Ridge' with the River Jumna, where the modern Civil Station now lies. The site of 'New Delhi' is about in the centre of this triangle, and 'Old Delhi', the first Muslim city, founded by Kutb-ud-dīn, at the south-west corner of the triangle. The second city, Sirī, lies north-east of Old Delhi, and the third, Tughlakābād, founded in 1321, in the south-east corner of the triangle. The fourth and fifth cities, Jahanpannah (1327) and Fīrozābād (c. 1354), were also established during the rule of the Tughlak dynasty, which provided a number of interesting buildings, very different in character from the earlier architecture just described.

The tomb of Ghiyās-ud-dīn Tughlak (d. 1325), first of the line, is a square structure of red sandstone with sharply battered walls, enormously thick, crowned with a simple white marble dome. This building, massive and severe, is surrounded by an enceinte of lofty stone walls with bastions. Nothing more like a warrior's tomb, and nothing less like 'Alā-ud-dīn's gateway, could be imagined. The other tombs of the period are no less stark in their aspect and the walls of Tughlakābād are equally impressive, while the surviving parts of the walls of Jahānpannah and Fīrozābād show a dour disregard of architectural prettiness that seems to indicate a rigid puritanism of outlook as well as a consciousness of defensive needs. Among Delhi mosques of the fourteenth century the most important is the Kalan Masjid (finished 1387), a citadel-like building of forbidding aspect with domed bastions at its angles and acutely tapered cylindrical minarets on either side of the main entrance. It stands within Shāhjahānabād, i.e. the present native city of Delhi. The remaining mosques are at Jahānpannah and elsewhere. Recently the 'Hall of a Thousand Pillars' erected at Jahānpannah by Muhammad-bin-Tughlak (1325–51) has been excavated,[1] and it is likely that the results will considerably extend our knowledge of the period.

Outside Delhi the chief Muslim buildings of the fourteenth century were erected in Gujarāt, Bengal, and the Jaunpur area. Gujarāt was a seat of Hindu craftsmanship, and such mosques as the Jāmiʻ Masjid at Cambay (1325) and the mosque of Hilāl Khān Kāzī at Dholka near Ahmadābād (1333) contain numerous Hindu fragments as well as Hindu ideas, the columnar or trabeated effect being frequently produced. At Gaur in Bengal the enormous Adina Masjid near Pandua (c. 1360) has a huge courtyard surrounded by five aisles of arches on the Mecca side and three aisles on the remaining sides. These arcades, constructed of brick, originally carried 378 domes of identical size and design, a most unimaginative and monotonous conception. Nothing could be less characteristic of Hindu art, yet Havell takes the opportunity to argue that 'it is much more than probable that in this brick-building country Indian builders were using radiating arches, either round or pointed, for struc-

[1] Reported in *The Times* of 28 December 1934.

tural purposes before the Muhammadans came. The pointed arch was not an invention of Saracenic builders.'[1]

At Gulbarga in the Deccan is another large and very remarkable mosque, the only one of its kind in India, built about the middle of the century. There is a tradition or legend to the effect that it was designed by an architect from Cordova, and certainly it resembles the famous mosque in that city to the extent that the whole area is covered. There are the usual arcades on the north, south, and east, with domes at each angle and a large dome over the *mihrāb*; but the roof over the remaining area (normally occupied by the open court) and over the sanctuary consists of 63 small domes resting on arcades. With its stilted domes, its foliated battlements, and its fine arcades of Persian arches this striking building is essentially 'Saracenic'. One wonders why the type was not reproduced elsewhere, and it has been suggested that the innovation of having the external arcade open to the public gaze was unpopular with the mullahs, who preferred the usual type enclosed within blank walls.

Returning to north India we find two interesting mosques at Jaunpur, near Benares: the mosque of Ibrāhīm Nāib Barbak in the fort, completed in 1377, and the fine Atala Masjid (1408). The latter has a truly impressive propylon or central feature in the Persian style, with a great Persian arch over the entrance, but the walls of the square flanking towers, which look as though they ought to carry minarets, are battered and are frankly Hindu, as are the colonnades on either hand. Yet the interior arches and domes are distinctly Muhammadan in character.

The next century, from 1421 to 1526, was interrupted by frequent wars, and Delhi ceased to occupy its predominant position of control over the semi-independent kingdoms of Bengal, Jaunpur, Gujarāt, Mālwā, the Deccan, &c. Nevertheless many notable buildings were erected in the area, most of them being tombs. The group of three, known as Tīn Burj

[1] Havell, *Indian Architecture*, p. 55.

('Three Towers') are rough and massive square structures with blank arcading on their exteriors, the Persian arch being used. The domes are rather lower than the typical high Saracenic dome, and thus approximate nearer to the Hindu form. The tombs of Mubārik Shāh Sayyid and Muhammad Shāh Sayyid,[1] in or near Khairpur, are plain octagonal structures with domes, 'kiosks' surrounding the domes, and external arcading. There is another fine but nameless tomb of the same type, square on plan, in Khairpur, with Hindu brackets over the doors and blue glazed tiles used in the Persian fashion. All these are works of the Sayyid period (1421–51). Rather later is the plain but impressive tomb of Sikandar Lodī (1517) at Khairpur, surrounded by a fortified enclosure. The chief Delhi mosques of the period are the beautiful Motī-ki-Masjid, a remarkable composition with high blank walls flanked by arcaded pavilions and with effective domes, and the splendid domed mosque of Khairpur.

The two chief mosques of this century at Jaunpur are the fine Jāmi' Masjid (begun in 1438) and the small Lāl Darwāza mosque. Both have been frequently illustrated, and both have the characteristics already mentioned in connexion with Jaunpur mosques of the preceding period.

Gaur, the capital of Bengal at this time, similarly followed and developed its fourteenth-century tradition of brick arcuated construction, a curious medley of Muslim and Hindu methods. Among its buildings may be mentioned the so-called Fīroz Shāh Minār (dated 1490) a curious structure resembling an Irish 'round tower' rather than a minaret; the Eklākhī mosque and tomb, a fine domed building 80 feet square of uncertain date; and the Sona Masjid or 'Golden Mosque', so styled because of its gilded domes, erected in 1526, and now the finest ruin in Gaur. It has no less than 44 brick domes over the principal *līwān* and there are six minarets, but the courtyard has prac-

---

[1] This is the 'nameless sepulchre' illustrated by Fergusson, *Indian and Eastern Architecture*, vol. ii, pp. 216–17 and fig. 379.

tically disappeared. The exterior is a monumental and most unusual design, combining both Hindu and Saracenic elements, yet remaining decidedly original.

Another great centre of building activity at this period was Māndū, the capital of the old kingdom of Mālwā, in the modern principality of Dhar. The Jāmiʿ Masjid, finished in 1454, is a magnificent congregational mosque, of which Fergusson says that 'for simple grandeur and expression of power it may, perhaps, be taken as one of the very best specimens now to be found in India'.[1] The great courtyard is surrounded by five arcades of pointed arches on the Mecca side, two on the east, and three on the north and south. There are large domes over the *mihrāb* and the north-west and south-west corners, the remainder of the arcades being covered by an enormous number of small domes. This is an essentially Muslim building, free from Hindu trabeated construction, and is carried out in red sandstone with marble enrichments. In south India the most notable Muhammadan architecture of the period 1421–1526 is to be found in the city of Bīdar, which supplanted Gulbarga in 1428. Here there are many interesting royal tombs, and a fine *madrasa* and mosque.

But the most important architectural centre of the time was Ahmadābād, the capital of the kingdom of Gujarāt. Here the mosques and other buildings erected by the Muslims are predominantly Hindu in character, in spite of the occasional use of arches for symbolical purposes. The Jāmiʿ Masjid (begun *c.* 1411) is a huge mosque of this type, all interest being concentrated on the Mecca *līwān*, which has 260 slender pillars supporting 15 symmetrically arranged stone domes, built up of horizontally projecting courses in the Hindu fashion. Dr. Burgess justly says that the result is 'a style combining all the beauty and finish of the native art with a certain magnificence which is deficient in their own works'. The method of lighting

---

[1] Fergusson, op. cit., vol. ii, p. 249.

the *līwān* is ingenious and admirably suited to climatic needs. At Sarkhej, about five miles from the city, is another large mosque completed in 1451, which is skilfully designed and is devoid of arches. The smaller mosques of Ahmadābād include those of Muhāfiz Khān, Sīdī Sayyid, and Rānī Sipari: all of this period and all characterized by Hindu tradition. The Jāmiʿ Masjid at Dholka (*c.* 1485) is another interesting example, and the Jāmiʿ Masjid at Champanīr (finished in 1508) is a large mosque resembling the Ahmadābād example in general arrangement but with two graceful minarets flanking the central doorway of the *līwān*, which has 11 domes in its roof as against 15 at Ahmadābād. This is one of the largest and finest of Indian mosques; certainly one of the most Indian. The Nāgīna Masjid at Champanir is a small and beautiful mosque of the same period. The most notable of many fine tombs in Ahmadābād are those of Sayyid Usmān (1460), Sayyid Mubārak (1484) and Rānī Sipārī (1514); and the tomb of Ahmad Ganj Baksh at Sarkhej, begun in 1446. The second of these has arches, but for the most part the tombs of Gujarāt have domes carried on an arrangement of columns in the Hindu manner.

With the year 1526, when Bābur the Mongol king of Kābul, with the aid of 700 field-guns, defeated the vast army of the Sultan of Delhi on the plain of Pānīpat, we enter on the Mogul or Mughal period of architecture which lasted nominally until 1761, but which may more conveniently end for our purpose at the death of Aurangzīb in 1707. The Muslim buildings of these two centuries form a more distinctive and homogeneous group than the architecture described hitherto, which varied greatly between province and province, and they are more familiar to English students—all of whom have at least heard of the Tāj Mahal. The term 'Mogul' as applied to architecture has its drawbacks, but the fact remains that the buildings erected under the Mughal emperors were more definitely Muhammadan or 'Saracenic' in character than those which preceded them and

need to be classified as a separate school. The chief monuments
were erected by Akbar (1556–1605) and Shāhjahān (1628–58);
during the reign of Aurangzīb (1658–1707) architecture pro-
gressively declined.

Most of the buildings of this important period are to be found
in the north-western part of India, especially at Delhi, Agra,
Lahore, Fatehpur-Sīkrī, and Allāhābād, with an isolated group
at Bījāpuɪ. Bābur established his capital at Agra, but his stormy
reign only lasted four years, and only two of his numerous
buildings remain: the mosques at Pānɪpat and at Sambal in
Rohilkand. His son Humāyūn ruled from 1530 to 1540 and
again from 1555 till his death in 1556, the intervening period
being occupied by the reign of an Afghan usurper, Sher Shāh.
Of buildings erected between 1526 and 1556, the best known
are in Delhi. They include the Jamāli Masjid (1528–36); the
mosque of 'Isā Khān (1547); and his richly decorated tomb
adjoining with 'kiosks' grouped round the central dome, altogether a bold combination of Hindu and Saracenic elements.
Then there is the walled 'sixth city' of Delhi known as the
Purāna Kīla, in which stands the splendid mosque of Sher Shāh,
a clever blending of richness and refinement. At Fathābād,
in the Hissār district of the Punjab, is a mosque (*c.* 1540) of
massive proportions, well designed and decorated with tiles
in Persian fashion. Sher Shāh's tomb stands on a high platform
or podium of masonry in the middle of a lake at Sahasram in
the Shāhābād district of Bengal. At the corners of this podium
are little domed kiosks, while two tiers of still smaller kiosks are
grouped round the great octagon beneath the dome. This is a
picturesque and delightful group, thoroughly Indo-Muslim.

One of the first monuments erected during Akbar's reign was
the tomb of his father Humāyūn at Delhi, built in 1565–9 by
Humāyūn's widow who was afterwards buried there. It is surrounded by a formal garden which still retains its original lay-
out though many of the trees have vanished. The base of the

tomb consists of a huge podium of red sandstone 22 feet high, with arches ornamented with white marble. From this noble foundation rises the tomb itself, 156 feet square and 125 feet high to the top of the dome. But though the building forms a square on plan, in fact it consists of a central domed octagon buttressed by four octagonal towers. The facing material is red sandstone, picked out with white marble, and the dome is faced with white marble. In shape the dome is slightly bulbous, thus introducing into India for the first time a feature characteristic of late work in Persia and Turkestan, and in construction it is double, another innovation. Its summit is crowned with the Arab finial, not the Hindu *kalasha*, and indeed it is a decidedly 'Saracenic' design. The exterior of the building has Persian arches and severely flat surfaces, relieved only by the brilliant marble inlay; and the kiosks on the angle towers are the sole legacy from Hindu tradition. Everything here suggests the experienced hand of a Muslim architect from Persia, or more probably from Samarkand, where the Tartar or Mughal princes had developed tomb-building to a fine art. It is generally considered that this splendid monument was the prototype of the Tāj Mahal. Other tombs in Delhi of Akbar's reign were erected in memory of Adham Khān and Atgah Khān (1566), two deadly rivals; and at Gwalior is the large and very fine tomb of Muhammad Ghaus. It is an Indo-Muslim hybrid, with Hindu kiosks at the angles of its podium.

Akbar resided in several cities: among them Allāhābād, Lahore, where he held his court from 1585 to 1598, and Agra, where he remained from that date until he died in 1605. At Agra he began building the famous fort in 1566, and within it he laid out the first part of the palace, which was continued by his successors and has since been so much altered that the various stages of extension are difficult to trace. The courtyard of the Jahāngīri Mahal, probably Akbar's work in spite of its name, is an Indian design with square pillars and bracket-capitals, richly

PLATE 14

DELHI: TOMB OF HUMĀYŪN

carved; and rows of small arches constructed in Hindu fashion without voussoirs. Other parts of Akbar's palace are slightly more Persian in style. The hall of the palace at Allāhābād (1583), with its boldly projecting veranda roof supported on rows of Hindu pillars, is a definitely Indian design, with hardly a single 'Saracenic' feature in it.

But the chief centre of Akbar's building activity is the city of Fatehpur-Sīkrī, twenty-three miles from Agra, which he founded in 1569 and was the seat of his court until 1584 or 1585. It was systematically laid out by him, has hardly been altered since, and is now deserted. It originally had a circumference of nearly seven miles, with walls on three sides pierced by nine gateways and a very large artificial lake on the fourth side. The Jāmi' Masjid of the city has a quadrangle 433 feet by 366 feet, surrounded by cloisters, with a vast number of small domed cells, one behind each bay of the cloister, which accommodated the Muslim teachers and their pupils, for this mosque served as the university of Fatehpur. The Mecca *līwān* with its three domes, its rows of pillars supporting the roof, and its lofty central propylon, follows an Indo-Muslim type we have met before. Two tombs stand in the quadrangle on the north side; there is a central gateway in the east colonnade; and in the middle of the south side the magnificent Buland Darwāza ('high gateway'), 130 feet wide, 88 feet deep, and 134 feet high. Built to commemorate Akbar's conquests, it is universally recognized as one of his greatest buildings. Though its huge recessed and vaulted portal, with a wide rectangular frame of flat ornament, is essentially Persian in character, the kiosks on its roof give it an Indian flavour. The palace of Fatehpur-Sīkrī contains a number of remarkable buildings, including Akbar's office or Dīwān-i-'Ām, a Hindu design with a projecting veranda roof over a colonnade; and the wonderful Hall of Private Audience (Dīwān-i-Khās), a masterpiece of planning, construction, and ornament, all of a distinctly Indian character. The city also contains two large houses of notable and unusual form, the palaces of Rāja Birbal and of Jodh Bāī.

Akbar's mausoleum (*c.* 1593–1613) is at Sikandara near Agra. It is a colossal structure standing on an enormous arcaded podium 30 feet high and 320 feet square. The mausoleum proper is rather more than 150 feet square and several stories high, with stepped walls of marble pierced with delicate trellis-work. The roof of this structure is flat, with a small kiosk at each corner, and it seems probable, if not certain, that a central dome was originally intended to complete the group. Fergusson is justified in suggesting that this remarkable Indo-Muslim design was inspired by the Buddhist-Hindu *vihāra*,[1] but others have advanced the theory that its origin is to be found in the Khmer temples of Cambodia.

Akbar was followed by Jahāngīr (1605–28), who lived mainly at Lahore, where he carried out the charming Motī Masjid ('Pearl Mosque') and a considerable amount of extension to the palace in the fort. Jahāngīr, even more than Akbar, was a lover of gardens, some of them laid out in patterns like a Persian carpet. He built 'paradises' at Udaipur, Srīnagar, and Fatehpur-Sīkrī; but the chief examples were the Shāh-Dāra or 'Garden of Delight' near Lahore, surrounding his own mausoleum, and the garden of the tomb of I'timādu-d-daula at Agra. This last monument (1621–8) is noteworthy less for its general design than for its decoration, the exterior being covered with an inlay of *pietra dura*, a fashion which may have been imported and thereafter became popular.

The reign of Shāhjahān (1628–58) was the golden age of Mughal architecture in India and produced a series of noble buildings. By far the most magnificent of all these was the celebrated Tāj Mahal at Agra (1631–53), erected at a cost estimated as $4\frac{1}{2}$ millions sterling in modern currency in memory of his favourite queen, Mumtāz-i-Mahal ('the elect of the

[1] Fergusson, op. cit., vol. ii, p. 300.

PLATE 15

THE BULAND DARWĀZA, FATEHPUR-SĪKRĪ

A.D. 1575

PLATE 16

THE TĀJ MAHAL, AGRA

A.D. 1632

palace'), after whom it is named. The frequently quoted statement that the architect was an Italian has been denied by some
historians. It is not incredible, though insufficiently docu-
mented, and may be a legend invented by those who consider
the design of the building so marvellous that they wish to find
a non-Hindu authorship for it. Admittedly it is the greatest
work of the Mughals, but it is a natural growth from the tomb
of Humāyūn and to a less extent from certain others. But it is
far superior to any of them in the dignity of its grouping and
disposition, in the masterly contrast between the central dome
and the slender minarets, in the chaste refinement and pains-
taking craftsmanship of its details, and above all in the splendour
of its materials. The design is more Persian and less Indian than
any building we have encountered hitherto, yet nothing quite
like it is to be found in Persia. The mausoleum itself closely
resembles the tomb of Humāyūn, being a square (of 186 feet)
with canted angles rather than an octagon. The square is composed of a high central block, octagonal within, buttressed at
each angle by projections, with a great Persian portal between
each pair. The slightly bulbous dome rises from a circular
drum. All the arches are of Persian type. On each angle of the
substructure stands a small domed kiosk. The beautiful central
chamber is restfully lit through marble trellis-work in the window openings, to break the glare of the sun. The mausoleum
stands on a terrace 22 feet high and 313 feet square with a
cylindrical minaret, divided into stages by galleries, at each angle.
The whole of these buildings are in dazzling white marble and
large parts of them are inlaid with coloured marbles and precious
stones in delicate Persian patterns. The group is surrounded by
a lovely formal garden, with avenues of cypresses and long lily-
ponds leading up the mausoleum, and the river which bounds the
garden on the north provides marvellous reflections. The Tāj
Mahal is one of the great buildings of the world, and has inspired
every serious critic who has seen it to express his admiration.

Only second in importance to the Tāj is Shāhjahān's work in the palace at Agra, carried out between 1638 and 1653, and including the Dīwān-i-ʿĀm, the Dīwān-i-Khās, and the Motī Masjid. In these various buildings, though red sandstone is used to some extent, white marble with coloured inlay is the prevailing material. Opulent elegance pervades the whole scheme, and the effect is a satisfactory blending of Indo-Muslim elements. Some writers indeed profess to rate the Motī Masjid higher than the Tāj. Shāhjahān also laid out charming gardens at Delhi and Lahore, and in the latter city the mosque of Wazīr Khān (1634) was built in his reign. It is the chief mosque of the town, Persian in general character, and freely decorated with coloured and glazed tiles. At Ājmīr are some beautiful marble pavilions on the embankment of the lake, also due to Shāhjahān.

His work at Delhi, too, was considerable. It included the walls of the present native town: the 'seventh city' of Delhi, called after him 'Shāhjahānābād', and built between 1638 and 1658. Its fine walls and gates have been well preserved, as have his Fort and the palace within it. Bounded on one side by the river, this vast complex of buildings, covering an area over 1,000 yards by 600 yards, is admirably laid out in an ordered sequence of courts, but suffered severely from military occupation in the unimaginative period before Lord Curzon came on the scene. As in the other Mughal palaces described, the two chief buildings are the Dīwān-i-ʿĀm and the Dīwān-i-Khās, and here they are of great beauty, richly decorated with marble inlay and Indo-Muslim in character.

Shāhjahān also built in 1644–58 the huge Jāmiʿ Masjid near the Fort at Delhi, with a quadrangle 325 feet square and two fine cylindrical minarets. Its outstanding feature is its commanding position, for it is placed on a high podium, a most unusual arrangement for a Muhammadan mosque. Whereas the domes, the minarets, and certain other parts of the building are Persian, the general effect is hybrid, and the angle pavilions are definitely Indian. Marble is used here too, but in combination with red sandstone.

At Bījāpur, which was the capital of an independent kingdom from 1489 until it was taken by Aurangzīb in 1686, there was a flourishing school throughout the Mughal period, characterized by many distinctive features of design. These included the use of purely ornamental minarets—the call to prayer being chanted by the muezzin from a small platform elsewhere—rich cornices, and ingenious dome-construction in which pendentives were employed. Fergusson writes of the architecture of Bījāpur in terms of the highest eulogy. Cousens, whose survey of the buildings of Bījāpur provides a mine of information, says that 'there is abundant evidence to show that first-class architects were induced to come south from Northern India' to Bījāpur, while there are traces of Hindu tradition in some of the buildings, proving that the Hindu craftsmen retained some of their individuality. Bījāpur at the height of its prosperity, early in the seventeenth century, is said to have contained nearly a million inhabitants and some 1,600 mosques; but during the Marātha supremacy in the eighteenth century it fell into ruin and its buildings were freely plundered for stone and other material. They were then smothered in jungle up to 1883, when Bījāpur became a British head-quarters, and they have since been cleared and partly restored.

Lack of space forbids more than a mention of the chief examples. The large but incomplete Jāmiʿ Masjid, commenced about 1576, is one of the finest mosques in India, severely plain but relieved by delicate *claire-voies* (pierced windows.) In front of the *mihrāb* is a large dome of unusual construction, the external appearance of which would be improved by the addition of a drum. The rest of the Mecca *līwān* is covered with a number of small stone domes supported on piers and arches but concealed externally by a flat terrace roof. The gorgeous gilt and coloured *mihrāb* is of later date (1636). The numerous halls, pavilions,

and mosques in the Citadel include the graceful Mihtar Mahal
(*c.* 1620), a small mosque with a striking gate-tower, said by
Fergusson to be 'equal if not superior to anything in Cairo';
the Sāt Manzil, a small palace of many stories; the Gegen Mahal
(? 1561), an assembly hall with a noble archway; and the Jala-
mandir, a dainty water-pavilion. Elsewhere in the city are two
large isolated monuments: the tomb of Ibrahim II and his
family (1626–33), commonly called the 'Ibrahim Rauza', and
the mausoleum (Gol Gumbaz) of Muhammad, his successor,
which was finished in 1659. The former is chiefly notable for
its rich decoration, the latter for the remarkable and daring
construction of its enormous dome, which is explained at some
length by Fergusson.[1]

Shāhjahān, whose private life was less creditable than his
architecture, was deposed in 1658 by Aurangzīb, his third son.
The buildings of Aurangzīb's reign are inferior in all respects
to those of Shāhjahān. Among them may be mentioned the
Motī Masjid at Delhi (1659) with delicate marble decoration;
and the Badāshī mosque at Lahore (1674), which is almost a
copy of the Jāmi' Masjid at Delhi, though inferior to it in several
respects. From that date onwards Muslim architecture in
India declined, but never died. The superb standard set by the
Tāj was imitated in buildings of all kinds—mosques and tombs,
palaces and houses—till the British finally introduced Indo-
Muslim railway-stations and hotels. Thus the well-known
buildings erected by Tīpū Sultān at Seringapatam in the
eighteenth century are Muslim architecture of a sort, though in
its most Indian form, but they are decadent in their elegance.

Undoubtedly the long occupation of the chief Muslim cities
of India by British army officers with little sympathy for historical architecture led to clumsy and sometimes barbarous
treatment of certain buildings, such as those royal palaces which
lay inside forts. But things have steadily improved for many

[1] Fergusson, op. cit., vol. ii, pp. 273–7.

PLATE 17

THE PEARL MOSQUE, AGRA
A.D. 1653

years, and under the enlightened administration of Lord Curzon the care of ancient monuments received really serious attention. It seems that historical buildings in India may now be regarded as sacrosanct, but neither the official mind nor the intelligentsia in India appears to have any clear idea as to the proper relation between traditional architecture and modern needs in that country. Was it really desirable, as Havell so fiercely contended, that the New Delhi should be designed on old Hindu lines, with its secretarial offices and its sanitary conveniences hidden behind imitation temple façades? Is the style of the Tāj Mahal, erected by an enormously rich emperor three centuries ago, suitable in any way to the severely economical requirements of modern commerce and industry?

At a recent London exhibition of Indian architects' designs it was evident that the Indian architect of to-day is producing schemes and erecting buildings in every shade of fashion from the archaic Hindu temple style to the latest fad in reinforced concrete and stainless steel, while the outstanding design in the exhibition—for a mosque at Bhopal, with a charming Cairene minaret and admirable traditional detail—bore a Muslim signature and an office-address in Baker Street, London. It will be interesting to see how India will regard her architectural legacy in the next generation: whether she will continue and revive the Indo-Muslim style of the Moguls; whether she will follow a modified European fashion, with domes and minarets added here and there; or whether she will evolve some new formula, not necessarily based on any European precedent, to meet the changed economic conditions and social habits of the day.

MARTIN S. BRIGGS.

HINDUISM

The Spirit of Hinduism

HISTORY is not a mere sequence of events but is the activity of the Idea or Spirit struggling to be born, endeavouring to realize itself through events. The Idea, however, is never and cannot ever be perfectly realized. Goethe in his *Conversations* tells us that 'no organism corresponds completely to the Idea that lies at its root: behind every one the higher Idea is hidden. That is the God we all seek after and hope to find, but we can only feel him, we cannot see him.' If we look at the various and sometimes conflicting creeds we may wonder whether Hinduism is not just a name which covers a multitude of different faiths, but when we turn our attention to the spiritual life, devotion, and endeavour which lie behind the creeds, we realize the unity, the indefinable self-identity, which, however, is by no means static or absolute. Throughout the history of Hindu civilization there has been a certain inspiring ideal, a certain motive power, a certain way of looking at life, which cannot be identified with any stage or cross-section of the process. The whole movement and life of the institution, its entire history, is necessary to disclose to us this idea and it cannot therefore be expressed in a simple formula. It requires centuries for ideas to utter themselves, and at any stage the institution has always an element that is yet to be expressed. No idea is fully expressed at any one point of its historical unfolding.

What is this Idea of Hinduism, this continuous element that runs through all from the earliest to the latest, from the lowest to the highest stages, this fundamental spirit which is more fully and richly expressed in the highest though it is present in the very lowest? Life is present in every stage of a plant's growth and it is always the same life though it is more fully expressed in the developed tree than in the first push of the tender blade. In the Hindu religion there must be a common element that makes every stage and every movement an expression of the religion. The different phases and stages have proper content and meaning only in so far as this common element exists. With the perception of the unity which runs through error and failure up the long ascent towards the ideal, the whole achievement of Hinduism falls into coherent perspective. It is this essential spirit that any account of Hinduism would seek to express, the spirit that its institutions imperfectly set forth, the spirit that we need to develop more adequately and richly before a better age and civilization can be achieved.

Historical Outline

The spirit is not a dead abstraction but a living force. Because it is active and dynamic the Hindu civilization has endured so long and proved so capable of adaptation to the growing complexity of life. The great river of Hindu life, usually serene but not without its rapids, reaches back so far that only a long view can do justice to its nature. From prehistoric times influences have been at work moulding the faith. As a result of the excavations in Harappa and Mohenjodāro we have evidence of the presence in India of a highly developed culture that 'must have had a long antecedent history on the soil of India, taking us back to an age that can only be dimly surmised'.[1] In age and achievement the Indus-valley civilization is comparable to that of Egypt or Sumeria. The noteworthy feature of this civilization is its continuity, not as a political power but as a cultural influence.[2] The religion of the Indus people is hardly dis-

---

[1] Sir John Marshall, *Mohenjo-Dāro and the Indus Civilization* (1931), vol. i, p. 106.

[2] Professor Childe writes: 'India confronts Egypt and Babylonia by the third millennium with a thoroughly individual and independent civilization of her own, technically the peer of the rest. And plainly it is deeply rooted in the Indian soil.' Again 'it has endured; it is already specifically Indian,

tinguishable, according to Sir John Marshall, from 'that aspect
of Hinduism which is bound up with animism and the cults of
Śiva and the Mother Goddess'.[1] These latter do not seem to
be indigenous to the Vedic religion. In the *Kulālikāmnāya* or
Kubjikāmala Tantra there is a verse which reads: 'Go forth to
India and assert your authority in the whole country. I will
not get to you until you establish yourself there.' Though the
Śakti cult was later accepted by the Vedic people, their original
opposition to it is not altogether suppressed. To the sacrifice
of Daksha, all the Vedic deities are said to be invited except Śiva,
who soon gained authority as the successor of the Vedic Rudra.
Even so late as the *Bhāgavata Purāna* the opposition to Śiva-
worship is present. 'Those who worship Śiva and those who
follow them are the opponents of holy scriptures and may be
ranked with pāshandins. Let the feeble-minded who, with matted
locks, ashes, and bones, have lost their purity, be initiated into
the worship of Śiva in which wine and brewage are regarded
as gods.'[2]

It is a matter for conjecture whether the Indus people had
any relation to the Dravidians, who, according to Risley, are 'the
earliest inhabitants of India of whom we have any knowledge'.[3]
Nor can we say whether the Dravidians were natives of the soil
or came from outside. Besides the Āryans and the Dravidians
there was also a flat-nosed, black-skinned people who are commonly known as *dāsas* or slaves. The religion, in the first literary

and forms the basis of modern Indian culture'. *New Light on the Most
Ancient East* (1934).

[1] Sir John Marshall, *Mohenjo-daro and the Indus Civilization* (1931), vol. i,
p. viii.

[2] *Bhāgavata Purāna*, iv. 2. In the *Padma Purāna*, pāshandins are said to
be 'those who wear skulls, ashes, and bones, the symbols contrary to the
Vedas, put on matted locks and the barks of trees, even without entering into
the third order of life and engage in rites which are not sanctioned by the
Vedas.' *Uttara-khanda*, ch. 235.

[3] *Census of India Report* (1901), vol. i, pt. 1, p. 508.

PLATE 18

ŚIVA NĀTARĀJĀ
Copper casting, Ceylon. 8th century A.D.

records that have come down to us, is that of the Āryans, though it was much influenced by the Indus people, the Dravidians, and the aborigines. The simple hymns of the *Rig-Veda* reveal to us an age when Pan was still alive, when the trees in the forest could speak and the waters of the river could sing and man could listen and understand. The spells and the charms to be found in the tenth book of the *Rig-Veda* and the whole of the *Atharva-Veda* suggest a type of religious practice based on fear and associated with the spirits of the dark. A religious synthesis of the different views and practices on the basis of monistic idealism is set forth in the early *Upanishads*. Soon after, Hellenistic culture springing from a union of Greek with Persian and Bactrian influences dominated north-western India. Successive descents of Muslim conquerors from about A.D. 1000 affected Hindu life and thought. The Parsee fugitives who were expelled from Persia by Muslim invaders found a welcome shelter in India. St. Thomas brought the Christian faith from Syria to south India and for over a thousand years this remained the only Christian centre of influence. In the sixteenth century St. Francis Xavier introduced Latin Christianity. The modern Christian missionary movement started over a century ago. The cultural invasion of the West has been vigorous, thanks to its political superiority and industrial efficiency.

Jainism, Buddhism, and Sikhism are creations of the Indian mind and represent reform movements from within the fold of Hinduism put forth to meet the special demands of the various stages of the Hindu faith. Zoroastrianism, Islam, and Christianity have been so long in the country that they have become native to the soil and are deeply influenced by the atmosphere of Hinduism.

India was a thorough 'melting pot' long before the term was invented for America. In spite of attacks, Hellenic, Muslim, and European among others, Hindu culture has maintained its tradition unbroken to the present day from the fourth millennium B.C. The spiritual life of the Hindus at the present time has not precisely the same proportion or orientation as that of either the Indus people or the Vedic Āryans or even the great teachers, Śamkara and Rāmānuja. Its changes in emphasis reflect individual temperaments, social conditions, and the changing intellectual environment, but the same persistent idea reappears in different forms. Hinduism grows in the proper sense of the word, not by accretion, but like an organism, undergoing from time to time transformation as a whole. It has carried within it much of its early possessions. It has cast aside a good deal and often it has found treasures which it made its own. It took what it could whence it could, though it adhered to its original vision. The more it changes the more it remains the same thing. The history of Hinduism is chequered by tragic failures and wonderful victories, by opportunities missed and taken. New truth has been denied and persecuted occasionally. The unity of its body realized at the cost of centuries of effort and labour now and then came near being shattered by self-seeking and ignorance. Yet the religion itself is not destroyed. It is alive and vigorous and has withstood attacks from within and without. It seems to be possessed of unlimited powers of renewal. Its historic vitality, the abounding energy which it reveals, would alone be evidence of its spiritual genius.

Universality

In its great days Hinduism was inspired to carry its idea across the frontiers of India and impose it on the civilized world. Its memory has become a part of the Asiatic consciousness, tinging its outlook on life. To-day it is a vital element in world thought and offers the necessary corrective to the predominantly rationalistic pragmatism of the West. It has therefore universal value.

The vision of India, like that of Greece, is Indian only in the sense that it was formulated by minds belonging to the Indian soil. The value of that vision does not reside in any tribal or provincial characteristics, but in those elements of universality which appeal to the whole world. What can be recognized as peculiarly Indian is not the universal truth which is present in it, but the elements of weakness and prejudice, which even some of the greatest of Indians have in common with their weaker brethren.

Religion as Experience

Hinduism represents a development from the beliefs and practices of the Indus-valley civilization to the complex of changing aspirations and habits, speculations and forms which are in vogue to-day. There are, however, certain governing conceptions, controlling ideas, deep dynamic links which bind together the different stages and movements. The unity of Hinduism is not one of an unchanging creed or a fixed deposit of doctrine, but is the unity of a continuously changing life. In this essay we can only deal with the general drift of the current of Hindu religion as a whole, not with the many confusing cross-currents and sects.

Religion for the Hindu is experience or attitude of mind. It is not an idea but a power, not an intellectual proposition but a life conviction. Religion is consciousness of ultimate reality, not a theory about God. The religious genius is not a pedant or a pandit, not a sophist or a dialectician, but a prophet, a sage, or a *rishi* who embodies in himself the spiritual vision. When the soul goes inward into itself it draws near its own divine root and becomes pervaded by the radiance of another nature. The aim of all religion is the practical realization of the highest truth. It is intuition of reality (*brahmānubhava*), insight into truth (*brahmadarśana*), contact with the supreme (*brahmasamsparśa*), direct apprehension of reality (*brahmasākshātkāra*).

In emphasizing the experiential as distinct from the dogmatic or credal character of religion, Hinduism seems to be more adequate than other religions to the history of religion as well as to the contemporary religious situation. Buddhism in its original form did not avow any theistic belief. Confucius, like Buddha, discouraged his disciples from occupying their minds with speculations about the Divine Being or the Unseen World. There are systems of Hindu thought, like the Sāmkhya and the Pūrva Mīmāmsā, which, in some of their characteristic phases, cultivate a spirit and attitude to which it would be difficult to deny the name of religion, even though they may not accept any belief in God or gods superior to oneself. They adopt other methods for achieving salvation from sin and sorrow and do not look to God as the source of their saving. We cannot deny to Spinoza the religious spirit simply because he did not admit any reciprocal communion between the divine and the human spirits. We have instances of religious fervour and seriousness without a corresponding belief in any being describable as God. Again, it is possible for us to believe in God and yet be without any religious sense. We may regard the proofs for the existence of God as irrefutable and yet may not possess the feelings and attitude associated with religion. Religion is not so much a matter of theoretical knowledge as of life and practice. When Kant attacked the traditional proofs of God's existence, and asserted at the same time his faith in God as a postulate of moral consciousness, he brought out the essentially non-theoretical character of life in God. It follows that the reality of God is not based on abstract arguments or scholastic proofs, but is derived from the specifically religious experience which alone gives peculiar significance to the word 'God'. Man becomes aware of God through experience. Rational arguments establish religious faith only when they are interpreted in the light of that religious experience. The arguments do not reveal God to us but are helpful in removing obstacles to the acceptance by our minds of a revelation mediated by that capacity for the apprehension of the Divine which is a normal feature of our humanity.[1] Those who have developed this centre through which all the threads of the universe are drawn are the religious geniuses. The high vision of those who have penetrated into the depths of being, their sense of the Divine in all their exaltation of feeling and enrichment of personality, have been the source of all the noblest work in the world. From Moses to Isaiah, from Jesus and Paul on to Augustine, Luther, and Wesley, from Socrates and Plato to Plotinus and Philo, from Zoroaster to Buddha, from Confucius to Mahomet, the men who initiated new currents of life, the creative personalities, are those who have known God by acquaintance and not by hearsay.

The Vedas

What is final is the religious experience itself, though its expressions change if they are to be relevant to the growing content of knowledge. The experience is what is felt by the individual in his deepest being, what is seen by him (*drishti*) or heard (*śruti*) and this is valid for all time. The Veda is seen or heard, not made by its human authors. It is spiritual discovery, not creation. The way to wisdom is not through intellectual activity. From the beginning, India believed in the superiority of intuition or the method of direct perception of the super-sensible to intellectual reasoning. The Vedic *rishis* 'were the first who ever burst into that silent sea' of ultimate being and their utterances about what they saw and heard there are found registered in the *Vedas*. Naturally they attribute the authorship of the *Vedas* to a superior spirit.

Modern psychology admits that the higher achievements of men depend in the last analysis on processes that are beyond and deeper than the limits of the normal consciousness. Socrates speaks of the 'daimōn' which acts as the censor on and speaks

[1] See Clement Webb, *Religion and Theism* (1934), p. 36.

through him. Plato regards inspiration as an act of a goddess. Ideas are showered on Philo from above, though he is oblivious of everything around him. George Eliot tells us that she wrote her best work in a kind of frenzy almost without knowing what she was writing. According to Emerson, all poetry is first written in the heavens. It is conceived by a self deeper than appears in normal life. The prophet, when he begins his message 'Thus saith the Lord', is giving utterance to his consciousness that the message is not his own, that it comes from a wider and deeper level of life and from a source outside his limited self. Since we cannot compel these exceptional moments to occur, all inspiration has something of revelation in it. Instead of considering creative work to be due to processes which take place unwittingly, as some new psychologists imagine,[1] the Hindu thinkers affirm that the creative deeds, the inspiration of the poets, the vision of the artist, and the genius of the man of science are in reality the utterance of the Eternal through man. In those rare moments man is in touch with a wider world and is swayed by an oversoul that is above his own. The seers feel that their experiences are unmediated direct disclosures from the wholly other and regard them as supernatural, as not discovered by man's own activity (*akartrika, apaurusheya*). They feel that they come to them from God,[2] though even God is said to be not their author but their formulator. In the last analysis the *Vedas* are without any personal author.[3] Since they are not due to personal activity they are not subject to unlimited revision and restatement but possess in a sense the character of finality (*nityatva*).

While scientific knowledge soon becomes obsolete, intuitive wisdom has a permanent value. Inspired poetry and religious scriptures have a certain timelessness or universality which intellectual works do not share. While Aristotle's biology is

---

[1] See Rivers, *Instinct and the Unconscious.*

[2] *Rig-Veda*, x. 90. 9; *Brihadāranyaka Upanishad*, ii. 4. 10.

[3] Purushābhāvāt . . . nishthā, *Mīmāmsā-nyāya-prakāśa*, 6.

no longer true, the drama of Euripides is still beautiful. While Vaiśeshika atomism is obsolete, Kālidāsa's *Śakuntalā* is unsurpassed in its own line.

There is a community and continuity of life between man in his deepest self and God. In ethical creativity and religious experience man draws on this source or rather the source of power is expressing itself through him. In Tennyson's fine figure the sluices are opened and the great ocean of power flows in. It is the spirit in man that is responding to the spirit in the universe, the deep calling unto the deep.

The *Vedas* are more a record than an interpretation of religious experience. While their authority is final, that of the expression and the interpretations of the religious experience is by no means final. The latter are said to be *smriti* or the remembered testimonies of great souls. These interpretations are bound to change if they are to be relevant to the growing content of knowledge. Facts alone stand firm, judgements waver and change. Facts can be expressed in the dialect of the age. The relation between the vision and its expression, the fact and its interpretation, is very close. It is more like the body and the skin than the body and its clothes. When the vision is to be reinterpreted, what is needed is not a mere verbal change but a readaptation to new habits of mind. We have evidence to show that the *Vedas* meant slightly different things to successive generations of believers. On the fundamental, metaphysical, and religious issues the different commentators, Śamkara, Rāmānuja, and Madhva, offer different interpretations. To ascribe finality to a spiritual movement is to bring it to a standstill. To stand still is to fall back. There is not and there cannot be any finality in interpretation.

Authority, Logic, and Life

Insight into reality which is the goal of the religious quest is earned by intellectual and moral discipline. Three stages are

generally distinguished, a tradition which we have to learn
(*śravana*), an intellectual training through which we have to
pass (*manana*), and an ethical discipline we have to undergo
(*nididhyāsana*).[1]

To begin with, we are all learners. We take our views on
the authority of a tradition which we have done nothing to
create but which we have only to accept in the first instance.
In every department, art or morality, science or social life, we
are taught the first principles and are not encouraged to exercise our private judgement. Religion is not an exception to
this rule. Religious scriptures are said to have a right to our
acceptance.

The second step is logical reflection or *manana*. To understand the sacred tradition we should use our intelligence.
'Verily, when the sages or *rishis* were passing away, men in-
quired of the gods, "who shall be our rishi?" They gave them
the science of reasoning for constructing the sense of the
hymns.'[2] Criticism helps the discovery of truth and, if it
destroys anything, it is only illusions that are bred by piety that
are destroyed by it. *Śruti* and *Smriti*, experience and interpretation, scripture and logic are the two wings given to the
human soul to reach the truth. While the Hindu view permits
us to criticize the tradition we should do so only from within.
It can be remoulded and improved only by those who accept
it and use it in their lives. Our great reformers, our eminently
original thinkers like Śamkara and Rāmānuja, are rebels against
tradition; but their convictions, as they themselves admit, are
also revivals of tradition. While the Hindus are hostile to those
who revile their tradition and repudiate it altogether and condemn them as *avaidika* or *nāstika*, they are hospitable to all
those who accept the tradition, however critical they may be
of it.

The authoritativeness of the *Veda* does not preclude critical

[1] *Vivarana-prameya-samgraha*, p. 1.   [2] *Nirukta-parisishta*, XIII. ii.

examination of matters dealt with in it. The Hindus believe that the truths of revelation are justifiable to reason. Our convictions are valuable only when they are the results of our personal efforts to understand. The accepted tradition becomes reasoned truth. If the truths ascertained by inquiry conflict with the statements found in the scriptures, the latter must be explained in a way agreeable to truth. No scriptures can compel us to believe falsehoods. 'A thousand scriptures verily cannot convert a jar into a cloth.' We have much in the *Vedas* which is a product not of man's highest wisdom but of his wayward fancy. If we remember that revelation precedes its record, we will realize that the *Veda* may not be an accurate embodiment of the former. It has in it a good deal of inference and interpretation mixed up with intuition and experience. Insistence on Vedic authority is not an encouragement of credulity or an enslaving subjection to scriptural texts. It does not justify the conditions under which degrading religious despotisms grew up later.

The Vedic testimony, the logical truth, must become for us the present fact. We must recapture something of that energy of soul of which the *Vedas* are the creation by letting the thoughts and emotions of that still living past vibrate in our spirits. By *nididhyāsana* or contemplative meditation, ethical discipline, the truth is built into the substance of our life. What we accept on authority and test by logic is now proved by its power to sustain a definite and unique type of life of supreme value. Thought completes itself in life and we thrill again with the creative experience of the first days of the founders of the religion.

God

If religion is experience, what is it that we experience? What is the nature of reality? In our knowledge of God, contact with the ultimate reality through religious experience plays the same part which contact with nature through sense perception plays in our knowledge of nature. In both we have a sense of the other, the trans-subjective, which controls our apprehension. It is so utterly given to us and not made by us. We build the concept of reality from the data of religious experience, even as we build the order of nature from the immediate data of sense.

In the long and diversified history of man's quest for reality represented by Hinduism, the object which haunts the human soul as a presence at once all-embracing and infinite is envisaged in many different ways. The Hindus are said to adopt polytheism, monotheism, and pantheism as well as belief in demons, heroes, and ancestors. It is easy to find texts in support of each of these views. The cults of Śiva and Śakti may have come down from the Indus people. Worship of trees, animals, rivers, and other cults associated with fertility ritual may have had the same origin, while the dark powers of the underworld, who are dreaded and propitiated, may be due to aboriginal sources. The Vedic Āryans contributed the higher gods comparable to the Olympians of the Greeks, like the Sky and the Earth, the Sun and the Fire. The Hindu religion deals with these different lines of thought and fuses them into a whole by means of its philosophical synthesis. A religion is judged by what it tends towards. Those who note the facts and miss the truth are unfair to the Hindu attempt.

The reality we experience cannot be fully expressed in terms of logic and language. It defies all description. The seer is as certain of the objective reality he apprehends as he is of the inadequacy of thought to express it. A God comprehended is no God, but an artificial construction of our minds. Individuality, whether human or divine, can only be accepted as given fact and not described. It is not wholly transparent to logic. It is inexhaustible by analysis.[1] Its inexhaustibility is the proof of

---

[1] Cf. Augustine's statement that if one knows the object of one's belief, it cannot be God one knows.

objectivity. However far we may carry our logical analysis, the
given object in all its uniqueness is there constituting a limit
to our analysis. Our thinking is controlled by something beyond
itself which is perception in physical science and the intuition
of God in the science of religion. The eternal being of God
cannot be described by categories. An attitude of reticence
is adopted regarding the question of the nature of the Supreme.
Those who know it tell it not; those who tell it know it not. The
Kena Upanishad says: 'The eye does not go thither, nor speech
nor mind. We do not know, we do not understand how one can
teach it. It is different from the known, it is also above the unknown.'[1] Śamkara quotes a Vedic passage where the teacher tells
the pupil the secret of the self by keeping silent about it. 'Verily, I
tell you, but you understand not, the self is silence.'[2] The deeper
experience is a 'wordless' doctrine. The sages declare that 'wonderful is the man that can speak of him, and wonderful is also
the man that can understand him'.[3] Buddha maintained silence
about the nature of ultimate reality. 'Silent are the Tathā-
gatas. O, Blessed one.'[4] The *Mādhyamikas* declare that the
truth is free from such descriptions as 'it is', 'it is not', 'both',
and 'neither'. Nāgārjuna says that Buddha did not give any
definition of the ultimate reality. 'Nowhere and to nobody
has ever anything been preached by the Buddha.'[5] A verse
attributed to Śamkara reads: 'It is wonderful that there under
the Banyan tree the pupil is old while the teacher is young. The
explanation of the teacher is silence but the doubts of the pupil
are dispersed.' This attitude is truer and nobler than that of
the theologians, who construct elaborate mansions and show
us round with the air of God's own estate agents.

When, however, attempts are made to give expression to the
ineffable reality, negative descriptions are employed. The real

[1] i. 2–4.   [2] *Bhāsya on Brahma Sūtra*, iii. 2. 17.
[3] See *Katha Up.* i. 2. 7; also *Bhagavad-gītā*, ii. 29.
[4] *Lankāvatāra-sūtra*, 16.   [5] *Mādhyamika-kārikā*, xv. 24.

is the wholly other, the utterly transcendent, the mysterious being which awakens in us a sense of awe and wonder, dread and desire. It not only fascinates us but produces a sense of abasement in us. Whatever is true of empirical being is denied of the Real. 'The Ātman can only be described by "no, no". It is incomprehensible for it cannot be comprehended.'[1] It is not in space or time; it is free from causal necessity. It is above all conceptions and conceptional differentiations. But on this account it is not to be confused with non-being.[2] It is being in a more satisfying sense than empirical being. The inadequacy of intellectual analysis is the outcome of the incomparable wealth of intrinsic reality in the supreme being. The eternal being is utterly beyond all personal limitation, is beyond all forms though the sustainer of all forms. All religious systems in which mankind has sought to confine the reality of God are inadequate. They make of God an 'idol'.

While the negative characteristics indicate the transcendent character of the real, there is a sense in which the real is also immanent. The very fact that we are able to apprehend the real means that there is something in us capable of apprehending it. The deepest part of our nature responds to the call of the reality. In spiritual life the law holds that only like can know like. We can only know what is akin to ourselves. Above and beyond our rational being lies hidden the ultimate and highest part of our nature. What the mystics call the 'basis' or 'ground' of the soul is not satisfied by the transitory or the temporal, by the sensuous or the intellectual.[3] Naturally, the power by which we acquire the knowledge of God is not logical thought,

---

[1] *Bṛhad-āraṇyaka Up.* iii. 9, 26.

[2] See Śaṁkara's commentary on *Chāndōgya Upanishad*, viii.

[3] 'In us too, all that we call person and personal, indeed all that we can know or name in ourselves at all is but one element in the whole. Beneath it lies even in us, that wholly other, whose profundity impenetrable to any concept can yet be grasped in the numinous self-feeling by one who has experience of the deeper life.' Rudolf Otto, *The Idea of the Holy*, E.T., p. 36.

but spirit, for spirit can only be spiritually discerned. While the real is utterly transcendent to the empirical individual, it is immanent in the ultimate part of our nature. God's revelation and man's contemplation are two aspects of one and the same experience. The Beyond is the Within. Brahman is Ātman. He is the *antaryāmin*, the inner controller. He is not only the incommunicable mystery standing for ever in his own perfect light, bliss, and peace but also is here in us, upholding, sustaining us; 'Whoever worships God as other than the self, thinking he is one and I am another, knows not.'[1] Religion arises out of the experience of the human spirit which feels its kinship and continuity with the Divine other. A purely immanent deity cannot be an object of worship and adoration; a purely transcendent one does not allow of any worship or adoration.

Hindu thinkers are not content with postulating a being unrelated to humanity, who is merely the Beyond, so far as the empirical world is concerned. From the beginnings of Hindu history, attempts are made to bring God closer to the needs of man. Though it is impossible to describe the ultimate reality, it is quite possible to indicate by means of symbols aspects of it, though the symbolic description is not a substitute for the experience of God. We are helpless in this matter and therefore are obliged to substitute symbols for substances, pictures for realities. We adopt a symbolic account when we regard the ultimate reality as the highest person, as the supreme personality, as the Father of us all, ready to respond to the needs of humanity. The *Rig-Veda* has it: 'All this is the person, that which is past and that which is future.'[2] It is the matrix of the entire being. The Vaishnava thinkers and the Śaiva Siddhāntins make of the supreme, the fulfilment of our nature. He is knowledge that will enlighten the ignorant, strength for the weak,

---

[1] *Brhad-āranyaka Upanishad*, i. 4, 10.

[2] The Supreme is 'all that which ever is, on all the world' (*Sarvam idam yatkiñca jagatyām jagat*).

mercy for the guilty, patience for the sufferer, comfort for the comfortless. Strictly speaking, however, the supreme is not this or that personal form but is the being that is responsible for all that was, is, and shall be. His temple is every world, every star that spins in the firmament. No element can contain him for he is all elements. Your life and mine are enveloped by him. Worship is the acknowledgement of the magnificence of this supreme reality.

We have accounts of the ultimate Reality as both Absolute and God, Brahman, and Īśvara. Only those who accept the view of the Supreme as personality admit that the unsearchableness of God cannot be measured by our feeble conceptions. They confess that there is an overplus of reality beyond the personal concept. To the worshipper, the personal God is the highest. No one can worship what is known as imperfect. Even the idol of the idolater stands for perfection, though he may toss it aside the moment he detects its imperfection.

It is wrong to assume that the Supreme is either the Absolute or God. It is both the Absolute and God. The impersonal and the personal conceptions are not to be regarded as rival claimants to the exclusive truth. They are the different ways in which the single comprehensive pattern reveals itself to the spirit of man. One and the same Being is conceived now as the object of philosophical inquiry or *jnānā*, at another as an object of devotion or *upāsana*. The conception of ultimate reality and that of a personal God are reconciled in religious experience, though the reconciliation cannot be easily effected in the region of thought. We cannot help thinking of the Supreme under the analogy of self-consciousness and yet the Supreme is the absolutely simple, unchanging, free, spiritual reality in which the soul finds its home, its rest, and completion.

Hospitality of the Hindu Mind

A religion that is based on the central truth of a comprehensive universal spirit cannot support an inflexible dogmatism. It adopts an attitude of toleration not as a matter of policy or expediency but as a principle of spiritual life. Toleration is a duty, not a mere concession. In pursuance of this duty Hinduism has accepted within its fold almost all varieties of belief and doctrine and treated them as authentic expressions of the spiritual endeavour, however antithetic they may appear to be. Hinduism warns us that each of us should be modest enough to realize that we may perhaps be mistaken in our views and what others hold with equal sincerity is not a matter for ridicule. If we believe that we have the whole mind of God we are tempted to assume that any one who disagrees with us is wrong and ought to be silenced. The Hindu shared Aristotle's conviction that a view held strongly by many is not usually a pure delusion. If any view has ennobled and purified human life over a wide range of space, time, and circumstance, and is still doing the same for those who assimilate its concept, it must embody a real apprehension of the Supreme Being. For Hinduism, though God is formless, he yet informs and sustains countless forms. He is not small and partial, or remote and ineffable. He is not merely the God of Israel or of Christendom but the crown and fulfilment of you and me, of all men and all women, of life and death, of joy and sorrow. No outward form can wholly contain the inward reality, though every form brings out an aspect of it. In all religions, from the lowest to the highest, man is in contact with an invisible environment and attempts to express his view of the Divine by means of images. The animist of the *Atharva-Veda*, who believes that nature is full of spirits, is religious to the extent that he is convinced of the Divine presence and interpenetration in the world and nature. The polytheist is true to the extent that the Divine is to be treated on the analogy of human consciousness rather than any other empirical thing. The gods of the *Vedas* resemble the Supreme no more than shadows resemble the sun, but even as the shadows indicate where the sun is, the Vedic deities point to the direction in which the Supreme reality is. All forms are directing their steps towards the one God, though along different paths. The real is one, though it is expressed in different names, which are determined by climate, history, and temperament. If each one follows his own path with sincerity and devotion he will surely reach God. Even inadequate views help their adherents to adapt themselves more successfully to their environment, to order their experiences more satisfactorily, and act on their environment more creatively. In the great crises of life, our differences look petty and unworthy. All of us have the same urge towards something of permanent worth, the same sense of awe and fascination before the mystery that lies beyond and within the cosmos, the same passion for love and joy, peace and fortitude. If we judge the saving power of truth from its empirical effects we see that every form of worship and belief has a strange power which enables us to escape from our littleness and become radiant with a happiness that is not of this world, which transforms unhappy dens into beautiful homes and converts men and women of easy virtue and little knowledge into suffering servants of God. All truth is God's truth and even a little of it can save us from great troubles.

Besides, the truth of religion is, as Troeltsch declared, 'polymorphic'. The light is scattered in many broken lights and there is not anywhere any full white ray of divine revelation. Truth is found in all religions, though in different measures. The different revelations do not contradict but on many points confirm one another. For the Hindu, religions differ not in their object but in their renderings of its nature.

The Hindu attitude to religious reform is based on an understanding of the place of religion in human life. A man's religion is something integral in his nature. It is like a limb, which grows from him, grows on him, and grows out of him. If we take it away from him we mutilate his humanity and force it into an unnatural shape. We are all prejudiced in favour of what is our own. In spite of all logic we are inclined to believe that the home into which we are born is the best of all possible homes, that our parents are not as others are, and we ourselves are perhaps the most reasonable excuse for the existence of the human race on earth. If strangers are sceptical, it is because they do not know. These prejudices serve a useful purpose within limits. Mankind would never have progressed to this high estate if it had not been for this partiality for our homes and parents, our art and culture, our religion and civilization. If each pushes this prejudice to the extreme point, competition and warfare will result, but the principle that each one should accept his own tradition as the best for him requires to be adopted with due care that it is not exaggerated into contempt and hatred for other traditions. Hinduism admits this principle of historical continuity, recognizes its importance for man's advancement, and at the same time insists on equal treatment for others' views. Trying to impose one's opinions on others is neither so exciting nor so fruitful as joining hands in an endeavour after a result much larger than we know.

Besides, truth will prevail and does not require our propaganda. The function of a religious teacher is only to assist the soul's natural movement towards life. The longing for an ideal life may be hidden deep, overlaid, distorted, misunderstood, ill expressed, but it is there and is never wholly lacking. It is man's birthright which he cannot barter away or squander. We have to reckon with it and build on its basis. It does not matter what conception of God we adopt so long as we keep up a perpetual search after truth. The great Hindu prayers are addressed to God as eternal truth to enlighten us, to enable us to grasp the secret of the universe better and better. There is no finality in this process of understanding. Toleration in Hinduism is not equivalent to indifference to truth. Hinduism does not say that truth does not matter. It affirms that all truths are shadows except the last, though all shadows are cast by the light of truth. It is one's duty to press forward until the highest truth is reached. The Hindu method of religious reform or conversion has this for its aim.

Conversion is not always by means of argument. By the witness of personal example, vital changes are produced in thought and life. Religious conviction is the result, not the cause of religious life. Hinduism deepens the life of spirit among the adherents who belong to it, without affecting its form. All the gods included in the Hindu pantheon stand for some aspect of the Supreme. Brahma, Vishnu, and Śiva bring out the creative will, saving love and fearful judgement of the Supreme. Each of them to its worshippers becomes a name of the Supreme God. *Harivamśa*, for example, tells us that Vishnu is the Supreme God, taught in the whole range of the Scriptures, the *Vedas*, the *Rāmāyana*, the *Purānas*, and the Epics. The same description is given of Śiva, who has Rudra for his Vedic counterpart.[1] He becomes the highest God. Śakti, the Mother Goddess, in her different forms represents the dynamic side of Godhead. Whatever form of worship is taken up by the Hindu faith it is exalted into the highest. The multiplicity of divinities is traceable historically to the acceptance of pre-existing faiths in a great religious synthesis where the different forms are interpreted as modes, emanations, or aspects of the one Supreme. In the act of worship, however, every deity is given the same metaphysical and moral perfections. The labels on the bottles may vary, but the contents are exactly the same. That is why from the *Rig-Veda* Hindu thought has been characterized by a distinctive hospitality. As the *Bhagavadgītā* has it: 'Howsoever men approach me, so do I welcome them, for the path men take from every side is mine.' Hinduism did not shrink from the acceptance of every aspect of God conceived by the mind of man, and, as we shall see, of every form of

[1] *Atharva-śiras Up.* v. 3.

devotion devised by his heart. For what counts is the attitude of sincerity and devotion and not the conception which is more or less intellectual. Kierkegaard says: 'If of two men one prays to the true God without sincerity of heart, and the other prays to an idol with all the passion of an infinite yearning, it is the first who really prays to an idol, while the second really prays to God.'[1] Dominated by such an ideal, Hinduism did not believe in either spiritual mass-production or a standardized religion for all.

The great wrong, that which we can call the sin of idolatry, is to acquiesce in anything less than the highest open to us. Religion is not so much faith in the highest as faith in the highest one can reach. At whatever level our understanding may be, we must strive to transcend it. We must perpetually strive to lift up our eyes to the highest conception of God possible for us and our generation. The greatest gift of life is the dream of a higher life. To continue to grow is the mark of a religious soul. Hinduism is bound not by a creed but by a quest, not by a common belief but by a common search for truth. Every one is a Hindu who strives for truth by study and reflection, by purity of life and conduct, by devotion and consecration to high ideals, who believes that religion rests not on authority but on experience.

Perfection

Whatever view of God the Hindu may adopt, he believes that the Divine is in man. Every human being, irrespective of caste or colour, can attain to the knowledge of this truth and make his whole life an expression of it. The Divinity in us is to be realized in mind and spirit and made a power in life. The intellectual apprehension must become embodied in a regenerated being. The Divine must subdue us to its purpose, subject the rebellious flesh to a new rhythm, and use the body

[1] Quoted in *The Tragic Sense of Life* by Unamuno (3rd imp.), p. 178.

to give voice to its own speech. Life eternal or liberation or the kingdom of heaven is nothing more than making the ego with all its thought and desires get back to its source in spirit. The self still exists, but it is no more the individual self but a radiant divine self, deeper than the individual being, a self which embraces all creation in a profound sympathy. The *Upanishad* says: 'The liberated soul enters into the All.'[1] The heart is released from its burden of care. The sorrows and errors of the past, the anxiety of unsatisfied desire, and the sullenness of resentment are no more. It is the destiny of man where there is a perfect flowering of the human being. To embody this eternal greatness in temporal fact is the aim of the world. The peace of perfection, the joy of heaven, is realizable on earth. Perfection is open to all. We are all members of the heavenly household, of the family of God. However low we may fall, we are not lost. There is no such thing as spiritual death. As long as there is a spark of spiritual life, we have hope. Even when we are on the brink of the abyss, the everlasting arms will sustain us, for there is nothing, not even an atom of reality where God does not abide. Men of spiritual insight take upon themselves the cross of mankind. They crown themselves with thorns in order that others may be crowned with life immortal. They go about the world as vagrants despising the riches of the world to induce us to believe in the riches of their world. When they gaze into men's eyes, whatever their condition of life, they see something more than man. They see our faces not merely by the ordinary light of the world but by the transfiguring light of our divine possibilities. They therefore share our joys and sorrows.

Yoga

To gain this enlightenment, this living first-hand experience of spiritual illumination, the aspirants submit themselves to long years of distracted search, to periods of painful self-denial.

[1] *Mundaka Up.* iii. 2. 15.

To be made luminous within we have to pay a heavy price. We must reduce the vast complex of actions and reactions we call human nature to some order and harmony. The appetites which call for satisfaction, the zest for life and the animal propensities, our unreasoned likes and dislikes, pull us in different directions. This raw material requires to be subdued into the pattern of self. We must attain an integrated vision, a whole life, health and strength of body, alertness of mind, and spiritual serenity. A complete synthesis of spirit, soul, flesh, and affections requires a radical change over, so that we think and live differently. We have to endure a violent inward convulsion. As a first step we are called upon to withdraw from all outward things, to retreat into the ground of one's own soul and find in the inmost depth of the self the divine reality. The world of things in its multiplicity is revealed as a unity. The vision of the true self is at the same time vision of unity (*ekatvam anupaśyati*). He beholds all beings in himself and himself in all beings.[1] 'There one perceives no other, hears no other, recognizes no other, there is fulness.'[2] A life that is divided becomes a life that is unified. Yoga is the pathway to this rebirth or realization of the divine in us.

There are not only many mansions in God's house but many roads to the heavenly city. They are roughly distinguished into three—Jñāna, Bhakti, and Karma. God is wisdom, holiness, and love. He is the answer for the intellectual demands for unity and coherence, the source and sustainer of values, and the object of worship and prayer. Religion is morality, doctrine as well as a feeling of dependence. It includes the development of reason, conscience, and emotion. Knowledge, love and action, clear thinking, ardent feeling and conscientious life, all lead us to God and are necessary for spiritual growth. A relatively greater absorption in one or the other depends on the point we have reached in our inner development. When the goal is

[1] *Īśa Up.* 6.　　　　　[2] *Chāndogya Up.* vii. 24.

reached there is an advance in the whole being of man. Religion then ceases to be a rite or a refuge and becomes the attainment of reality.

Jñāna

When *jñāna* is said to lead to *moksha* or liberation, it is not intellectual knowledge that is meant but spiritual wisdom. It is that which enables us to know that the spirit is the knower and not the known. By philosophical analysis (*tattva-vichāra*) we realize that there is in us a principle of awareness by which we perceive all things, though it is itself not perceived as an object in the ordinary way. Not to know that by which we know is to cast away a treasure that is ours. Yoga in the sense of the stilling of outward activities and emotions and concentration on pure consciousness is adopted to help the process of development. When we attain this *jñāna* there is a feeling of exaltation and ecstasy and a burning rage to suffer for mankind.

Bhakti

While Hinduism is one of the most metaphysical of religions, it is also one that can be felt and lived by the poor and the ignorant. By the pursuit of *bhakti* or devotion we reach the same goal that is attained by *jñāna*. The devotees require a concrete support to their worship and so believe in a personal God. *Bhakti* is not the love which expects to be reciprocated. Such a love is a human affection and no more. Prayer becomes meditation, the worshipful loyalty of will which identifies itself with the good of the world. If you are a true devotee of God you become a knowing and a virtuous soul as well. The *bhakta* knows how to identify himself completely with the object of devotion, by a process of self-surrender.

> My self I've rendered up to thee;
> I've cast it from me utterly.
> Now here before thee, Lord, I stand,
> Attentive to thy least command.

> The self within me now is dead,
> And thou enthroned in its stead
> Yea, this, I, Tuka, testify,
> No longer now is 'me' or 'my'.[1]

The distinction between God and worshipper is only relative. Love and knowledge have one and the same end. They can only be conceived as perfected when there is an identity between lover and beloved, knower and known.

Karma

Ethical obedience is also a pathway to salvation. Hinduism desires that one's life should be regulated by the conception of duties or debts which one has to discharge. The debts are fourfold: (i) To the Supreme Being. One's whole life is to be regarded as a sacrifice to God. (ii) To the seers. By their austerities and meditations the sages discovered truth. We become members of a cultured group only by absorbing the chief elements of the cultural tradition. (iii) To our ancestors. We repay these debts by having good progeny. The Hindu social code does not ask us to impose an unnatural order on the world. We discover the intentions of nature in the constitution of men and women and it is our duty to act agreeably to them. Marriage is not merely of bodies but of minds. It makes us richer, more human, more truly living, and becomes the cause of greater love, deeper tenderness, more perfect understanding. It is an achievement which requires discipline. If it is not the expression of spirit, it is mere lust. There are innumerable shades between love, the spiritual unity expressed in physical unity, and lust which is mere physical attraction without any spiritual basis, and which has created prostitution both within and without marriage. The great love stories of the world, even when they involve a breaking of human laws, are centred, lifted up, and glorified by their fidelity, by the fact that they do not pass. (iv) To humanity.

[1] Nicol Macnicol, *Psalms of Marāthā Saints*, p. 79.

We owe a duty to humanity which we discharge by means of
hospitality and goodwill. Those who adopt this view are not
content with merely earning their bread or seeking their comfort, but believe that they are born not for themselves but for
others. Hinduism does not believe that the use of force is
immoral in all circumstances. The *Bhagavad-gītā*, for example,
lays stress on the duties of the warrior and the claims of the
nation. There is a place for politics and heroism, but wisdom
and love are more than politics and war. In order to remain
within the bonds of a class or a nation we need not free ourselves from the bonds of humanity. Real democracy is that
which gives to each man the fullness of personal life. Animals
are also included under objects to be treated with compassion.
All life is sacred, whether of animals or of fellow men. We
shudder at cannibalism and condemn the savage who wishes
to indulge in this habit of our ancestors, though the slaughter-
ing of animals and birds for human consumption continues to
be regarded as right. The Hindu custom allows meat-eating
but prefers vegetarianism. On days dedicated to religious functions meat-eating is disallowed. Our right to take animal life
is strictly limited by our right to self-preservation and defence.
The true man is he in whom the mere pleasure of killing is
killed. So long as it is there, man has no claim to call himself
civilized. The time will soon come, I hope, when public opinion
will not tolerate popular amusements which depend on the ill-
treatment of animals. While Hinduism has within its fold
barbarians inheriting the habits of wild ancestors who slew
each other with stone axes for a piece of raw flesh, it aims at
converting them into men whose hearts are charged with an
eager and unconquerable love for all that lives.

In the priestly codes there is a tendency to confuse virtue
with ceremonial purity. To kill a man is bad, but to touch his
corpse is worse. The great scriptures, however, disregard technical morality and insist on the spirit of self-control and love of

humanity. The law of self-sacrifice is the law of development for man. To be able to fulfil the obligations expected of man he must exercise self-control. Not only what we accept but what we renounce contributes to our making. Threefold is the gate of hell that destroys the self: lust, anger, and greed. We must make war upon them with the weapons of spirit, opposing chastity to lust, love to anger, and generosity to greed. The *Veda* says: 'Cross the bridges hard to cross. Overcome anger by love, untruth by truth.' The *Mahābhārata* says: 'The rules of *dharma* or virtuous conduct taught by the great seers, each of whom relied on his own illumination, are manifold. The highest among them all is self-control.'[1] Unfortunately, in our times, the man of self-control is regarded as a weak man.[2] It is for developing self-control that austerities and asceticism are practised, but when self-control is attained these rigorous practices are unnecessary. Insistence on discipline or self-control avoids the two extremes of self-indulgence and asceticism. Discipline does not mean either the starving of the senses or the indulgence of them.[3]

There is enough scope for repentance also. 'If he repents after he commits the sin, the sin is destroyed. If he resolves that he will never commit the sin again, he will be purified.'

The *sannyāsi* is not one who abstains from work. Meditation and action both express the same spirit. There is no conflict between wisdom and work. 'It is the children of this world and not the men of learning who think of wisdom and work as different. The peace that is won by the knower is likewise won by the worker. He sees in truth who sees that wisdom and work are one.'[4]

Karma and Rebirth

The world is not only spiritual but also moral. Life is an education. In the moral sphere no less than the physical, what-

---

[1] *Śāntiparva*, clx. 6. [2] Ibid. 34.
[3] See *Bhagavad-gītā*, vi. 16–18. [4] Ibid. x. 3; v. 4–5.

soever a man soweth that shall he also reap. Every act produces its natural result in future character. The result of the act is not something external to it imposed from without on the actor by an external judge but is in very truth a part of the act itself. We cannot confuse belief in *karma* with an easy-going fatalism. It is the very opposite of fatalism. It deletes chance, for it says that even the smallest happening has its cause in the past and its result in the future. It does not accept the theory of pre-determination or the idea of an over-ruling providence. If we find ourselves helpless and unhappy we are not condemned to it by a deity outside of ourselves. The *Garuḍa Purāṇa* says: 'No one gives joy or sorrow. That others give us these is an erroneous conception. Our own deeds bring to us their fruits. Body of mine, repay by suffering.' God does not bestow his favours capriciously. The law of morality is fundamental to the whole cosmic drama. Salvation is not a gift of capricious gods but is to be won by earnest seeking and self-discipline. The law of *karma* holds that man can control his future by creating in the present what will produce the desired effect. Man is the sole and absolute master of his fate. But so long as he is a victim of his desires and allows his activities to be governed by auto-matic attractions and repulsions he is not exercising his freedom. If chains fetter us, they are of our own forging and we ourselves may rend them asunder. God works by persuasion rather than by force. Right and wrong are not the same thing and the choice we make is a real one.

About future life there are three alternatives possible: (i) The soul dies with the body since it is nothing more than a function of physical life. Hindu religion does not accept this mechanical view. (ii) The soul goes either to heaven or eternal bliss or to hell or eternal torment and remains there. For the Hindu, the doctrine that the soul has only one life, a few brief years, in the course of which it determines for itself an eternal heaven or an eternal hell, seems unreasonable and unethical.

(iii) The soul may not be fit for eternal life and yet may not deserve eternal torment and so goes from life to life. This life is not the end of everything. We shall be provided with other chances. The soul does not begin with the body nor does it end with it. It pursues its long pilgrimage through dying bodies and decaying worlds. The great purpose of redemption is carried over without break from one life to another. All systems of Hindu thought accept the idea of the continuous existence of the individual human being as axiomatic. Our mental and emotional make-up is reborn with us in the next birth, forming what is called character. 'When a man dies, what does not forsake (*na jahāti*) him is his soul (*nāma*).'[1] Our strivings and endeavours give us the start. We need not fear that the spiritual gains of a long and strenuous life go for nothing. This continuity will go on until all souls attain their destiny of freedom, which is the goal of human evolution. If there is not a shred of empirical evidence for it the same is true of other theories of future life also.

Conclusion

From the beginnings of Hindu history the culture has been formed by new forces which it had to accept and overcome in the light of its own solid and enduring ideas. In every stage there is an attempt to reach a harmony. Only the harmony is a dynamic one. When this dynamic harmony or organic rhythm of life is missing it means that the religion stands in need of reform. We are now in a period of social upheaval and religious unsettlement the world over, in one of those great incalculable moments in which history takes its major turns. The traditional forms are unable to express the growing sense of the divine, the more sensitive insight into the right way of life. It is wrong to confuse the technique of a religion with its central principles. We must reform the technique so as to make it embody the

[1] *Brihad-āranyaka Upanishad*, iii. 2, 12

fertile seeds of truth. In my travels round the country and abroad I have learnt that there are thousands of men and women to-day who are hungry to hear the good news of the birth of a new order, eager to do and dare, ready to make sacrifices that a new society may be born, men and women who dimly understand that the principles of a true religion, of a just social order, of a great movement of generosity in human relations, domestic and industrial, economic and political, national and international, are to be found in the basic principles of the Hindu religion. Their presence in growing numbers is the pledge for the victory of the powers of light, life, and love over those of darkness, death, and discord.

S. RADHAKRISHNAN.

THE CULTURAL INFLUENCES OF ISLAM[1]

MODERN Indian civilization has developed from the action and reaction of so many different races and creeds upon each other that it is extremely difficult to say which of its features is due to a particular influence. Hardest of all to assess is the influence of Islam, for the various Muslim incursions into India brought comparatively few people of an alien race into India. Even the great Bābur, when he 'put his foot in the stirrup of resolution' and set out to invade India, in November 1525, only took with him some 12,000 soldiers and merchants. Of the eighty odd million Muslims, who to-day form a quarter of the population, the great majority are descended from Hindu stock, and retain certain characteristics common to Indians as a whole. Yet because the Muslim invaders came as conquerors, rulers, and missionaries they made such an impression, especially in the north, that to many Europeans and Americans the characteristic life and architecture of India must seem to be Musulman. Muslim culture in India, being a blending of two civilizations, is something *sui generis*, and as such has its special contribution to make to the Western world, as well as to the rest of Islam. The process by which the blending took place is of special interest. A passage in the *Cambridge History of India*, by Sir John Marshall (vol. iii, p. 568), well describes the influence of Hindu and Muslim culture on one another. He observes:

'Seldom in the history of mankind has the spectacle been witnessed of two civilizations, so vast and so strongly developed, yet so radically dissimilar, as the Muhammadan and the Hindu, meeting and mingling together. The very contrasts which existed between them, the wide divergence on their culture and their religions, make the history of their impact peculiarly instructive.'

[1] This chapter is based on the Birdwood lecture, delivered by the author before the Royal Society of Arts, 13 Dec. 1935.

The earliest contact of Islam with India began in the second half of the seventh and the beginning of the eighth centuries of the Christian era, through Sind and Baluchistan. The Arabs, who conquered Sind and remained there, have left a lasting impress on the manners and customs of the people. Later on, another stream of Muslim people came to India, through its north-west frontier. They were racially and culturally different from the Arab invaders, who had come to the western coast. Representatives of various tribes and dynasties of Central Asia, who felt the spell of Islam and embraced the faith, started a long series of invasions of India. It is obvious, however, that invasions like those of Tīmūrlane or Mahmūd of Ghaznī were not calculated to produce marked cultural results or to leave many permanent traces of their influence. These contacts did not last long and offered no opportunities of any intimate relations between the people of the country and their unwelcome visitors from the north. The real contacts began when Muslims began to settle down in the country as their adopted home.

Several dynasties of Muslim kings preceded the establishment of the Mughal Empire in India, and undoubtedly contributed much to the grafting of Muslim culture on the ancient civilization of the country, but there is very little material available for making a definite estimate of their contributions. Attention has to be confined mainly to the Mughal period, which has contributed most to the development of an Indo-Muslim culture.

Some of the influences which have come to India through Muslims may not have been essential ingredients of Islam when it originated in Arabia, but they came to be identified with it in course of time, in its onward march from Arabia to Persia and Central Asia. Of these countries Persia has had a dominating influence on Islam and through it on India. The Arabs conquered Persia, but Persian civilization made such a profound impression on them that the Persian language and literature became a necessary part of Islamic culture in many Eastern lands. The Central Asian dynasties, which came to India and established kingdoms in it, had come under the influence of Persian literature before they came to India, and the result was that Persian was adopted by them as the language of the Court and of literature. In the time of the Mughals the study of the Persian language was eagerly taken up by Muslims as well as non-Muslims. The Hindus, who possess a great capacity for adaptation in matters intellectual, took kindly to Persian literature, just as they are now eagerly studying the English language and its literature. The Northern Provinces of India furnish many brilliant examples of Hindu scholars of Persian, who could use the language very effectively in prose as well as in poetry. Two classes of Hindus have particularly distinguished themselves in this respect—the Kashmīrī Pandits and the Kāyasthas. Recently a large book has been published containing selections from Persian poems composed by Kashmīrī Pandits. It was through the medium of Persian, which, in its turn, had been largely influenced by the Arabic language and the texts of the sacred books of the Muslim faith, that the best ethical thought of Islam influenced the educated Hindus of the period. One great result of this influence was the gradual prevalence of a widespread belief in the Unity of God and the growth of indigenous monotheistic faiths. The second remarkable result was the creation of a new indigenous language, called Urdū, which was a mixture of Persian and Hindī, and which has become, in course of time, the most commonly used language in India.

These two influences have had far-reaching effects in the past and are fraught with great possibilities in the future. They require, therefore, to be discussed at some length. Other influences are too numerous to be noticed in detail, as they cover a very wide range. You see them in the style of buildings and houses, in music and painting, in arts and crafts, in dress and costume, in games and sports, in short, in the whole life of the country. We shall have to be content with passing references to these commemorations of a happy blending of two cultures, the streams of which decided, long ago, to take a common course.

Let us first consider religious thought. A large majority of educated people in India, even among non-Muslims, believe in one God, as the Creator and Preserver of the Universe, with no rivals and no equals. Though this belief is to be found in almost all the great religions of the world, in one form or another, it cannot be denied that no other faith has laid so much emphasis on it as Islam. We have to remember that the systems of belief prevailing among the Hindus at the time of the advent of the Muslims had largely drifted away from the original purity of the doctrines in their earliest sacred books, and various forms of idolatry had been substituted for divine worship. Things have so changed now that, in spite of the fact that orthodox Hindus have still got idols in their temples, their attitude towards the worship of idols is very different from what it used to be. The intelligent and the educated among them declare that idols are only meant to serve as aids to concentration of thought, and that those who appear to worship them are, in reality, offering worship to Him to whom alone it is due. In this greatly changed attitude the influence of Islam can be easily traced, though in recent times the influence of Christianity has been another great force working against idolatry and superstition. It is also noteworthy that forces have sprung up inside Hinduism itself to combat the tendency to worship idols or to blindly follow designing priests. The Ārya Samāj, founded by the late Swāmī Dayānanda Sarasvatī in the Punjab, in the second half of the nineteenth century, may be mentioned as the most striking instance of the revolt of Hinduism against idol worship. This movement purports to be a revival of the ancient Vedic faith. Though it sometimes adopts a militant attitude towards Islam, in order to counteract its influence, it is significant that some of its reforms run on lines parallel to the teachings of Islam. Besides condemning idol worship, it denounces priests, it allows the admission of people of other religions into the fold of the Āryan faith, and commends the marriage of widows.

Apart from these indications of Islamic notions, gradually and imperceptibly influencing the modes of religious thought in India, Islam has had a more direct influence in bringing into existence monotheistic systems of faith in India. The Sikh religion, founded by the saintly Guru Nānak, is a remarkable instance of this influence. This holy man believed in the Unity of God as strongly as any Muslim, and desired to smooth the differences between Hinduism and Islam. The *Granth Sahib*, the sacred book of the Sikhs, bears testimony to the fact that the founder of the religion loved God and loved his fellow men and had great respect for the Prophet of Arabia and other holy men of Islam. A well-known Sikh gentleman, Sardār Umrāo Singh of Majītha, has recently published a book which clearly shows that the essential beliefs of the Sikhs and the Moslems are very similar to one another. This book is a Persian translation of Sukhmani, which is a part of the sacred book of the Sikhs and every verse in it breathes the love of God. Sardār Umrāo Singh luckily lighted on the Persian manuscript of this book in the Bibliothèque Nationale of Paris and copied it. He took the copy to India and has taken great pains in comparing the translation with the original and editing it carefully. It is highly regrettable that, for want of sufficient knowledge and appreciation of each other's beliefs, the Sikhs and Muslims have drifted so far apart from one another.

Another great religious teacher who may be specifically mentioned in this connexion is Kabīr, the best exponent of what is known as the *Bhakti* movement. In the words of a recent writer this movement 'recognized no difference between Rām and Rahīm, Kaaba and Kailash, Qurān and Purān and inculcated that Karma is Dharma. The preachers of this creed,

Rāmānanda, Kabīr, Dādū, Rāmdās, Nānak, and Chaitanya, who flourished in different parts of India and preached the principles of Unity of God, were immensely influenced by Islam.'

In more recent times the religious movement that showed the strongest signs of Muslim influence is the Brahmo-Samāj, founded by the late Rājā Rām Mohan Rāy and carried on and strengthened by the late Keshab Chandra Sen. Rājā Rām Mohan Rāy was a good scholar of Persian and very well versed in the literature of Islam. His study of English brought him into touch with Christian beliefs also, and he conceived the idea of an eclectic religion, combining the best points of the teachings of the Vedas, the Bible, and the Qurān, and holding all the great spiritual teachers of the world in equal veneration, as the best solution of the difficulties of India. The Brahmo-Samāj, as a strictly unitarian faith, shows the predominance of the most essential doctrine of Islam in its beliefs. This Samāj has included in its fold men of the highest intellectual calibre in our country, though, for obvious reasons, the number of its members has never been very large.

Language, Literature, and Art

The Urdū language is another proof of the union of Hindu and Muslim cultures, though it is strange that there is a tendency in some quarters to look upon it as something imported from outside, which might be got rid of as foreign to the soil. This mistaken view is due to want of sufficient information as to the origin of the language and its development. It is gratifying to note a growing recognition of its value even in provinces where provincial languages are spoken. The following passage taken from an article by Mr. Anilchandra Banerjee on Indo-Persian literature and the contributions made to it by the famous poet, Amīr Khusrū, of Delhi, embodies the opinion of a fair-minded Hindu writer as to the place of Urdū in the culture of our country. He says:

'Almost every work in Indo-Persian literature contains a large number of words of Indian origin, and thousands of Persian words became naturalized in every Indian vernacular language. This mingling of Persian, Arabic, and Turkish words and ideas with languages and concepts of Sanskritic origin is extremely interesting from the philological point of view, and this co-ordination of unknowns resulted in the origin of the beautiful Urdu language. That language in itself symbolized the reconciliation of the hitherto irreconcilable and mutually hostile types of civilization represented by Hinduism and Islam.'

The language thus developed by the combined efforts of Hindus and Muslims now boasts of a fairly varied and wide literature, which may be claimed as a common heritage by both, and is gaining every day in importance and strength.

Urdū literature is rich in poetry. It must be admitted, however, that Urdū poetry has been considerably restricted in its scope in the past and it is only recently that efforts have been made to widen its sphere. The most popular form of versification in Urdū was the *ghazal*, consisting of stray thoughts on such subjects as love, beauty, and morality. Each line was in the same metre, and the endings of each line rhymed with one another. This style of writing has found numerous votaries among Muslims as well as Hindus. In the collections of the *ghazals* of many of our eminent writers you can find literary gems bearing comparison with some of the best pieces of literature in other languages, though for the bulk of this kind of verse no merit can be claimed. Hence it was that some of the poets of the second half of the nineteenth century who realized the limitations of the *ghazal* and its shortcomings felt the need of literary reform. In Delhi, Ghālib was the first to realize this, but it fell to the share of his distinguished pupil, Hālī, to inaugurate the reform. He started a new school of Urdū poetry, which has had many adherents among his contemporaries and successors. In Lucknow a departure from the ordinary style of poetry was introduced by two great poets, Anīs and Dabīr, who wrote *marsiyas*, or elegies, about the martyrdom of Imām Husain. Anīs and Dabīr vastly enriched the store of Urdū literature and greatly refined and polished the Urdū language. It is very interesting to note that these two eminent literary men were not only great as writers, but were equally remarkable for the wonderful effect they could produce by giving public readings of their works. They made reading an art, which has since been imitated, but has not so far been excelled in India. Large gatherings of people of all classes, Muslims and Hindus, used to assemble to hear their recitations, and this brought about a cultural *entente* between the two, which still exists. A noteworthy influence of this form of literature was an adoption of the style of the *marsiyas* by distinguished Hindu writers for depicting the charming story of the Rāmāyana, concerning the sacrifices made by the heroic Rāma in the performance of his pious filial duty and the unselfish love of Lakshman, his brother, and of Sītā, his wife. Munshī Jawāla Pershād (*Barq*) and Pandit Brij Nārāyan (*Chakbast*) are among the Hindu writers who have effectively used the style originated by the two great masters of *marsiya* writing.

This reference to the Lucknow school of Urdū literature will not be complete without a brief mention of the famous *Fisāna-i-Āzād*, a remarkable work of fiction in Urdū, written by the late Pandit Ratan Nāth (*Sarshār*), who holds a unique position among the writers of Urdū prose. He has given graphic pictures of the life of the rich as well as the poor in Lucknow. In this book of his, as well as in many of his other works, the influence of Muslim literature, which he had read widely, is clearly visible.

Among the literary institutions popularized by the Muslims may be mentioned the *Mushaira*, which means a symposium or a meeting for a poetical contest. This contest is ordinarily held in order to judge who excels in writing a *ghazal* in a given metre. The poets joining the *Mushaira* all recite their respective compositions. It is not customary in high-class *Mushairas* for the meeting or its chairman to declare who wins the laurels of the day, but in most cases the audience is not left in doubt as to the merits of the best poem, the indication of opinion being given by the loud applause of the listeners or by expressions of approbation uttered in the course of the recitations by those in a position to judge. This institution, though not enjoying the vogue which it did in days gone by, is still fairly popular and often brings together people of different classes and communities, who manage to forget their differences for the time being, in their admiration for a common literature.

A separate chapter in this book has dealt with Muhammadan architecture. Of all branches of art this has always appealed most strongly to Muslims. One reason is that painting of human beings and animals was discouraged on religious grounds during the first period of proselytism and of Islamic expansion, and the tradition survived for many centuries afterwards. In India the building of mosques, tombs, and palaces was the most characteristic activity of the early Muslim rulers. This allowed great scope both to those artists who came from other parts of Asia, and also to the indigenous craftsmen who worked under Muslim inspiration and orders. They found vent for their artistic genius in drawing beautiful mural designs in letters and figures, and cultivating symmetry and proportion in buildings. Mausoleums and mosques thus became an inspiration to artists in every form of art. They came from every part of the country to take sketches of these buildings. Floral designs adorning the walls of these structures have been copied for embroidery and textile work. It would be impossible to estimate the immense educative value of these buildings in forming and developing the tastes, the standards of craftsmanship, and the imaginative scope of millions of Indians all over northern India, Bengal, and the Deccan. The structure of Indian society tends to make artistic production dependent upon the continuous patronage of rulers and of the very wealthy. This patronage the Mughals, and, to a far lesser extent, the earlier Muslim rulers, were able to provide. They brought not only new ideas, but also a new urge to produce. A modern writer, Mr. Ja'far, in his *History of the Mughal Empire*, has laid great stress upon the influence which the Emperors exerted on their courtiers, and through them on the rest of India.

'Bābur displayed a remarkable taste for painting. He is said to have brought to India with him all the choicest specimens of painting he could collect from the library of his forefathers, the Timurides. Some of these were taken to Persia by Nādir Shāh after his invasion of India and the conquest of Delhi, but as long as they remained in India they exerted a great influence on and gave a new impetus to the art of painting in India.'

As we know, Bābur did not live long enough to carry out his schemes for the development of India. His somewhat unfortunate son, Humāyūn, also had an unsettled reign. It was left to Bābur's grandson, Akbar, to bring to perfection the love of art which he had inherited. He proved a great patron of art in all its branches. According to Abul Fazl, the well-known Minister of Akbar, the Emperor had more than a hundred *Karkhānajāt* (i.e. workshops of arts and crafts) attached to the royal household, each like a city. (See *Āīn-i-Akbarī*—Text 9). Interesting details about these institutions have been collected by a modern writer, Mr. Abdul Azīz, in his remarkable book on the reign of Akbar's grandson, Shāhjahān.[1] I am indebted to this book for the following extract from an old historical work of Father Monserrate, who was at the Court of Akbar in 1580–2. He writes:

'He has built a workshop near the palace, where also are studios and workrooms for the finer and more reputable arts, such as painting,

---

[1] *History of the Reign of Shāhjahān*. It is being published serially in the *Journal of Indian History*.

goldsmith work, tapestry making, carpet and curtain making, and the manufacture of arms. Hither he very frequently comes and relaxes his mind with watching at their work those who practise these arts.'

The lead given by Akbar in the patronage of art was followed by his son, Jahāngīr, who was himself fond of painting. Shāhjahān was also artistic, and his personal interest encouraged his courtiers to imitate him and thus his influence further filtered down to those who came in contact with them. This tendency was particularly strong among the nobility of the Mughal Court. Mr. Abdul Azīz, writing about this tendency in the book above mentioned, observes:

'The Mughal nobility constituted a sort of agency through which the ideals of art and morals and manners were diffused among the lower classes. . . . The habits and customs of the people, their ideas, tendencies, and ambitions, their tastes and pleasures, were often unconsciously fashioned on this model. The peerage acted as the conduit-pipe for this stream of influence. The patronage of art and culture followed the same lines; and even where the interest was not genuine the enlightened pursuits were followed and encouraged as a dogma dictated by fashion.'

The merits of the paintings done under Muslim patronage during the Mughal period have been the subject of several monographs. Their value as an aid to history has been discussed in a lecture, given by the late Sir Thomas Arnold, before the Royal Society of Arts. There are considerable numbers of admirable miniatures in various European collections. The India Office in London, the British Museum, and the Bodleian at Oxford have many rare and beautiful specimens of an art which has hardly been properly appreciated by the Western world. We give two specimens of this delicate and wholly delightful work.

Closely allied to the art of painting is the art of illuminating books. This found great encouragement under the influence of Islam in India. Muslims, who could afford to do so, liked to adorn manuscripts of the Qurān and other books of religion or classic literature with gold borders on every page and to have the bindings of books adorned with gold. The taste for possessing such books was shared by their Hindu countrymen. Artists of both communities derived amusement as well as profit from illuminating books of Arabic, Sanskrit, and Persian.

Caligraphy, or the art of writing a beautiful hand, was also very widely cultivated, and though a good many people adopted it to earn a livelihood, there was a sufficient number of well-to-do people who practised it as a relaxation from other pursuits, and liked to copy in an attractive form the books they wished to treasure. It is recorded that the Emperor Aurangzīb was not only an accomplished master of this art, but that he used to earn a livelihood by making copies of the Quran and offering them for sale, as he did not like to spend the money of the State on his personal requirements.

In connexion with the subject of manuscripts, it may be mentioned that paper was brought into India by Muslims. This was a very material contribution to the advancement of learning. It appears that originally the manufacture of paper came to Central Asia from China. There was a great manufactory of it in Samarqand and it was from there that paper came to India about the tenth century A.D.

We may now consider the contribution made by Muslims to another branch of art, i.e. music. As observed by Mr. Ja'far, in his *History of the Mughal Empire*, 'Indian music, like other fine arts, proved a new channel of intercourse between the Hindus and Mussulmans. The process of co-operation and intermutation was not a new thing in the time of Akbar. It had begun centuries before. In the domain of music it became distinctly perceptible how the two communities were borrowing from each other the precious share they possessed in this art, and thereby enriching each other. *Khiyāl*, for example, which was invented by Sultān Husain Shāh (*Sharqī*) of Polpur, has become an important limb of Hindu music. *Dhrupod*, on the other hand, has engrafted itself on Muslim music.'

Abul Fazl tells us that Akbar paid much attention to music and patronized those who practised this art.

It is significant that though in the beginning of Islam this branch of art had also been discouraged like painting, yet the contact of Islam with Persia brought about a change in the attitude of Muslims towards it, particularly under the influence of *Sūfīs*, or Muslim mystics, who believed in the efficacy of music as a means of elevating the soul and as an aid to spiritual progress. This attitude became more pronounced when Muslims settling in India found that their Hindu countrymen were fond of music and made use of it in their religious ceremonies. The result was that though Divine worship in mosques continued to be performed on the rigid lines of orthodox Islam, without any extraneous aids of singing or playing on musical instruments, music became quite popular among Muslims in India. The fondness of the rich for it made it a favourite amusement, so that it was customary to have musical performances on all festive occasions. The liking which the *Sūfīs* had for music started the custom of semi-religious congregations assembling to hear songs of divine love sung by professional singers. This class of musicians is known as *Qawwāls* and the tunes which they sing are called *Qawwālī* and are very popular.

A number of new musical instruments were either introduced by Muslims or were given Persian names, after some modifications in their appearance. Instruments like *Rabāb*, *Sarod*, *Tāūs*, *Dilrubā*, are instances in point.

The Mughal gardens of northern India are almost as well known in Europe as Mughal buildings. Centuries earlier the Arabs had introduced into southern Spain the idea of the well-ordered garden, as a place in which to find repose, beauty, recreation, and protection from the heat of the day. Water, preferably flowing, was an essential feature, not only to irrigate plants and shrubs, but to bring coolness, and in the plains to bring the illusion of the mountain streams. These would call back memories of their original homes to the Mughals as much as they did to the expatriated Moors. The rediscovery in Northern India of these rather formalized gardens undoubtedly had an influence upon Italy and England.

The Mughals had undoubtedly a great feeling for natural beauty, and a certain nostalgia afflicted them in the dry arid plains of the Punjab, before the days when widespread irrigation had done something to relieve its monotony. At times they eagerly went to distant places in search of natural beauty, incurring great trouble and expense in doing so, at other times they incurred even more trouble and expense in bringing beauty to places where it did not exist before. It is interesting to read in the letters of Abul Fazl an account of the journeys of the Emperor Akbar from Agra to Kashmir, to enjoy the wonderful scenery and climate of that beautiful valley. We are told that he used to go there for the summer, attended by his courtiers and troops, and used to take a new route every time, so that sappers and miners had to go before him making roads where no roads existed. His son, Jahāngīr, kept up this practice and was as fond of the beauties of Kashmir as his father. The famous garden, known as Shālamār, in Kashmir, still exists as a thing of beauty and a joy for ever, and contributes to the pleasure of thousands of visitors every year. So does the other equally beautiful garden there, called the *Nishat*. The journeys to Kashmir are thus instances of Muslim kings going to the beauty spots of India, while the creation of a Shālamār garden in Lahore illustrates their enterprise in bringing to the plains of India the beauties of Kashmir. This garden is, to this day, one of the great sights of Lahore. The stages into which the garden at Srīnagar (in Kashmir) is divided were made possible by the natural situation of the site chosen for it. It was at the foot of a mountain and water gushing down from the hillside flowed into the garden

PLATE 19

DOMESTIC SCENE

By MUHAMMAD FAKĪRULLĀH KHĀN

Mogul school, 17th century A.D.

and enriched its soil. The natural ups and downs of the locality easily lent. themselves to being shaped as stages of the garden. At Lahore, however, the garden was divided into three stages by artificial means, which added very much to the difficulty of the task. There was no water available near the site chosen for it and it had to be brought by means of a canal, but still the beauties of the garden in Kashmir were reproduced in the heart of the Punjab. I have specifically mentioned these gardens to illustrate the point that the love of gardening displayed by so many Moslem kings in India was a valuable cultural influence and has left a lasting impression on the taste of the well-to-do classes in India, Hindus as well as Muslims. This taste has now had a further stimulus with the advent of the English, who are behind no other people in their love of gardens.

The Emperor Jahāngīr was specially keen on horticulture, and was fond of gaining knowledge and collecting information about trees, plants, and flowers. In his time he imported many new trees and plants into India. A part of Lahore which is known as the *Badāmī Bāgh* was full of almond trees which were successfully planted there. In the private collection of paintings I have seen an old book, containing hand-painted illustrations of leaves of trees and fruit-plants, indigenous as well as imported, which was prepared in Jahāngīr's time and, presumably, at his instance.

The beauty and tranquillity of the Mughal gardens undoubtedly struck the imagination of contemporary scholars and travellers, as well as of the Indians in whose midst they were placed. They provided a new conception of life and its aims which influenced literature both in India and in Europe. There are poems in Indo-Persian literature as well as in Urdū, which were professedly inspired by the gardens in Kashmir and Lahore. Our distinguished Indian poet, Iqbāl (or to give him his full name, Dr. Sir Muhammad Iqbāl) has several exquisite poems in

Persian, which were inspired by a visit to Srīnagar. A famous couplet in Persian, improvised by a Mughal princess, owed its inspiration to the sight of the beautiful waterfall which adorns the centre of the Shālamār at Lahore. She was watching with admiration the sparkling water of the *Abshar* falling on the slope of the marble, which constituted the artificial fall, and was listening to the sound so produced, when the following improvised song came to her lips:

> Ai Abshar nauha gar az bahr-i-kīstī.
> Sar dar nigūn figanda zi andoh-i-kīstī.
> Āyā chi dard būd ki chūn mā tamām shab
> Sar rā ba sang mī zadī o mī giristī.

It is not possible to bring out in translation the beauty of the original, but the words may be freely translated as follows:

Whose absence, O Waterfall, art thou lamenting so loudly,
Why hast thou cast down thy head in grief?
How acute was thy pain, that throughout the night,
Restless, like me, thou wast striking thy head against the stone and
shedding tears profusely!

So far we have dealt chiefly with the amenities of life, but the Mughals also brought new ideas of administration into India. Many of these, like the land revenue system, have been absorbed into the ordinary government of the country under British rule. Although much of the Mughal administration had collapsed before the battle of Plassey, there were the rudiments of a postal system, and the Muslims had made roads, dug irrigation canals, and encouraged gardening from well-water. They had covered the land with *kārāvan serais*, and almost certainly made it easier for Indian or European to travel in India. They had established a rule of law, which was in many ways more humane than that administered in contemporary Europe. The death sentence, which was inflicted for theft in contemporary England, was reserved for far more serious offences under the Mughal administration in India. There is abundant evidence to show that the Bengalis, in the latter half of the eighteenth century, found Muhammadan criminal law much easier to understand than the uncodified and exotic law which was enforced by the English High Court. A famous passage from Macaulay describes the devastating effect of the introduction of the new system. The merits of Muhammadan law have been fully recognized by colonial administrators in Africa.

There is some question as to how far the Mughals initiated and how far they merely adapted the elaborate court ceremonial and etiquette which so struck many travellers. From Milton onwards there are numberless references to this side of Mughal civilization. It is possible that the Mughals, like the English who followed them, believed in the psychological effect of this pomp upon the popular mind. It may be open to doubt whether this impressive show of power and wealth was really conducive to any development of culture. I must say, however, that these spectacles have an irresistible hold on the imagination of the people, and even countries boasting of the highest modern civilization cannot do without them. A peculiar feature of a Darbar in India was that poets used to come and recite *Qasīdas*, or panegyrics, praising the ruler presiding over the function, and used to be rewarded for doing so. This custom is not forgotten yet and prevails in Indian States and to a smaller extent in British territory, where *Qasīdas* are sometimes read in honour of Governors and Viceroys. These poems are not always of a very high order from a literary point of view, but there are instances of *Qasīdas* possessing real literary merit having been presented on such occasions.

The libraries that came into existence in India, as a result of the love of learning of many of its Muslim rulers, had a great influence on Indian culture. It was not only kings and princes who collected rich stores of literature for their enlightenment, but noblemen of all classes vied with one another in owning such collections. Of the Mughal kings, Humāyūn was very fond of his books and the stone building that housed his library still stands in Delhi. It was from its narrow stairs that Humāyūn fell when he died. Among the Mughal princes, Dārā Shikoh, the eldest son of Shāhjahān, a scholarly and broad-minded prince, was a great lover of books and left behind a large library, the building of which survived for a long time and the site of which is still pointed out. The ruin that followed the terrible period of the Mutiny of 1857 swept away most of these stores of literature. A few private collections of that period may still be found in some ancient families in India or in Indian States, but thousands of valuable books were lost or destroyed or sold cheap by those who got them as loot. A large number of them have travelled west and are fortunately preserved in the libraries of Europe. Among these may be found manuscripts bearing the seals or signatures of Muslim kings and noblemen who owned them. They furnish a silent but eloquent testimony to culture of days gone by, when in the absence of modern facilities for propagation of literature and for the multiplication of books, human patience endured great hardships to preserve for posterity the best thoughts of the learned men of antiquity.

ABDUL QADIR.

MUSIC

Music arises when irregular sounds are made regular, indiscriminate sounds periodic. Musical systems are the various attempts of man to get the experience which will enable him to do this. His experience divides into two aspects of time, as opposed to space: relative duration, which is time in succession, and relative pitch, which is time in simultaneity, i.e. two different frequencies, or periodicities, are instantaneously related.

His early attempts have often been described; but as we were not there to hear them it will be better to describe this particular system, the Indian, as it is known to-day, and for this purpose to assume in the reader such musical instincts as the cultivated European ordinarily possesses and no more technical knowledge than is supplied by the articles on 'Time' and 'Interval' in Grove's *Dictionary*.

Perhaps we may best begin by taking a glance at folksong, where we are not cumbered by any theory or convention. We know our own: it is a little square in structure compared with the more fanciful Irish, homely compared with the adventurous Highland Scot, of extended compass compared with the French songs, which are almost talked, naïve as compared with the sophisticated German, smooth compared with the angular Scandinavian, cheerful compared with the melancholy Russian, busy compared with the leisurely Italian, vocal compared with the Spanish, in which we hear the constant thrumming of the guitar. In India the plains and the hills seem to contrast. In the plains we hear the Irish fancy, chiefly rhythmical; an ultra-smoothness which creeps from note to note scarcely risking a leap of any kind, and, like the French, with a short compass thoroughly well explored; lugubrious, not unlike the Russian according to our views though not perhaps according to theirs, for that is a thing that foreigners never can really judge; decidedly leisurely, as one expects in a country where *kal* means both yesterday and to-morrow; and purely vocal, without a hint of the influence of any instrument.

In the hills it is more cheerful; the steps become leaps, the rhythm is accented, though it has not so many resources; it is as busy as you could wish, almost breathless in its excitement; it is pure singing, revelling in the sound, though one song is very much like another. But there is one characteristic of the hill tribes which should be noticed: they sing in the pentatonic. We think at once of the Scottish Highlanders and the Swiss yodelers and say it is the mountain air that makes these invigorating leaps in the melody; but when we find these same leaps equally in the plains of China and among the Sioux along the Missouri we think there must be some other explanation. Perhaps it is that instruments are not easily to be had in the mountains; for it is the instrument that first makes possible the division of the tone into two semitones. At any rate, whatever the reason, the fact is that the pentatonic, though not confined to, is characteristic of the Himālaya.

Some such might perhaps be the characteristics of hills and plains anywhere. What is especially Indian is the ubiquity of 'variation' and of 'grace notes'. There is no such thing as 'the' tune of a song; there is merely 'a way of singing' it. I listened to a Madrāsī singing a couple of dozen variations of a short phrase in half an hour; to three or four crowds in Calcutta singing 'Bande Mātaram' all to different tunes, though they no doubt believed them to be the same; and to a party of Gonds in the Central Provinces dealing out their 'graces' so lavishly and promiscuously as to quite obscure the tune.[1]

---

[1] There is practically no concerted singing, because, as Mendelssohn found with the Italians when his trombone-player put in twiddles of his own in a melody carefully calculated for subsequent development, their *contrappunto alla mente* is incalculable.

The same sort of thing happens with these grace-notes as happens with the ornaments of the chattri: they tend to occupy any available space. A Kadar at Trichur could not play me the simple scale of his instrument, he graced all the notes; I had to take his fingers and put them down in succession on the holes. The graces are not something definite added to the note that can be written as a part of a fixed scale; they are a kind of warble, above and below it, almost part of it, and quite essential to it. An early book (by Somanāth, 1609) enumerates, and the author's commentary explains, nineteen different kinds of grace-notes for the *vīnā*; and an Indian is ashamed if his vocal cords cannot do as much as some one else's fingers.

There is an obvious reason for grace-notes wherever there is no harmony. For a melody is a sentence with important 'words' and unimportant, and grace-notes and harmonic texture are the only two things that can always be applied to enhance this importance. For stress and quantity, which serve this purpose in verse, are not so well adapted to music. Stress, which is additional volume, is difficult to achieve with low notes; and quantity, which is additional duration, alters the melody itself, imposing on it from without something which should come from within. But grace, like harmony, can be applied anywhere, and in *Rāga*, which we shall presently consider, some of the notes of the scale—two, as a rule—receive this enhancement, as it were, *ex officio*.

And now we turn to the system of this music and watch these folk-song instincts shaping themselves. We take the element of *time* first, as being the most deep-rooted.

The earliest measurements of time follow the scansion of verse, as we should expect from the history of our own music. The earliest extant record (the *Ratnākara*, thirteenth century) gives a very miscellaneous list of 'times', several of which are identifiable with the 'feet' of poetry, while some show signs of systematic tabulation. The present system is, as we may say, a tidying up of that, the bar representing the foot.

First, we have the bar of one beat, which has 3, 4, 5, 7, or 9 units. This is new to us: we have seldom conceived *in a single sweep* more than 3 or 4; we think of 5 usually as 3+2 or 2+3.

After that come bars of two beats, but each beat with a different number of units: 3+2, 4+2, . . . 9+2. These represent the trochee (– ◡), but in different proportions; or, when the music begins on the offbeat, the iambus (◡ –).

Next, two forms of dactyl, the ordinary (– ◡◡) and the cretic (⌐ ◡ –), and the amphimacer (– ◡ –); thus:

$$\text{dactyl } 3+2+2,\ 4+2+2\ .\ .\ .\ 9+2+2$$
$$\text{cretic } 3+1+2,\ 4+1+2\ .\ .\ .\ 9+1+2$$
$$\text{amphimacer } 3+2+3,\ 4+2+4\ .\ .\ .\ 9+2+9$$

Lastly, there are bars of four beats representing presumably the various feet of the *śloka*, which is syllabic, not quantitative, such as 3+2+3+3, 3+3+2+2, &c.

The peculiarity of this system is that a different proportion between long and short notes is allowed for, not instead of, but as well as, the way in which we allow for it. We take multiples; they can also take sums. That is the theory, a beautiful thing arranging for a host of cases that seldom occur. And there are 'figurative' times—1+2+3+4+5—and geometrically progressive times—1+2+4 (like the first seven bars of the Overture to *Figaro*)—and others. But in practice a couple of dozen kinds are chosen and kept to.

These chosen times are again varied by the drum. The drummer usually keeps a time-foundation going in his left hand and varies detail with his right; the ball of the thumb, the palm of the hand, the first finger and the other fingers give four different qualities of sound; his two drums are at different pitches; he carries on with his singer in the same rhythm for several minutes, then cross-rhythms begin, until there is every appearance of their being at cross purposes as well. So variety is amply provided for. Unity is provided in a way that has hardly occurred to us, though in Handel's time they did something of the same sort at the cadence of a song. The cross-rhythms begin to converge, up to the triumphant moment when they coincide on a down-beat, and an appreciative audience duly applauds.

What the drum is *not* used for, as it is with us, is to accentuate. There is little accent in Indian music, which is all made up of proportioned lengths, discriminated by silences. This comes out in the time-beating. Putting numbers for the beat and zero for the silence, four-time is beaten

$$\text{♩ ♩ ♩ ♩} = 1\ 2,\ 0\ 3$$

and three time

$$\text{♩ ♩ ♩} = 1\ 2,\ 0\ 3,\ 0\ 4$$

and so on. In some of the folk-dances the beats are represented by forward steps and the silences, or 'empty' times, by a backward. Consequently, our four-time is called *tīntāl* (three-time) and our three-time *chautāl* (four-time).

And after time, tune. When millions of songs have been invented and sung in a countryside or a country, it is found that these follow a general tendency which can be written down as a scale. It is open to any one to invent a song which ignores this scale, but if he goes on inventing long enough he will generally come back to it. Songs travel, and travel faster and further than speech; what does *not* travel is this musical scale. When a song travels to another country it is apt to adopt the scale of that country.

The one thing that every one can tell you about Indian melody is that 'it is all quarter-tones'; but there are some reservations to be made about this statement. (1) 'Quarter-tone' is not a very good name, since nine of the intervals between the twenty-two notes are of one-ninth of a tone, and the remaining thirteen are semi-tones of different sizes. 'Microtone' would be a better word. (2) All non-harmonic peoples use microtones of some sort; the Arabs rather oftener than the Indians, and English folk-singers occasionally, and we blandly say they sing 'out of tune'; though if the mere facts of Nature are the test they are all of them more in tune than Europeans. (3) The *śrutis* are all equal in size, but not in the way people usually think when they offer to sing the octave 'putting in the *śrutis*'. These are equal increments and decrements of certain chosen notes, a very different thing. Those who sing the octave halving every semitone perform a remarkable feat, but it has nothing to do with Indian music, which never employs two successive *śrutis* in the same melody. Messrs. Bloch, Haba, Foulds, and a host of others believe that we may look forward to a 24-note system, and are entitled to their view so long as they do not quote India as their precedent; such a system will be guesswork (and a very lucky guess if two fiddlers ever manage to strike the same microtone), but so, of course, is equal temperament, though there is more to go upon in that.

Let us have a look at this microtone (*śruti*).

Suppose we ask a violinist and a viola-player to tune to one another. And suppose, now, the violinist bows his open E-string, and the viola plays an E as follows:

Ex. 1.

C   G   D $\left.{\begin{matrix}A\\D\end{matrix}}\right\}$ strings.

—in perfect tune, then the violin E will be one-ninth of a tone sharp on the viola E.[1] This is a fundamental fact which nothing

---

[1] The mathematics of it is as follows. Both start with the same A. The violin E is a fifth above it ($\frac{3}{2}$ = 702 cents). The viola has dropped three-fifths and risen two octaves and a major third:

$$\left(\tfrac{2}{3}\right)^3 \left(\tfrac{2}{1}\right)^2 \tfrac{5}{4} = \tfrac{40}{27}; \text{ or } 2,400 + 386 - 2,106 = 680 \text{ cents.}$$

The discrepancy therefore is:

$$\tfrac{3}{2} \cdot \tfrac{27}{40} = \tfrac{81}{80}, \text{ or } 702 - 680 = 22 \text{ cents.}$$

can alter except one or other player of the two being out of tune. This interval of 22 cents is the *śruti*-interval, our 'comma', and the following table shows how it is employed to form the Indian scale of to-day.

	Euro-pean notes	Euro-pean semi-tones	Euro-pean scale	Śruti	Hindu additions		North Indian terms translated
					Scale	Deriva-tion	
	1	*2*	*3*	*4*	*5*	*6*	*7*
22	C		1200				C natural
21		112		+22	1110	B+	⎰ sharp
20	B		1088				B ⎱ natural
19		92		+22	1018	B♭+	flat
18	B♭		996				very flat
17		112		+22	906	A+	A ⎰ four-*śruti* ⎱ (from G)
16	A		884				⎱ three-*śruti* ⎰
15	A♭	70	814				flat
14				−22	792	A♭−	very flat
13	G	112	702				G natural
12	G♭	92	610				⎧ very sharp
11	F♯		590				⎪ sharper
10		92		+22	520	F+	sharp
9	F		498				F ⎩ natural
8		112		+22	408	E+	⎧ sharp ('violin E')
7	E		386				E ⎨ natural ('viola E')
6	E♭	70	316				⎩ flat
5		112		−22	294	E♭−	very flat
4	D		204				D ⎧ natural
3		92		−22	182	D−	soft
2	D♭		112				flat
1		112		−22	90	D♭−	⎩ very flat
0	C		0				C natural

The twenty-two *śrutis* are arranged upwards. Column *1* gives the European notes as we name them, distinguishing F♯ and G♭ but not naming other sharp notes, since they have nothing to do with the Indian scale. As far as it goes it is the same as the Indian, except that they consider A+, whereas we consider A, to be the 'natural' note.

Column *3* gives in cents (see Grove) in Just Intonation the European chromatic scale.

Column *2* shows the semitones between the notes. They are of three sizes: diatonic semitone, 112, and two chromatic, 92 and 70. Francesco Tosi, who wrote in 1742, says that European singers could then distinguish accurately between diatonic and chromatic semitones; now that Equal Temperament has been adopted they no longer can.

Column *4* gives the increment and decrement of the *śruti* as against the normal note. It is of one size only.

Column *5* gives the notes affected by it, the *śruti*—nine out of our thirteen in the octave, all shown in heavy type.

Column *6* shows the notes from which these are derived.

Column *7* gives the North Indian nomenclature. C and G are unalterable. F has four degrees sharpwards, and the other notes four degrees flatwards. The South Indian system counts them all sharpwards. The north is historical, the south phonetic.

A line is drawn below G to assist the eye to note symmetries. Notes distant by nine *śrutis* are fourths, by thirteen are fifths.

The *vīnā* is fretted by semitones, and the *śruti* is got by stopping the string in front of or behind the fret, also by a lateral pull of the stopping finger.

We said that the *śruti* was a fundamental fact of scale; it must therefore appear somewhere in our own. It occurs in the simplest modulation. In

Ex. 2.   BEETHOVEN.

—that asterisked note is taken as A (major third from F) and left as A+ (fifth from D); and it is because we want to be able to understand it in both senses, to be able in fact to modulate, that we take, in equal temperament, a note which is between A and A+.

Indian music does not need to modulate, and therefore does not temper. The way they negotiated the *śruti* was by having two scales, one with A and the other with A+, so that the two could not clash. But then, as these scales came to be started from different tonics, the *śruti* spread all over them. For instance, as from a tonic C the sixth place is A and A+, so from

D♭ it is B♭ and B♭+, from D it is B and B+ and so on. This makes a series of pairs of notes, *plus* or *minus* to one another; and that fact gives us an important date.

In the *Rkprātiśākhya* (13. 17), which is of the fourth century B.C., perhaps earlier, occurs this sentence;

The twin-note is not to be distinguished without the other note; the seven notes are the twins, or, the twins are different from the seven.[1]

That is fairly enigmatic, and Max Muller, who edited the book, could make nothing of it, since the Indian scale was then practically unknown to the Western world. What was 'the other note'? How could the seven notes of the octave be both twins and not twins? But in the light of what we have just seen the difficulties vanish. The brilliance of A+ in the song we are singing is not to be tasted except in contrast with the sedateness of A elsewhere: A+ and A are therefore twins. And when we plot the two scales (the scale with A and the scale with A+) on an instrument, and play them from one tonic after another, the 'twin-ness' is obvious; but when we sing or play in one of the scales we forget all about the other, and the twin-ness disappears.[2]

The Indian scale, then, existed in principle twenty-four centuries ago, and that principle included, as we have seen, the recognition of the major third as a consonance. Of that recognition we have no documentary evidence in Europe till a treatise

---

[1] anantaraścātra yamo 'viśeshah sapta svarā ye yamaste prthagvā.

[2] Before we leave the word *śruti* it should be mentioned that it has in course of time acquired two other distinct meanings. (1) Since grace-notes always involve the microtones of the note graced, *śruti* was used to mean grace-note. On the *vīnā* there are two ways of getting it—by sliding the stopping finger along the string, or by pulling the string aside with that finger. (2) Since the being exactly in tune is a matter of getting the microtone right, the tuning of the *vīnā* is called the *śruti*; the *vīnā* is said to 'stand in the G-tuning', or the F (*pañchama śruti*, or *madhyama śruti*).

by Ptolemy in the second century A.D. But this Indian treatise is quite different. Not only is it contemporary, but it offers this same major third not as a theoretical solution but as a substantive element of a scale already in being. That opens a vista.

We are ready now to investigate *Rāga*, or mode, the glory of Indian music. There has been some hesitation in so translating the word, because mode as we know it in Europe is altogether a poorer thing. We usually assume it to be the 'white' notes taken from any one of them as tonic. This is inaccurate. Our 'mode' is in essence pentatonic, comprising the notes C, D, E, G, A and starting on any one of them: B and F were added gradually, but were unessential. Within this pentatonic one note was predominant besides the tonic, and the melody was pivoted on these two. Some day our pundits will examine the Gregorian and folk-song melodies critically from this point of view and will discover *several* dorians and *several* mixolydians, each with special characteristics.

That has long been the state of things in India. If we take the dorian, as it is sung at Gwālior, a famous centre, it is, under the name of *Kāfī*, the same as ours,

Ex. 3.

but if we go to Poona, *Kāfī* has an alternative B♮, and if to Calcutta, we find the E♭ ornamented with a grace-note. Returning to Gwālior, *Kāfī* has G for its predominant, but *Bāgeshrī*, with the same notes, has F, and *Shahāna*, with the same notes again, has D (but at Poona and Gujerat E♭, and at Calcutta E♭ and G).

Merely stated like that, these details seem of little account; but it is extraordinary how completely it changes the whole

PLATE 20

RĀGMĀLĀ

Rājput school, 18th century A.D.

atmosphere of the tune when the predominant is at F, perhaps, instead of G; a mere alteration of pitch, from B♭ to B♮, for instance, is a small thing in comparison. We have looked only at two or three cases of one diatonic mode. But there are many more cases, and the Indians employ all the chromatic notes as well, even the enharmonic notes whenever these have *śruti* applied to them, which usually takes place in pairs (D♭–A♭, or E♭–B♭). Again, round the predominant note a recognizable phrase—like the Ecclesiastical 'Trope'—springs up and recurs, which characterizes the *Rāg*; and while some *Rāgs* have five notes, others six, seven (or even eight, two being alternatives), a *Rāg* is not usually the same in ascent and descent. Lastly, the F may be natural or sharp. The whole thing is a very magnificent convention, inside which there is room for abundant art.

To realize that it is an art takes time. It is best to begin with a few *Rāgs* and get to know them, before venturing further; book-knowledge amounts to little. At first we sadly miss the accustomed harmony, which prepared for us the notes that were coming; and we try mentally to supply it—with fatal results. The thing must be taken as it is. Presently it begins to dawn on us that harmony would only spoil it. An example may help. The words and music are by Rabindranath Tagore: I can still hear him singing it. His own translation is:

I know, I know thee, O thou Bideshini; thou dwellest on the other shore of the ocean. I have seen thee in the autumn, I have felt thee in the spring night. I have found thee in the midst of my heart, O thou Bideshini. Putting my ear to the sky I have heard thy music, and I have offered to thee my life, O thou Bideshini. I have roamed through the world and have come at last into the strange country. Here I am a guest at thy door, O thou Bideshini.

A translation into English would be too accentual, and we all like singing Latin—it commits us to nothing—besides, it is quite as sonorous as the Bengali. I persuaded Dr. J. W. Mackail to write one; he said it was an impossible task, but he would do his best. The melody is in *Behāg* (an Ionian, we should

Ex. 4.

I Behag.

R. TAGORE.

A - mi chi-ni go chi - ni to - ma - re O go bi - de - shi -
Mi - hi no - ta tu, mi-hi no - ta O di - va de - vi -

- ni Tu-mi tha - ko sind - hu pa - re O
- a Trans ae-quor im - ma - ne re - mo - - ta O

go bi - de - shi - ni To-may-e de-khe-cchi sha-ra-da
di - va de - vi - a Tu mi-hi sub fo-li - is ca-

pra-te To-may de-khe-cchi madha-vi ra-te To-may
-du - cis Tu mi-hi ver - nis cog-ni-ta lu - cis Tu

de-khe - cchi . . . hri-di ma - jha - re hri-di
mi-hi com-ples . . mi-hi in-ti-ma vo - ta mi-hi

ma . . . jha - re O go . . bi-de - shi - ni
in-ti-ma vo - ta O di - va de - vi - a

A-mi a-ka-she pa-ti-ya kan su-ne-cchi su-ne-cchi to-ma-ri
Au-rem cœ-li-tus di - re - xi vox est tu-a de-la-ta mi-

gan A-mi to-ma-re sam-pecchi pran . . . . O
- hi Ti-bi to-tum me . . . de - - tu-li O

say, with a strong third of the scale, and a weak fourth and seventh).

A mere example or two on paper does little to convey the penetrating quality of good Indian music. A great part of the charm consists in its being usually an extemporization. The *Rāg* has been sung thousand of times; this particular instance of it now and here for the first time. We easily understand, therefore, how the mere notation of a melody has been, as a rule, quite a secondary matter; there has been nothing to write down, because the next man would sing it quite differently, at least, if he was worth his salt. Still, there are notations, all tonic-solfa, in the different scripts; the Bengali, that, at least, in which Tagore's songs are printed, is the only one I have seen in which the symbols have precision, and in which type, proof-reading, printing, and paper are even respectable. They are aware of these shortcomings; 'your notation must be very good', said one of them, 'if you can read off a song like that.' It is possible that with some adaptation the best notation for India would be the plainsong: with only four lines, and with the clefs (which are easily learnt) it economizes space; it is not, like the staff, based on the keyboard; and the general line of the melody is easily seen ahead of the moment of performance, which is a help to the singer in economy of breath and in interpretation.

Any notation can only give the letter of the musical experience, and what is wanted is to convey its spirit. A portrait of the mode is therefore painted, usually a portrait of the presiding deity, called a *Rāgmāla*. This is frankly mythological, usually artistic, sometimes well executed. Only the well-known *Rāgs* are honoured in this way, for the appeal is popular, not scientific. The North American Indians do the same thing in a more elementary way, the actual portraitures of man, house, river, being half-way towards hieroglyphs; with them it is a story that is to be conveyed as a reminder not of the notes but of the spirit of the song, whereas in India not so much a story as a sentiment. This is not mere fancy: there have been moments at Leighton House and elsewhere when one has felt a picture before the eyes to be a real help to the music, though one was not prepared to say why it was so, except that in some way it unified the variety of the sounds.

This picture of the *Rāg* portrays, then, not the tune, which is ephemeral, but the sentiment, which is eternal. It is—would it be too much to say?—a turning from the illusions of this earth, from the things which take one shape or another, to the 'I am That' which is behind all shapes. But without looking so deep, the picture is a recognition of the truth that the quintessence of an art is not to be expressed by descriptive words, but only to be re-created, in that art or in another, and, if by words at all, only in poetry. It is not, therefore, merely a pictorial substitute for the suggestive titles and mottoes with which we deck instrumental pieces, nor for the words of song and opera, nor for the programme of a symphonic poem, all of which take any real value they may have ultimately from the music itself, and all of which yield in themselves no more than a title we give to the music in preference to a mere number. It is rather a conscious dedication of mind and heart to the wonder that music is there to symbolize, to which they, quite simply, give the name of the deity to whom that particular wonder is an attribute.

But the Hindu race has changed the names and confused the attributes of its gods so often that there are many to whom this appeal means little. Wonder has gone, and so, largely, has association. *Rāgs* could once be sung only on occasion: this in the morning when man is bracing himself for the day, that in the evening when he relaxes; or they recognized the bodily rhythms —that in the spring when the sap rises, that in the rains when the long looked-for relief has come. Breach of these observances was visited with dire penalties, the stories of which were passed from father to son and lost nothing in the telling. All this goes to show that the endeavour to derive the *ethos* of mode, whether in India, ancient Greece, or Europe of the Middle Ages, directly from its tonal constituents is beside the mark. The *ethos* comes from association, whose nature is now forgotten, which has been crystallized in myth, and which had originally as much to do with the traditional time as with the traditional tune of the music sung in that mode.

We turn now to the tonal structure of *Rāg*.

We have seen the complete octave of twenty-two notes. *Rāg* takes five, six, or seven of these within the octave with an alternative or two. We recognize in Europe five modes, which are arrived at by taking the 'white' notes from C and successively flattening B, E, A, D, and G; or, alternatively, by keeping them all 'white', but beginning the mode successively on C, G, D, A, and E. In addition, we recognize five pentatonic modes consisting of the notes C, D, E, G, A taken from any one of them as tonic. And thirdly, in our 'ascending' minor we flatten the E, and in our 'harmonic' minor the E and the A, without flattening the B.

India has all these modes, but goes further. First, it may flatten the A, *or* the D, or the A *and* the D, or the B, E, A, and D, *alone*. Secondly, it may substitute F♯ for F♮, which of itself at once doubles the number of *Rāgs*. Thirdly, any note except C and G is subject to enharmonic treatment, i.e. it can be raised, or else lowered, by a comma (*śruti*). They do not avail themselves of all these possibilities, but select from them; and we might describe a *Rāg* as a chosen path of the seven (or so) notes among the twenty-two, G being never altered, though it may be omitted. The alternatives alluded to above are for ascent or descent. Hamirkaliān has F♮ in ascent and F♯ in descent; Bilāval has B♮ as a rule both ways, but occasionally B♭ in descent, and so on.

Now the first thing to say about this astonishing complexity is that it did not come from caprice but from the determination to sing absolutely in tune. In Europe there have not been, since the popularization of keyboard music and particularly of the pianoforte, many singers who can sing in tune habitually; for the compromise of equal temperament, which a keyboard necessitates, has dulled their ear. Still, there are some singers and many violinists who can appreciate and produce the just major scale when they wish to. What they do not all realize is that there are two just major scales, and it is from this and what it implies that the complexity of Indian *Rāg* arises. In order to understand this the reader's close attention is bespoken for the next paragraph. The *Rāgs* concerned are *Bilāval* (just major i), *Kedāra* (Lydian mode), and *Behāg* (just major ii).

Referring back to the table of the scale on p. 311 and using the ordinal numbers of the notes (on the left hand) we may plot the just major as:

	C		F			B♮	C
(*Bilāval*)	0	4	7	9	13	16	20	22

From this we can get the Lydian mode (i.e. with occasional sharp fourth) by beginning at F, and subtracting 9 from (or adding 13 to) all the numbers:

	F		B♮	C			F
(*Kedāra*)	0	4	7	11	13	17	20	22

Again, we can get back the just major in a new form by substituting B♭ for this B♮:

	F		B♭			F	
(*Behāg*)	o	4	7	9	13	17	20	22

Putting *Bilāval* and *Behāg* on the same tonic we find

		C			A	C	
(*Bilāval*) just major i	o	4	7	9	13	**16**	20	22
(*Behāg*) just major ii	o	4	7	9	13	**17**	20	22

This **16, 17** is our old friend, the *śruti*, again; but what we have added to our knowledge is that the scale with and the scale without the *śruti* are recognized and maintained as two different things, whereas Europe merges them by equal temperament, and that the complexity of *Rāg* is arrived at by simply singing in tune.

That example was easy. Now we take one with a more forbidding look.

Māravā (or *Dīpak*).

C	D♭	E	F♯+	A̳	B+	C
o	2	7	12	16	21	22

(A̳ is the predominant).

It will be easier to understand if we write it out with C in the middle,

F♯+ A̳ B+ C D♭ E

when we find that

C	to D	is a diatonic semitome.
C	to B+	„ chromatic semitone.
C	to E	„ major third.
C	to A	„ minor third.
F♯+	to B+	„ fourth.
F♯+	to D♭	„ fifth.
A	to E	„ fifth.
B+	to D♭	„ major tone.

(All these intervals can be verified by the cents given in the table on p. 311.)

Māravā is therefore full of harmony, and the songs sung in it produce, in fact, an effect of arpeggio. Incidentally, *Dīpaka*, the 'kindler', or 'exciter', is the *Rāg* which consumed in flame the body of its singer even when immersed in the Jumna, which then proceeded to boil.

It is the difficulty of remembering accurately that stands between us and the singing of *Rāg*. We are accustomed to *read* whatever we have to sing, or if not, to memorize it as a particular tune, not as a type of many tunes, i.e. as a mode. All that we can, as a rule, *remember*, i.e. can sing without having to think too much about it, is the major and minor scale. If we were asked to sing such a *Rāg* as *Māravā* we should have to think very hard to get the notes in tune. And when we had at last succeeded in that, we should still be a long way from being able to sing a song in it, which means dodging about among its notes with extreme accuracy. But the Indian has the 'type' of it, and of a hundred other *Rāgs*, in his mind, and to him it is child's play. As Heine remarks somewhere: 'The Romans would never have had time to conquer the world if they had had first to learn (what they knew from their cradles) which nouns make their accusative in -*im*—*cucumis, tussis, buris, amussis,* and the rest of them.'

But it is not out of extreme cases like *Māravā* that the European will at first get pleasure, for he has nothing to compare it with. The pleasure comes from noting, without necessarily being able to account for, minute differences such as those between *Behāg* and *Bilāval* (above), or between the pentatonics,

Kalyān	0	4	7	13	16	22
and						
Deshkar	0	3	7	13	16	22
and						
Jeshtkalyān	0	4	7	13	17	22

When 'Ye banks and braes' is sung over to an Indian musician, he will say it is in *Kalyān*, and will play variations not on the tune but in the mode. This is a little disconcerting until the European recognizes that to the Indian the *mode* is everything and the *tune* nothing; whereas if the singer flattened the second of the scale (as in *Deshkar*) the Indian would at once object that it was quite a different song.

As we see from Italian and French singers, Russian and Czechoslovak choirs, French and German pianofortes, each country prefers and cultivates one sort of tone rather than another. The Indian preference is for a nasal tone, not pronouncedly nasal, but more so than we should accept. In singing the more advanced songs, the Muhammadan *Khyāl*, for instance, which may take twenty minutes and extend over two or more octaves, good tone is neither attained nor is it to be looked for. In such passages as the following attention has to be concentrated on time and tune, and the tone must be what it may.

Ex. 5 *a*.

Ex. 5 *b*.

The Sanskrit books particularly warn singers against this nasal
tone, and the singers no doubt are not aware that they are
disobeying the injunction. That they like its quality is clear
from the hautboy having driven out the flute in India, from the
practice of *surbahār* players who insert threads between the
strings to produce a nasal twang, and from the indifference to
the nasal tone of the harmonium (apart, of course, from its
other vices). They are averse to loud tone. From the *vīnā* downwards, through *sitār* (tinny tone), *surbahār* (booming), *sārangī*
(viol tone), *rabob* (banjo tone), *tambūra* (humming), *kinnāri* and
ekatāra (thin), the actual volume is never great, although, as with
the European clavichord, the amount of gradation between
piano and forte is surprising. The drums, again, being used not
for intensifying accent but for rhythmic definition, formidable
as they look in array, make little noise, except perhaps in temples
and rock-caves (where I have not heard them). The hautboy
(*surnāī* in the north, *nāgasāram* in the south) has a most imposing
sound in such places. In concerted music the small cymbals
(*tāla*) are prominent, and other rattling, whispering, tapping
sounds are heard from instruments too slight and too numerous
to mention.

The object of this chapter is to show in what respects Europe
is indebted to India. But the indebtedness of Europe in the

matter of music is rather to Greece and Arabia. When after the fall of Rome music began to be cultivated again, the attempt to systematize it was based on an imperfect understanding of the Greek theory and of some remains of Byzantine practice. In the early Middle Ages some knowledge of Al Farābī's system percolated through the Romance countries and in particular the Arabian 'Ud was acclimatized in the form of the lute. No direct contact was made by Europe with India until the fifteenth and sixteenth centuries, and the arts of that country began to be known in the eighteenth. In the last years of that century the writings of Sir William Jones, founder and first president of the Royal Asiatic Society, gave Europe its first inkling of Indian music. This lead was not followed until in 1891 C. R. Day published his *Music and Musical Instruments of the Deccan and Southern India*, and in 1913 E. Clements his *Study of Indian Music*.

Indian music is entirely independent of ancient Greece and modern Europe, but touches Arabia through the Persian and Muhammadan influences: the Arabian *maqām* is in principle the Indian *Rāg*, though there is no sign that the one is borrowed from the other. The account of the *vīnā* in Bhārata's *Nātya-śāstra* (early centuries A.D.) has been aptly compared by R. Lachmann, *Zeitschrift für vergleichende Musikwissenschaft* (i. 4), to the principle though not necessarily to the form of the Chinese horizontal psaltery, the *K'in*, which is known to have been in use as early as the Chou dynasty (1122–225 B.C.).

But the fact that there has been no collusion between India and Europe is valuable in another way. The modal system has permeated Europe, but we have no records of how it behaved in its palmy days, because the Church kept the records, and mode was there early affected by incipient harmony. In India, where harmony never proceeded beyond the drone bass, melody was unfettered and could evolve its own laws. These may be summed up in the following propositions.

1. Melody is pivoted in the first instance on a tonic and a

predominant note (*amśā*); and though the tonic is the Ecclesiastical Final, the predominant by no means coincides with the Ecclesiastical Dominant; the variety of its position contributes to the character of the mode.

2. That position counts for more, aesthetically, than the constitution of the mode in sharps and flats.

3. The comma and other microtones which arise in the process of scale-construction are attached to particular notes and utilized to elate or depress the character of the mode.

4. A drone is essential for all but very well-known modes.

5. The best-known modes are further characterized by traditional phrases of a few notes (which Europe calls tropes) which recur and are easily recognizable.

6. The pivotal notes of mode, the predominant, and the fifth or fourth note from it, are frequently emphasized by gracenotes, though these may also occur elsewhere.

7. When the music is in a high state of cultivation modes are numerous; a good musician can sing in a hundred different ones, or more, with accuracy.

8. This is a remarkable feat of memory and a surer guide than notation; the arrival of notation is a sign that the modes are dying out.

9. The singer (player) is intent not on a specific tune, but on 'displaying' the mode; hence when distinct tunes are occasionally hit upon, and 'varied', they do not often survive, because the next displayer of the mode does it in another way.

10. Such relics as have been preserved of the *Sāmaveda*, the oldest known liturgical music in the world, show remarkable correspondences with plainsong. In India the grammatical accents develop into musical notes, which are marked, however, by numerals instead of by neumes; a system of cheironomy was invented (not unlike Guido's); the text is divided into strophes and stanzas; syllables are prolonged by vocalises or by farsing, or by the introduction of jubilations; the strains are as much as

can be taken in one breath, and the last note is accented or lengthened; the words determine the rhythm; there are three time-units only; there are ligatures, stereotyped 'endings', and the cadence is downwards; the harmonic unit is the fourth (fifth), not the third; and great care is taken not to deviate from the original types. In all this the plainsong singer will recognize a good deal that is familiar.

The value, then, to us of this system of music lies in the light it throws on folksong and plainsong, which are now intensively studied in the West. It is difficult to say whether the likenesses or the unlikenesses are the more enlightening.

A. H. Fox Strangways.

ADDITIONAL NOTE ON THE HARP AND FLUTE IN INDIA AND ON THE INDIAN ORIGIN OF THE VIOLIN BOW

In the previous pages of this chapter attention has been mainly directed to the growth of the musical scale with its many graces and embellishments; but allusion has also been made to the wealth of musical instruments, especially of the stringed type, which abounds in India. Yet it is not merely the multiplicity of form or the beauty of workmanship or even the skilfulness of the performers which renders them so attractive. They have themselves become divine attributes, accredited in the ancient treatises to the lofty strains of the world unseen and peculiarly associated with the religious cults of this vast country.

The musical instruments of India reflect the varying aspirations of mankind whether in primitive Nature worship, in Brahmanism with its 'gods many', or in the simpler and more practical appeal of Buddhism. In fact we should recognize that it is to these changes in the religious outlook of the people that the rise or fall, the use or disuse of many of these instruments must be attributed. Hence we obtain an unusual opportunity for psychological research—from the rattles, drums, and primitive musical bows of most remote times to the intricate and many-toned lutes and mandolines of the present day.

In this additional note, however, we do not propose to enter into this wide panorama of history: the description of the musical instruments of India has already been ably done by such authorities as the late Captain C. R. Day (*The Music of Southern India and the Deccan*, 1891), by Dr. Kurt Sachs (*Die Musikinstrumente Indiens und Indonesiens*, 1923), and the late M. V. Mahillon (Descriptive Catalogue of the Museum of the *Conservatoire de Musique*, Brussels, 1893, seq.), whilst learned treatises have also appeared from the pens of Indian writers. We will only remark that, as regards the many varieties of *vīnās* or lutes, &c., the majority have been evolved from simpler forms within recent centuries and that several instruments, especially of the *sitār*, *tambūri*, and oboe classes, have been introduced from Persia and Arabia. On the other hand, the use of the drum alone as an accompaniment to the voice must have come down from times most remote; for it is frequently mentioned in the Sumerian temple-ritual of the third millenium B.C.

There is one stringed instrument, however, which claims more than a passing notice, because, although no longer in use in India proper, it has been recently hailed as an original production of that country and the true *vīnā* of the Vedic literature; we therefore give the following facts.

1. *The Harp in India*

In its construction this instrument, generally known as the bow-harp, shows that it must have originally been developed from the hunting bow, to which a boat-shaped sound-box and additional strings have been attached: it is often figured in the hands of musicians on the early Buddhist sculptures as at Bhaja, Bharhŭt, and Sānchī (second century B.C.) and is still in use in Burmah and Assam: in Africa it survives amongst many Nilotic tribes.

PLATE 21

b. VĪNĀ IN THE HANDS OF SĀRASVATĪ

c. A.D. 900

a. BOW-HARPS AND FLUTES. AMARĀVATĪ

c. A.D. 200

Dr. Coomaraswamy (*Journal of the American Oriental Society*, vol. l) has endeavoured to prove that all the early literary allusions to the Indian *vīnā* refer to this instrument: he relegates the modern *vīnā* in its inception to the seventh or eighth centuries A.D. But, in doing so, he has been compelled either to divest the terms used in the Vedic writings from the middle of the first millenium B.C. of their natural meaning or to reject them altogether as inexplicable, which is unnecessary if the instrument referred to was of the modern *vīnā* type with a finger-board. Careful collation of these early descriptions provides convincing evidence on this point: moreover Dr. Lachmann (*Zeitschrift für vergleichende Musikwissenschaft*, Jahr. II) has recently shown that the elaborate tone-system attributed to Bhārata (206 B.C.–A.D. 100) must have been evolved from and demonstrated on an instrument with a 'fretted' finger-board and not on the open strings of a harp: only upon such an instrument could the famous musician Pañchaśikha have been able to produce the seven notes and the twenty-one modes 'on *one* string'.

The history of the bow-harp has become clearer since representations of it have been discovered in Babylonia dating from before 3000 B.C. and actual specimens have been unearthed at Ur of almost as early a date.

That it may have been used in India at a very distant period is undoubted: the dances of the primitive Ghonds in honour of their national hero, Lingal, are still accompanied by a rudimentary bow-harp called *pinga*. That it may have been called *bīnā* or *vīnā* is also probable as it is suggested by the present name *p'hin* for the Siamese instrument.

The word, whether applied to a harp or a lute, is evidently derived from the Sumerian BAN or PAN, 'a hunting bow', which is found too in the ancient Egyptian name *bain* or *ban* for the same instrument, lingering also in the Coptic *vini* and the Indian *bīn* (the northern *vīnā*) and *pināka* (the musical bow). The reason for its appearance on the Buddhist works of art seems to be this: when the popular revulsion from Hinduism took place in the fourth century B.C. the exclusive instruments of the Brahmin priests were banned and the bow-harp, with other instruments of the people, was adopted as more suitable for the *samājas* or festal celebrations in praise of Gautama: when, however, Buddhism lost its prestige and Brahmanism again triumphed in the sixth century of our era, the bow-harp disappeared and its rival, the 'fretted' *vīnā*, took its place in the art of the period. The same may be said of the pear-shaped lute often depicted by Buddhist artists and now only remaining in the extreme south of India though, as the *p'i p'a*, it is still used by Buddhist priests in China.

Apart, however, from these interesting details which the musical instruments of India offer us toward the study of their evolution, there are two ways at least in which our Western orchestras are indebted to her; one for the gift of the violin bow and the other for the development of the cross-blown concert flute. As the latter was the earlier in date it shall receive first consideration.

2. *The Flute*

The flute is frequently mentioned in Sanskrit books under the name *vamśi*: it was in its earliest stage a long reed, open at both ends and played *vertically* like the Sumerian *ti-gi*, the ancient Chinese *ti* or *yo*, and the modern Arabian *nay*. This, it appears, was the type of flute popular amongst the Asiatic peoples from prehistoric times and in general use during the earlier Egyptian dynasties. In eastern Asia, however, it had a rival, with flute-like tone and blown in the same way, but consisting of a closed resonating chamber with 5 or 6 holes for the fingers. This instrument was known in China as the *hsüan* and took its place with the *ti* in the temple ritual music. From this the Chinese evolved a variant form called the *ch'ih*, in which the resonator was no longer a truncated cone but tubular; both ends were closed with plugs, a mouth-hole placed in the middle of the length of the tube, and at right angles to it, on the side of the tube away from the player, six finger holes, three on either side of the central mouth-hole. Owing to the closed ends the resonator principle was still retained and by opening one or more of the side holes a diatonic scale of an octave and two tones (with a sharp fourth) was obtained. When Buddhism reached China in the first century A.D. it was at once approved as one of the State religions: thence this *ch'ih* was taken to other centres of the new cult and, reaching India, was transformed into a cross-blown flute. The transverse position was accepted, but the mouth-hole was moved to the left, the lower end unblocked, and the six finger holes transferred to points between the mouth-hole and the open end. Here the resonator principle no longer obtains but the result is a vertical flute blown transversely. As such it is frequently figured in Buddhist art of the first century A.D. at Sānchī, and later at Amarāvatī, Kafir Kot, and elsewhere: at the present time it is represented by the *bānsalī*, *pillagōvī*, or *muralī* ascribed to Krishna. On its return to China in due course it became the 'foreign' *ti-tzŭ*, while westward it travelled in the early Middle Ages through Byzantium and, later still, through North Africa to become the beautiful instrument of the modern orchestra.

3. *The Violin Bow*

The origin of the violin bow has been and still is a constant source of discussion, but it is becoming more and more evident that, not to the Germanic peoples, as has been recently suggested, but to India we owe its existence. Dr. Sachs supports the view originally propounded by Fétis as to this source and, although in his work on Indian instruments he hesitates to determine the method of its evolution and deprecates an addition to the many 'guesses' already made, we may perhaps suggest the following facts as an aid to its solution.

It is generally agreed that the earliest form of stringed instrument in India was some type of musical bow—that is, a hunting bow on which a tightly drawn string was twanged by the finger or struck with a short stick: to increase the resonance, either the back of the bow was held across the mouth of the performer or else the end rested on a hollow gourd. For further particulars of this widely spread instrument we need only refer readers to *The National History of the Musical Bow* by H. Balfour (1899) or to Dr. Kirby's work on *The Musical Instruments of the Native Races of South Africa* (1934).

In India several forms are to be found, from the simple *pināka*, already mentioned, to the more elaborate giant bow of Travancore. Out of its primitive state a stringed instrument emerged, consisting of a small half-gourd or coco-nut with a skin table or cover, through which longitudinally a bamboo-stick was passed bearing a string of twisted hair resting on a little wooden bridge placed on the skin table. This is the *ekatāra* or one-stringed lute of India, which soon produced its close relative, the *dvitāra* or two-stringed lute. Amongst primitive tribes these early attempts are still to be found; as for the *rāvanastron*, however, of which so much has been heard in these discussions, Dr. Sachs has definitely stated that the word does not occur in India or Ceylon: in fact, it has probably arisen through confusion with a six-stringed *sārangī*, an Indian violin, decorated with the Rāvanahasta or the Hand of Ravana, chief of the spirit world.

Now of the musical bow one form used in India is peculiar: we cannot say unique, for a similar form exists in South Africa, introduced possibly by Malabar slaves. On one side of the bow-staff little notches are cut and when a small rod is passed rapidly over them the bow-string vibrates and emits a musical sound. It must soon have become evident to the performer that he could produce the same effect by notching his little rod and rubbing it on the plain bow-staff or, more easily still, by rubbing the string itself with his rudimentary bow, as in the *bum-bass* of medieval Europe—a step to which the African native has also attained.

That this is not mere supposition is shown by the fact that when the *hsi-ch'in*, a form of the two-stringed *hu-ch'in* or Chinese fiddle, was introduced into that country, probably towards the end of the T''ang Dynasty (A.D. 618–907), a Chinese Encyclopaedia compiled about the year 1300 states that 'the two strings between (them) use a slip of bamboo to sound them'. This is a literal translation given by Professor Moule of the original passage, which he had previously alluded to in his description of 'The Musical Instruments of the Chinese' (*Journal of the Royal Asiatic Society*, North China Branch, vol. xxxix), and he adds that the word *ya* ('to sound') appears to denote the production of sound 'by rubbing or friction'. Moreover in the orchestra of this T''ang Dynasty there was a form of Psaltery called *ya-chêng* which was also played by rubbing the strings with a slip of bamboo: this was afterwards replaced by a wooden rod, and now, under the name of *la-ch'in*, it is played, like the *ch'in*, with a hair-strung bow. Many foreign instruments were introduced into China during the T''ang Period and the *ya-chêng* came through Tibet.

It is interesting to observe that, although the Chinese use a hair-strung bow for the 'foreign' *hu-ch'in*, the hair is still passed between the two strings like the original bamboo slip.

Here we surely have an indication of the evolution of the bow. China lays no claim to it, for the name *hu*, given to this simple violin, is applied by Confucian writers to outsiders, natives of India, and elsewhere. Indeed the *hu-ch'in* is exactly similar to the two-stringed *vitāra* of India and practically indistinguishable from the little folk-instruments, used with the bow, in Ceylon, Assam, Siam, and even Turkestan, as well as throughout India.

From this great country, so rich in musical emotion, its little offspring was borne by Arab traders from the western coast to their own land and to Persia in the seventh or eighth centuries and there also applied to the small lutes already in use; like the flute, it soon afterwards sped westward again, through Byzantine commercial routes and North African invasions, to adorn, as the legacy of India, the highest attainments of our European music.

F. W. GALPIN.

SCIENCE

AT present it is impossible to give any adequate account of early Indian achievements in science and technology. An exaggerated idea of the part played by religion and philosophy in the life of ancient India has led to the neglect of Indian *Realien*. But we know that there was in ancient India a large amount of literature dealing with the practical affairs of life, with technical arts and crafts, and with specific sciences. Much of this has been lost; a large part of what has been preserved is still unedited; and most of the edited texts have not yet been studied critically.

There are no good discussions of Indian science as a whole. Brajendranāth Seal's *The Positive Sciences of the Ancient Hindus* and Benoy Kumār Sarkār's more popular *Hindu Achievements in Exact Science* are unhistorical and uncritical, and the titles are misnomers. Most of Seal's book is devoted to logic and philosophical speculation rather than to matters of positive scientific method. His constant mixture of science and philosophical theory tends to obscure the issues.

Critical study is difficult because of the unhistorical character of Sanskrit literature. Many of our texts are anonymous, have been handed down in schools, contain accretions made over a long period of time, and no particular passage in them can be dated with precision. Many of the works which bear the names of individual authors have been subject to this same process, are really composite, and cannot be used for historical purposes except with the greatest caution. This lack of precise dating makes it difficult to compare Indian achievements with the achievements of the Greeks and Arabs, or to determine priority of invention or the direction of borrowing if borrowing can be proved. Rarely can we prove specific borrowing at definite dates and have to content ourselves with possibilities, probabilities, and vague generalizations.

For the period between Pythagoras in the sixth century B.C. and Ptolemy in the second century A.D. there is no certain proof of Indian influence on Greek thought or of Greek influence on Indian thought. Historically the way was open for influence in either direction, and there may have been much mutual influence, but at present the problem is still an open one. Those who go furthest in repudiating all Indian claims to scientific invention and in asserting that all Indian science was borrowed from Greece have made much of the supposed esoteric knowledge of Neoplatonists and Neo-Pythagoreans. For this they have adduced no historical evidence. In order to prove borrowing by India from Greece, Kaye has even gone so far as to postulate the contents of Greek works which have been lost.[1]

For the period during which India may have exerted a formative influence on Persian and Arabic thought we lack detailed and accurate historical information concerning Indian contacts with the Sāsānian Empire of Chosroes Nūshīrwān at Jundēshāpūr in south-west Persia (A.D. 531–79) and with Baghdād under the caliphs al-Mansūr (A.D. 754–75), Hārūn ar-Rashīd (A.D. 786–809), and al-Ma'mūn (A.D. 813–33).

Little is known of the scientific aspects of Sāsānian civilization and of the activities of the great academy at Jundēshāpūr, where Greek, Jewish, Christian, Syrian, Hindu, and Persian ideas met and syncretized. We have only the story of the physician Burzōe's journey to India,[2] his study of medicine there, his return to Persia with a version of the Indian *Pañchatantra*, which was translated into Pahlavi (Middle Persian), and of the wide diffusion of this Indian work throughout the West by means of Syriac, Arabic, and other versions based on this Pahlavi translation. Little is known of the culture, during Sāsānian rule, of the great cities of north-eastern Persia, in which Chinese

[1] *Scientia*, xxv (1919), 1–14.
[2] Th. Nöldeke, 'Burzōes Einleitung zu dem Buche Kalīla wa Dimna', *Schriften der Wissenschaftlichen Gesellschaft in Strassburg*, 1912.

and Indian influences seem to have been strong. We may suspect but cannot prove the translation into Pahlavi at this time of many other works of Indian literature both popular and scientific, which later may have been translated into Arabic and may have influenced early Arabic thought. At least one medical work, the *Charaka-Samhitā*, was translated from Sanskrit into Persian and from Persian into Arabic.[1]

Carra de Vaux[2] explains away the word *hindī* in the title of al-Khwārizmī's work on arithmetic, preserved only in the Latin translation *Algoritmi de numero Indorum*, as due to a confusion with the word *hindasī* (relating to geometry) 'because the word Hindī is easily confused in the Arabic script with *hindasī*', and 'in various cases in which the word Hindī is used, the meaning of *hindasī* fits better'. It may be argued just as plausibly that in many of the later works *hindasī* does not mean geometrical, but that in some cases where the word *hindasī* is used the meaning *hindī* fits better. Indian arithmetic and numerals are frequently referred to in Arabic works written between the ninth and thirteenth centuries. The same textual error would have to be assumed in all these later works also, or the original error in al-Khwārizmī's book would have been tacitly accepted by these later authors, and all their references to Indian science would be mistaken and illusory ones. This point of view has not been made even plausible.

Later Arabic tradition indicates that there was a large amount of Indian influence on early Arabic mathematics, astronomy, and medicine during the late eighth and early ninth centuries. Then attention turned toward Greek science, which became dominant in later Islamic thought. Few of the earliest Arabic scientific works have been preserved, but it is likely that there is a much larger Indian factor in the *Legacy of Islam* than is generally recognized. The older Indian methods were transformed

[1] On the authority of the *Fihrist* as quoted by Flügel, *ZDMG*, xi (1857), 149.
[2] *Scientia*, xxi (1917), 273–82; *The Legacy of Islam*, pp. 384–5.

and developed and replaced more and more by Greek methods. We happen to be better informed about the way in which Greek science came to the Arabs than we are about the way in which Indian science spread westward. A vast amount of detailed critical work on Indian and Arabic scientific manuscripts will have to be done before we shall be in a position to draw many definite conclusions.

For the early period of Indian history down to the fourth and fifth centuries A.D., the time of the *Sūrya-Siddhānta* and the *Āryabhatīya* of Āryabhata, in which for the first time Indian astronomy and mathematics appear in their fully developed classical form, there is little scientific literature which can be dated accurately. But a people which was capable of making the Iron Pillar of Delhi and the Sultānganj copper colossus of Buddha, and of hewing out blocks of sandstone 50 feet long and 4 feet square, carving them into a perfect roundness, giving them a wonderful polish which cannot be duplicated even to-day, and transporting them over distances of several hundred miles, must have attained considerable proficiency in metallurgy and engineering. The Iron Pillar of Delhi[1] measures 23 feet 8 inches from the top of the bell capital to the bottom of the base; and the diameter diminishes from 16·4 inches below to 12·05 inches above. The material is pure, rustless, malleable iron. It was made by some sort of welding process, and the weight is estimated to exceed six tons. V. Ball in his *Economic Geology of India*, p. 338, 1st ed., 1881, remarked: 'It is not many years since the production of such a pillar would have been an impossibility in the largest foundries of the world, and even now there are comparatively few where a similar mass of metal could be turned out.' The Sultānganj colossus[2] is made of very pure copper, cast in two layers over an inner core

[1] V. A. Smith, 'The Iron Pillar of Delhi', *JRAS*, 1897, 1–18.
[2] *JASB*, xxxiii (1864), 365–67.

by a sort of *cire perdu* process. It is 7½ feet high and weighs about a ton. Both date from about A.D. 400. The monolithic pillars of Aśoka (3rd century B.C.)[1] average about 50 tons in weight, are from 40 to 50 feet long, from 35½ to 49½ inches in diameter at the base, and from 22 to 35 inches at the top.

Among the scientific achievements of the Hindus their work on grammar occupies a high place. In the systematic analysis of language they reached a much higher point than any other people of antiquity. The date of Pānini is uncertain, but it cannot be later than the fourth century B.C. His grammar is the earliest scientific grammar in the world, the earliest extant grammar of any language, and one of the greatest ever written. It was the discovery of Sanskrit by the West at the end of the eighteenth century and the study of Indian methods of analysing language that revolutionized our Western study of language and grammar and gave rise to our science of comparative philology. The most striking feature of Sanskrit grammar is its objective resolution of speech and language into their component elements, and the definition of the functions of these elements. Long before Pānini, who names over sixty predecessors, the sounds represented by the letters of the alphabet had been arranged in an orderly, systematic form, vowels and diphthongs separated from mutes, semivowels, and sibilants, and the sounds in each group arranged according to the places in the mouth where they are produced (gutturals, palatals, cerebrals, dentals, and labials). Words were analysed into roots, out of which complex words grew by the addition of prefixes and suffixes. General rules were worked out defining the conditions according to which consonants and vowels influence each other, undergo change, or drop out. The study of language in India was much more objective and scientific than in Greece or Rome. The interest was in empirical investigation of language rather than in philosophical theories about it. Greek

[1] V. A. Smith, *Asoka*, 3rd ed., pp. 117 ff.

grammar tended to be logical, philosophical, and syntactical. Indian study of language was as objective as the dissection of a body by an anatomist.

It would be very strange if this analytical and empirical spirit had been confined entirely to the study of language. There are reasons for believing that it extended into other matters as well.

The discovery in 1909 of the *Kautilīya-Arthaśāstra*[1] has opened up an entirely different world of life and thought in ancient India from that represented by the religious and philosophical literature of the *Veda*. Accounts of ancient Indian civilization based entirely on this religious literature are as misleading as would be accounts of early European civilization based entirely on the Church Fathers.

The book deals with every phase of government as regulating all matters of worldly life—a government which was not dominated by the priesthood, but which was highly practical and empirical. Sections are devoted to precious stones, ores, metallurgy and mining, roads, trade routes and irrigation, medicine, trees, plants and poisons, ships and shipping, cattle, horses, and elephants, chemistry, mechanical contrivances, and other technical matters.

This treatise is ascribed to Kautilya, who was the prime minister of Chandragupta, the first of the Maurya emperors, at the end of the fourth century B.C. Critical study has convinced most Western scholars that only the nucleus can be so early, and that the present work is a composite based on the tradition of a school; but no one has argued for a date later than the third century A.D. for any part of it.

Undoubtedly the oldest works of Indian mathematics are the *Śulva-Sūtras*,[2] 'the Sūtras of the cord', which form a part

[1] Translated by R. Shamasastry, Bangalore, 1915 (3rd ed., Mysore, 1929), and by J. J. Meyer, Leipzig, 1925–6.

[2] G. Thibaut, 'On the Śulvasūtras', *JASB*, xliv (1875), 227–75.

of the Vedic *Kalpa-Sūtras*. These texts are primarily geometrical but seem to indicate also the beginnings of mathematics. Their geometry is largely of a practical and empirical sort, dealing with the measurement and construction of altars and sacrificial places by stretching cords between stakes.

They deal with such matters as the construction of squares and rectangles, the relation of the sides to the diagonals, the construction of equivalent squares and rectangles, the construction of equivalent circles and squares, the construction of triangles equivalent to squares and rectangles, and the construction of squares equal to two or more given squares or equal to the difference of two given squares.

They make systematic use of a considerable number of right-angled triangles whose sides can be expressed in whole numbers (Pythagorean triangles) but give no general proof, only a sort of generalizing from a few examples. How far calculation may have played a part in this generalizing is uncertain.

For obtaining the diagonal of a square the following rule is given: 'Increase the measure by its third part and this third by its own fourth less the thirty-fourth part of that fourth.' This gives the formula $1 + \frac{1}{3} + \frac{1}{3.4} - \frac{1}{3.4.34}$ (which is equivalent to 1.4142156) as an approximation to $\sqrt{2}$. It is doubtful, however, whether the irrational as such was recognized.[1]

For constructing a circle which is equal to a given square Baudhāyana gives the following rule: 'If you wish to turn a square into a circle, draw half of the cord stretched in the diagonal from the centre toward the *prāchī* line (the line passing through the centre of the square and running exactly from the west toward the east); describe the circle together with the third part of that piece of the cord which will lie outside the circle.'

For turning a circle into a square Baudhāyana gives the following rule: 'If you wish to turn a circle into a square, divide the

[1] H. Vogt in *Bibliotheca Mathematica*, vii (1906–7), 6–23.

diameter into eight parts, and again one of these eight parts into twenty-nine parts; of these twenty-nine parts remove twenty-eight, and moreover the sixth part (of the one part left) less the eighth part (of the sixth part).' This is equivalent to the formula $\frac{7}{8} + \frac{1}{8.29} - \frac{1}{8.29.6} + \frac{1}{8.29.6.8}$ as giving that part of the diameter of a circle which forms the side of a square the area of which is equal to the area of the circle.

The first of these two rules is purely geometrical; the second rule seems to give merely the reverse of the first rule treated arithmetically. Taking 16 *angulis* as the half-diagonal and 12 *angulis* as the perpendicular to the side (one *anguli* equals thirty-four *tilas*), the half-side would be equal to 408 *tilas* and the radius to $464\frac{1}{3}$ *tilas*; multiplying by 3 to remove the fraction, the half-side would be 1224 and the radius would be 1393. The rule given above expresses what fractional part 1224 is of 1393.

The date of the *Śulva-Śūtras* is unknown, but it is probable that they are as early as the third or fourth century B.C. Further, it is to be noted that altars and sacrificial places of the same shapes and constructions are described in the *Śatapatha-Brāhmana* and the *Taittirīya-Samhitā*; so that Śulva methods must be several centuries older than the redaction of our present *Śulva-Śūtras*. In all probability, therefore, geometry in India was independent of Greek influence, and this geometry seems to imply the development of some of the elementary operations of arithmetic.

These texts did not continue on into the later period as a formative influence on the further development of geometry. None of their geometrical constructions, which pertained to the old Vedic ritual, occur in later Indian works. The ritual had disappeared, to be replaced by temple worship. The later development was along the lines of arithmetic and algebra. What geometry is found later was subsidiary to arithmetical calculations.

Noteworthy in India is the early preoccupation with problems involving numbers, and the early development of names for classes of numbers mounting by powers of 10.[1] Āryabhata (A.D. 499), in dealing with mathematics, gives names for classes of numbers mounting by powers of 10 up to the tenth place; but the peculiar alphabetical notation which he devised for the brief expression of large numbers in verse reaches to the eighteenth place at least, and as interpreted by some might be extended indefinitely. The largest number which he actually uses runs only to the tenth place. Of the later mathematicians, Mahāvīra gives names for twenty-four places, Bhāskara gives names for eighteen places.

As early as the *Vājasaneyi-Samhitā* (xvii. 2) and the *Kāthaka-Samhitā* (xxxix. 6) we find names for classes of numbers mounting by powers of 10 up to the fourteenth place. This is extended two places further by the *Mahābhārata*, ii. 2143–4 (Calcutta edition), and in Gorresio's edition of the *Rāmāyana*, vi. 4, 56–9, we have the statement that a hundred times a thousand hundreds makes a *koti*, that a hundred times a thousand *kotis* makes a *śankha*, and so on up to the seventh time. Such large numbers are referred to frequently in the Vedic *Samhitās, Brāhmanas*, and *Sūtras*.

The *Śatapatha-Brāhmana*, x. 4, 2, 4–17, gives the division of 720 by 2, 3, 4, 5, 6, 8, 9, 10, 12, 15, 16, 18, 20, and 24.

The *Śatapatha-Brāhmana*, xii. 3. 2, 5, refers to 12 months, 24 half-months, and 360 days and nights; then it continues by saying that these 360 days and nights contain 10,800 *muhūrttas*, that these multiplied by 15 give *ksipras*, that these multiplied by 15 give *etarhis*, that these multiplied by 15 give *idānis*, and that these multiplied by 15 give *prānas* (breathings).

The *Lalita-Vistara* (ed. Lefmann, pp. 147–8) gives names for classes of numbers from 10^9 mounting by hundreds to 10^{53}.

[1] A. Weber, 'Vedische Angaben über Zeittheilung und hohe Zahlen', *ZDMG*, xv (1861), 132–40.

Then this is said to be one numeration above which there are seven other numerations.

The *Lalita-Vistara* (ed. Lefmann, p. 149) also gives a calculation for the number of atoms which, when placed one against the other, would form a line a *yojana* long ($4 \times 1,000 \times 4 \times 2 \times 12 \times 7^{10}$). The result is expressed in words, but this is so different from the number actually given by the above multiplication that we must assume either complete ignorance of multiplication or corruptions in the text. Discussion and ingenious emendations are given by Woepcke.[1] This problem is very similar to the famous *arenarius* of Archimedes.

The dates of our present text of the *Lalita-Vistara* and of the passages from the *Mahābhārata* and *Rāmāyana* are unknown. They are at least as early as the first centuries of the Christian era. The passages from the *Vājasaneyi-Samhitā*, the *Kāthaka-Samhitā*, and the *Śatapatha-Brāhmana* must be earlier than the sixth century B.C.

Such enumerations, mounting by powers of 10, lead much more naturally to the discovery of place value than the Greek method of counting by myriads would do.

It is to be noted that the *Chāndogya-Upanishad*, vii. 1. 2, 4, includes in a list of knowledges and sciences the name *rāśi*, 'heap, number', a word which is commonly used later in connexion with arithmetical operations, and which probably is equivalent to *ganita*, 'arithmetic', here.

In Buddhist books there is frequently mentioned in connexion with the education of a boy a list of subjects of study beginning with *lipi*, *mudrā*, *gananā*, and *samkhyā*, 'writing, expressing numbers by means of the fingers, counting, calculation', in which the last two words must refer to arithmetic of some kind. Many of these passages are certainly pre-Christian.

Important mathematical material from Jaina canonical texts

[1] *Journal Asiatique*, 1863, i. 258–65.

has been collected recently by Bibhutibhūshan Datta,[1] but he makes extravagant claims (300 and 500 B.C.) for the dates of certain texts which he uses. The two main Jaina sects differ radically in their accounts of the formation of Jaina literature. The Digāmbara Jains reject the authority of the whole Śvetāmbara canon on the ground that all of the old canonical Jaina literature had disappeared. According to the tradition of the Śvetāmbara Jains themselves, the old literature had fallen into such confusion and so much of it had been lost that a new canon was formed about 300 B.C., and this also fell into such confusion that a new one was formed during the fifth century A.D. How much of this canon is based on material preserved from the old literature, how much of it may be valid for the pre-Christian period, is very uncertain. Our present knowledge of this Jaina literature is too uncritical and too slight to warrant the use of it for historical purposes. Interesting is the statement of the *Anuyogadvāra-Sūtra* (142) that the total number of human beings in the world is a number which occupies 29 places, is obtained by multiplying the sixth square (of 2) by the fifth square ($2^{64}+2^{32} = 2^{96}$), and can be divided by 2 ninety-six times. Charpentier[2] is inclined to ascribe this text to a period before the beginning of the Christian era. This dating, although not improbable, is too positive. Its validity depends on the validity of the dates which he assigns to the *Kautilīya-Arthaśāstra* and to Vātsyāyana's *Kāmasūtra*.

Jaina works such as the *Jambudvīpaprajñapti*, in giving detailed descriptions of parts of the earth, which is described as being circular and having the diameter of 100,000 *yojanas*, (using $\sqrt{10}$) give dimensions which involve the relations of circumference, arc, and diameter of a circle (the approximation

[1] 'The Jaina School of Mathematics', *Bulletin of the Calcutta Mathematical Society*, xxi (1929), 114.

[2] 'The Uttarādhyayanasūtra', p. 30 in *Archives d'Études Orientales*, xviii (Upsala, 1921).

to the square root of a surd being necessary), and which involve
the arc of a circle, the height of the arc, the chord of the arc,
and the diameter of the circle (solutions of quadratic equations
being necessary).

The Jaina *Bhagavatī* deals with permutations and combinations. In connexion with this it is to be noted that in the
Chandassūtra of Pingala are given rules for calculating all the
possible varieties of metres with a given number of syllables.
These lead to very large numbers.[1] Permutations and combinations continued to form a favourite topic in later Indian mathematics. Square and square root are implied by certain rules of
Pingala and of the *Jyotisha-Vedānga*.[2] The dates of these works
are unknown, but they are generally thought to be as old as the
second century B.C

The nature of early Vedic astronomy is problematical, but
the material which has been preserved does not warrant the
conclusion that it reached any high state of development.[3]

The earliest astronomical texts which have been preserved
are the Vedic *Jyotisha-Vedānga*[4] and the Jaina *Sūryaprajñapti*,[5]
the dates of which are unknown. They must be considerably
earlier than the classical astronomy of the fourth or fifth centuries A.D., and may be pre-Christian.

The *Jyotisha-Vedānga* has been preserved in two recensions,
that of the *Rig-Veda* (36 stanzas) and that of the *Yajur-Veda*

[1] A. Weber, *Indische Studien*, viii. 432 ff., and H. T. Colebrooke, *Life and Essays*, ii. 88 (London, 1873).

[2] A. Weber, *Indische Studien*, viii. 323-4.

[3] For Indian astronomy, astrology, and mathematics see G. Thibaut, 'Astronomie, Astrologie und Mathematik' in *Grundriss der indo-arischen Philologie und Altertumskunde*, Strassburg, 1899.

[4] G. Thibaut, 'Contributions to the Explication of the Jyotisha Vedānga', *JASB*, xlvi (1877), 411-37.

[5] G. Thibaut, 'On the Sūryaprajñapti', *JASB*, xlix (1880), 107-27, 181-206.

(43 stanzas). Their style is of almost algebraical brevity, and the texts have come down to us in an exceedingly corrupt form.

It deals primarily with the calendar, describes the five-year cycle, the places of new and full moon in the 27 *nakshatras*, and gives rules for the calculation of these places. The five-year cycle consists of 5 years of 366 days (= 1,830 days). This is equal approximately to 67 sidereal months, and contains 62 synodical months. In order to keep the traditional 12 months in a year, 2 months were omitted in each cycle (the 31st and the 62nd). Thus lunar and solar reckoning coincided at the beginning and middle of a cycle. This system was used also in Jaina works, in the old *Paitāmaha-Siddhānta* described by Varāhamihira, and in the lost works of Garga and other ancient astronomers. The distinction between the true and mean motions of the heavenly bodies was unknown.

The origin of the lunar zodiac of 27 or 28 *nakshatras* or lunar mansions, which is found also among the Chinese and the Arabs, is still undetermined. The first complete enumeration of all the *nakshatras* seems to be given by the *Taittirīya-Samhitā* (7th century B.C. or earlier).

It is still uncertain whether a knowledge of the motions of the five planets is to be ascribed to this period or not.

The cosmology of this period, as described in the *Sūrya-prajñapti*, in chapters of the *Purānas* which continue this old cosmology, and in other early texts, assumes that the earth is flat and circular. In the centre of the earth, to the north, is Mount Meru with the Pole Star directly over it. The heavenly bodies are at the same elevation above the earth and revolve, in smaller or larger circles, from east to west around Mount Meru. When they are invisible at night, it is due to the fact that they go behind Mount Meru. Around Meru are four quadrants (like the petals of a lotus), of which India is the southern one. Around this central continent are seven concentric oceans and continents. This is the basic conception of Brāhman, Buddhist, and Jaina texts, although they differ in details.

In the astronomical literature of the third period, which begins in the fifth century A.D. at the latest, the earth is described as a motionless globe, of which Mount Meru becomes the axis, and around which the sun, the moon, the five planets, and the other heavenly bodies revolve. The sun, the moon, and the planets move more slowly than the stars and therefore change their places with reference to them. The true places of the planets in relation to their mean places are calculated by means of epicycles and eccentric circles. The inclination of the ecliptic to the equator is known and the positions of the heavenly bodies with reference to both are calculated. The precession of the equinoxes is known. The real causes of the eclipses of sun and moon are recognized, and the motions of these bodies are so well known that eclipses are calculated with great accuracy. The sexagesimal division of the circle is used.

This represents substantially the point reached by Greek astronomy by the time of Ptolemy in the second century A.D., and is on an entirely different plane from that of the *Vedānga*. Are these basic changes in point of view due to Greek influence, or do they represent a gradual internal development in Indian thought? Most of the old astronomical literature of India has been lost, but the nature of the *Jyotisha-Vedānga* and of the cosmography described above does not seem to give much support to the view that classical Indian astronomy was entirely a natural development from within.

Varāhamihira's *Pañchasiddhāntikā*[1] (*c.* A.D. 505) preserves summaries of five old astronomical *Siddhāntas*, the dates of which are unknown:

1. The *Paitāmaha*, which is on practically the same level as the *Jyotisha-Vedānga*.

---

[1] Edited and translated by G. Thibaut and Sudhākara Dvivedī, Benares, 1889.

2. The *Vāsishtha*, which seems to represent a transitional stage.

3. The *Pauliśa*, which is ascribed by Al-Bīrūnī[1] to 'Paulisa, the Greek, from the city of Saintra, which I suppose to be Alexandria'. Some think that this *Siddhānta* is a translation of the astrological work of Paulus Alexandrinus. It is to be re-marked, however, that the *Siddhānta* seems to have been purely astronomical and not astrological. If it does go back to some unknown Greek work, it has been so thoroughly Hinduized that no decisive traces of Greek influence are left.

4. The *Romaka*, in which the presence of Greek influence may be argued most plausibly. Its elements are almost exactly identical with those of Hipparchus and Ptolemy. In place of the great cycle of 4,320,000 years, which is in general use for purposes of astronomical calculations from the time of the *Pauliśa*- and *Sūrya-Siddhāntas*, it employs a cycle of 2,850 years, and its results are true for the meridian of Yavanapura (Greek city), not for that of Ujjayinī.

In some manuscripts of the *Sūrya-Siddhānta* is given a stanza in which Sūrya, the sun, says to the *asura* Maya, 'Go therefore to Romaka city, thine own residence; there, undergoing in-carnation as a barbarian, owing to a curse of Brahma, I will impart to thee this science.' If the stanza does not really belong here, it must be a fragment of an ancient account of the origin of some other treatise. In Indian astronomical works from the time of the *Sūrya-Siddhānta* the city of Romaka is situated on the equator 90° west of Lankā, which is south of Ujjayinī.

5. The *Sūrya-Siddhānta*, which is the only one of the five that has been preserved. Our present text, however, shows some discrepancies from the text described by Varāhamihira and must be a re-worked version of the original. Whitney[2]

---

[1] Sachau, *Alberuni's India*, i. 153, 266 (London, 1910).
[2] Whitney-Burgess, 'Translation of the Sūrya-Siddhānta', *JAOS*, vi (1860), 470–1. Reprint pp. 330–1.

decides that the work shows so many divergences from the numerical elements of Ptolemy that the Greek influence must have come from some work of the pre-Ptolemaic period, not far from the commencement of the Christian era.

The system of the *Sūrya-Siddhānta* continued in substantially the same form through the works of Āryabhaṭa (A.D. 499), Brahmagupta (7th century), and other lesser works to Bhāskara (12th century), whose *Siddhāntaśiromaṇi* is the last great work of Indian astronomy.

During the whole of this period there was little development in theory, the methods of calculation continued unchanged in essentials, and only minor corrections in the numerical elements were made. Noteworthy is the theory of Āryabhaṭa that the earth rotates on its axis, but this theory remained isolated and was not followed by any of the later works.

The earliest works of Indian astrology which have been preserved, such as the *Bṛhajjātaka* and the *Laghujātaka* of Varāhamihira (A.D. 505), contain many words which are undoubtedly of Greek origin.[1] A stanza preserved by Varāhamihira[2] from an older work by Garga says, 'The Greeks are Mlecchas, but amongst them this science is duly established; therefore even they (although Mlecchas) are honoured as Rishis; how much more then an astrologer who is a Brāhman.' The exact source of Varāhamihira's astrology has not been traced, but it seems to represent about the same stage of Greek astrology that is found in Firmicus Maternus in the fourth century A.D. The twelve signs of the zodiac appear in Varāhamihira in the form of Sanskrit transliteration from the Greek and of literal translation into Sanskrit. Although Greek influence on Indian astrology is undeniable, it is to be noted that only a few words of Greek origin are found in the works on

---

[1] A. Weber, *The History of Indian Literature*, 3rd ed., pp. 254–5 (London, 1892); J. Burgess, *JRAS*, 1893, 746–8.

[2] H. Kern, *The Bṛhat Saṃhitā*, p. 35 (Calcutta, 1865).

astronomy. Of these the most significant, since it is at the central point of this whole system of astronomy, is *kendra* (κέντρον) 'the mean anomaly', since the centre of the epicycle coincides with the mean place of the planet.[1] It has been argued by some that India did not borrow astronomical ideas directly from Greek astronomical works, but indirectly from works on astrology.

Even if the impetus toward a new astronomy was received by India from Greece by the acceptance of some general ideas, these were cleverly adapted to the older Indian cosmography and modes of reckoning. What had been borrowed was thoroughly Hinduized and completely assimilated into Indian culture.

Classical Indian astronomy is now only of historical interest, although there seems to be no doubt that it exercised a formative influence on early Arabic astronomy and therefore had some formative influence on the medieval astronomy of Europe.

The beginnings of Indian medicine[2] can be traced back to the magical charms of the *Atharva-Veda*, and *āyurveda* (medicine) has always been regarded as one of the *upāngas* of the *Atharva-Veda*. The earliest Buddhist books frequently refer to medicine and report stories of the wonderful surgical operations of the physician Jīvaka. Passages of the *Mahāvagga* and of the *Majjhima-Nikāya*, which must be at least as old as the third century B.C., refer to surgery. The inscriptions of Aśoka (3rd century B.C.) refer to the cultivation of medicinal plants, and to hospitals for men and for beasts. Corroboration of this is found in Megasthenes and other Greek writers who deal with the India of the Mauryan period. A passage of Strabo, xv. 1. 34 (C 701), 'they make no accurate study of the sciences

---

[1] Whitney-Burgess, *The Sūrya-Siddhānta*, chap. ii, pp. 30 n., 45 n.

[2] J. Jolly, 'Medicin' in *Grundriss der indo-arischen Philologie und Altertumskunde*, Strassburg, 1901.

except that of medicine', has been taken by some as referring to the Indians in general. As a matter of fact it is based on a description given by Onesicritus of the kingdom of Musicanus in Upper Sind. The *Kautilīya-Arthaśāstra* refers to ordinary physicians, physicians who dealt with poison, midwives, army surgeons and nurses, ointments and bandages, surgical instruments and other appliances. Patañjali's *Mahābhāshya* (ed. Kielhorn, i. 9) of the second century B.C. names *vaidyakam* (medicine) as one of the sciences.

The earliest work of Indian medicine which can be dated accurately is the Bower MS.[1] This was found in the year 1890 in Chinese Turkestan and dates from the fourth century A.D., but was probably copied from an older work. It proves the existence of a well-developed school of Indian medicine at that date.

The earliest medical works which have been preserved are those of Charaka and Suśruta. The Bower MS. refers to Suśruta as an ancient legendary author of medical works, and quotes many extracts from Charaka, Suśruta, and other authors whose works have been lost. By the fourth century A.D. the *Samhitās* of Charaka and Suśruta had already become standard works. The twenty-eight quotations from Charaka are practically identical with passages in the older part of our present text of Charaka. The six quotations from Suśruta are fairly close to passages in our present text.

According to the *Fihrist*, Charaka and Suśruta were translated into Arabic about A.D. 800, and about sixteen other Indian works on medicine were known to the Arabs in translation.[2] Both Charaka and Suśruta are frequently referred to by Rhazes, Avicenna, and other later Arabic physicians. Arabian medicine was the chief authority and the guiding principle of European

[1] Edited and translated by A. F. R. Hoernle in the *Archaeological Survey of India*, vol. xxii (Calcutta, 1893–1912).

[2] Flügel in *ZDMG*, xi (1857), 149, 325.

physicians down to the seventeenth century. Although later Arabian medicine was largely based on Greek medicine, it is certain that Indian medicine, which had been introduced into Baghdād at the end of the eighth and the beginning of the ninth century, formed part of the *Legacy of Islam*. Further it is to be noted that the Persian word *bīmāristān*, which was used for 'hospital' throughout the Islamic world, probably indicates that Arabian hospitals were modelled on the famous hospital at Jundēshāpūr, which seems to have been the point of intersection of Greek and Indian medicine. It may be that this in turn owed something to the Indian hospitals referred to in the inscriptions of Aśoka.

It is significant that although linguistically Indian texts on astrology and astronomy bear certain or possible traces of Greek influence there is nothing in Indian medical texts which might suggest Greek influence. There are some general resemblances to Hippocratic medicine, but the whole materia medica is Indian and there is no reference to Greek medicine and no proof of borrowing from Greece.

Much detailed critical work must be done on Arabian and Indian medical texts before a final judgement can be rendered concerning the relationship of Indian and Arabian medicine.[1]

About a third of our present text of Charaka was written by Drdhabala (about the 9th century A.D.), and the present text is guaranteed only by the commentary of Chakrapānidatta of the eleventh century. However, the many quotations given by the Bower MS. guarantee that the older part of our text is earlier than the fourth century A.D., probably considerably earlier, for its style is archaic, and it contains nothing of Puranic mythology.

The main part of the book is supposed to be a re-working by Charaka of a book by Agniveśa, a pupil of Ātreya, who is believed

---

[1] A. Müller, 'Arabische Quellen zur Geschichte der indischen Medizin', *ZDMG*, xxxiv (1880), 552–6.

to have been the founder of scientific Indian medicine. Hoernle[1] places Ātreya in the sixth century B.C. on the basis of Buddhist traditions that the famous Jīvaka studied medicine with Ātreya at Taxila in north-western India. It is a commonplace in the old Buddhist books for a boy to be sent to Taxila in north-western India to study arts and crafts. Benares in the east became a centre of learning at a much later date. This old tradition may indicate that from the end of the Vedic period Taxila continued for many centuries to maintain its prestige for learning, and that the arts and crafts implied by the *Kautilīya-Arthaśāstra* may represent the accumulated learning of several centuries during which the political centres shifted from the eastern Punjab down the Ganges valley to Magadha at the end of the fourth century B.C. There is nothing inherently improbable in connecting the author of our text with the Charaka who, according to a tradition preserved in the Chinese *Tripitaka*, was physician to King Kanishka in the first century A.D., or in dating Ātreya in the sixth century B.C. That is all that can be said at present.

As contrasted with the *Charaka-Samhitā*, which is medical, the *Suśruta-Samhitā* deals primarily with surgery. Tradition connects Suśruta with Benares in eastern India. The text seems to be later than the text of Charaka. Its language is less archaic, and its treatment is more concise, more developed, and more systematic. As in the case of Charaka, the text is guaranteed only by commentaries of the eleventh century, but the Bower MS. guarantees for parts of it at least a date earlier than the fourth century A.D. About a hundred and twenty surgical instruments are described, and a large number of surgical operations are referred to.

The osteology of Charaka, Suśruta, and other early texts, as described by Hoernle, *The Medicine of Ancient India*, proves

[1] *Studies in the Medicine of Ancient India*, Part I, 'Osteology', pp. 7–8 (London, 1907).

that careful empirical observations must have been made. How far actual dissection was practised is uncertain. Suśruta remarks (Hoernle, p. 116): 'No accurate account of any part of the body, including even its skin, can be rendered without a knowledge of anatomy; hence anyone who wishes to acquire a thorough knowledge of anatomy must prepare a dead body, and carefully examine all its parts. For it is only by combining both direct ocular observation and the information of text-books that thorough knowledge is obtained', and continues with considerable detail concerning methods of procedure.

The *Śatapatha-Brāhmana* (viii. 6. 2, 7–10; x. 5. 4, 12; xii. 2. 4, 9–14; xii. 3. 2, 3–4) and the *Atharva-Veda* (x. 2), texts which are believed to belong to the period between 1000 and 600 B.C., contain enumerations of the bones of the human body, which although associated with a good deal of religious symbolism, are very similar to those of Charaka and Suśruta.[1]

It is uncertain whether these early Vedic passages actually indicate dissection or not. But all the characteristic tendencies of later Hinduism warn us against ascribing to any very late period the passage concerning dissection just quoted from Suśruta. It bears the mark of antiquity rather than lateness. A mystical intuitive tendency which settled down over every branch of Hindu thought during the medieval period discouraged the development of any scientific objective attitude. As Wilson remarks,[2] 'We must therefore infer that the existing sentiments of the Hindus are of modern date, growing out of an altered state of society, and unsupported by their oldest and most authentic civil and moral as well as medical institutes.'

The third great name in Indian medicine is that of Vāgbhata. His *Astāngasamgraha* is probably to be placed at the

---

[1] For opposite views of the priority of the medical schools of Ātreya and Suśruta to the *Śatapatha-Brāhmana* see Hoernle, *The Medicine of Ancient India*, pp. 106–7, and A. B. Keith, *ZDMG*, lxii (1908), 137–9.

[2] H. H. Wilson, *Works*, iii. 392 (London, 1864).

beginning of the seventh century, for the Chinese traveller I-tsing, without giving the name, refers to a writer who shortly before his time had composed a compendium dealing with the eight branches of medicine. It is suspected that this may be the *Asānkar* referred to in Arabic works.

It has been conjectured that the famous *Mādhavanidāna* (of the 8th or 9th century) may be the *Badān* of Arabic writers.

After this period the arts and crafts were left more and more to the lower castes, and anatomy and surgery fell into disuse. Empirical medicine decayed as diseases came to be regarded as the inevitable result of *karma*.

There is not much that can be said at present about Indian chemistry and alchemy.[1] Little critical work has been done in editing the texts which have been preserved or in trying to sift out the early elements from the later accretions.

The origins of chemistry are lost in the mist of prehistory. Indian chemistry developed in connexion with medicine, metallurgy, and the technical arts. Alchemy in the narrow sense, with its theory of the transmutation of metals and of the elixir of life, is of comparatively late historical development. At present we lack material to make any comparison of Indian alchemy with that of the Chinese, the Alexandrian Greeks, and the Arabs. The very derivation of the word alchemy is uncertain. The claims of Chinese alchemy, which evolved out of Taoist speculations, to have played a part in the development of Persian and Arabic alchemy are becoming stronger and stronger.

Metallic preparations as medicines are casually referred to in the *Charaka-* and *Suśruta-Samhitās* and in Varāhamihira's

[1] For a brief and inadequate account of Indian chemistry and alchemy see E. O. von Lippmann, *Entstehung und Ausbreitung der Alchemie*, pp. 429–48 (Berlin, 1919). Praphulla Chandra Ray, *A History of Hindu Chemistry*, 2 vols. (Calcutta, 1902, 1909), contains much undigested and uncritical material.

Bṛhatsamhitā (mercury and iron), but the wide extension of their use does not seem to have taken place before the seventh century. Alchemy and the *rasāyana* doctrine of mercury as the elixir of life seem to have flourished especially in connexion with the Tantric cults of Hinduism, but the origin of these and their historical development are obscure. Jolly[1] sees in the *rasaviddham* of the *Kautilīya-Arthaśāstra* (ed. 2, p. 85) a possible reference to the transmutation of metals into gold.

The relationship between the musical systems of Greece, Arabia, Persia, and India is uncertain. There is much resemblance in several essential features. In the Vedic *Vedānga* on metrics (the *Chandassūtra* of Pingala) the seven notes of the octave (*grāma*) are referred to by the seven initial syllables of the Sanskrit names of the notes, *sa ri ga ma pa dha ni*.[2] In the *Jyotisha-Vedānga* the *naksatras* are referred to by comparable abbreviations, which are typical of the Indian *sūtra* style. The same method of naming the notes, but with differences in particular names, is found in Persia. Was it borrowed by the Arabs from Persia and transmitted to Europe? It has not been demonstrated conclusively that the syllables of the *solfeggio* are purely Greek or purely Latin or purely Arabian in origin.[3]

It has been generally conceded that the Arabic numerals are so called only because Europe learned them from the Arabs in the tenth century, that they are Indian in origin, that the Arabs admit that they learned them from India, and that the

[1] *Festschrift Windisch* (Leipzig, 1914), pp. 103–4.

[2] A. Weber, *Indische Studien*, viii. 256.

[3] A. Weber, *The History of Indian Literature*, 3rd ed., p. 272 (London, 1892). The Indian origin is accepted by Lévi, *La Grande Encyclopédie*, xx. 710. See H. G. Farmer, *Historical Facts for the Arabian Musical Influence*, pp. 72–82 (London, n.d.), who argues for Arabic origin. Considering our dense ignorance of Sāsānian Persia, he presses the argument from silence too far.

method of reckoning by means of nine signs and zero with place value was invented by the Indians.[1] A theory proposed by Bubnow[2] that the forms of the numerals first employed in medieval Europe are derived from ancient symbols used on the abacus in Europe, but that the zero is Indian in origin, has not been favourably received. Of recent years Kaye[3] and Carra de Vaux[4] have argued on the following grounds that the nine digits and zero with place value are not Indian in origin but were borrowed by the Indians from the Arabs, and that they are of Greek Neoplatonist origin:

1. No Indian literary evidence is valid for the period before the date of the actual copying of the manuscripts, and all coins and inscriptions which use digits with place value before the end of the ninth century are spurious.

2. The Arabic *hindasī* (geometrical) was misread as *hindī* and gave rise to the later myth among the Arabs of an 'Indian way of reckoning'.

3. References to India in medieval works may refer vaguely to 'the East' and not necessarily to India.

4. The digits with place-value notation were brought to the court of Chosroes by the Neoplatonists who sought refuge in Persia after the closing of the schools at Athens in A.D. 529.

The negative side of this argument is based on an unfair and hypercritical treatment of Indian inscriptions and literary tradition, and no evidence has yet been produced which would make the positive side of the argument even plausible.

Between A.D. 595 and the end of the ninth century about twenty inscriptions are known in which numerals with place

[1] Cf. D. E. Smith and L. C. Karpinski, *The Hindu-Arabic Numerals*, Boston, 1911, and W. E. Clark, 'Hindu-Arabic Numerals' in *Indian Studies in Honor of Charles Rockwell Lanman*, pp. 217–36.

[2] *Arithmetische Selbständigkeit der europäischen Kultur* (Berlin, 1914).

[3] Cf. *Indian Mathematics*, pp. 15–16, 45 (Calcutta, 1915); *Scientia*, xxiv (1918), 53–5; *JASB*, iii (1907), 475–503, and vii (1911), 801–13.

[4] *Scientia*, xxi (1917), 273–82.

value are used. The authenticity of some of these inscriptions has been questioned, but it is by no means certain that they are all to be brushed aside as forgeries. The matter will have to be decided by the judgement of expert epigraphists. The earliest epigraphical instance of the use of a sign for zero in India[1] is from the year A.D. 876, in Arabic[2] inscriptions from the year A.D. 873.

Brahmagupta (7th century) gives rules for different arithmetical operations with zero, and Varāhamihira's *Pañchasiddhāntikā* (A.D. 505) refers frequently to the addition and subtraction of zero. These do not necessarily prove the existence of a symbol for zero, but in a passage of Vasubandhu's *Vāsavadattā* (*c*. A.D. 600) is the statement that the stars in the sky are like zeros put there by the Creator to indicate the nothingness of this world of transmigration. The *Yogabhāshya* (*c*. 6th century A.D.) remarks that the same stroke is termed one in the unit's place and ten in the ten's place and a hundred in the hundred's place. Moreover, the alphabetical notation of Āryabhata (A.D. 499), his method for the extraction of square and cube roots, and the numerical words used by Brahmagupta, Lallā, Varāhamihira, and the *Sūrya-Siddhānta* seem to imply nine symbols with place value and probably a sign for zero as early as the fifth century A.D. The epigraphical use of numerical words begins in the eighth and ninth centuries, unless Kaye is correct in claiming that all such inscriptions previous to the tenth century are forgeries. But their use in inscriptions in Indo-China goes back to A.D. 604, and the usage there is doubtless derived from India.

It is generally assumed that the Indian numerals with place value were introduced to the West about A.D. 773, at the time when an Indian pandit brought the astronomical *Sindhind* to the court of al-Mansūr at Baghdād, but a passage from the

[1] Smith and Karpinski, *The Hindu-Arabic Numerals*, p. 52.
[2] Karabacek in *WZKM*. xi (1897), 13.

Syrian writer Severus Sebokt (A.D. 662) furnishes the earliest known reference outside of India to Indian numerals:[1] 'The subtle discoveries of the Hindus in astronomy, discoveries which are more ingenious than those of the Greeks and the Babylonians, and their clever method of calculation, their computation which surpasses words, I mean that which is made with nine signs. . . .' It is to be noted that the reference to nine signs does not necessarily prove the absence of zero. Up to the sixteenth century there was maintained a distinction between the nine signs and the zero.

If credence is given to this statement, Indian astronomy and arithmetic were known in a Syrian monastery on the upper Euphrates over a century before the Indian *Siddhānta* (*Sindhind*) was brought to the court of al-Mansūr at Baghdād in A.D. 773. There is nothing inherently improbable in this statement, and nothing has been adduced to prove that it should be brushed aside as worthless.

It has been suggested that this passage of Sebokt is to be interpreted as meaning that the Hindu numerals, without the zero, had reached Alexandria at some time before the seventh century, perhaps early enough to explain the mention in a passage of the *Geometry* of Boethius of nine numerical symbols which are called *apices*. Present opinion, however, seems to favour the view that this passage of Boethius is an insertion of later date.

Whereas the eastern Arabs in their 'Indian reckoning' used signs for nine numerals plus a symbol for zero, the western Arabs, as early as the tenth century, used somewhat different forms, without a symbol for zero, called *gobār* (dust) numerals and ascribed their origin to India. In Brahmagupta's *Brahma-sphutasiddhānta*, x. 62, 66, 67, the word *dhūlikarma*, 'dust work', is used as a synonym of *ganita*, 'calculation'. Whether these *gobār* numerals indicate an earlier and different stream of Indian

[1] Cf. Nau in *Journal Asiatique*, 1910, ii. 225-7.

influence or whether in some circles the symbol for zero was not adopted until later is uncertain.

In 1881 there was discovered at Bakhshālī, in extreme north-western India, fragments of some seventy folios of a buried birch-bark manuscript which contained a mathematical text.[1] It is a practical, not a theoretical work, consisting of rules and examples but without proof of the rules. It is written in an old form of Sāradā characters such as were in use between the ninth and thirteenth centuries. On the basis of paleography Hoernle dated the actual copying of the present manuscript in the eighth or ninth century; on the basis of the language, which seems to bear a certain relationship to the so-called Gāthā dialect, speci-mens of which have been preserved in old Buddhist works, he placed the composition of the work in the third or fourth cen-tury A.D. This dating, if it could be substantiated, would have an important bearing on the history of Indian mathematics.

The work deals with fractions, square roots, arithmetical and geometrical progressions, income and expenditure, profit and loss, computation of money, interest, the rule of three, summation of complex series, simple equations, simultaneous linear equations, quadratic equations, some indeterminate equations of the second degree, and many miscellaneous prac-tical problems. The algebraical symbolism is clumsy and in-adequate. Solutions are often given in such a general form as to imply a general solution—a generalized arithmetic.

The nine digits and zero (a dot) are used with place value. The negative sign is $+$ placed after a number, a usage which is not found in any other Indian work. In calculation large numbers up to 23 digits are easily manipulated.

Kaye assigns the work to the twelfth century A.D., and as-sumes Western influence because of the use of place-value

[1] G. R. Kaye, 'The Bakhshālī Manuscript', *Archaeological Survey of India*, vol. xlii (Calcutta, 1927).

notation, the occurrence of a general rule for the square root of surds, the frequent use of the *regula falsi* ('false position'), and one example of the transformation of a simple fraction expressed in the ordinary way to the sexagesimal notation.

It has not yet been proved that place-value notation is a criterion of late date, or that it is due to Western influence. A rule for the square root of surds is not found definitely expressed until after the time of Bhāskara (12th century), but approximation to the square root of a surd is found in the *Śulva-Sūtras*, in Āryabhata, and in Brahmagupta. In the *Śulva-Sūtras* the result may have been reached by a purely geometrical construction; in the other cases, even though no rule is given, it is by no means certain that an arithmetical method was not used.

The *regula falsi* is in common use in the works of most of the Arabic algebraists, beginning with al-Khwārizmī (*c.* A.D. 825), and is employed in India by Bhāskara (12th century) and sparingly by Mahāvīra (9th century). It is not used by Brahmagupta (7th century) or by Āryabhata (A.D. 499). But according to Smith, *History of Mathematics*, ii. 437, n. 1, Rabbi Ben Ezra (11th century) ascribes the origin of this rule to India. False position is a natural way of solving simple equations before the development of an adequate algebraical symbolism. It may have been used in India before Bhāskara and Mahāvīra, especially in works of a practical arithmetical nature.

The supposed sexagesimal fraction occurs in the solution of a problem in which the answer is expressed in days and in parts of days, each succeeding unit being one-sixtieth of the one preceding it. Therefore it can hardly be looked upon as the transformation of a simple fraction expressed in the ordinary way to the sexagesimal notation.

Kaye's late dating, based on arguments from silence, is unconvincing, and Hoernle's early dating is based on uncertain general linguistic considerations. At present the work, although important, cannot be used for historical purposes.

For the classical period of Indian mathematics the most important works are the following:

1. A short section in thirty-three stanzas in Āryabhata's astronomical work the *Āryabhatīya* (written A.D. 499).[1]

2. Two chapters in Brahmagupta's *Brahmasphutasiddhānta*, a general work on astronomy written in A.D. 628.[2]

3. Two chapters in the *Mahāsiddhānta*[3] of the second Āryabhata (between Brahmagupta and Bhāskara).

4. Mahāvīra's *Ganitasārasamgraha* (*c*. A.D. 850).[4]

5. Śrīdhara's *Ganitasāra* (*c*. A.D. 1020).[5] This is a compendium extracted by him from a large work which has not been preserved. This larger work must have dealt with algebra, for Bhāskara and others quote algebraical rules from Śrīdhara, in particular a general rule for the solution of quadratics.

6. The *Līlāvatī* and the *Bījaganita*,[6] which form the arithmetical and the algebraical part of Bhāskara's great work on astronomy, the *Siddhāntaśiromani*.

At the end of the *Bījaganita* Bhāskara remarks that he has composed a compendium since the treatises of algebra by Brahmagupta, Śrīdhara, and Padmanābha are too diffusive.

Āryabhata deals with the following matters: square root and cube root, area of triangle and volume of pyramid, area of circle and volume of sphere, area of trapezium and length of perpendiculars from intersection of diagonals to parallel sides, area of any plane figure; the chord of one-sixth circumference equal

---

[1] Prabodh Chandra Sengupta in *Journal of the Department of Letters* (Calcutta University), xvi (1927), and W. E. Clark, *The Āryabhatīya of Āryabhata* (Chicago, 1930).

[2] Colebrooke, *Algebra with Arithmetic and Mensuration from the Sanskrit of Brahmagupta and Bhāskara* (Calcutta, 1817).

[3] Edited in *Benares Sanskrit Series* (1910); for brief summary of the mathematical chapters see pp. 14–19, 21–3.

[4] Cf. *Bibliotheca Mathematica*, xiii (1912–13), 203.

[5] Translated by M. Rangāchārya (Madras, 1912)

[6] Translated by Colebrooke in work referred to above.

to radius, relation of circumference of circle to diameter; method of constructing sines by forming triangles and quadrilaterals in quadrant of circle, calculation of table of sine differences from the first sine; construction of circles, triangles, and quadrilaterals, determination of horizontal and perpendicular, shadow problems, hypotenuse of right-angled triangle, relation of half-chord to segments of diameter which bisects chord, calculation of *sampātaśaras* when two circles intersect; arithmetical progressions, sum of series formed by taking sums of terms of an arithmetical progression, sums of series formed by taking squares and cubes of terms of an arithmetical progression, product of two factors is half the difference between square of their sum and sum of their squares, to find two factors when product and difference are known; interest, rule of three, fractions, inverse method, to find sum of several numbers when results obtained by subtracting each number from their sum are known, to find value of unknown when two equal quantities consist of knowns and similar unknowns; to calculate their past and future conjunctions from distance between two planets; general solution in whole numbers of indeterminate equations of the first degree (to which Brahmagupta gave the name *kuttaka*).

Many elementary operations seem to be taken for granted, and no rules are given for them. For instance, one rule concerning the number of terms in an arithmetical progression implies the solution of a quadratic equation, although no rule is given for this operation. No rules are given for addition, subtraction, multiplication, division, square, and cube. It would surely be fallacious to argue from silence that these operations were unknown to Āryabhata. The value of π is given as 3.1416. The *kuttaka* or 'pulverizer' consists in finding a multiplier such that, if a given number is multiplied by it and a given number added to or subtracted from the product, the sum or difference may be divisible, without remainder, by a given divisor. This is substantially equivalent to Euler's method of solving the equation $ax+by = c$ in whole numbers by the use of continued fractions.

Brahmagupta gives formulae for the area and diagonals of any cyclic quadrilateral, rules for operations with zero, a rule which gives one root for quadratic equations, a partial solution in whole numbers of indeterminate equations of the second degree (with particular treatment of the special case $ax^2+l = y^2$ or so-called Pellian equation). He knew negative numbers, and by using negative terms in algebra reduced all quadratic equations to one form. He solved the equation $ax+by+c = xy$ in whole numbers by reducing $ab+c$ into $m \cdot n$ and putting $x = m+b$ and $y = n+a$.

Bhāskara extends into a general rule for quadratic equations a rule quoted from Śrīdhara, whose arithmetic has been preserved but whose algebra has been lost, special treatment of the Pellian equation $ax^2+l = y^2$, a solution for the general Pellian equation $ax^2+bx+c = y^2$ by completing the square and then applying the method for solving the Pellian equation, solutions of several other types of indeterminate equations of the second degree, and of some special equations of the third and fourth degree, and knew the negative roots of quadratics but disapproved of them. Of his cyclic method of solving indeterminate equations of the second degree Hankel[1] remarks that it is the finest thing in the theory of numbers before Lagrange.

The Hindus developed the sine function in computations connected with angles and with the circle. The Greeks used a trigonometry of chords (the ratio of the chord to the diameter). The Hindus considered the ratio of the half-chord to the radius as fundamental. Our whole modern trigonometry rests on this foundation. Hindu computations with shadows (with gnomon of length 12) were later utilized by the Arabs in forming their tables of the tangent function. If the Hindus borrowed the use

[1] H. Hankel, *Zur Geschichte der Mathematik*, p. 202 (Leipzig, 1874).

of chords from Greek astronomy, they improved and revolutionized the idea and made it wholly their own. Ptolemy's
chords were based on a radius of 60. In the *Pañchasiddhāntikā*,
in a passage which may be based on the *Pauliśa-Siddhānta* and
which may be the first Indian text to deal with half-chords, is
given a table of twenty-four sines at intervals of 3° 45', based
on a radius of 120, thus converting Ptolemy's table of chords
into a table of sines without changing the values.

The word *jyā* or *jīva*, from which our word 'sine' is ultimately
derived, is first used by Āryabhata, who gives a table of sines
at intervals of 3° 45' from 225' to 3438' (the radius), a table
of versed sines, and a formula for calculating these. With
$\pi = 3\cdot1416$ the radius of a circle of 360° (21,600') would be
3438' in round numbers, the arc of 3° 45' equals 225', and this is
taken as identical with the half-chord. There seems to have been
little further development until the time of Bhāskara, who gives
a table of sines by degrees. The word *jyā* or *jīva* (abbreviated
from *ardhajyā* or *ardhajīva*, 'half-chord') means the bow-string.
This was transliterated into the meaningless Arabic *jība*, the
consonants of which allowed later writers to substitute the word
jaib, 'bay or curve', and this word was translated into Latin as
sinus, from which is derived our word 'sine'.

According to Arabic tradition, an Indian pandit, Kankah
or Mankah, brought to the court of al-Mansūr about the year
A.D. 773 a book which is called by the Arabs *Sindhind* and which
probably represents the Sanskrit word *Siddhānta*. Tables based
on this *Sindhind* were composed by Ya'qūb ibn Tāriq and a
translation was made by al-Fazārī. This latter formed the basis
of the astronomical tables of al-Khwārizmī. Al-Khwārizmī
(died *c.*850) also wrote a book on the Indian method of reckoning, which continued for two or three centuries to form a large
part of the basis of Arabic mathematics. Was this book based
on chapters of the *Sindhind* or of some independent Indian book

on arithmetic concerning which we have no information? Karpinski[1] remarks of al-Khwārizmī's arithmetic, which has been preserved only in a Latin translation *Algoritmi de numero Indorum*:[2] 'Through his arithmetic preserving the Hindu art of reckoning he revolutionized the common process of calculation, and through his algebra he laid the foundations for modern analysis.' According to D. E. Smith and J. Ginsburg,[3] Rabbi Ben Ezra (born 1095) remarked that al-Khwārizmī 'and all later Arabic scholars do their multiplications, divisions, and extraction of roots as is written in the book of the (Hindu) scholar which they possess in translation'.

Al-Khwārizmī did much to make a synthesis of Greek and Hindu mathematics and astronomy. There appears to have been a large Indian element in his arithmetic. How much Indian influence is to be traced in his algebra is uncertain. The work seems to be neither purely Indian nor purely Greek. Ruska[4] has shown pretty conclusively that there are certain Indian elements in his algebra, that he had no knowledge of Diophantus, but that his geometrical proofs are based on some Greek source.

It is useless to surmise what Indian book the *Sindhind* represented or whether other works were brought with it. If it represented, as some think, the Indian *Sūrya-Siddhānta*, that work contains no chapters on mathematics. If, as others think, it represented Brahmagupta's *Brahmasphutasiddhānta* (and it is to this that the numerical data of later Arabic astronomy correspond most closely), it is strange that the chapter on arithmetic should have been so influential while the chapter on

---

[1] *Robert of Chester's Latin Translation of the Algebra of Al-Khowarazmi*, p. 33 (New York, 1915).

[2] Edited by Boncompagni in *Trattati d'Aritmetica* (Rome, 1857).

[3] *The American Mathematical Monthly*, xxv (1918), 103.

[4] 'Zur ältesten arabischen Algebra und Rechenkunst' in *Sitzungsberichte der Heidelberger Akademie*, viii (1917).

algebra made such a comparatively slight impression. The Arabs seem to have made much of Indian arithmetic with its methods of calculation based on nine digits and zero, but their algebra seems to have been based on a Greek rather than an Indian model. From the time of Brahmagupta the Indians had a much better system of algebraical notation than the Greeks and had gone further than the Greeks in general methods for the solution of indeterminate equations. Arabic adoption of Indian methods in algebra would have led to a much more rapid development of algebra in Europe. Were they ignorant of these Indian methods, or were they attracted rather to the more practical and geometrical Greek form of algebra than to the more speculative and generalizing Indian algebra? Al-Khwārizmī makes constant use of geometry to illustrate his equations.

Al-Kindī (*d*. 873) wrote four books on the use of the Hindu numerals. Between the ninth and thirteenth centuries Hindu numerals are mentioned repeatedly by Arabic writers, and several treatises based on them were written.

The *Sindhind*, and astronomical tables based on it, continued to be influential for several centuries. A clear proof of Indian influence on Arabic astronomy seems to be furnished by the fact that for centuries Arabic astronomy reckoned longitudes from the meridian of Arin, apparently a distortion of Sanskrit Ujjayinī (Ujjain), from the meridian of which the Indians reckoned longitude. Ujjain became Ozein (Ptolemy's Ozene), this became Azin, and this became Arin through omission of the point over the letter z.[1] The idea of a 'cupola of the earth' located at Arin continued on into the *Imago Mundi* of Cardinal Peter of Ailly (1410), from which Columbus learned an Islamic geographical theory which may have had a share in his discovery of the New World.

WALTER EUGENE CLARK.

[1] Reinaud, *Mémoire . . . sur l'Inde* (Paris, 1849), pp. 373–4, and *The Legacy of Islam*, pp. 93–4, 388 n.

VERNACULAR LITERATURES

THE vernacular literatures grew out of the theistic movement known as Vaishnavism. The movement makes its first appearance about the second century B.C., when the *Rāmāyana* and the *Mahābhārata* are found to be losing their original character of heroic poems through the interpolation of sectarian religious matter by Vaishnava priests. Vaishnava influence becomes more pronounced in the subsequent recensions of those poems, expanding them into encyclopaedias of theology, law, philosophy, and politics, and giving them, in their final form, the character of Vaishnava scriptures. The *Bhagavad-gītā* gives the most authoritative exposition of the Vaishnava creed about the third century B.C., and the *Bhāgavata Purāna*, next only to the *Gītā* in influence, appeared about the tenth century A.D. The movement reaches its highest development through the preachings of Rāmānuja in the twelfth century A.D., of Rāmānanda and Madhvachārya in the thirteenth, and of Chaitanya in the sixteenth. It then became what it has remained since, viz. the most important branch of Hinduism, both in the number of adherents and the impulse it has given to vernacular literature.

Vishnu, from whose worship the creed derives its name, arose out of the craving in the average human being for a personal god to whom love and devotion could be offered as to another human being. The Vedic deities, such as Indra, Varuna, or Agni, whom Vishnu supplanted, were personifications of natural phenomena, to be appeased, whether cruel or kind, with sacrificial offerings and prayer. No intimate spiritual communion could be established with them. More distant was the Supreme or Absolute of Vedic philosophy, resting on metaphysical heights attainable only by the highly cultured Brahmin. The vast masses required a god less neutral,

impersonal, and intellectual. Vaishnavism met their require-
ment with its doctrine of Bhakti (devotion) to Vishnu. Because
it was a popular religion, it used the vernaculars more than
Sanskrit for its literature.

The Vaishnava movement found a special source of strength
in the attempt made by Hinduism to reassert itself during the
decadence of Jainism and Buddhism. In some parts of India,
as in Bengal and the Kanarese country, the earliest vernacular
literature was the work of Jain or Buddhist priests. But Jainism
in those days had degenerated into exhibitionism and maso-
chism, spirituality being equated with physical torture by its
adherents, and death through self-inflicted starvation being
regarded as the consummation of a virtuous life. Buddhism
had lost the austere moral code and introspection of its days of
glory, and got mixed up with the degenerate aspects of such
cults as Tāntrism and Sahajīya. Against the looseness and law-
lessness, into which Jain and Buddhist free-thinking had sunk,
the pioneers of reawakened Hinduism imposed the necessity
of absolute obedience to a personal god. They encountered the strongest opposition not from the decadent Jains
and Buddhists, but from within Hinduism, from a section of
Hindus who were fighting the same corruptions from a different
camp. From the ninth to the twelfth century A.D. the religious
thought of India was dominated by Śamkara's doctrines of
Advaitavāda (monism) and Māyā (badly translated as illusion).
The intellectuality of Śamkara's doctrines which strikes us to-day
as among the noblest achievements of mankind was thought by
the Vaishnava reformers to be as dangerous as the grossness into
which Jainism and Buddhism had sunk. They taught that the
Supreme, 'the only one without a second', was not an intellectual
abstraction as Śamkara had made it out to be, but a Being capable
of stirring man's love and devotion, and of fulfilling his craving
for worship, sympathy, and communion.

Political events helped the development of Vaishnavism. The

Maurya Empire, the stronghold of Buddhism, declined in the second century B.C. After that there was a fairly continuous succession of Hindu kingdoms in all parts of India. The new Hinduism flourished under the patronage of Hindu kings. The Muhammadan conquest of India, too, helped the cause of Vaishnavism, though in an indirect way. The conquest introduced a period of ruthless oppression which went on unmitigated from the thirteenth to the sixteenth century, until the ascendancy of the emperor Akbar. Religion, especially of an emotional kind, is always the anodyne of a people in distress, and there can be no doubt that Vaishnavism took deeper hold as the country grew more wretched.

The orthodox forms taken by the Vaishnava cult of Bhakti were two, in accordance with the two incarnations of Vishnu as Rāma and Krishna. In North India through the teaching of Rāmānanda, who was inspired by Rāmānuja and followed by Kabīr and Tulasī Dās, it was the worship of Rāma and his wife Sītā that prevailed. In parts of South India through the influence of Madhvachārya, in Mathurā and Bihar, and in Bengal through the influence of Chaitanya, it was Krishna and his mistress Rādhā who received the widest devotion. Besides expressing itself in these orthodox forms, the Bhakti cult deeply influenced an earlier, and in many respects a rival, Hindu creed. This was Śaivism, or the worship of Śiva, which obtained wide vogue in the south, especially in the Tamil country. After Vaishnavism was introduced there from the north the two creeds existed side by side, sometimes in rivalry, but more often on parallel and separate lines, the Śaivas being known as Adiyārs and the Vaishnavas as Ālvārs. But when Śamkara's Advaitavāda attempted to impersonalize both Śiva and Vishnu, the Adiyārs and Ālvārs rose against the common enemy and joined forces. One result of this was that in some parts of the country the two creeds were reconciled by building temples consecrated to a hyphenated Śiva-Vishnu deity. But the more important result was that Śaivism underwent radical change by accepting the Vaishnava doctrine of Bhakti. Personal devotion henceforth became the keynote of Śaivism, replacing such earlier methods as Tapas (austerity) and Yoga (self-concentration).

The Bhakti cult, and consequently the literature it has produced, thus manifests itself in three main forms: Rāma-worship, Krishna-worship, and Śiva-worship. In some parts of India, especially in Bengal, it has had a fourth form which is of sufficient interest to be noted, because of the influence it has had on literature. This is derived from the Tāntric cult of Śāktism, or the worship of Śakti, either in her beneficent aspect as Durgā (or Pārvati or Umā) or in her maleficent aspect as Kālī (or Chandī or Tārā). The goddess is sometimes worshipped alone, but more often in conjunction with her consort Śiva. The philosophical principle running through the worship is that Śakti, the female, is the earth-force, ever active, ever changing and perpetually creating the illusions that constitute the phenomenal world; while Śiva, the male, is the soul-force, neutral, abstract, and eternally abiding.

The Śakti literature of Bengal is large but monotonous. The two most important writers it has produced it will be convenient to notice here, though out of chronology. The first is Mukundarām of the sixteenth century, the writer of a long narrative poem, *Chandī*, which has enjoyed considerable reputation in the past, though it might strike the modern reader as dull in places. But it is of great value for the picture it gives of contemporary Bengal. The realistic, even documentary, art of Mukundarām is of exceptional interest, because of the predominantly sentimental character of Indian vernacular poetry. Rāmprasād Sēn, the devotional song-writer of the eighteenth century, has enjoyed immense popularity in the past, and there is no village or town in Bengal to-day where his songs are not sung. He invented for them a special tune which has been named after him. He is the typical village poet, confined within a narrow range of ideas and experience, and content with a naïve manner of expression which is at once his strength and weakness. His interest lies primarily in his devotional fervour.

This day will surely pass, Mother, this day will pass, and only rumour linger . . . . I came to the market of the world, and by its bathing-*ghāt* I sat to sell my wares. Mother, the Sun our Lord is seated on his platform, the ferryman has come. The load of the many fills the boat, he leaves behind the wretched one. They seek a cowrie from this poor man; where shall he get it?

Prasād says: Stony hearted Girl, look back. Give me a place, O Mother! Singing thy glory, I will plunge in, into the sea of the world.[1]

In point of time Tamil takes the place of precedence among vernacular literatures. In the high standard of development it attained during the first ten centuries of the Christian era it is comparable with Sanskrit. In consideration of this long history it is at least arguable that Tamil should more properly be regarded as a classical literature. Possessing a civilization as early as, if not earlier than, the Āryan, the Tamils, the chief of the Dravidian people, were the last to be Āryanized. Hence their literature shows least trace of Sanskrit influence. Even in pre-Christian days we hear of three Sangams (academies of scholars) at Madurā, the capital of the Pāndya, and how they adjudicated on new literary works. Tradition mentions a Sangam poet, Nakkīrar, who is supposed to have flourished about the second century B.C. The earliest extant Tamil work is the *Tol-kāp-piyam*, a versified grammar of about the first century A.D. But the literature really begins with the *Kural* of Tiru-Vulluvar, the date of which is supposed to be between the first and the fifth century A.D. It is a didactic poem, written in terse epi-grammatic couplets reminiscent of the Sanskrit Sutra form. The *Kural* is the most venerated and popular book of South India and has even been spoken of as the Tamil Veda.

[1] *Bengali Religious Lyrics*, by E. J. Thompson and A. M. Spencer.

The show of power of one, who has no power within,
Is like a cow in tiger-skin, which quietly grazes on.

Be like the heron when 'tis time for lying low,
But like its strike when time for action comes.

The link of soul and body, say the wise,
Is but the fruit of man's own link with love.

Of the other Tamil poets before the tenth century, the Śiva-worshipping or Adiyār group includes such well known names as Tirujñāna Sambandar, Apparswami, Sundaramurti, and Mānikka Vāsahar. The first three are the authors of the collection of hymns known as *Devāram*, the earliest canonical literature of the Tamil Śaivas. The hymns were composed between the sixth and the eighth centuries and collected by Nambi Āndār Nambi about the eleventh century. Mānikka Vāsakar's chief work is the *Tiru-Vāchakam* (sacred utterances) of about the ninth century. It stands higher in popular affection than even the *Devāram*. The Tamil Vaishnava or Ālvār poets of the same period are twelve in number, the chief of whom are Nammālvār, Kulasekara Ālvār, Tirumangal Ālvār, and Āndāl who is of special significance as a woman. They are the authors of the collection called *Nālāyira Prabandham*, the great devotional classic of the Tamil Vaishnavas. The most important portions of it, the *Tiruppallāndu* and the *Tiruppāvai*, are recited daily in the temples.

To Hindi belongs the credit of possessing the earliest secular literature. The Rajput clans of central and western India who had come into prominence between the seventh and the twelfth centuries offered the most stubborn resistance to the Muhammadans, both before their conquest of India and after. The story of this struggle and the heroism and chivalry displayed by the Rajputs have been chronicled in the bardic lays with which Hindi literature makes its bow. The Chārans or Bhāts (professional bards) who were the authors of these lays were maintained at the courts of Rajput chiefs, and it was their duty to celebrate in song the heroic achievements of their patrons and their clans. It is traditionally supposed that these verse chronicles existed as early as the eighth century, but the earliest extant work is that of Chand Bardai of the twelfth. He was the court poet of Prithvī Rāj, the last Hindu king of Delhi, and is supposed to have lost his life in the same battle of Tarāin in which his master was killed. Chand's chief work, the *Prithvī Rāj Rāsō*, is a long narrative poem describing in a spirited manner the life and times of Prithvī Rāj, though not always to be trusted for historical accuracy. The story rises to tragic heights when Padmāvati marries Prithvī Rāj against her father's wish. The infuriated father, himself a Hindu king, conspires with the Muhammadan invaders against Prithvī Rāj, and Hindu rule permanently disappears from northern India. Chand Bardai was succeeded by several bards such as Jagnāyak and Sārang Dhar, the author of *Hammīr Rāsō* and *Hammīr Kāvya*, but they had no influence on subsequent Hindi or any other literature. When the vernacular literatures appear again after the twelfth or thirteenth century they are in the full spate of Bhakti.

From the twelfth to the fifteenth century may be described as the seed-time of the vernacular literatures. The establishment of Muhammadan rule in northern India in the thirteenth century brought about the disruption of Sanskrit learning. Academies were dissolved, temples desecrated, scholars dispersed, and priests persecuted. Sanskrit never recovered from this blow, though there was a classical revival in the fifteenth and sixteenth centuries. The vernaculars, however, benefited from the Muhammadan conquest, finding room to grow in the gap left by Sanskrit. Persian was the new classical language introduced by the Muhammadans, but it remained confined within the royal courts and the upper class Muhammadans and Hindus who learned it for professional and cultural purposes. The bulk of the people, both Muhammadan and Hindu, remained outside the influence of Persian which, lacking roots in the Indian soil, became in course of time as dead a language as Sanskrit. The vernaculars were the only living organs for both the communities, and many Muhammadan writers have contributed to the vernacular literatures of the past, as they continue to do in the present. A conspicuous example is Malik Muhammad Jayasi of the sixteenth century, the author, in Hindī, of the allegorical narrative poem *Padmāvatī*. The common needs of Hindus and Muhammadans even evolved the new vernacular language known as Urdū (literally meaning camplanguage). It was a compromise between Hindī and Persian, and may be described as the Persi..nized form of western Hindī, spoken near Delhi. Its vocabulary is largely Persian, its grammar Hindī. Another thing that helped the growth of the vernaculars was the patronage of Muhammadan kings. Apathetic to Sanskrit, if only out of their affinity with Persian, they were kind to the vernaculars of the people they ruled. Akbar is the greatest example of this, but many other Muhammadan rulers have been noted for their encouragement of vernacular literature. This was as much a matter of statecraft with them as of genuine interest. The first Bengālī translation of the *Mahābhārata*, for instance, was undertaken in the court of Nāsir Shāh, king of Gauda in the fourteenth century. The same king and the Sultan Ghiyās-ud-dīn are eulogized by the poet Vidyāpati as patrons of vernacular literature. The Hindu kings, on the contrary, were as a rule anxious to encourage Sanskrit, as the sacred books of Hinduism were in that language.

Bengālī, Hindī, and Gujarātī are the most important vernacular literatures of the north after the Muhammadan conquest. The southern Indian vernaculars of the same time are of secondary importance. In the history of Indian literature the south has always been influenced by the north, but never influenced it. The oldest Bengālī works, dated about the eleventh or twelfth century, give a good view of what the vernacular literatures were like in the earliest stage of their growth. The language, for instance, is found to be very close to the Māgadhi Prākrit from which Bengālī is descended, and to have developed very few modern forms. The authors are almost entirely Tāntric Buddhist priests. There is some semi-religious, mythological, and legendary matter, but the most interesting works, such as *Dākēr Bachan*, *Khanār Bachan*, and *Bāra Māsī*, are on topics such as would be of value to a rustic people in their daily life on the fields and at home. Some of the observations are delightful in their quaintness and *naïveté*, as for instance the following advice to husbands:

The woman who ties her hair loose; who throws away water so that she may go out to fetch it from the pond; who frequently looks over her shoulders as she goes, and casts furtive glances at passers by; who sings while lighting the evening lamp;—such a woman should not be kept in the house. (*Dākēr Bachan*.)

The Buddhist priests were pioneers, but they could not raise the language to literary status. For that, Bengālī, as well as the other vernaculars, had to wait until the fifteenth and sixteenth centuries, the golden period of Bhakti.

The afflorescence of Hinduism in that period had its literary counterpart in a great revival of interest in Sanskrit learning. Numerous translations and adaptations from Sanskrit were the result, and it was these that really started the vernaculars on their literary career. It should be remembered, however, that the classical influence operated indirectly through religion, that the resources of Sanskrit were explored chiefly because the religious works were in that language. This explains the almost universal demand for such religious works as the *Gītā* and the *Bhāgavat Purāna*, and the frequency with which they were translated. It also explains why semi-religious, or even secular, Sanskrit originals got a definitely religious character in their vernacular versions.

Of the two sources, classical and indigenous, from which the northern Indian vernaculars have sprung, the first, which is the older, may be said to have supplied the body, and the second the spirit. Sanskrit gave the vernaculars their vocabulary, grammar, system of rhetoric and prosody, literary types and modes, and almost all the themes on which they subsisted previous to the nineteenth century when the Western influence began to operate. But though their materials were mostly derived from the classical source, the vernaculars remained essentially indigenous in spirit. They never acquired the adult and civilized consciousness of Sanskrit, its high culture and intellectuality. As in the days of their primitive origin, their essential spirit still remains dark and mystical, semi-conscious and semi-articulate, religious rather than artistic, musical rather than poetic, sentimental and emotional rather than intellectual. This gives them a certain amount of freshness and charm, and enables them, at exceptionally rare moments of intuitive experience, to have direct vision into the life of things. But the main bulk of such literature, relying almost entirely on the heart and the spirit and almost entirely devoid of objectivity and intellectuality, is bound to be uninteresting.

When after the Muhammadan conquest Sanskrit ceased to be a living language, it came under the exclusive care of the pandits (schoolmen). It then became, like Greek and Latin in medieval Europe, over-sophisticated, hide-bound, and snobbish. This was inevitable in view of the unfavourable surroundings in the midst of which the pandits preserved the classical tradition, but it was also inevitable that the literary spirit could only thrive by rebelling against the rigidity and pedantry into which that tradition degenerated. The history of the vernacular literatures may be studied as a long fight between the puritanism of the pandit and the libertinism of the vernacular writer. The fight is by no means over yet, though the pandit has got the worst of it so far. One reason why Bengālī has developed more than

Hindī is that it has been less influenced by Benares, the principal seat of Sanskrit learning in India.

Yet a virile classicism, purged of pedantry and untrammelled by religion, will be necessary before Bengālī or the other vernacular literatures can hope to attain maturity of body and mind. So far the classical and the vernacular literatures have met at their weakest points. Adaptation into the vernaculars has, as a rule, meant emasculation and vulgarization of the Sanskrit originals. The *Rāmāyana* and the *Mahābhārata*, for instance, comparable to mighty rivers in their epic grandeur and richness, have shrunk into faint trickles of rustic piety in their vernacular versions. The types of Sanskrit literature that have been most sought after by vernacular writers are such debased ones as the Nakh-sikh and the Nāyak Nāyika Bhed, which describe every physical feature of the hero and the heroine from toe-nail to top-knot, and every shade of their amatory sentiment, with almost grotesque minuteness and ingenuity. Bihārī Lāl Chaubē, the seventeenth-century Hindī poet, turned out in his *Sat Sai* no less than seven hundred such slot-machine poems, though he was not the only purveyor of that species. The exaggerated eroticism and lusciousness of Jayadēva's *Gītā-Govinda*, itself a work of Sanskritic decadence, have been scrupulously emulated by the Krishna-Rādhā lyricists of north India, especially Bengal. The most inferior aspects of Sanskrit poetry, its stereotyped manner and ideology, and the trickeries of its clichés and conceits, have been copied *ad nauseam* by the vernacular writers. Even to-day a reader of vernacular poetry will find that the bird Chakōra drinks the rays of the moon in India, that the serpent has a jewel on its head, and that the river Jumna flows upstream when Krishna plays the flute.

The influence of Persian, the other classical literature, has been much less than that of Sanskrit. Persian poets, such as Hāfiz, Saʿdī, Jalāl-ud-Dīn Rūmī, and Omar Khayyam, have indeed inspired writers all over India, especially in the north, as have such themes from Persian literature as Leilah-Majnūn, Shīrīn-Farhād, Suhrāb-Rustam, Guli-Bakāwalī and Hātim Tai. The same is true of Persian verse-forms such as the *ghazal*, the *masnawī*, and the *rubā'ī*, which have made themselves at home in vernacular poetry. But the principal sphere of Persian influence was Urdū, and as such it was confined chiefly to the United Provinces in north India and to Bījapur and Golconda in the south. The last two states evolved a considerable body of Urdū poetry in the seventeenth and eighteenth centuries, known as the Ādil Allāhī and Qutb-Shāhī schools. The twofold misfortune of Persian in India was that its life was circumscribed within the royal courts, and that it lacked vital contact with the land of its birth. The Mughal courts of the seventeenth and eighteenth centuries, depraved and decadent, could foster only the corrupt aspects of the Persian tradition. That is why the bulk of Urdū poetry of that period, growing in the same atmosphere of disintegrating feudalism, is found to combine a high order of verbal ingenuity and prosodic dexterity with a range of subjects almost exclusively restricted to homosexuality, the cult of the courtesan, and rakish and sadistic cynicism. To say this is not to take a didactic or puritanic view of art, or to forget that great poetry, like Baudelaire's, may flower out of evil; but to point out that there is no Baudelaire among the Urdū poets in question.

Properly explored, the resources of Persian, like those of Sanskrit, will not fail to enrich the vernacular literatures. But such exploration will not be possible until Persian is divested of the communal and political interests within which a section of Indian Muhammadans have entrenched it at the present day. They are too proud of it as a symbol of Islam's glory in the past, and have too much faith in it as a means of reviving that glory in the present. That is what stands in the way of a proper critical approach towards Persian as an old literature with defects as well as merits, and of value to contemporary Indians principally in so far as it can be of use to Indian vernaculars. The pan-Islamists even run to such excess as to desire wholly to Persianize Urdū, though that is a major vernacular with possibilities of becoming the lingua franca of India, and only a small minority of the upper-class Muhammadans know Persian. In view of this it is regrettable that Sir Muhammad Iqbal, the most prominent Muhammadan poet of contemporary India, should have given up writing in Urdū and adopted Persian as the medium of his later works. As in the past, Persian is still serving the forces of reaction in India.

The renaissance of Sanskrit learning, which set the vernacular literatures on their feet, showed itself principally through translations and adaptations of Sanskrit epics, notably the *Rāmāyana* and the *Mahābhārata*. As a matter of fact, such was the preponderance of epic or semi-epic literature between the twelfth and the sixteenth centuries, that it would be right to say that the vernacular literatures began with an epic revival. The most outstanding works, selected out of a large multitude, were: the Telugu version of the *Mahābhārata* by Tīkkana, Nannaya and Erra Pragada; the Bengālī version of the *Rāmāyana* by Krittibās; the version in the same language of the *Mahābhārata* by Kāsīrām Dās; and above all, the Hindī version of the *Rāmāyana* by Tulasī Dās. The popularity enjoyed by the last work has given it the title of the Bible of the Hindī-speaking people of India. These versions make no attempt to reproduce the epic character of the originals and are to be classed as folk literature in sentiment and diction. Nor does their fidelity to the original story or characterization extend beyond the broadest outline. The most important change, however, is the note of devotion they introduce into the theme in accordance with the cult of Bhakti. In all the versions of the *Rāmāyana*, for instance, Rāma, the hero, is no longer a human being, but an incarnation of Vishnu. Devotion to Rāma is recommended in almost every page as the only means of attaining salvation. In the Introduction to his *Rāmāyana* Tulasī Dās does not hesitate to disregard the literary shortcomings of his work and proudly emphasizes its religious character as being of higher value. What he says in self-justification might have been said by all who made vernacular versions of Sanskrit epics in that age.

I am confident of one thing, that the good will be gratified to hear me though fools [i.e. Sanskrit scholars] may laugh. The laughter of fools will be grateful to me—as they have no taste for poetry nor love for Rama . . . If my homely speech and poor wit are fit subjects for laughter, let them laugh; it is no fault of mine. If they have no understanding of true devotion to the Lord, the tale will seem insipid enough; but to the true and orthodox worshippers of Hari and Hara the story of Raghubar [Rāma] will be sweet as honey.[1]

The note of devotion becomes more pronounced as the vernaculars attain the stage of original composition, the first period of which may be conveniently dated between the fifteenth and seventeenth centuries. The Bhakti movement reached its highest watermark in that period. A large number of the earliest as well as the most important specimens of Bhakti poetry written in Hindī in that period was collected in the *Ādi-Granth*, the scripture of the Sikh community, by Guru Arjun in the early years of the seventeenth century. The outstanding contributors were Rāmānanda, Nānak, and Kabīr, the last-named being the most important from the literary point of view. All three are Rāma-worshippers, with the difference that Kabīr went furthest of all in discarding sectarianism and orthodoxy. Traditionally supposed to have been born a Muhammadan, he fought with equal zeal against the shams and dogmas of both Hinduism and Muhammadanism, preaching the unity of God and enjoining sincerity of devotion as the essence of religious life. Large numbers of Hindus and Muhammadans became his disciples, calling themselves 'Kabīr-panthīs' or the followers of the path of Kabīr.

[1] *Hindi Literature*, by F. E. Keay.

> There is nothing but water at the holy bathing places; and I know
> that they are useless, for I have bathed in them.
> The images are all lifeless, they cannot speak; I know, for I have
> cried aloud to them.
> The Puran and the Koran are mere words; lifting up the curtain,
> I have seen.
> Kabir gives utterance to the words of experience; and he knows very
> well that all other things are untrue.[1]

The Krishna-worshipping form of Bhakti was more widespread
than the Rāma-worshipping, and inspired poetry of greater
literary merit. In the south it produced such Telugu works
as the *Āmuktā-mālyada* by Krishnadīva-Rāya and the *Manu-
charitra* by Allasāni Peddanna, and inaugurated the first period
of original work in that literature known as that of the Praband-
has. But the work produced in the north was more copious,
influential, and beautiful. Sūr Dās and Mīrā Bāī are the greatest
Krishna-poets in Hindī, Nāmdēv and Tukārām in Marāthī,
and Narasinha Mehta, Nākar, and Prēmānand in Gujarātī.
These names have been chosen out of a large number. Some of
them, such as Mīrā Bāī and Nāmdēv, wrote in two languages
or in a dialect that was a mixture of two. Mīra Bāī, 'the sweet
singer of Rājputānā', is the best woman poet of India before
the nineteenth century.

> God hath entwined my soul, O Mother, with his attributes, and
> I have sung of them.
> The sharp arrow of His love hath pierced my body through and
> through, O Mother.
> When it struck me I knew it not; now it cannot be endured, O
> Mother.
> Though I use charms, incantations, and drugs, the pain will not
> depart.
> Is there any one who will treat me? Intense is the agony, O Mother.
> Thou, O God, art near; Thou art not distant; come quickly to
> meet me.

[1] *Kabir's Poems*, trs. Rabindranath Tagore.

Saith Mīrā, the Lord, the mountain-wielder, who is compassionate, hath quenched the fire of my body, O Mother.

The Lotus-eyed hath entwined my soul with the twine of his attributes.

Mīra Bāī (trs. Macauliffe).

Specimens such as the above lose much through translation, especially as the original words were meant for music. The best work of these writers is as good as poetry of the kind can be. But restricted, as it is, to the one note of simple piety, their average performance leaves no other impression than that of monotony. One wonders at the patience and seriousness with which they go on repeating the same platitudes, such as the renunciation of earthly ties, the delusions of Māyā, and the value of reciting the name of God.

The finest flowering of the Krishna cult was in Bihār and Bengal, in the poetry of Vidyāpati, Chandīdās, Govinda Dās, and of the many later Padakartās (song-makers) who wrote under the great stimulus given to Vaishnavism by Chaitanya in the sixteenth century. They sing of the love of Krishna and Rādhā, than which there is no subject dearer to the heart of India. Krishna is a cowherd, Rādhā a princess, and their passionate encounters take place against a background of great romantic beauty on the banks of the river Jumna. According to the Vaishnavas only love can produce the highest state of spirituality in a man or a woman, and it does that best when it attains the utmost degree of intensification through the enhanced pain and pleasure of an illicit relationship. So Rādhā is represented as a married woman. The story is developed through the six stages of Pūrvarāg (dawn of love through hearing of each other), Dautya (message), Abhisār (tryst), Sambhōg-milan (union), Mathur (separation), and Bhāba-sammilan (reunion in spirit). The allegory running through the story is that Rādhā is the human soul, Krishna the god of love in human form, and that the human and the divine are restlessly seeking completion through union with each other. They achieve this completion by realizing each other through every form of physical and spiritual relationship: through affection, as between mother and son (*bātsalya*); through friendship, as between a man and a man and between a woman and a woman (*sakhya*); through devotion, as of a servant to his master (*dāsya*); through tranquillity, as between two souls polarized with each other (*sāntā*); and through the ecstatic oneness of a man and his mistress (*madhur*). To describe the last, which, according to the Vaishnavas, is the highest state, the poets range over all the physical aspects of love, including coition. The unhesitating frankness and wholehearted delight with which they do this free their work from the least suspicion of vulgarity and give it a naturalness which in itself is very beautiful. At the same time their crudity, their lack of detachment and of intellectual abstraction, render them incapable of transmuting their materials into poetic values of the highest order. Whether they are describing physical sensations with the joyousness of a Vidyāpati or pouring forth their most poignant feelings with the abandon of a Chandīdās, they are too much dominated by their material to make the greatest poetry out of it. They rely too often on overstatement to produce the impression of intensity, as on the many occasions when an ecstatic state is produced in Rādhā by trivial things remotely associated with Krishna; and are too fond of using the jaded conventionalities pilfered from erotic Sanskrit literature, such as the comparison of Rādhā's eye to a lotus and of the pupil to a bee. Only very rarely, in the best moments of Vidyāpati and Chandīdās, does the body seem to burst its bounds and feelings seem to become the fine flame of poetry.

> Ever since my birth have I beheld his beauty,
>   Yet my eyes are not appeased.
> For millions of ages have I pressed my heart to his,
>   Yet my heart is not appeased.
>
>   Vidyāpati.

In spite of the allegorical-religious setting of their work, these poets strike a human note that is altogether new in Indian vernacular literature. For the first time, in passages such as the above, is human love being valued for its own sake, and as something to be offered to another human being, not to a god. The human note is most intense in Chandīdās's poetry, inspired as it was by his love for a low-caste woman for whom he sacrificed social position, wealth, and religion. For the first time, too, is there indication of a genuine interest in natural sights and sounds. Stereotyped images from Sanskrit abound, but there are, especially in Vidyāpati, many instances of direct and loving observation of nature. The work of these poets is a green spot in the arid waste of devotional literature produced by the Indian vernaculars previous to the nineteenth century.

The eighteenth century was a period of stagnation. Mughal power was rapidly disintegrating, the British was not yet established. The country groaned under the heel of foreign and native adventurers who were constantly at war with one another, and whose barbarity, cruelty, and rapacity knew no bounds. The miserable plight of the people reflected itself in the scantiness and inferior quality of the literature of the period. Some vernaculars such as Telugu, Kanarese, and Gujarātī were almost barren, while the others, such as Bengālī, Urdū, and Hindī, accentuated their most defective aspects. The perversities and artificialities of Urdū increased as the Mughal courts became more and more decadent. In Bengal the healthy carnality and the ardent emotion of love of the Vaishnava poets considered above gave way to erotic sensationalism as in the *Vidyāsundar* of Bhārat Chandra Rāy, or to wishy-washy sentimentalism as in the many Krishna-Rādhā poems of the time. Poetic art became entirely a matter of facile versification, stilted metaphors and similes, and jingling puns and alliterations.

Bengālī literature entered its modern period in the year 1800, when the Fort William College was established in Calcutta. The nineteenth century is also the period of Western influence which operated through the introduction of English education among Indians. For the major vernaculars other than Bengālī the modern period did not begin until later in the century— not until 1852 for Gujarātī—and for the minor vernaculars, such as Assamese, Bihārī, Oriya, Punjābī, Sindhī, Kāshmīrī, and Malayālam, it cannot be said to have begun even to-day. The Fort William College was started with the object of teaching British civil servants the languages, law, history, and customs of India. There were facilities for teaching Sanskrit, Persian, Arabic, Bengālī, Telugu, Tamil, Kanarese, and Marāthī, though Bengālī received the most attention, being the local language. The college helped the development of Bengālī indirectly by bringing it within the pale of official recognition, and directly by the literary and linguistic activities undertaken by members of the staff. The most memorable name in this connexion is that of William Carey, professor of Sanskrit and Bengālī in the college, who rendered a great service to Bengālī by writing a grammar and compiling a dictionary of that language. The vernaculars were also helped by the Christian missionaries who established societies in all parts of India during the century. They adopted the language of the people as the best means of furthering propaganda. Their principal literary work was the translation of the Bible, but it was by introducing the printing press that they really helped the vernaculars. The press brought the vernacular literatures within the reach of a wide public, finally broke their oral tradition, and made conditions favourable for the growth of prose. Since then the vernaculars have rapidly developed in many directions, but the fact that the printing press came to India nearly four hundred years after it came to England will in itself explain the enormous difference, of quality and quantity, that exists between the literatures of the two countries.

The Christian missionaries have always played an important part in the cause of Indian education, and helped to create a taste for Western literature and culture through the schools and colleges they have established. But for her Western education India's thanks are principally due to Lord Macaulay, who urged on the Government the need for teaching Indians the English language and the Western arts and sciences with a view to creating an Indian intelligentsia which would form the connecting link between the imperial power and the masses ruled by it. The same view was held by the Christian missionaries, such as the Rev. Alexander Duff of the Scottish Mission in Calcutta, who saw in anglicizing the Indian the preliminary step to Christianizing him; and by progressive Indians such as Rājā Rām Mohan Rāy who sought the help of liberal ideas from Europe in order to combat the religious orthodoxies and social corruptions of their country. The policy advocated by these people was adopted by the Government and has continued to the present day.

The Hindu College of Calcutta was the premier seat of Western learning in the nineteenth century. Under the guidance of David Hare, the first principal, and H. L. V. Derozio and D. L. Richardson, professors of English, the college became a centre of great intellectual activity, in fact the nursery of the modern spirit in India. It inspired generations of young Indians with love for Western arts and sciences, and made them realize that only through the help of Europe could they hope to pull their country out of the decadence into which it had sunk. It is true that the new learning acted like strong wine on the young Indian intellectuals of the day, and they went to the extreme by trying to Westernize themselves completely, crying down everything Indian and exaggerating the value of everything European. But that was inevitable at the time, considering into what the country had degenerated. The tide turned towards the eighties of the century, when the movement began

for the revival of a national Indian culture with roots in the
past civilization of the country, but purged of the corruptions
of medieval and post-medieval times. This renaissance movement developed under the influence of the West, and its object
was the fusion of the best in Indian civilization with the
best of modern European. It was the offshoot of the spirit
of nationalism awakened by the impact of Europe, and its
knowledge of ancient India was derived from the researches of
European indologists and of Indian scholars trained by them.
Europe not only breathed life into the moribund India of the
eighteenth and nineteenth centuries, it also helped to recreate
ancient India, and so provided modern India with a background
and a perspective.

Previous to the nineteenth century none of the vernaculars
except Urdū had a secular literature. The impulse to write
came primarily from religious, not literary or artistic, motives.
Even if the theme was secular, as for instance the secret love of
Vidyā and Sundar in the Bengālī poems written about them, a
religious ending had to be foisted upon it. Poems were not
written to be read or recited, but to be sung as hymns or
devotional songs. Even the long narrative was meant to be
chanted. The authors were, as a rule, saints or devotees who
cared more for piety than poetry and whose chief concern was
to renounce the world rather than live intensely in it so as to
elicit artistic values out of it. This religious obsession—really
pseudo-religious, if we leave out the best devotional works—was
the permanent blight of Indian literature in the past, and it
continues to exist to the present day. Before the nineteenth
century India possessed no theatre, and consequently no drama,
of the type known to Europe since the Renaissance, and adopted
by India from Europe in recent times. What is worse, there was
no prose, and prose is the backbone of literature. There were
some translations of Sanskrit treatises on rhetoric and prosody,
but no work of proper literary criticism—it hardly exists even

to-day—no historical and scientific writing. In short, there was little literature of knowledge, none of thought. There was some biographical, narrative, theological, and descriptive work in both prose and verse, or in such mixed prose and verse form as the Champū of south India, but it is not to be regarded as literature. The same is to be said about the large body of popular verse floating about in all parts of the country in the lowest stratum of its life, e.g. the Bāul songs and boatmen's songs of Bengal; the Javali songs of Teluguland; the Garbhī songs of central India; the Holī songs of all parts of India; the dirges of Hussain and Hassan sung by Muhammadans at the time of the Muharram; and the verse-fables of Sītalā, Manasā, and Behulā in Bengal. These communal reservoirs of literature still exist, though they have shrunk considerably through the disruption of village life since the nineteenth century.

At the beginning of the nineteenth century the vernaculars were in a state somewhat similar to that of English at the time of Chaucer. Since then, principally by virtue of contact with England, they have been acquiring copiousness, variety, vitality, and modernity. The English language has given them access not only to the literature of England but, through translations, to that of Europe. Bengālī has been the quickest and most wholehearted in responding to the stimulus from the West and has, in consequence, acquired the position of the premier literature in modern India in output, original power—it is the only literature that manifests that—and in the vitalizing and modernizing influence it exerts on the other literatures. It has produced a large number of able writers, the best of whom are Rājā Rām Mohan Rāy, the pioneer of prose and of the literature of thought; Bankim Chandra Chatterjee and Romesh Chandra Dutt, novelists; and Madhusudan Dutt, poet, of the nineteenth century; and Sarat Chandra Chatterjee, novelist, and Rabindranath Tagore, the greatest Indian vernacular writer of the present day. The influence of Bengālī extends over all the other vernacular literatures and, next to English, Bengālī is the greatest modernizing force in contemporary India.

The vernacular literatures still reproduce in a considerable measure the outworn modes and conceptions that are their heritage from the past. But their main bulk bears the stamp of Western influence in some form or other. This literature of absorption, as it may be called, includes, among other things, the mass of fiction, lyric poetry, drama, and the immense journalistic matter that are either translated from English or almost entirely based upon English or European models. It also includes vernacular works such as the novels of Bankim Chandra Chatterjee and the devotional songs and many lyric poems of Tagore which are Indian in outlook and spirit but have adopted and absorbed European form and technique. The latter class is the result of the attempts made by Indian intellectuals since the eighties of the last century to bring about a fusion of Indian and European culture. So far the best vernacular writers have belonged to this class, though the synthesis made by them of the East and the West, of the old and the new, has as a rule been vague and superficial. Tagore, for instance, skims the surface of the old Indian spirituality and mysticism and of *fin de siècle* European aestheticism, and combines the two with a complacency that strikes us as amazing, though it endeared him to the pre-War world.

The future hope of Indian literature lies in more intensive assimilation of Western literature than has been achieved so far. As a matter of fact, except among a very small number of Indian intellectuals, the best elements of English or Western literature cannot be said to have arrived in India yet, or, having done so, to have struck root there. Language has been a bar, but, more than language, the difference in the ideals and modes of Western and Indian literature and, above all, the difference in the condition of life of the two countries. This is not to say that the increasing fertilization of India by the West is neither possible nor desirable, but to suggest the difficulties that lie in the way. So far it is the class of literature to be found in the railway bookstalls and the suburban libraries of Europe that have had the most vital and widespread influence in India. This is as much due to the inability of the majority of Indians to comprehend the best aspects of European literature as to the same inability in the majority of Europeans, drawn from the military and commercial classes, who go to India. The taste they diffuse for the Ethel M. Dells, Gilbert Frankaus, and similar stars of the journalistic and pseudo-literary world is freely acquired by the majority of educated Indians who know English. The regrettable result is not that this class of European literature enjoys the greatest popularity in India—it does that in Europe too—but that it is regarded seriously as specimens of European modernity and intellectuality. This does not mean that such European writers as Shaw, Proust, Eliot, or Aldous Huxley are unread in India, but that their influence on contemporary Indian literature is negligible in comparison with that of the class mentioned above. Tagore is the only writer in contemporary India whose work shows understanding and assimilation of higher class European literature. The Indian universities, under the guidance of Europeans and Indians trained in Europe, try to improve taste, but their influence hardly extends beyond the examination hall and their curriculum beyond Tennyson and Browning. In the field of creative work they seem to be able to do little more than to perpetuate the voice of Wordsworth's spirit of the woods and the trickle of Tennyson's idle tears. For the poetry of Wordsworth and Tennyson is reduced to little more than this in the text-books.

Intellectuality and realism are the two greatest things Western literature could give to India. Growing out of religion and remaining almost entirely confined to religion, vernacular literature of the past had little contact with the actualities of life. It had even glorified as virtue the depravity that had made it escape from life. The result was that it was platitudinous, convention-ridden, and devoid of substance, variety, and virility. Since the nineteenth century it has been more in touch with life than it was before, but not as much as one would wish it to be. Both in Tagore's poetry and elsewhere it still lives upon facile emotion and sentiment, and shirks the rigours of intellectual work. Tagore has not imported from Europe the intellectual and scientific objectivity which Indian literature needs, but only the sentimental langours and affectations of the Celtic Twilight and the misty vagueness of Maeterlinckian symbolism. As in the past, Indian writers are still seeking escape from reality, though not always into the old-fashioned devotionalism of native growth. The emasculated, demodé, decadent, or inferior aspects of European literature are providing a new refuge. Isolated groups of young writers, such as the *Parichaya* group of Calcutta, have perceived that a change is necessary, and are trying to bring it about with the help of the advanced literature of contemporary Europe. But they are not succeeding, mainly for the reason that there is no counterpart to that literature in Indian thought and life of the present day.

Indian literature will not acquire reality and vitality until it is rescued from the academic, priestly, and well-to-do classes in whose keeping it has degenerated so long, and becomes wide enough to include the consciousness of the working people of the country. Only the hard realities of life of those people, and the practicality, zeal, and freshness they possess, will effectively destroy the mystical-devotional obsession Indian literature has inherited from the past, and the sentimental-aesthetic posturings it has acquired from modern Europe. For that a radical change in the political, economic, and social structure of the country will be necessary. The chief hope for Indian vernacular literature lies in the struggle that has already commenced for such a change.

J. C. Ghosh.

INDO-BRITISH CIVILIZATION

MOST of the previous chapters have dealt with aspects of Indian civilization previous to the British occupation. Until the end of the eighteenth century physical and linguistic difficulties were sufficient to account for the comparatively small influence which India exercised upon the Western world. We must now consider the last phase of Indian history, during which the whole country has been brought, province by province, State by State, under the control or under the indirect influence of the British Government. Within the last century some millions of educated Indians have learnt English, and the physical barriers preventing easy intercourse with the West have been substantially reduced. It might have been expected that Indian philosophy, literature, and art would have received at last a fuller appreciation in Europe; and that some new form of civilization might have developed from the close contact between England and India. Unfortunately it must be confessed that the last 150 years have proved the most disappointing, and in some ways the most sterile in Indian history. The English, working or domiciled in India, have not provided a good channel for spreading abroad the more valuable elements of Indian culture. Even more surprising is the poverty of the harvest from this hybrid civilization, from Indians working under English influence, or from English inspired by India and the Indian peoples.

The failure must be ascribed chiefly to the conditions of European colonization. Apart from temporary raiders India had usually absorbed and assimilated her Asiatic invaders. These entered from the north, and aimed at conquest and settlement. The Europeans, when they began to come east during the last three centuries, were not impelled by pressure of population, and only to a small extent by imperial ambitions. Neither France, Holland, nor England have ever seriously considered

India or the East Indies as *colonies de peuplement*, but only as *colonies d'exploitation*. Portugal, with her visions of mass conversion, began to colonize in India with some object of building up a new Christian civilization. Her government deliberately encouraged the growth of a hybrid Christian population, but her efforts did not pass the experimental stage. The other invaders from temperate climates came originally as traders, and continued as soldiers and administrators, but they never made much attempt to force their religion or civilization upon India. This typically nineteenth-century form of colonization tends to destroy the existing social structure, without encouraging the development of any new culture. There were special circumstances which exaggerated this defect in British India.

During the latter half of the eighteenth century, when the British Government began to accept some responsibility for the territorial commitments of the East India Company, Indian civilization was at its lowest ebb. The break-up of the Mughal Empire left the country at the mercy of adventurers and 'war lords'. Civil war and general disorder caused the complete submergence of all those arts which flourish in times of peace. The English who first went out to Bengal, Madras, and Bombay cannot be seriously blamed for neglecting such Indian culture as still survived. Most of the Company's servants were hardy adventurers, only anxious to 'shake the pagoda tree' and collect what profit they could out of the prevailing anarchy, but from the first there were a few who sought the company of educated Indians, and took an interest in their thought and achievements. Some account of this has been given in the first chapter of this book. It is enough for our purpose to recall that Warren Hastings encouraged Pandits and Maulvies. His motives may have been partly utilitarian, but he helped, in 1781, to found the Calcutta Madrasa for Islamic studies, while another of the Company's servants took a considerable share in launching the Sanskrit College at Benares in 1792. These early administrators were reprehensible from many points of view, but they did not suffer from the self-righteousness and strong Christian prejudices which were so marked amongst Englishmen in India from about 1830 onwards. They found Hindu religious thought and Muslim law in a state of decadence, and certainly did not discourage them. They even tried, without any great enthusiasm, to revive them. There was little literature being produced in any part of India during the later part of the eighteenth century—the Bengali renaissance was much later—but there was a definite school of orientalists amongst the Englishmen who first went to Bengal. Sir William Jones, Sir Charles Wilkins, and Colebrooke were followed by men like Horace Wilson and James Prinsep. They were all men of great erudition, who 'aimed at a union of Hindu and European learning', and did much to introduce the ancient Sanskrit classics to the Western world. If they failed to find much in contemporary Indian literature or philosophy which interested them, it is at least possible that the reason was because there was very little to find.

The question of English treatment of Indian craftsmanship has, unfortunately, been obscured by later political controversy, but the same general considerations apply. There have always been two distinct types of craftsmen in India—those making commodities needed by villagers, and the far smaller group working for the wealthy and for export. The history of the former, still a large proportion of the Indian population, is hardly relevant, and it was many years before they encountered serious competition from machine-made goods, either imported or made in India. The position of the specialist craftsmen had begun to degenerate before the battle of Plassey. The impetus which the Mughals had given to architecture was exhausted by the time of Aurangzīb, and there was little building during the unsettled period which followed his death. The tradition survived, but only obscurely. The makers of luxury goods suffered equally from the disturbed times which had ruined so many of the princes and landed aristocracy, replacing them by upstarts clinging precariously to place and power. The extension of direct rule over most of India only hastened a process which had already gone far before 1760. The export trade had also begun to decline before that date. Muslins from Dacca, brocades from Ahmadābād, *bandanas* from Murshidābād, shawls from Kashmir, and similar goods intended for a leisured class had been sent to Europe for hundreds of years, but by the eighteenth century 'mercantilist' theories were widely accepted, and a kind of 'economic nationalism' developed which became more intense during the Napoleonic period. The East India Company made a profitable business from the distribution of such goods throughout Europe—their sale in England itself had never been great—but they found themselves blocked by tariffs and prohibitions in nearly every country, including England itself. The Company encouraged the manufacture of such goods in the limited part of India over which it exercised control, and the British Government after 1760 merely maintained the same policy which it had adopted as early as 1720. The Indian 'luxury' export trade was ruined by the development of better craftsmanship in Europe, and by economic theories opposed to the export of bullion, especially for imports which were not strictly utilitarian.

The charge, so frequently made from nationalist platforms, that the British deliberately destroyed a flourishing Indian civilization, will not bear examination.[1] It has obscured the real charge against British rule, which is that after the restoration of peace throughout the peninsula, when the civilized arts might have been expected to flourish once more, and the craftsman return to his hereditary activities, the new rulers failed lamentably to achieve a 'union of Hindu and European learning', or

---

[1] This question, so far as it concerns craftsmen, is discussed at some length in Thompson and Garratt's *Rise and Fulfilment of British Rule in India*, pp. 430–5.

to give any scope to the technical skill and knowledge inherent amongst the people. With the gradual pacification and settlement of all India south of the Sutlej, there developed a new and most unfortunate attitude towards the Indian population amongst the Englishmen who began to come out East as administrators, business men, and soldiers. Former invaders had settled down, brought up their families in India, and either were absorbed by the Hindu system, or, like the Moslems, introduced a new religion which spread sufficiently to give them a real hold in the country. The English did none of these things. From the first the Eurasian and the 'country-bred' were despised. The tone of the administration and of the expatriated community was set by fresh contingents of Englishmen, coming from a land which was itself rapidly changing.

The East India Company in early days patronized both the Hindu and Muslim religions. Offices were open on Sunday but closed on Indian holidays. Troops were paraded in honour of Hindu deities. A coco-nut was solemnly broken at the beginning of each monsoon, and British officials assisted in the management of Hindu religious trusts. This phase ended early in the nineteenth century. The Company gave up being 'wet nurse to Vishnu', and 'churchwarden to Juggernaut'. The administration became strictly secular, and hence more and more aloof in a country where religion permeates every human activity. In the meantime the evangelical revival in England, the rapid development of industry and science, the social reforms of the thirties, and the breaking up of the English caste system were all reflected in the changed outlook of a new generation of officials. Like Macaulay they came to India, often for only a few years, endowed with a full consciousness of racial superiority. Already in 1817 some of the more broad-minded civilians, like Sir Thomas Munro, were protesting against the new tendency.

'Foreign conquerors have treated the natives with violence, but none has treated them with so much scorn as we; none have stigmatized the whole people as unworthy of trust, as incapable of honesty, and as fit to be employed only where we cannot do without them. It seems not only ungenerous, but impolitic, to debase the character of a people fallen under our dominion.'

The struggle over the employment of Indians in the administration was paralleled by the controversy between 'Anglicists' and 'Orientalists', which was to affect the whole future attitude of the British in India towards indigenous literature, art, and culture. The dispute came to a head over a comparatively small matter, the allocation of a grant of £10,000 a year which the Company had been forced to make to education at the time of the renewal of its charter in 1813. The grant had remained dormant for some years, but in the thirties its disposal brought to a head the differences between two schools of thought in the Indian Government, and in that small section of educated Bengalis who were articulate. It was not a matter of mass education, which few Governments then considered to be their responsibility, but of subsidizing higher education. Behind this minor dispute lay the fundamental question of policy—whether England should try to build upon the existing foundations of Indian language, philosophy, science, and craftsmanship, or whether the Government should start afresh, giving educated Indians a European education, which, according to the 'Filtration Theory' then popular, would gradually percolate down to the rest of the community.

Many factors helped in the defeat of the 'Orientalists'. Bengal was an unlucky field of battle. There were few of those visible signs of Indian skill and energy which abound in many parts of the country. The local Muslims were uneducated, their Maulvis were the decadent hangers-on left over from the collapse of Mughal rule. Hinduism was seen at its worst in Bengal, and a new generation of British officials was at last awakening to some of its less defensible aspects. The younger Englishmen believed firmly that they were dealing with 'a decomposed society', hopelessly corrupt, and they were supported in that idea by a group of reformist Bengalis, of whom Rām Mohan Rāy was the best known. The 'suttee' controversy had important reactions. The unhappy arguments against its abolition, which were used by a leader of the 'Orientalists', Horace Wilson, did much to ruin their cause. Besides the *sahamarana* rite other unfortunate aberrations of Hinduism were coming to light, as the British administration spread and became more settled. Female infanticide was discovered to be prevalent; child marriages, untouchability, and such savage survivals as the *meriah* sacrifices added to the general prejudice. On the positive side the 'Orientalists' were handicapped by the general decadence of Indian civilization. Such religious teaching as had survived was obscurantist, and neglected. Keshab Chandra Sen, writing of his boyhood, describes how

'the ancient scriptures of the country, the famous records of numerous Hindu sects, had long been discredited. The Vedas and Upanishads were sealed books. All that we knew of the immortal Mahabharata, Ramayana, or the Bhagavad Gita was from execrable translations into popular Bengali, which no respectable young man was supposed to read.'

Vernacular literature was at an equally low ebb. For two centuries there had been no Hindī or Marātha poetry to compare with the work of Tulasī Dās or Tukārām.

The rout of the 'Orientalists' was completed by one of the two Englishmen of literary genius who have spent any time in India. Macaulay entered into the fray with the most superficial knowledge, but with immense gusto. Like Mr. Rudyard Kipling half a century later, he lent his great powers to voicing the prejudices of his less articulate countrymen, marooned in a country for which they had little sympathy.

'The question now before us is simply whether, when it is in our power to teach this language, we shall teach languages in which by universal confession there are no books on any subject which deserve to be compared to our own; whether, when we can teach European science, we shall teach systems which by universal confession whenever they differ from those of Europe differ for the worse; and whether, when we can patronize sound philosophy and true history, we shall countenance at the public expense medical doctrines which would disgrace an English farrier, astronomy which would move laughter in girls at an English boarding-school, history abounding with kings thirty feet high and reigns 30,000 years long, and geography made up of seas of treacle and seas of butter.'

Macaulay's sonorous Minute on Education served a double purpose. It helped to win an immediate victory for the 'Anglicists', and its generalizations, coming from a man of such repute, appeased the conscience of those officials who dimly recognized a great field of learning from which they were cut off by linguistic and other obstacles. Nearly everything with which this present book has dealt was included in Macaulay's sweeping condemnation—the Indian epics, Hindu and Buddhist philosophy, the science and craftsmanship which raised and adorned her great buildings, the Ayurvedic system of medicine, and the traditions of a people 'civilized and cultivated; cultivated by all the arts of polished life while we were yet in the woods'. Macaulay in India might with advantage have recalled his Burke.

There were other reasons which account for the success of the 'Anglicists'. For the quarter of a century which preceded the Mutiny, although much of the country was settled, the administration remained chiefly occupied in minor wars, and the pacification of new territory. The Government was continually short of money and obsessed with the idea of building up a prosperous country upon the ruins of the old anarchy. It was typical of these times that Bentinck as Governor-General should have seriously considered the demolition of the Tāj Mahal and the sale of its marble. He 'was only diverted because the test auction of materials from the Agra Palace proved unsatisfactory'.[1] Indian civilization seemed a subject only fit for the antiquary, and had little interest for the new generation of keen and rather narrow Christians who began to fill the higher places in the administration—men like Charles Grant, Edwardes, Outram, Aitchison, and the Lawrences. They were wildly optimistic, and prepared to apply to all India Macaulay's astounding 'belief that if our plans of education are followed up, there will not be a single idolater among the respectable classes in Bengal thirty years hence. And this will be effected without any effort to proselytise; without the smallest interference in the religious liberty; merely by the natural operation of knowledge and reflection.' There was, of course, some reaction against these extravagances. English became the official language of India in 1835, but by 1855 the need for vernacular education was fully recognized, especially in the north. Those Indians who had supported the demand for an English education showed little inclination to become Christians, and Debendranath Tagore led a 'counter-reformation'. As the English spread over India they came into contact with more independent and stubborn types than they had met in Bengal, and they found in the north and the Deccan the visible evidence of a comparatively recent Indian administration and civilization. But again India's evil star was in the ascendant. Just as there were signs of a return to a more balanced outlook the Mutiny occurred. Its suppression, and the measures taken to prevent a recurrence, caused a breach between the two races which has never been adequately recognized by English historians. A flood of Englishmen came out to India after 1860 filled with a strong racial antipathy to the inhabitants of the country, and from the resulting bitterness developed Indian Nationalism, which has always been a racial as much as a political movement.

From this time until very recent years the administration

---

[1] E. B. Havell, *Indian Sculpture and Painting*, p. 246.

remained completely aloof. It was, in Dr. Tagore's phrase, brought from England and given to the people 'untouched by hand'. By the eighties British officials had given up any idea of educated Indians becoming Westernized Christians, and of the masses following humbly after them to find the light. The Government's sphere of action was strictly defined. Within certain limits the Indian States were to go their own way, thus leaving two-fifths of the country as a quiet backwater where the 'Old India' could survive as a horrid example to the Indians in British India. Over the remaining three-fifths we would enforce justice along the English model, provide certain utilitarian services, make canals, roads, and bridges, build offices and official residences, and a church or two for the English residents, but not interfere with the social or religious life of Indians. It was a policy which fitted in well with the *laissez-faire* philosophy of Victorian Liberalism, and with the commonly held view that the Mutiny had been caused by excessive Government activity. It killed any prospect of Indo-British civilization. The English community remained a separate caste, with several sub-castes, strictly preserving the usual characteristics of endogamy, commensality, and mutual control by members. The officials had little need, the traders and soldiers had little inclination, to co-operate with Indians in the subjects with which this book is mostly concerned. The Indian Christians, mostly living in the extreme south, were too few in numbers and too little accepted into Anglo-Indian life to provide any real contacts with the Indian population. Towards the end of the nineteenth century it was becoming obvious that the English in India had nothing in common with the growing mass of educated Indians, and as a measure of their failure they emphasized, without much justification, their special interest in the illiterate peasantry.

The history of Indian architecture during the last hundred years provides a useful commentary. The English have left a permanent mark upon India by their canals, roads, and railways

—honestly and efficiently made. They had, however, little urge to build for the future. Officials, business men, and soldiers were all birds of passage, intending to make their homes in England and seldom spending even their working life in the same Indian 'station'. Soon after the Mutiny they tended to give up the idea that India would become a Christian country, and during much of the century they were uncertain about the future of British rule. Some of the highest officers—Viceroys and Provincial Governors—only stayed five years in India.

It was sufficient to put up a bungalow in which to live, some offices in which to work, and, rather grudgingly, a few churches in which the expatriated Englishman could worship his expatriated deity. There were none of the usual motives for erecting fine permanent buildings, except possibly to provide an imposing residence for a Viceroy or Governor. The engineers, to whose department all building was entrusted, were dominated by the same ideas of Indian art as the higher officials who gave them their orders. To them Indian art 'meant no more than a pretty chintz, a rich brocade, or gorgeous carpet, fantastic carving, or curious inlay; and an ancient architecture fascinating to the archaeologist and tourist with its reminiscences of bygone pomp and splendour, but an extinct art useless for the needs and ideals of our prosaic and practical times'.[1] They came out East, with little technical training but some general ideas gathered from Victorian England. These they modified slightly to suit Indian materials and conditions, developing that unpleasing style which is irreverently known as 'dak bungalow Gothic'. The few eccentrics who suggested that India might still contain craftsmen with valuable traditions and a style better suited to the country were completely overwhelmed by official disapproval and scepticism. It was not until the time of Lord Curzon, well into the present century, that the ancient buildings were thought worthy of protection, preservation, or study,

[1] E. B. Havell, *Indian Sculpture and Painting*, p. 4.

and even Curzon's interest in Indian art was almost entirely archaeological. Of the two buildings in which he took a keen personal interest—the Victoria Memorial and the Military Secretariat in Calcutta—the first was entrusted to an English architect, who produced 'an archaeological essay on Kedleston Hall and the Radcliffe Library at Oxford'; the second, part of which was the subject of a prize competition, is a queer production in a 'pseudo-renaissance' style. Lord Curzon's term of office did, however, synchronize with the rise of a new school of artistic criticism in India. The last thirty years has been marked by a far better appreciation of the continuity and achievements of Indian craftsmanship.

The Public Works Department began to function after the Mutiny, at the height of the reaction against everything Indian. The highest officers were not inclined, the subordinates had no opportunity, to encourage indigenous knowledge and skill. Any Indian craftsman who might hope for a post worth more than three pounds a month had to go to Rurki for training. There he imbibed a contempt for Indian architecture, as having merely an archaeological interest, and he acquired a very inadequate knowledge of English architecture at one of its worst periods. Afterwards he would be used to erect offices and public buildings at a salary far smaller than the Mughal emperors had paid their master-masons. Government activities in India cover such a wide field, private building such a limited one, that this policy almost killed the Indian tradition. The hereditary craftsman, however, will continue at his trade until he is forced down to that dead level of Indian living, the standard of the small cultivator. In the Indian States he could still get work. Palaces, such as those built for Indian princes at Benares; temples at Brindaban, Hardwar, and Puri; private merchants' houses at Bikanir and Mewar show that all through the nineteenth century there were Indian builders, without any European training, capable of admirable religious and private architecture, well

suited to the climate, to the materials of the country, and to
the tastes of educated Indians.

The revival of interest and broader outlook which followed
Lord Curzon's term of office were reflected in Mr. Sanderson's
Report of 1913.[1] He found 'master masons of Bikanir working
at the rate of annas 8 to Rs 1 daily', and building a fine row of
merchants' houses on traditional lines. At Jodhpur a mosque,
at Alwar a railway station, at Jaipur a Hindu temple were being
built by men of this type. In each case their work makes one
regret the hideous buildings which deface every Indian town
where there is a cantonment or a civil station.

A note on modern Indian architecture prefaced to this Report
by the Consulting Architect to Government suggests that a
saner view on Indian master-builders had at least spread to
Simla, but it was too late to prevent the planning of the New
Delhi being entrusted to English architects, and the War discouraged any marked change of policy towards indigenous
talent.

'It would be a fitting thing if the architectural note we sound in
our new Capital were to type the reawakened India of the present and
future. In this matter practical and economical considerations seem
to me to join hands with those which are artistic and sentimental. We
have got our art—why waste it? We have got our craftsmen—why
employ them on work for which they have small aptitude—or (which
is what would happen) leave our best craftsmen out altogether? There
is nothing, as I have already said, in an Indian manner of design that
makes it costly, indeed my own experience goes to prove that the
costliest manner of building in India is a Renaissance or classical one.
Again, why should a Western manner be held to type most fittingly
the spirit of the Government of India? Why should the style of our
Capital be such as to express most strongly those alien characteristics in
the administration which every year tend more and more to disappear?
And lastly, why sound again a note that is sure to dwindle into decadence as it has done before, rather than one more likely to be worthily

[1] Report on Modern Indian Architecture.

sustained by the future generations of indigenous architects for whose advent we might well make it our duty to prepare?'

These are admirable sentiments, but old prejudices are strong. The future is still uncertain. The partial triumph of nationalism and the prospect of a Federation with some real measure of provincial autonomy provide grounds for hoping that the Government will now begin to use and organize the Indian craftsmen. It will, however, be difficult to revive in British India an art neglected so long. In the meantime New Delhi has been completed and stands vast, incongruous, and wholly alien to northern India. Its huge range of offices are so unsuited to the climate that they are only used for about half the year. Behind them stands the enormous Viceregal Lodge, which is occupied for two or three months during the cold weather. In front there are miles of bungalows and hostels, a hybrid collection. New Delhi is in many ways a fitting monument to our rule, but it will remain as a *damnosa hereditas* for the new Federation.

An alien Government must build, but has little need to patronize the other craftsmen who cater for a settled aristocracy. These hereditary weavers, silk-workers, and metal-workers suffered even more than the masons. The export trade for fine brocades and other products had vanished altogether. The internal demand was injured by the upset which followed the introduction of British rule and European standards of taste throughout most of the peninsula. The caste-craftsmen were not organized to stand the introduction of free competition.

'A great industry in gold-embroidered shoes', wrote that great authority Sir George ·Birdwood, 'flourished in Lucknow. They were in demand all over India, for the native kings of Oudh would not allow the shoemakers to use anything but pure gold wire on them. But when we annexed the kingdom, all such restrictions were removed and the bazaars of Oudh were at once flooded with the pinchbeck embroidered shoes of Delhi, and the Lucknow shoemakers were swept away for ever by the besom of free trade.'

Nearly all of these old crafts disappeared before the rush of cheap or showy articles from abroad, displayed before a new type of wealthy Indian. Even the princes were corrupted by their first contact with the West and preferred to spend their money on racehorses rather than on patronizing the hereditary craftsmen of their States. Some of these may still be found in Hyderabad, Gwalior, and other State capitals, producing beautiful work which they cannot sell and eking out their existence on the wages of a coolie.

The neglect of Indian craftsmanship can be partly ascribed to the policy of the Government and to the ignorance or the hubristic outlook of the expatriated Englishman. The sterility of Indian science and art was partly due to these same causes, but also to the hostility which developed between the Indian educated classes and the English community. The latter's habit of disparaging every kind of Indian enterprise is probably a symptom of their own consciousness that their position in India is false, and that the only justification for the kind of government imposed upon India would be a racial superiority which clearly does not exist. Enmity breeds enmity. Whatever may be the origin of the quarrel there is no doubt about its reality and bitterness since the middle of the nineteenth century. On the English side it led to the blind acceptance of such superficial generalizations as those of Macaulay; on the Indian side, especially after the Mutiny, there was a tendency to react against all Western ideas. In religion this led to the 'Back to the Vedas' movement; a return to an orthodox and sometimes obscurantist Hinduism which had its counterpart in many other walks of life.

The history of Indian medicine is typical. There were three indigenous systems—Ayurvedic, *Tibbī*, and *Yunānī*. These undoubtedly contained much that was valuable, including a number of useful drugs, but, as in European pharmacy of the eighteenth century, there was a considerable admixture of

PLATE 22

STENCILLED COTTON CLOTH FROM RĀJPŪTĀNĀ
18th century A.D.

superstition. The Ayurvedic system and practice were further vitiated by restrictions due to the Hindu rules of caste and ceremonial cleanliness. But English medical officers were not going to worry about 'medical doctrines which would disgrace an English farrier', and the indigenous methods were contemptuously rejected without the least consideration of the effect which such a policy would have upon the people or the older practitioners. Instead of a friendly development and modernization of the old systems, which were in some ways suited to the country, the Western and Eastern ideas of medicine became rivals. With the spread of an intense nationalism there was a reaction in favour of Ayurvedic methods, and competition between the two schools of thought became a political issue, which is not yet settled.

The recent history of Indian painting in some ways resembles that of architecture. Those old indigenous craftsmen, the court 'portrait painters', were sometimes employed by the early 'nabobs', but can now only be found in a few of the Indian States. Very few Englishmen who went to India in the nineteenth century had any interest in painting; the little patronage which they dispensed went to painters in a pseudo-European style. The kind of malaise which settled over educated India seems to have discouraged the development of modern art until the growth of the Calcutta school under Dr. Abinandranath Tagore. Much of their work is wholly admirable, but the Calcutta group has suffered from being too limited in numbers, too dependent on Dr. Tagore, his brother Goganendranath Tagore, and a few pupils like Asit Kumar Haldar and Nanda Lal Bose. Some examples of their work are reproduced in Dr. J. H. Cousins's *Modern Indian Artists*, and E. B. Havell's *Indian Sculpture and Painting*. Both Calcutta and Bombay have Art Schools and it is to be hoped that the great technical ability latent amongst so many Indian races will find better expression in the freer political atmosphere of the future. At present both

Indian art and Indian science tend to become 'one-man deep', relying upon the occasional individual who seems able to transcend the inertia into which the country has sunk.

Literature is the one field of Indo-British culture which has provided a comparatively large harvest, though the average quality is not very good. It is, perhaps, significant that India ceased to be a source of inspiration to English poets about the time when the country came wholly within our jurisdiction. Shakespeare, Dryden, Southey, Campbell, Moore, Shelley, and Wordsworth were all attracted by the glamour of an unknown India; a land of romantic dynasties, of luxury and exotic beauty, and of mystic religions. To their literary descendants India has become a dull and arid land in which some rather dull and arid compatriots spend their working life. Some mention has already been made of the Sanskrit scholars in the early days of the Company. Their connexion with the Bengali reformers might have led to a literature based on a common culture and tradition, but the interest taken by Western writers did not survive long into the nineteenth century. Schopenhauer's enthusiasm for the *Upanishads*, Goethe's appreciation of Kālidāsa, left no permanent mark on European literature. Emerson's *Brahma*, Lowell's *Mahmood the Image Breaker*, and Whittier's *Brewing of the Soma* continued the tradition in America, but the Western world did not really take kindly to Hindu thought and literature. Buddhism made a greater appeal in the nineteenth century, and has had a more definite effect on European thought. It cannot be said that the work of the early Sanskrit experts, or later that of Max Müller, really roused more than an immediate and superficial interest.

The reaction against Indian ideas can be traced amongst the succeeding generations of Englishmen in India who felt the urge to write. Sir William Jones not only produced some admirable translations—the best-known being of *Hitopadeśa* and *Śakuntala* —but he also wrote the original and very remarkable *Hymns* to

PLATE 23

THE EXILED YAKSHA

By A. N. TAGORE

Modern Bengal school

various Indian deities. They show a real attempt to understand and appreciate Hindu religious mentality.

> Wrapt in eternal solitary shade,
> Th' impenetrable gloom of light intense,
> Impervious, inaccessible, immense,
> Ere spirits were infus'd or forms display'd,
>   BREHM his own Mind survey'd,
> As mortal eyes (thus finite we compare
>   With infinite) in smoothest mirrors gaze:
> Swift, at his look, a shape supremely fair
>   Leap'd into being with a boundless blaze,
>   That fifty suns might daze.

This phase was not fated to last. His successors soon began to adopt that slightly hostile and superior attitude which characterizes the work of Englishmen writing on Indian subjects. John Leyden and Bishop Heber, at the beginning of the nineteenth century, wrote verse of some merit, but they both viewed India as a land of ancient decaying pomp and of dark mysteries. Leyden, like Wellesley, saw and was shocked by the infant sacrifices at Sagur. His verse has an undercurrent of hostility against all Hinduism.

> On sea-girt Sagur's desert isle
> Mantled with thickets dark and dun,
> May never morn nor starlight smile,
> Nor ever beam the summer sun.

From about 1836 this tradition had become firmly established. India was the 'Land of Regrets' in which Englishmen spent years of exile amongst a people half savage, half decadent. This idea runs through Leyden's *Ode to an Indian Gold Coin*, and the works of a number of Anglo-Indian poets, of whom Sir Alfred Lyall is probably the best remembered. His *Meditations of a Hindu Prince* and *Siva* show an attempt to appreciate the Indian point of view, but Lyall was always a stranger in a strange land, looking with contemptuous pity upon a people over whose heads

> the deities hover and swarm
> Like the wild bees heard in the tree-tops, or the gusts of a gathering
> storm.

There was no reason to expect any great output of literature from the small community of expatriated officials, soldiers, and business men. Lyall was an exceptionally versatile man, and the 'Services' chiefly·produced histories, works on administration, and occasional novels. A few, like Henry Meredith Parker, wrote light verse in the tradition of Mackworth Praed; these were the not unworthy forerunners of Kipling's *Departmental Ditties*. The one considerable Anglo-Indian poet of Victorian times was Sir Edwin Arnold who, after a short time spent in educational work, made a name for himself as a translator of Indian verse, and as the author of *The Light of Asia*. He wrote too easily and quickly to reach the highest rank, but hundreds of thousands in Europe and America have gained some appreciation of Buddhism from him.

> The Scripture of the Saviour of the World,
> Lord Buddha, Prince Siddhartha styled in earth—
> In Earth and Heavens and Hells Incomparable,
> All-Honoured, Wisest, Best, most Pitiful;
> The Teacher of Nirvana and the Law.

Amongst the historians, James Grant Duff and Mountstuart Elphinstone have left two classic works in their *History of the Mahrattas* and *History of India*; both belong to the generation before the Mutiny. William Hunter, G. O. Trevelyan, and the unconventional S. S. Thorburn were administrators who could write of their work and make it into literature. They have had many successors whose books have never been properly appreciated in England. No one can hope to understand the important formative years which followed the Mutiny without reading Trevelyan's *The Competition Wallah*; the great problem of Indian indebtedness without Thorburn's *Mussulmans and Money-lenders in the Punjab* and M. L. Darling's *The Punjab Peasant* and *Rusticus Loquitur*; or Indian education without Arthur Mayhew's work on that subject. A host of works of this kind are a by-product of a great bureaucracy.

Within the English community a new school of writers developed, attempting a wider field than history and administration. After the Mutiny the population of Anglo-India began to increase very rapidly. New types of Englishmen went out East, including journalists and schoolmasters; they brought their wives, and were visited by tourists; within India a domiciled English and Eurasian population was growing in numbers and developing a life of its own. These factors encouraged the production of fiction, partly for the Indian market and partly for those in England who liked to think of India as a country where Englishmen had strange adventures. The Victorian novelists and descriptive writers were really in the direct line from those travellers, like Tavernier and Manucci, who described India under the Mughals. Earlier British settlers in Bengal do not seem to have been much impressed by the hazardous nature of their life, but this aspect appealed forcibly to the generation which conquered central and northern India and later spread over the Punjab and up to the North-west Frontier. The early 'Nabobs' accepted the incidents of their life with the same indifference as they displayed towards 'suttee' or the corruption of the local rulers. Eighteenth-century Europe had so much more in common with contemporary India.

Colonel Meadows Taylor made his reputation by *The Confessions of a Thug*, a typical product of this new school. It was written about 1839, towards the end of the campaign against the *phānsīdārs*, of which Sleeman has also left a good account in his *Rambles and Recollections*. Taylor's later works were written after retirement. *Tara, Seeta, Tippoo Sultan*, &c., all contain passages of great vigour and show a real understanding of India, but are rather swamped by the conventional working out of their plots. *Seeta* has a special interest because it marks the transition which took place so rapidly after the Mutiny. Taylor was pre-Mutiny in his outlook, and he idealized a marriage between an Englishman and an Indian which shocked the Anglo-Indian of 1873, when it was published.[1] The British were rapidly developing into a separate caste, strongly reinforced by the new officials, planters, and business men who came crowding out East after 1860. There was a natural tendency for writers to concentrate more upon this colony of their expatriated countrymen, upon what was then called Anglo-Indian society. Rudyard Kipling had, of course, a long line of predecessors as well as imitators. Few of them are of much importance, but any one interested in this subject should consult a recent monograph by Bhupal Singh, *A Survey of Anglo-Indian Fiction*, in which the author pours coals of fire upon our English heads by rescuing from oblivion a large number of forgotten and unreadable books, nearly all of which are grossly offensive to his race.

A few of these are interesting. Mrs. Sherwood had peculiar opportunities for knowing the seamy side of pre-Mutiny Anglo-India. Her books are full of little incidental touches recalling that queer society which survived even after the 'clipping Dutchman', Lord William Bentinck, had begun his reforms. Matthew Arnold's brother, W. D. Arnold, went to India in Government service, and his rather stilted novel, *Oakfield*, shows how the new type of Englishman, coming out East in the fifties, revolted against the religious and social life of the times. After the Mutiny, when the old 'Brahmanized' Englishmen had

[1] Until the beginning of this century the word 'Anglo-Indians' was always used for the English community, resident but not settled in India. It is now officially applied to the Eurasian population—a change which has led to much confusion.

almost disappeared, the new expatriated community began to settle down comfortably to its allotted term of work, as part of a great administrative machine. It could afford to laugh at itself, sentimentalize over its love affairs, carried on under such artificial conditions, and take a mild interest in the native life which flowed round the 'stations', or the flora and fauna in the neighbouring jungle. Iltidus Pritchard's *Chronicles of Budgepore*, Sir Henry Cunningham's *Chronicles of Dustypore*, Philip Robinson's *Nugae Indicae*, and 'Eha's' later *Tribes on my Frontier* are typical of this period. They are still readable for their humour, and interesting for the light they throw upon the bureaucracy during the most static, self-satisfied, and sterile era of British rule, from about 1870 till the end of the century. The greater part of Rudyard Kipling's Indian work is directly in this tradition, though it is illuminated by his own genius and reinforced by his knowledge of Indian customs, animal fables, and jungle-lore. Much of this he probably acquired from his father, Lockwood Kipling, whose *Beast and Man in India* is a wonderful storehouse from which many have drawn inspiration.

Kipling's influence over his generation can hardly be exaggerated. Many Englishmen, especially amongst those directly connected with India, felt that some interpreter was needed for that curious phenomenon, British Rule in India. Kipling supplied the necessary exposition in a manner most flattering to English pride, and in forms—that of fiction and light verse—which were easily assimilated. Coming to India as a young man, he worked for a few years as a journalist in Lahore and Simla. From this rather slender acquaintance with the country his marvellously fertile mind poured out short stories and verse which were of such intrinsic brilliance that they gave a wholly disproportionate value to his interpretation of Indian life. He knew the garrison towns of northern India and the hill stations. His comparatively humble position on a local newspaper gave

him an insight into the sub-castes of Anglo-India—the subordinate railway employees and the domiciled European and
Eurasian families. Apart from his 'jungle' books, the greater
part of his Indian fiction and verse is concerned with these two
tiny communities, the officials and military officers, and the
subordinate Europeans and Eurasians. Round them surges the
immense sea of Indians, but nearly all of this subjected race
who appear as individuals are minor characters, mostly domestic
servants or women kept by Englishmen. The few educated
Indians who come into his pages seem to have been introduced
to satisfy the deep-seated prejudices of the English in India.
Almost all of them are, in the old school phrase, 'sent up for
bad', and Kipling allowed himself the most astounding generalizations about Indian duplicity and mendacity, or the physical
cowardice of certain races. Even in the two novels which take
a wider scope and deal more directly with Indian life—*Kim*
and *The Naulahka*—the Indians are all drawn 'in the flat', as
types, not human beings, whereas the Europeans or the country-
bred Kim are so indubitably drawn 'in the round'. The one
possible exception, the old Lama, is not really an Indian. Not
until he had left India for many years could Kipling rid himself
of that obsession, driven into the minds of all Englishmen who
went East before the War, that a denial of racial superiority was
the one deadly sin. *Kim* is a wise and also a comparatively
mellow book, but Kipling had to make his young hero assert his
superiority as a 'Sahib' over Hurree Chunder Mookerjee, the
Bengali, though the latter was his departmental superior.

Kipling can hardly be said to have founded a school, but his
attitude towards India is followed by nearly all of the novelists
who followed him. Some of these, like Mrs. Steel, Mrs. Perrin,
F. E. Penny, and 'Sydney Carlyon Grier', are very capable
writers, but they have the same tendency to make their real
characters Europeans, while Indians form a shadowy background, types rather than human beings. Edmund Candler's

Siri Ram, Revolutionist is a very interesting attempt to 'get inside the skin' of an Indian student, but is marred by the contemptuous dislike of the educated Indian which marks the same author's later work *Abdication*. Nor can it be said that English writers have been more successful in dealing with Indian peasants and craftsmen. Leonard Woolf's *Village in the Jungle* stands quite alone in this class, and was written about Ceylon. It may be interesting to compare other European literature in this respect. Couperus, writing of the Dutch East Indies, has something of Kipling's outlook, and a few French writers have dealt successfully with the higher-class Muslims in their Empire. There is, however, a definite group of French novelists, the *grande brousse* school, who have tried to portray the mentality of negroes and of illiterate Muhammadans. There are no English equivalents to René Maran's *Batouala*, Victor Salagen's *Les Immémoriaux*, and Eberhardt's *Dans l'ombre chaude de l'Islam*; or to such negro studies as Marius Lebland's *Ulysse Caffre* and *Zézère*, or Joseph's *Roman vrai d'un noir*.

Of later years E. M. Forster and Edward Thompson have written novels dealing with Anglo-Indian life in which the Indian characters have not been supernumerary actors, dragged on to the stage in various guises to add a little local colour. *A Passage to India* and *An Indian Day* are for this reason outstanding novels amongst the mass of post-Kipling fiction. A few Englishmen, working in India, have also attempted in literature the same Westernized forms of Indian art which are to be found amongst some of the modern Indian painters. By far the most successful are the works of F. W. Bain. *A Digit of the Moon* and *In the Great God's Hair* are admirable examples in a genre which would not bear much analysis, but in themselves stand out amongst the mass of Anglo-Indian literature as would a painting by Gogendra Nath Tagore in an exhibition of Anglo-Indian art. C. A. Kincaid is a less subtle writer, but his *Shri Krishna of Dwarka* and other stories show an appreciation of that mass of

Hindu folk-lore and fable which is a sealed book to most Englishmen.

In considering the Indian writers in English a tribute must be paid to the extraordinary brilliance with which certain Indian races overcome linguistic difficulties. Bengalis, Chitpavan and Kasmiri Brahmins, Madrassis, and Parsis have produced a succession of capable journalists and publicists, who have served the nationalist cause by writing clear and trenchant English prose—Tilak, Ghokhale, Arabindo Ghose, Ranade, Sarendra Nath Banerjee, R. C. Dutt, N. C. Kelkar, Pherozshah Mehta, and a host of other writers have shown that Indian English can develop into a powerful weapon of attack. But polemical writing can only with great difficulty reach the level of literature, and very little is likely to survive from the vast mass of political and economic articles and books which have been produced in India during the last half-century. It is unfortunate that the British connexion has not inspired many Indians to try their hands at fiction. Even written from the nationalist standpoint it might have been an effective alternative line of attack. S. M. Mitra, a Bengali writer of considerable versatility, wrote *Hindupore* during the height of the anti-Partition agitation, but it is not a success.

Rabindranath Tagore's novels were written in Bengali and so hardly come within the scope of this chapter, but translations of *The Home and World*, *The Wreck*, &c., have provided many Westerners with an insight into Indian life which is unobtainable from biographies, histories, or controversial writing, and add to one's regret that the few Indians who have written fiction should have usually adopted conventional themes and produced work which is only too clearly derivative. Dhan Gopal Mukerji's *My Brother's Face* is an admirable account, possibly autobiographical, of a Bengali returning to his country after some years' absence. It is perhaps significant that this book, with its remarkable freedom and scope, should have been written by an Indian who has spent so much of his life abroad. Sir Hari Singh Gour is a reformer of courage and originality, but this would hardly appear in *His Only Love*. Sir Jogindra Singh has written a capable but not very interesting historical romance, *Nur Jahan*; P. A. Madhaviah's *Thillai Govindan* approaches nearer to being the self-revelatory novel which would be so valuable; finally there are two new writers whose work suggests that Indian authors are beginning to see what an enormous field lies open to them in their villages, in the complications of their caste system, and in the lives of working men and women. K. S. Venkataramni's *Murgan, the Tiller* is excellent, while Mulk Raj Anand's *The Coolie* and *The Untouchable* are probably the most important and promising books ever written in English by an Indian.

The Indian poets who have written in English are a small but very interesting group. Perhaps it is fitting that one should first mention Henry Derozio, a Eurasian or, as he would now be called, an 'Anglo-Indian' poet who lived in Calcutta during the first quarter of the nineteenth century. He died when he was 22, but he managed to make his mark as a teacher, upset conventional Calcutta by his modern ideas, and leave a modest volume of verse—clever, facile writing, but obviously derivative, owing much to Keats and Shelley. He found Greece in the abstract more inspiring than India, but attempted one long poem called the *Fakeer of Jungheera*, which suggests that India might have found, in this lad of mixed parentage, a poet who could ultimately have given us the spirit of the traditional Indian culture fashioned into English verse. During the remainder of the century an occasional Bengali young man or woman would develop the authentic lyric note as a result of a contact with English literature, and in most cases with England itself. The two sisters Toru and Aru Dutt wrote extraordinarily fluent and graceful verse while they were still in their teens, and then died with their great promise unfulfilled. Some of their

best work appeared in *A Sheaf gleaned in French Fields*, a series
of adaptations and translations. This includes those lines by
Aru Dutt which first attracted the attention of Edmund Gosse:

> Still barred thy doors! The far east glows
> The morning wind blows fresh and free.
> Should not the hour that wakes the rose
> Awaken also thee?
>
> All look for thee, Love, Light, and Song,
> Light in the sky deep red above,
> Song, in the lark of pinions strong,
> And in my heart, true Love.
>
> Apart we miss our nature's goal,
> Why strive to cheat our destinies?
> Was not my love made for thy soul?
> Thy beauty for mine eyes?
> No longer sleep,
> Oh listen now!
> I wait and weep,
> But where art thou?

Toru Dutt's *Ancient Ballads of Hindustan* seldom reaches
such heights, but the longest of her poems, *Savitri*, suggests
that, like Derozio, she also might have found inspiration in her
own country, if she had reached to a more mature age. She
and her sister were lost between two worlds. The same also
must be said of a later Bengali poet, Manmohan Ghose. Like
his brother Arabindo, the great nationalist, he was educated in
England, and most of his *Love Songs and Elegies* and *Songs of Love
and Death* spring from this early experience, and many from his
affection for the English countryside. He returned to India and
an academic life. He had that extra portion of sensibility which
made him an exile in England, and then doubly an exile in India.

> Art thou in the cornfields lonely?
> Oh, to be
> Where the wide earth ripples green
> Like a sea.

> There, possessed of verdure only,
> Watching dost thou lean?
> No not there; for thou wouldst meet
> By some stile, some hedgerow fair,
> Sweet objects, ah! too keenly sweet
> With the memory of her;
> Her, that from their perfume knows
> Not a woodbine, not a rose!
> No, not there!

From those Indians who are 'English educated', and more especially from those educated in England, there has been a constant succession of minor poets, the excellence of whose work has hardly been appreciated in post-War Europe or America. The trouble is that they are definitely minor poets, admirable in their technique, but without very much to say; living in an age not much interested in a form of art which so many have acquired. Harindranath Chattopadhaya, Ananda Coomaraswamy, Feridoon Kabraji, and many others have written thoroughly competent verse, which in Victorian times might have received a recognition which would have encouraged them to write more. The best of these later poets is undoubtedly Sarojini Naidu. Like so many of her generation she has found politics more enthralling than poetry, but like Manmohan Ghose she has the authentic lyrical note, and was fortunately persuaded by Sir Edmund Gosse to write of Indian life:

> What longer need hath she of loveliness,
> Whom Death has parted from her lord's caress?
> Of glimmering robes like rainbow-tangled mist,
> Of gleaming glass or jewels on her wrist,
> Blossoms or fillet-pearls to deck her head,
> Or jasmine garlands to adorn her bed?

Possibly English is not a good medium for expressing Indian thought. Certainly no verse in this language has the essential greatness or the permanent importance of Rabindranath

Tagore's Bengali poems, or Muhammad Iqbal's extraordinarily interesting Persian mystical poetry.[1]

The future of Indo-British culture is as uncertain as its past has been disappointing. There are no signs that the exaggerated nationalism of the present day is a phase likely to pass quickly away. The next ten years may well see Hindī substituted for English as the lingua franca of India, and modern Europe shows how easily Governments and nationalist movements can set up artificial barriers which more than counterbalance the effects of easier communications. Nothing is gained by ignoring the enmity which exists between educated Indians and educated Englishmen. Much of the world's future depends upon a solution of this futile and unnecessary quarrel. It is hoped that this small book, written by Indian and English hands, may help to remove one cause of that quarrel, which is the Englishman's failure to appreciate the old traditional culture of the people with whose destiny that of his own country is so closely intermingled.

G. T. GARRATT.

[1] Both, of course, have been translated. Unfortunately Dr. Tagore has allowed abbreviated and very banal versions of his poems to appear in English. Muhammad Iqbal's *Secrets of the Self* was published by Messrs. Macmillan & Co.

INDEX

PRINTED IN GREAT BRITAIN AT THE UNIVERSITY PRESS, OXFORD
BY CHARLES BATEY, PRINTER TO THE UNIVERSITY